NEONATAL DECISION MAKING

Clinical Decision Making™ Series

Berman:
    Pediatric Decision Making
Bready, Smith:
    Decision Making in Anesthesiology
Bucholz, Lippert, Wenger, Ezaki:
    Orthopaedic Decision Making
Callaham, Barton, Schumaker:
    Decision Making in Emergency Medicine
Cibis, Tongue, Stass-Isern:
    Decision Making in Pediatric Ophthalmology
Cohn, Doty, McElvein:
    Decision Making in Cardiothoracic Surgery
DeCherney, Polan, Lee, Boyers:
    Decision Making in Infertility
Greene, Johnson, Maricic:
    Decision Making in Medicine
Karlinsky, Lau, Goldstein:
    Decision Making in Pulmonary Medicine

Korones, Bada-Ellzey:
    Neonatal Decision Making
Levine:
    Decision Making in Gastroenterology
Marsh:
    Decision Making in Plastic Surgery
Nichols, Hyslop, Bartlett:
    Decision Making in Surgical Sepsis
Ramamurthy, Rogers:
    Decision Making in Pain Management
Resnick, Caldamone, Spirnak:
    Decision Making in Urology
Schein:
    Decision Making in Oncology
van Heuven, Zwaan:
    Decision Making in Ophthalmology
Weisberg, Strub, Garcia:
    Decision Making in Adult Neurology

NEONATAL DECISION MAKING

Sheldon B. Korones, M.D.

Alumni Distinguished Service Professor
of Pediatrics and Obstetrics and Gynecology
Director of Newborn Center
The University of Tennessee, Memphis, College of Medicine
Memphis, Tennessee

Henrietta S. Bada-Ellzey, M.D.

Professor of Pediatrics and Obstetrics and Gynecology
The University of Tennessee, Memphis, College of Medicine
Memphis, Tennessee

B.C. Decker
An Imprint of Mosby–Year Book, Inc.

Publisher: George Stamathis
Executive Editor: Susan M. Gay
Senior Managing Editor: Lynne Gery
Production Supervisor: Jolynn Gower
Production Coordinator: Pete Hausler

NOTICE: The authors and publisher have made every effort to ensure that the patient care recommended herein, including choice of drugs and drug dosages, is in accord with the accepted standard and practice at the time of publication. However, since research and regulation constantly change clinical standards, the reader is urged to check the product information sheet included in the package of each drug, which includes recommended doses, warnings, and contraindications. This is particularly important with new or infrequently used drugs.

Printed in the United States of America

Mosby−Year Book, Inc.
11830 Westline Industrial Drive
St. Louis, Missouri 63146

ISBN 1-55664-148-6

Korones, Sheldon B., 1924−
    Neonatal decision making / Sheldon B. Korones, Henrietta S. Bada −Ellzey. —1st ed.
        p.   cm. — (Clinical decision making series)
    Includes bibliographical references and index.
    ISBN 1−55664−148−6
    1. Infants (Newborn)—Medical care—Decision making.   I. Bada −Ellzey, Henrietta S. II. Title. III. Series.
    [DNLM: 1. Infant, Newborn, Diseases—diagnosis. 2. Infant, Newborn, Diseases—etiology. 3. Infant, Newborn, Diseases—therapy. WS 420 K84n]
RJ253.K67   1993
618.92′01—dc20
DNLM/DLC
for Library of Congress   92−49370
                                                                      CIP

92 93 94 95 96 CL/MY 9 8 7 6 5 4 3 2 1

Some children thrive happily;
others languish sadly.
Are they not all ours?

PREFACE

Clinical decision trees fall into three categories. The first addresses conceptual decisions, largely diagnostic and predicated on data derived from the history, the physical findings, and the results of diagnostic procedures. The second concerns decisions of action; these are largely therapeutic. The third category combines the first two. We have utilized all three types, depending on the subject presented. Common to all three categories, however, are the indispensable considerations of pathogenesis, whether these be distinctly demonstrable or tentatively presumed. The comments that accompany each decision tree are the most useful and pertinent ones that we could discern from the literature, while maintaining a commitment to be succinct.

These decision trees are road maps. They are intended for use by individuals who are actively responsible for the care of sick neonates. They are also intended as descriptions of clinical problems that confront and confound care providers. Abnormal physical findings in the sick neonate are not often subtle, but virtually always they are nonspecific. Hence, there is the need for a road map to indicate directions of thought and action. In their application, however, any of these indications may well serve as points of departure. We have of course relied heavily on the accumulated literature for the construction and explanation of these algorithms, but we have also utilized our long (and ongoing) experience as teachers of hundreds of trainees and as practitioners responsible for the care of thousands of babies. Thus we appreciate the constructive comments of our nurse practitioners, residents, and fellows as we progressed in the preparation of this book.

We express gratitude to Marion Haynes and Rosalind Griffin for their patient correction of recurrent errors, for their expertise in executing the lines and labels of each decision tree, and for their steadfast pleasantness born of a long-time understanding of our goals and temperaments.

Finally, we salute the incredible patience of our publisher.

Sheldon B. Korones, M.D.
Henrietta S. Bada-Ellzey, M.D.

CONTENTS

THE FETUS

Intrauterine Growth Retardation .2

Intrauterine Growth Acceleration 4

Infant of a Diabetic Mother 6

Twins 8

Polyhydramnios: Associated Fetal and Neonatal
Disorders 10

Oligohydramnios: Associated Fetal and Neonatal
Disorders 12

Hydrops Fetalis: Antenatal Diagnosis and
Managment 14

Hydrops Fetalis: Postnatal Diagnosis 16

Hydrops Fetalis: Postnatal Management 18

LABOR AND DELIVERY

Management in the Delivery Room: Apgar Score 0-3
(Severe Asphyxia) 22

Managment in the Delivery Room: Apgar Scores 4-6
and 7-10 24

Breech Birth 26

Abruptio Placentae/Placenta Previa 28

Prolapsed Cord and Cord Compression 30

Trauma: Peripheral Nerves .32

Birth Injury: Viscera and Soft Tissue 34

Trauma: Bones 36

HEAT AND WATER BALANCE

Hypothermia 40

Hyperthermia 42

Maintenance of Fluid Balance 44

Oliguria 46

Oliguria: Management 48

Polyuria 50

PHYSICAL SIGNS
Color

Jaundice: Diagnosis 54

Jaundice: Management 56

Cyanosis 58

Pallor 60

Breathing

Apnea 62

Tachypnea 66

Stridor 68

The Head

Large Head 70

Small Head 72

Misshaped Head 74

Wide Sutures 76

Bulging Fontanelles 78

The Chest

Abnormal Contour of Chest .80

Retractions and Respiratory Distress 82

The Abdomen

Vomiting/Excessive Gastric Aspirate: Differential
Diagnosis 84

Bloody Stools: Differential Diagnosis 86

Abdominal Enlargement Due to Gaseous Distention . . .88

Abdominal Masses 90

Abdominal Enlargement Due to Isolated Ascites
(Intraperitoneal Fluid Accumulation) *92*

Hepatomegaly *96*

Splenomegaly *98*

Enlarged Kidneys and Bladder *100*

INFECTION

Maternal-Fetal Transmission of Bacterial Infection
(Vertical Transmission) *104*

Bacterial Infection: Risks, Clinical Signs, and
Etiology *106*

Bacterial Infection: Diagnosis and Management *108*

Congenital Syphilis *112*

Nonbacterial Infections: Viruses and Toxoplasmosis . .*114*

Fungus Infection: *Candida* *118*

DISORDERS BY ORGAN SYSTEM

Pulmonary Disorders

Respiratory Distress Syndrome: Pathogenesis and
Diagnosis *122*

Respiratory Distress Syndrome: Management *124*

Respiratory Distress Syndrome: Specific Therapy *126*

Meconium Aspiration *128*

Transient Tachypnea of the Newborn (RDS Type II) . .*130*

Bronchopulmonary Dysplasia *132*

Pleural Effusion (Hydrothorax and Chylothorax) *134*

Massive Pulmonary Hemorrhage *136*

Diaphragmatic Hernia *138*

Complications of Mechanical Ventilation *140*

Pulmonary Air Leak (Extraneous Air Syndromes) *142*

Cardiovascular Disorders

Bradycardia *144*

Tachycardia *146*

Diminished Heart Sounds *148*

Mediastinal Shift *150*

Hypertension *152*

Hypertension: Therapy *154*

Abnormal Central Venous Pressure *156*

Shock *158*

Patent Ductus Arteriosus *162*

Persistent Fetal Circulation *164*

Myocardial Ischemia *166*

Gastrointestinal Disorders

Necrotizing Enterocolitis: Diagnosis *168*

Necrotizing Enterocolitis: Management *170*

Intestinal Obstruction *172*

Esophageal Atresia and Tracheoesophageal Fistula . . .*174*

Ineffective Suck and Swallow *176*

Hematologic Disorders

Anemia Due to Blood Loss *178*

Anemia Due to Hemolysis *180*

Polycythemia/Hyperviscosity *182*

Platelet Disorders: Thrombocytopenia *184*

Platelet Disorders: Thromboyctosis *186*

Neutropenia *188*

Disseminated Intravascular Coagulation *190*

Bleeding Infants *192*

Neurologic Disorders

Seizures *194*

Seizures: Therapy *196*

Jitteriness *198*

Hypotonia *200*

Hypoxic-Ischemic Encephalopathy: Pathophysiology
and Clinical Signs.............................202

Hypoxic-Ischemic Encephalopathy: Therapy........204

Periventricular-Intraventricular Hemorrhage:
Pathophysiology...............................206

Periventricular-Intraventricular Hemorrhage:
Therapy.......................................208

Ocular Abnormalities

Pupillary Opacities (White Pupils)................210

Retinopathy of Prematurity.....................212

Skin and Subcutaneous Tissue

Petechiae, Ecchymoses, and Bruises..............214

Blisters.......................................216

Edema, Sclerema, and Lymphedema.............218

Hemangiomas..................................220

Lymphangiomas...............................222

Pigmented Lesions............................224

NEONATAL SEQUELAE OF MATERNAL DRUG ABUSE

Maternal Cocaine Abuse........................228

Maternal Heroin/Methadone Abuse..............230

Maternal Alcohol Consumption..................232

Maternal Amphetamine Use.....................234

BLOOD CHEMISTRY ABNORMALITIES

Transient Neonatal Hypoglycemia: Clinical and
Biochemical Screening.........................238

Transient Neonatal Hypoglycemia: Therapy........240

Acidosis......................................242

Alkalosis.....................................244

Hyponatremia.................................246

Hypernatremia................................248

Potassium Disorders...........................250

Hyperkalemia: Therapy........................254

Hypocalcemia.................................256

Hypercalcemia................................260

Hypomagnesemia..............................262

Hypermagnesemia.............................264

Hyperammonemia.............................266

Hyperammonemia: Therapy.....................268

THE FETUS

Intrauterine Growth Retardation
Intrauterine Growth Acceleration
Infant of a Diabetic Mother
Twins
Polyhydramnios: Associated Fetal and
    Neonatal Disorders

Oligohydramnios: Associated Fetal and
    Neonatal Disorders
Hydrops Fetalis: Antenatal Diagnosis and
    Management
Hydrops Fetalis: Postnatal Diagnosis
Hydrops Fetalis: Postnatal Management

INTRAUTERINE GROWTH RETARDATION

A. Similar to infant mortality, the incidence of low birthweight is highest in low socioeconomic circumstances. The inherent maternal variables that enhance the likelihood of low birthweight include high parity, short stature, extremes of age, and lifestyle. Toxemia (pregnancy-induced hypertension) is a generalized vascular disease in which reduced uteroplacental perfusion impairs function of the fetal lifeline, particularly in the last trimester. Advanced diabetes also causes generalized vascular damage that diminishes placental blood flow. The role of maternal malnutrition is identifiable in underweight pregravid women and in those whose weight gain is subnormal during pregnancy (<20 pounds). Both of these factors, separately and synergistically, probably increase the likelihood of low birthweight. Growth in early pregnancy is infrequently impaired. When early pregnancy growth is impaired, symmetrical undergrowth results. Generally, growth impairment occurs late in pregnancy, resulting in asymmetrical undergrowth. Cigarette smoking is associated with twice the incidence of small for gestational age (SGA) babies if indulgence is moderate, triple the incidence if heavy. The impaired growth may be due to marginal fetal hypoxia because carbon monoxide in smokers' blood (carboxyhemoglobin) precludes optimal red cell oxygen content (oxyhemoglobin). Alcohol consumption is associated with the fetal alcohol syndrome, a constellation of structural abnormalities that are combined with notable growth deficiency. Among drug-addicted gravida the incidence of low birthweight infants is 50%. Of these, 40% are SGA and 60% are appropriate for gestational age premature babies. The SGA infants are usually hypoplastic (see the following discussion). Mothers who reside at higher altitudes tend to have lower birthweight infants, but length of infant is apparently unaffected. Smoking at high altitudes increases two to three times the likelihood of fetal undergrowth compared with smoking at sea level.

B. Multiple fetuses are more likely to be SGA after 30–32 week's gestation, at which time deceleration in growth rate occurs. Congenital malformations (chromosomal and nonchromosomal) are associated with symmetrical (hypoplastic) undergrowth. Chronic nonbacterial fetal infections, notably rubella and cytomegalovirus, also produce hypoplastic growth retardation.

C. Placental insufficiency implies impaired maternal-fetal exchange, particularly in regard to the suboptimal provision of nutrient material to the fetus. In most instances placental dysfunction is not associated with dysmorphic fetuses. Placental arteriovenous anastomosis occurs in identical twins and results in twin-to-twin transfusion (parabiotic syndrome), which is characterized by marked discrepancy in the sizes and hematocrits of both fetuses. However, the discrepancy in size is not a regular feature of the parabiotic syndrome.

D. Postnatal abnormalities can be hypoplastic or hypotrophic. Symmetrical (hypoplastic) undergrowth is characterized as follows:
   1. Universally diminutive size; head, length, weight percentile reduced proportionately.
   2. Reasonably nourished appearance; subcutaneous fat appropriate for size, skin taut.
   3. Palpable liver, sometimes enlarged.
   4. Hematocrit generally normal.
   5. Congenital malformation frequent.
   6. Fetal nonbacterial infection frequent.
   7. Hypoglycemia, hypoproteinemia infrequent.

Asymmetrical (hypotrophic) undergrowth is characterized as follows:
   1. Disproportionately reduced size; weight percentile significantly more reduced than head circumference and length.
   2. Subcutaneous fat diminished for size; skin redundant.
   3. Liver usually diminished in size.
   4. Hematocrit often high.
   5. Congenital malformation infrequent.
   6. Fetal nonbacterial infection rare.
   7. Hypoglycemia, hypoproteinemia common.

At the cellular level, hypoplastic undergrowth is characterized by a paucity of cells, each of which has an approximately normal volume of cytoplasm. Hypotrophic undergrowth is characterized by a near-normal number of cells and a paucity of cytoplasm.

SBK

References

Davies DP. Physical growth from fetus to early childhood. In: Davis JA, Dobbing J, eds. Scientific foundations of Paediatrics. Baltimore: University Park Press, 1982: 303.

Kliegman RM. Intrauterine growth retardation: Determinants of aberrant fetal growth. In: Fanaroff AA, Martin RJ, eds: Neonatal-perinatal medicine: diseases of the fetus and infant, 5th ed. St Louis: Mosby–Year Book, 1992:149.

Korones SB. Significance of the relationship of birthweight to gestational age. In: Korones SB: High-risk newborn infants: The basis for intensive nursing care, 4th ed. St Louis: Mosby–Year Book, 1986: 111.

Winick M. Malnutrition and brain development. New York: Oxford University Press, 1976.

INTRAUTERINE GROWTH RETARDATION

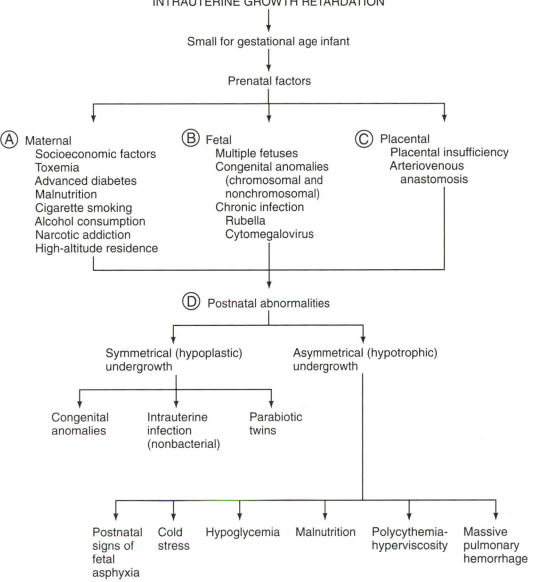

Small for gestational age infant

Prenatal factors

(A) Maternal
  Socioeconomic factors
  Toxemia
  Advanced diabetes
  Malnutrition
  Cigarette smoking
  Alcohol consumption
  Narcotic addiction
  High-altitude residence

(B) Fetal
  Multiple fetuses
  Congenital anomalies
    (chromosomal and
    nonchromosomal)
  Chronic infection
    Rubella
    Cytomegalovirus

(C) Placental
  Placental insufficiency
  Arteriovenous
    anastomosis

(D) Postnatal abnormalities

Symmetrical (hypoplastic)
undergrowth

Asymmetrical (hypotrophic)
undergrowth

Congenital
anomalies

Intrauterine
infection
(nonbacterial)

Parabiotic
twins

Postnatal
signs of
fetal
asphyxia

Cold
stress

Hypoglycemia

Malnutrition

Polycythemia-
hyperviscosity

Massive
pulmonary
hemorrhage

INTRAUTERINE GROWTH ACCELERATION

A. Birthweight is considered high at 4000 g or more. An infant is large for gestational age (LGA) at any gestational age when plotted above the 90th percentile on the Colorado Growth Curves. Abnormalities intrinsic to the mother rarely cause overgrowth. An obvious exception is maternal diabetes. Large mothers have large babies. These mothers also tend to be older, taller, and heavier; they often gain weight excessively during pregnancy. Furthermore, they have little if any history of troublesome pregnancies. Large infants are born to multiparous mothers three times as often as primipara. Of all infants, 5% are >4000 g at birth; 0.4% − 0.9% are >4500 g.

B. Intrinsic fetal disorders are rare causes of growth acceleration. Exceptions are transposition of the great vessels and the Beckwith-Wiedemann syndrome.

C. Perinatal asphyxia is associated with difficult labor and delivery. The incidence of asphyxia is higher in large babies than in those of normal weight.

D. The incidence of birth trauma is high in large babies delivered vaginally. Shoulder dystocia has been observed in 10% of overgrown infants delivered vaginally. Other trauma include fractured clavicle, depressed skull fracture, brachial plexus palsy, and facial paralysis. Together these occur in approximately 15% of oversized infants.

E. Beckwith-Wiedemann syndrome is characteristically associated with oversized hypoglycemic infants. The syndrome consists of macroglossia; enlargement of liver, pancreas, and kidneys; and an omphalocele. Other common components are nevus flammeus of the face, microcephaly, and renal hypoplasia. Hypoglycemia occurs in 30% − 40% of affected infants. The hypoglycemia is caused by high plasma insulin levels from islet cell hyperplasia. A hyperresponsive insulin response to glucose has been observed. Hypocalcemia and polycythemia have also been observed.

F. Transposition of the great vessels occurs in 1:2100 − 1:4500 births and is generally associated with higher than average birthweight. Transposition is a relatively common cardiac anomaly and the only one known to be associated with oversized neonates. Dextrotrans-

position is usually associated with patent foramen ovale, patent ductus arteriosus, and a ventricular septal defect. Dextrotransposition occurs ten times more frequently than levotransposition, which is often associated with situs inversus, dextrocardia, and asplenia in the newborn period. The anterior-posterior chest film of dextrotransposition is characterized by a narrow mediastinum, cardiac enlargement, and hypervascularity of the lungs.

G. Infants of diabetic mothers (IDMs) are oversized by virtue of excessive fat deposits, mostly in subcutaneous tissue. Fat deposits are enhanced by fetal overproduction of insulin. The extracellular fluid compartment is contracted in IDMs. The length and head size are no greater than those of average term babies. In contrast, the size of large infants of nondiabetic mothers is greater by virtue of larger head circumferences and greater linear growth.

H. Advanced postmaturity is frequently associated with oligohydramnios (p 12) and unmistakable fetal undergrowth, but up to one-fourth of postmature infants, not as advanced in gestational age, may be macrosomic. The sharp difference in fetal outcome is apparently associated with placental status, which if undisturbed often accommodates continued growth past 40 weeks.

SBK

References

Hohn AR, Stanton RE. The cardiovascular system. In: Fanaroff AA, Martin RJ, eds: Neonatal-perinatal medicine, 5th ed. St Louis: Mosby−Year Book, 1992:883.

Horger EO, III, Miller C, III, Conner ED. Relations of large birthweight to maternal diabetes mellitus. Obstet Gynecol 1975; 45:150.

Iffy L, Chatterton RT, Jakobovits A. The "high weight for dates" fetus. Am J Obstet Gynecol 1973; 115:239.

Korones SB. High-risk newborn infants: The basis for intensive nursing care, 4th ed. St Louis: Mosby−Year Book, 1986:148.

Stubblefield PG, Berek JS. Perinatal mortality in term and post-term birth. Obstet Gynecol 1980; 56:676.

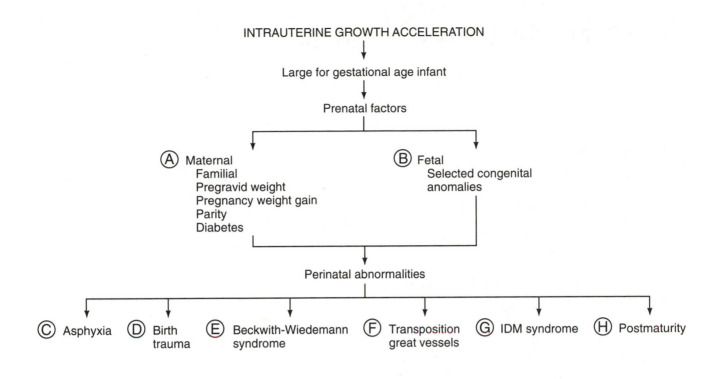

INTRAUTERINE GROWTH ACCELERATION

Large for gestational age infant

Prenatal factors

(A) Maternal
  Familial
  Pregravid weight
  Pregnancy weight gain
  Parity
  Diabetes

(B) Fetal
  Selected congenital
  anomalies

Perinatal abnormalities

(C) Asphyxia (D) Birth trauma (E) Beckwith-Wiedemann syndrome (F) Transposition great vessels (G) IDM syndrome (H) Postmaturity

INFANT OF A DIABETIC MOTHER

Diabetic pregnancies are classified according to White's criteria. Class A refers to chemical diabetes or abnormal glucose tolerance before or during pregnancy. In class B diabetes, onset is after age 20 years and duration <10 years. In class C, onset of diabetes is between 10 and 19 years of age with duration of 10–19 years. In class D, onset is before age 10 and duration is >20 years. Additional findings may include calcification of big vessels, benign retinopathy, and hypertension. Pelvic vessels are calcified in class E. Nephropathy is present in class F. Class G is associated with reproductive failures. Cardiopathy is present in class H, and malignant retinopathy is present in class R.

A. Improved obstetric management and good diabetic control during pregnancy have resulted in decreased fetal death. Perinatal mortality depends on associated maternal complications such as ketoacidosis, hydramnios, preeclampsia, and urinary tract infection. With good diabetic control, an infant of a diabetic mother (IDM) may be a normal infant with mild or no metabolic complications.

B. The typical IDM is a macrosomic or large for gestational age (LGA) baby. Macrosomia is observed in 20–40% of class A, B, and C diabetic pregnancies. Maternal hyperglycemia leads to fetal hyperglycemia and consequently fetal pancreatic islet cell hypertrophy, hyperplasia, and hyperinsulinism, an in utero growth-promoting factor.

C. Traumatic birth injuries (e.g., brachial plexus palsy, fractures) are some of the complications observed in the macrosomic IDM.

D. The risk of hyaline membrane disease (HMD) in an IDM is five to six times greater than in infants of similar gestational age born after normal pregnancies. Insulin has been shown to slow lung maturation, antagonize action of cortisol in surfactant synthesis, or inhibit key enzymes in phospholipid synthesis. Small for gestational age (SGA) babies are less likely to develop HMD; prenatal stress is associated with accelerated surfactant synthesis.

E. Among pregnant diabetics with vascular disease, intrauterine fetal growth retardation is common because of decreased nutrient supply to the fetus.

F. Metabolic complications are common to both LGA and SGA IDMs. Specific glucose values have been used in the past to define hypoglycemia. However, there is no consensus as to the level of plasma glucose, below which neurological dysfunction occurs. Thus it is best to maintain plasma glucose above 40 mg/dl. Hypoglycemia, although often asymptomatic, occurs in 40–50% of IDMs. Screening for hypoglycemia may be accomplished by Dextrostix or Chemstrip. Confirm borderline values by quantitative glucose oxidase method. Treatment is by bolus injection (over 1 minute) of 10% dextrose solution (2 ml/kg) or 200 mg/kg. This is followed by maintenance solution of 10% dextrose at a glucose load of 8 mg/kg/min. Use of 25% or 50% dextrose solution may lead to rebound hypoglycemia. Feeding as early as 1 hour of age is instituted to supplement intravenous therapy. Hydrocortisone 10 mg/kg/day divided into two doses administered IV or IM may be effective if hypoglycemia persists in spite of a glucose load of 12 mg/kg/min. Glucagon (300 µg/kg/dose) may raise glucose levels but only transiently; it may not be effective in SGA babies with minimal glycogen stores.

G. The incidence of hypocalcemia (serum Ca level <7 mg/dl or ionized Ca ≤3.5 mg/dl) in IDMs ranges from 15–30%, with peak onset at 24 hours of life. Etiology of the suppressed fetal parathyroid function is not known. For treatment, bolus of calcium gluconate IV (200 mg/kg of 10% solution) is given. Maintenance therapy is by a continuous drip of 400–500 mg/kg/day of 10% calcium gluconate.

H. Hypomagnesemia (serum Mg <1.6 mg/dl), which occurs in 30% of IDMs, probably also relates to suppressed parathyroid function. It is corrected by 0.1–0.3 ml/kg of 50% $MgSo_4$ IM repeated in 8–12 hours.

I. Bilirubin levels are slightly higher in IDMs. Contributing factors include prematurity, polycythemia, excessive weight loss, and delayed clearance and increased production rates of bilirubin, possibly as a result of hemolysis (increased carboxyhemoglobin), increased erythropoiesis, and catabolism of nonhemoglobin hemes.

J. Cardiomegaly is seen on chest radiography in 50% of IDMs. In 5–17%, congestive heart failure is observed. Forty percent may have ECG abnormalities; infants have thickened ventricular septa. Cardiomegaly is thus due to myocardial hypertrophy. Some infants may have only transient left ventricular function abnormalities that resolve in 5–7 days. Propranolol will decrease ventricular contractility. Digitalis is contraindicated.

K. Polycythemia/hyperviscosity with venous hematocrit ≥65% is a finding in 15–30% of IDMs. Treatment is by partial exchange transfusion with plasma, saline, or 5% albumin solution.

L. The risk of congenital malformations in IDMs is three to four times that in infants of normal pregnancies. A wide spectrum of malformations is reported. Proposed pathogenetic mechanisms include genetic factors, teratogenic agents, maternal vascular disease, and metabolic effects of diabetes. Some studies of HbA_{1C} suggest positive correlation between degree of control of diabetes and incidence of anomalies, but more recent data showed no correlation between glycosylated hemoglobin and malformations or between good glycemic control and prevention of malformation.

HSB

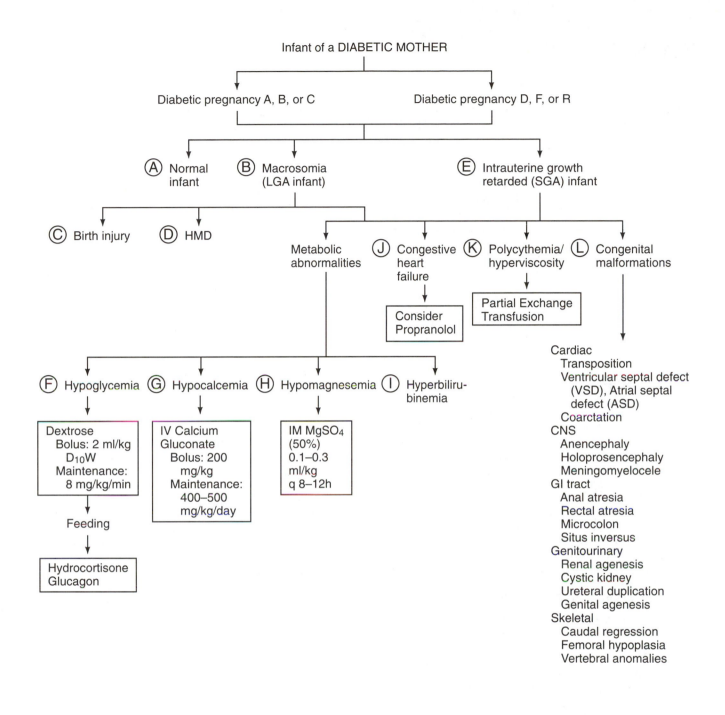

Infant of a DIABETIC MOTHER

Diabetic pregnancy A, B, or C

Diabetic pregnancy D, F, or R

(A) Normal infant

(B) Macrosomia (LGA infant)

(E) Intrauterine growth retarded (SGA) infant

(C) Birth injury

(D) HMD

Metabolic abnormalities

(J) Congestive heart failure

(K) Polycythemia/ hyperviscosity

(L) Congenital malformations

Consider Propranolol

Partial Exchange Transfusion

(F) Hypoglycemia

(G) Hypocalcemia

(H) Hypomagnesemia

(I) Hyperbilirubinemia

Dextrose
Bolus: 2 ml/kg
$D_{10}W$
Maintenance:
8 mg/kg/min

IV Calcium
Gluconate
Bolus: 200
mg/kg
Maintenance:
400–500
mg/kg/day

IM $MgSO_4$
(50%)
0.1–0.3
ml/kg
q 8–12h

Feeding

Hydrocortisone
Glucagon

Cardiac
   Transposition
   Ventricular septal defect
      (VSD), Atrial septal
      defect (ASD)
   Coarctation
CNS
   Anencephaly
   Holoprosencephaly
   Meningomyelocele
GI tract
   Anal atresia
   Rectal atresia
   Microcolon
   Situs inversus
Genitourinary
   Renal agenesis
   Cystic kidney
   Ureteral duplication
   Genital agenesis
Skeletal
   Caudal regression
   Femoral hypoplasia
   Vertebral anomalies

References

Hollingsworth DR, Moore TR. Diabetes and pregnancy. In: Creasy RK, Resnik R, eds. Maternal-fetal medicine: Principles and practice. Philadelphia: WB Saunders, 1989:925.

Mills JL, Simpson JL, Driscoll SG, et al. Incidence of spontaneous abortion among normal women and insulin-dependent diabetic women whose pregnancies were identified within 21 days of conception. N Engl J Med 1988; 319:1617.

Pedersen JF, Molsted-Pedersen L. Early fetal growth delay detected by ultrasound means increased risk of congenital malformation in diabetic pregnancy. Br Med J 1981; 283:269.

Pildes RS. Infants of diabetic mothers. In: Avery GB, ed. Neonatology: Pathophysiology and management of the newborn. Philadelphia: JB Lippincott, 1987:332.

White P. Diabetes mellitus in pregnancy. Clin Perinatol 1974; 1:331.

TWINS

Reported incidence of twin pregnancies ranges from 1.05% to 1.35%. Rate of dizygotic twins varies widely (4%–50%) compared with usually constant monozygous twinning rate of 3.5–4/1000. There are two types of twins: monozygous twins and dizygous twins.

A. Monozygous twins are of similar gender and blood grouping. Placentation is of monochorionic-diamniotic type in 20%–30% of cases; in another 30% dichorionic diamniotic placentation is observed; i.e., twins that separated in the first two days after fertilization. Least common placentation is that of a monochorionic-monoamniotic variety.

B. In dizygous or fraternal twins, gender and blood groups are different. Incidence increases with increasing maternal age, parity, coital frequency, and may be related to genetic factors leading to double ovulation.

C. Mortality is highest with monochorionic-monoamniotic twins (50%–60%); knots in the umbilical cord result in cessation of umbilical blood flow. Mortality with monochorionic-diamniotic twins is lower, approximately 25%. Lowest mortality (8.9%) is reported with dichorionic twins. Twinning may be diagnosed in utero early by ultrasound. Death of a twin may result in "disappearance" of the twin as the pregnancy approaches term. Careful examination of the placenta should confirm twin pregnancy. Fetus papyraceus results from death of a twin before birth wherein the fluid of the dead twin's tissue is absorbed and the fetus is compressed and becomes incorporated into the membranes (membranous twin). Fetus papyraceus is also associated with aplasia cutis (diffuse and patchy) in the surviving twin. Intrapartum death or death in the neonatal period may be attributed to morbidity and various complications associated with twin deliveries.

D. Mortality may be attributed to difficulties during delivery. Incidence of operative delivery is increased with the second twin, and so are the risks of longer period of hypoxia, greater length of exposure to anesthesia, development of hyaline membrane disease (HMD), and intracranial hemorrhage after prolonged labor. The chance for survival diminishes with longer interval from delivery of the first to the second twin.

E. Compared with single pregnancies, vasa previa and velamentous insertion of the cord occur six to nine times as frequently in twin placentas. They occur at a greater frequency with higher order multiple births. These conditions are associated with exsanguination during delivery and/or fetal distress (sinusoidal fetal heart rate pattern) because of vessel compression during labor or thrombosis. Exsanguination leads to death in the first twin and in over 60% of the second twin.

F. Cord prolapse and entanglement are more common with twin births, which could result in perinatal asphyxia and death.

G. Vascular shunts or anastomoses are of three types: (1) artery-to-artery, (2) vein-to-vein, and (3) artery-to-vein. These anastomoses are common in monochorionic-diamniotic placentae and less common in the monochorionic-monoamniotic placentae. Artery-to-artery anastomosis is more common than vein-to-vein anastomosis. Interfetal large vessel anastomosis may lead to significant shift of blood between fetuses, particularly with the death of one fetus. Large volume of blood from the surviving fetus may shift into the dead fetus upon relaxation of the vessels, thus severe anemia is observed in the surviving fetus. This differs from the twin-to-twin transfusion, which is usually the result of artery-to-vein anastomosis through a shared cotyledon. In twin-to-twin transfusion, the donor twin is smaller and anemic, and the recipient twin is larger with hypervolemia and polycythemia (plethora), which leads to cardiac decompensation.

H. Multiple fetuses in utero may restrict growth potential.

I. Congenital anomalies occur twice as frequently in twin pregnancies as in singletons. Anomalies may be concordant but could be discordant even with monozygotic twins. Etiologies for the malformation include interfetal vascular embolization, vascular coagulation, and deformation as a result of crowding. Other discordant malformations such as anencephaly and sirenomelia and the so-called heterokaryotic monozygotic twins may be related to the twinning process itself. Acardiac twin (no heart or misshapen heart) is a bizarre malformation wherein its perfusion is maintained by the normal twin through an artery-to-artery and a vein-to-vein anastomosis. Acardiacs do not survive.

HSB

References

Antoine C, Young BK, Silverman F, et al. Sinusoidal fetal heart rate pattern with vasa previa in twin pregnancy. Obstet Gynecol 1982; 27:295.

Benirschke K. Multiple gestation: Incidence, etiology, and inheritance. In: Creasy RK, Resnik R eds. Maternal-fetal medicine: Principles and practice, Philadelphia: WB Saunders, 1989:565.

Benirschke K, Driscoll SG. The pathology of the human placenta. New York: Springer-Verlag, 1967.

Benirschke K, Kim CK. Multiple pregnancy. N Engl J Med 1973; 288:1276.

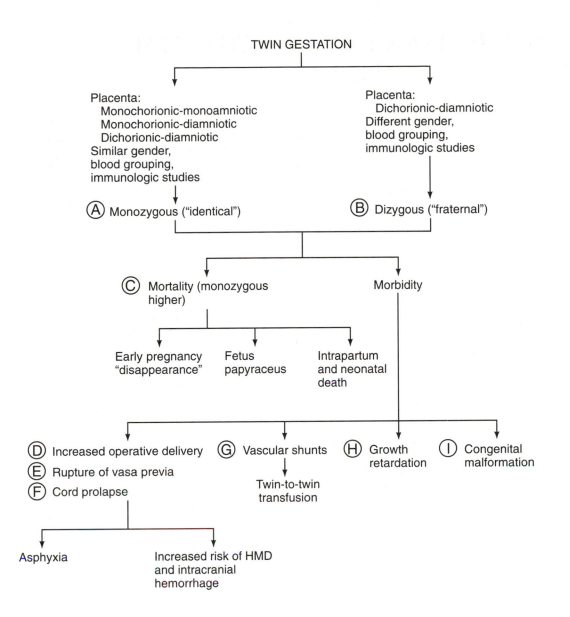

TWIN GESTATION

Placenta:
   Monochorionic-monoamniotic
   Monochorionic-diamniotic
   Dichorionic-diamniotic
Similar gender,
blood grouping,
immunologic studies

Placenta:
   Dichorionic-diamniotic
Different gender,
blood grouping,
immunologic studies

(A) Monozygous ("identical")

(B) Dizygous ("fraternal")

(C) Mortality (monozygous higher)

Morbidity

Early pregnancy "disappearance"

Fetus papyraceus

Intrapartum and neonatal death

(D) Increased operative delivery
(E) Rupture of vasa previa
(F) Cord prolapse

(G) Vascular shunts

Twin-to-twin transfusion

(H) Growth retardation

(I) Congenital malformation

Asphyxia

Increased risk of HMD and intracranial hemorrhage

POLYHYDRAMNIOS: ASSOCIATED FETAL AND NEONATAL DISORDERS

A. Polyhydramnios is an overaccumulation of amniotic fluid, generally considered to be in excess of 2000 ml at term. Expected proportions of amniotic fluid in total uterine volumes at various gestational weeks have been approximated by ultrasound examination. Large areas of echolucency are prominent in a generally enlarged uterus. Fetal parts are widely separated.

B. Polyhydramnios is thought to result from impaired fetal swallowing in the presence of normal urine output. It has been observed in fetal diabetes insipidus in the presence of presumably normal swallowing and excessive urine output. Swallowing is impaired by structural obstruction (esophageal atresia, duodenal atresia) or by neuromuscular dysfunction (anencephaly). In other associated maternal and fetal disorders (maternal diabetes, trisomy 18) the mechanism of fluid accumulation is unknown.

C. Anencephaly is the most frequent of all malformations associated with polyhydramnios. Polyhydramnios has been identified in half such cases. Hydrocephalus is also common. Diabetes is probably the most frequent maternal disorder that has been observed with excessive accumulation of amniotic fluid. When polyhydramnios is present in erythroblastosis fetalis, hydrops is usually also present. Obstructions above the ileum are the most common gastrointestinal abnormalities. They impair passage of amniotic fluid sufficiently to cause accumulation in the amniotic sac. Esophageal atresia is frequently implicated whether associated with a tracheoesophageal (TE) fistula. Obstructive lesions of the duodenum and jejunum are identified by ultrasound in utero and by abdominal radiograph after birth.

SBK

References

Boylan P, Parisi V. An overview of hydramnios. Semin Perinatol 1986; 10:136.

Lotgering FK, Wallenburg HCS. Mechanisms of production and clearance of amniotic fluid. Semin Perinatol 1986; 10:94.

Prindle RA, et al. Maternal hydramnios and congenital anomalies of the central nervous system. N Engl J Med 1955; 252:555.

Queenan JT. Polyhydramnios. In: Queenan JT, Hobbin JC, eds. Protocols for high-risk pregnancies, 2nd ed. Oradell, NJ: Medical Economics Books, 1987:288.

Queenan JT. Polyhydramnios, oligohydramnios, and hydrops fetalis. In: Fanaroff AA, Martin RJ, eds. Neonatal-perinatal medicine: Diseases of the fetus and infant. 5th ed. St Louis: Mosby-Year Book, 1992:244.

Wallenburg HCS, Wladimiroff JW. The amniotic fluid. II. Polyhydramnios and oligohydramnios. J Perinat Med 1977; 6:233.

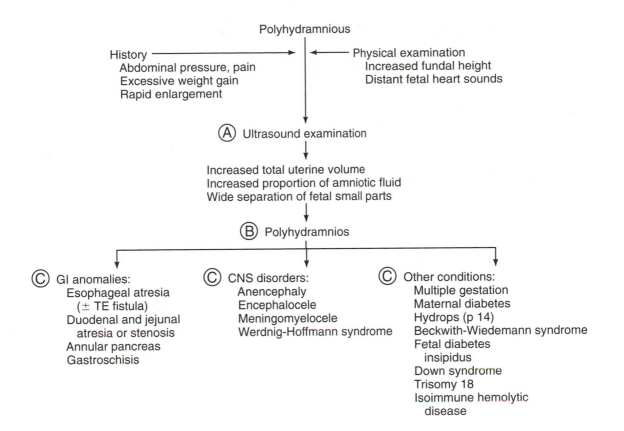

Polyhydramnious

History ──────────────→ | ←────── Physical examination
    Abdominal pressure, pain   Increased fundal height
    Excessive weight gain   Distant fetal heart sounds
    Rapid enlargement

Ⓐ Ultrasound examination

Increased total uterine volume
Increased proportion of amniotic fluid
Wide separation of fetal small parts

Ⓑ Polyhydramnios

Ⓒ GI anomalies:
    Esophageal atresia
      (± TE fistula)
    Duodenal and jejunal
      atresia or stenosis
    Annular pancreas
    Gastroschisis

Ⓒ CNS disorders:
    Anencephaly
    Encephalocele
    Meningomyelocele
    Werdnig-Hoffmann syndrome

Ⓒ Other conditions:
    Multiple gestation
    Maternal diabetes
    Hydrops (p 14)
    Beckwith-Wiedemann syndrome
    Fetal diabetes
      insipidus
    Down syndrome
    Trisomy 18
    Isoimmune hemolytic
      disease

OLIGOHYDRAMNIOS: ASSOCIATED FETAL AND NEONATAL DISORDERS

A. Progressive accumulation of amniotic fluid results in a volume at term that normally varies between 400 ml and 1.5 L. After 16 weeks the fetal urinary contribution to amniotic fluid volume increases progressively; in the last trimester fetal urine is the principal source of amniotic fluid. Fluid egress occurs largely by absorption into fetal blood from the gastrointestinal tract, where fluid gains entry by fetal swallowing. If little or no urine is excreted, the volume of amniotic fluid is greatly reduced. Chronic leakage of amniotic fluid, usually beginning in the second trimester, may also cause diminished volume. In its fullest expression, the oligohydramnios syndrome includes severe malformation of the urinary tract sufficient to preclude normal urine flow, plus several nonrenal abnormalities that result directly from the diminished volume of amniotic fluid. In a normal obstetric population, the incidence of oligohydramnios is approximately 0.5%. It is infrequently identified in the second trimester because maternal symptoms are absent. When clearly in evidence in the second trimester, oligohydramnios is almost invariably associated with severe malformations that are often incompatible with survival. Diminished amniotic fluid volume is one of the parameters for evaluation for fetal growth retardation by serial ultrasound assessments.

B. Urinary tract abnormalities are the primary defects that secondarily cause oligohydramnios because of diminished urine output. These abnormalities include renal agenesis (which may be the only underlying anomaly), severe renal hypoplasia, polycystic kidneys, and obstructive lesions of the lower urinary tract such as urethral dysplasia.

C. Secondary effects of oligohydramnios seem to be related to fetal compression and pulmonary hypoplasia. The typical face is characterized by a wizened appearance, a nose that appears beaked because the tip is fattened, low-set ears close to the head and often folded on themselves, a receding chin, and prominent skin folds that course downward and laterally along the cheek from the inner canthus. A variety of positional defects involve the limbs; talipes is most common.

Amnion nodosum is an indication of oligohydramnios, although its presence is not consistent. The nodules are several millimeters in diameter, cream-colored, and clearly visible on the placental surface of the amnion. They are composed of fetal epidermal cells, skin appendages, and vernix that presumably become attached to the surface of the amnion by direct contact in the absence of intervening fluid.

Potter syndrome is the oligohydramnios tetrad that includes renal agenesis, typical facies, positional limb abnormalities, pulmonary hypoplasia, and amnion nodosum.

Pulmonary hypoplasia associated with oligohydramnios is bilateral and of varying severity. It is characterized by a diminished number of alveoli, bronchioles, and arterioles. Depending on the extent of anatomical paucity, respiratory symptoms are moderate and amenable to mechanical ventilatory support or are severe and incompatible with life beyond several hours after birth.

D. Nonrenal factors associated with oligohydramnios are those of deficient fetal growth (IUGR, postmaturity). Severe fetal undergrowth from any cause (p 2) is often associated with diminished amniotic fluid volume. Chronic amniotic fluid leakage, particularly with early onset at midgestation, has also been observed to cause oligohydramnios and the associated fetal syndrome.

E. Other abnormalities are intrinsic to the disorders that underlie oligohydramnios. Parabiotic syndrome most prominently entails a severe discrepancy in hematocrits between the twins (p 8). The broad spectrum of abnormalities involved in IUGR is presented on p 2.

SBK

References

Jones KL. Oligohydramnios sequence (Potter syndrome): Primary defect—Development of oligohydramnios. In: Jones KL: Smith's recognizable patterns of human malformation, 4th ed. Philadelphia: WB Saunders 1988:572.

Lawrence S, Rosenfeld CR. Fetal pulmonary development and abnormalities of amniotic fluid volume. Semin Perinatol 1986; 10:142.

Leveno KJ. Amnionic fluid volume in prolonged pregnancy. Semin Perinatol 1986; 10:154.

Queenan JT. Polyhydramnios, oligohydramnios, and hydrops fetalis. In: Fanaroff AA, Martin RJ eds. Neonatal-perinatal medicine: Diseases of the fetus and infant, 5th ed. St Louis: Mosby—Year Book, 1992:244.

Rayburn WF, Motley ME, Stempel LE, Gendreau RM: Antepartum prediction of the postmature infant. Obstet Gynecol 1982; 60:148.

OLIGOHYDRAMNIOS

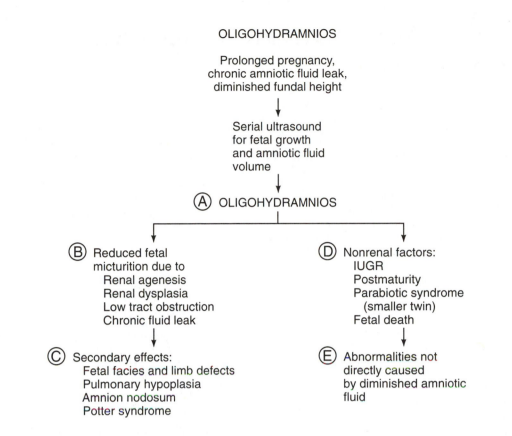

Prolonged pregnancy,
chronic amniotic fluid leak,
diminished fundal height

↓

Serial ultrasound
for fetal growth
and amniotic fluid
volume

↓

Ⓐ OLIGOHYDRAMNIOS

Ⓑ Reduced fetal
micturition due to
Renal agenesis
Renal dysplasia
Low tract obstruction
Chronic fluid leak

↓

Ⓒ Secondary effects:
Fetal facies and limb defects
Pulmonary hypoplasia
Amnion nodosum
Potter syndrome

Ⓓ Nonrenal factors:
IUGR
Postmaturity
Parabiotic syndrome
(smaller twin)
Fetal death

↓

Ⓔ Abnormalities not
directly caused
by diminished amniotic
fluid

HYDROPS FETALIS: ANTENATAL DIAGNOSIS AND MANAGEMENT

A. Diagnosis by ultrasound is feasible in virtually all hydropic fetuses. Early sonographic signs include pericardial effusion, placental enlargement (edema), and dilation of the umbilical vein. Scalp and body wall edema plus pleural effusion and ascites are virtually always identifiable either singly or in combination. Polyhydramnios has been observed repeatedly; oligohydramnios occurs infrequently. Ultrasound may detect a variety of congenital anomalies known to be associated with fetal hydrops such as congenital heart disease. The presence of hydrops fetalis in twins suggests twin-to-twin transfusion, particularly if their sizes show significant discrepancy later in pregnancy (intrauterine parabiotic syndrome).

B. Antenatal search for the etiology of hydrops should begin with identification of isoimmune blood incompatibility. Maternal antibody screen early in pregnancy, bilirubin content of amniotic fluid, and fetal blood sampling from the umbilical cord identify the progressive severity of immune fetal hydrops. If blood incompatibility is excluded, etiology of a nonimmune hydrops should be established by the tests listed.

C. Fetal management is still restricted to a few measures. Maternal digoxin has been effective in suppressing fetal tachycardia. Abdominal paracentesis may be necessary to accomplish delivery when the fetal abdomen is severely distended. Some authors advocate maternal administration of dexamethasone to accelerate lung maturity just before delivery. The progress of fetal anemia and thus the need for transfusion can be identified by repeated venipuncture of the umbilical cord. A planned delivery requires in-house availability of neonatal intensive care with all essential laboratory and imaging procedures and access to a broad spectrum of consultants in the pediatric subspecialties.

SBK

References

Davis CL. Diagnosis and management of nonimmune hydrops fetalis. J Reprod Med 1982; 27:594.

Etches PC. Part V: Hydrops fetalis. In: Roberton NRC, ed. Textbook of neonatology. New York: Churchill Livingstone, 1986.

Giacoia GP. Hydrops fetalis (fetal edema). Clin Pediatr 1980; 19:334.

Holzgreve W, Holzgreve B, Curry CJR. Nonimmune hydrops fetalis: Diagnosis and management. Semin Perinatol 1985; 9:52.

Hutchinson AA, Drew JH, Yu VYH, et al. Nonimmunologic hydrops fetalis: A review of 61 cases. Obstet Gynecol 1982; 59:347.

Turkel SB. Conditions associated with nonimmune hydrops fetalis. Clin Perinatol 1982; 9:613.

HYDROPS FETALIS: ANTENATAL DIAGNOSIS AND MANAGEMENT

Maternal risks:
    Abnormal uterine enlargement
    Polyhydramnios
    Isoimmune hemolytic disease-positive
      antibodies, history
    Diabetes
    Pregnancy-induced hypertension
    Diminished fetal activity
    Fetal cardiac arrhythmia
    Anemia, unknown cause

(A) Ultrasound diagnosis:
      Hydrops fetalis

(B) Antenatal assessment:

Maternal antibody screen	→ Isoimmune blood incompatibility
Kleihauer-Betke syndrome	→ Feto-maternal hemorrhage
Serology for syphilis	→ Fetal syphilis
Alpha fetoprotein	→ Neural tube defects, sacrococcygeal teratoma, fetal nephrosis
TORCH antibodies	→ Fetal infection
G6PD, pyruvate kinase	→ Maternal carrier state
Hemoglobin electrophoresis	→ Maternal alpha-thalassemia trait
Amniocentesis	→ Fetal chromosomal abnormalities
	Bilirubin for isoimmune hemolytic disease
Glucose tolerance	→ Maternal diabetes
Ultrasound	→ Multiple gestation
	Fetal malformation
	Fetal cardiac status
Fetal echocardiography	→ Arrhythmias

(C) Fetal management:

Fetal tachycardia →	Maternal Digoxin, Propranolol
Fetal abdominal distention (severe) →	Paracentesis Preceding Delivery
Pulmonary immaturity →	Maternal Dexamethasone
Hemolytic anemia (isommune) →	Fetal Transfusion

Delivery after 30 weeks' gestation

Hydrops fetalis in the neonate (pp 16, 18)

HYDROPS FETALIS: POSTNATAL DIAGNOSIS

A. The typical "blown-up" appearance of hydrops fetalis is caused by accumulation of subcutaneous edema, accentuated by ascites. Both may be sufficiently mild to be overlooked at the first inspection. Respiratory distress regularly is obvious; there may indeed be no respiratory effort. Pallor is most often the result of anemia, but it may also be impressive in the presence of a normal or slightly diminished hematocrit because subcutaneous edema blocks normal transmittance of color. Hydrops resulting from isoimmune hemolytic disease (or other hematological disorders) is associated with significant edema. Birthweight is excessive for gestational age because of fluid accumulation. Thus calculations of fluid and pharmacological dosages should be based on the 50th weight percentile of estimated gestational age. Tachycardia (supraventricular tachycardia) is the most frequent cardiac arrhythmia. Bradycardia not caused by profound fetal asphyxia is the result of heart block. Enlarged liver and spleen are difficult to perceive if ascites is extensive even though they are enlarged in hematological and infectious disorders. Hepatomegaly can be expected in the presence of cardiac failure, but the spleen is not enlarged in these circumstances. The placenta is swollen because it is water loaded. Placental exchange is presumably impaired because of gross edema, contributing significantly to fetal asphyxia, tissue hypoxia, and thus to profound depression at birth.

B. Laboratory studies are essential for identification of the primary disorder (if it has not been diagnosed antepartum) and for assessing the status of a hydropic infant. Over one hundred disease states have been reported in association with hydrops fetalis. The most frequently encountered are cardiac disorders (principally arrhythmias and a variety of cardiac malformations), homozygous alpha-thalassemia, and twin-to-twin transfusion in utero. The incidence of primary disorders varies considerably from one report to another, depending on the population under study. In a population with large numbers of Asians, homozygous alpha-thalassemia is a frequent primary disorder. A diversity of these disease states has been identified. In most, one or more of a few basic mechanisms seem to be responsible for the hydropic state. Edema is the result of disturbed pressure relationships between intravascular and extravascular compartments plus disrupted function of capillary walls (increased permeability). Hemodynamic disorders that increase capillary hydrostatic pressure include heart failure because of intrinsic myocardial disease (infection and hypoxia), high output failure in anemia, and obstructed venous return. Diminished intravascular oncotic (colloid osmotic) pressure is a consequence of diminished serum albumin concentrations, which are probably the result of hepatic dysfunction, or of fetal nephrosis, which entails massive loss of albumin in the urine. In Rh disease, hypoalbuminemia has been shown to be more consistently related to fetal hydrops than heart failure or anemia. Although anemia, heart failure, hypoalbuminemia, and increased capillary permeability are the known major pathogenic factors, their relationship (singly or in combination) to the occurrence of hydrops fetalis and its severity is nevertheless inconsistent.

C. Postnatal imaging entails use of ultrasound and radiographs to diagnose the primary disorder and to assess neonatal status. The extent of fluid accumulation in pleural, pericardial, and peritoneal cavities and the severity of pulmonary edema must be demonstrated. Echocardiography is required to assess severity and nature of cardiac dysfunction. Radiographs of the skull and long bones may reveal brain calcification and structural abnormalities of bone. Cranial ultrasound is essential for demonstration of structural abnormalities of the brain and for the presence of periventricular-intraventricular and parenchymal hemorrhage. Abdominal ultrasound is used to identify masses and gross anomalies of the urinary tract.

SBK

References

Davis CL. Diagnosis and management of nonimmune hydrops fetalis. J Reprod Med 1982; 27:594.

Etches PC. Part V: Hydrops fetalis. In: Roberton NRC, ed. Textbook of neonatology. New York: Churchill Livingstone, 1986.

Giacoia GP. Hydrops fetalis (fetal edema). Clin Pediatr 1980; 19:334.

Holzgreve W, Holzgreve B, Curry CJR: Nonimmune hydrops fetalis: Diagnosis and management. Semin Perinatol 1985; 9:52.

Hutchinson AA, Drew JH, Yu VYH, et al. Nonimmunologic hydrops fetalis: A review of 61 cases. Obstet Gynecol 1982; 59:347.

Turkel SB. Conditions associated with nonimmune hydrops fetalis. Clin Perinatol 1982; 9:613.

HYDROPS FETALIS: POSTNATAL DIAGNOSIS

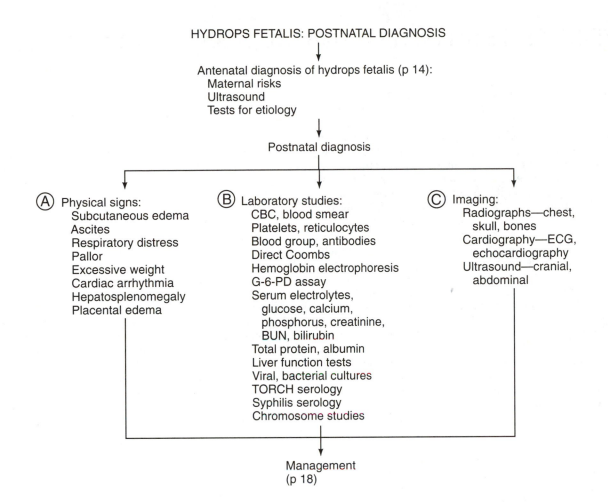

Antenatal diagnosis of hydrops fetalis (p 14):
    Maternal risks
    Ultrasound
    Tests for etiology

Postnatal diagnosis

Ⓐ Physical signs:
    Subcutaneous edema
    Ascites
    Respiratory distress
    Pallor
    Excessive weight
    Cardiac arrhythmia
    Hepatosplenomegaly
    Placental edema

Ⓑ Laboratory studies:
    CBC, blood smear
    Platelets, reticulocytes
    Blood group, antibodies
    Direct Coombs
    Hemoglobin electrophoresis
    G-6-PD assay
    Serum electrolytes,
        glucose, calcium,
        phosphorus, creatinine,
        BUN, bilirubin
    Total protein, albumin
    Liver function tests
    Viral, bacterial cultures
    TORCH serology
    Syphilis serology
    Chromosome studies

Ⓒ Imaging:
    Radiographs—chest,
        skull, bones
    Cardiography—ECG,
        echocardiography
    Ultrasound—cranial,
        abdominal

Management
(p 18)

HYDROPS FETALIS: POSTNATAL MANAGEMENT

A. Amelioration of life-threatening factors is the immediate concern in managing hydrops fetalis. Intrauterine asphyxia is virtually the rule, accentuated by labor if it has occurred, and by progressive dysfunction of an increasingly edematous placenta. Tissue hypoxia becomes more profound in utero when hemolysis is progressive, when the liver fails to generate albumin, and when permeability increases as a result of continued capillary wall damage. Direct effect on the myocardium adds abnormal hemodynamic phenomena to exacerbate tissue hypoxia. Resuscitation first requires an airway to introduce oxygen and eliminate CO_2. In the delivery room, positive end expiratory pressure by bag and endotracheal tube or by ventilator is an absolute requirement, as well as the application of sufficient peak inspiratory pressures to expand edematous noncompliant lungs. Severe ascites splints the diaphragm; paracentesis may be required for its relief. Ascitic fluid should be drained cautiously until diaphragmatic mobilization has been accommodated. Similarly, large pleural effusions must be drained promptly. Anemia may be incompatible with life. Hydropic infants are usually normovolemic. A partial exchange transfusion with packed red blood cells (hematocrit at least 70) is advisable, rather than a simple transfusion that could further impair a dysfunctional myocardium because of volume overload. Hydropic infants are not often hypervolemic; diminution of blood volume during the exchange transfusion is therefore illadvised. If hypervolemia is later demonstrated by elevated central venous pressure in the absence of cardiac failure, cautious blood letting while monitoring venous pressure may be appropriate. Initial treatment for stabilization also requires correction of metabolic acidosis, but first hypoxia must be minimized and severe anemia corrected. Administration of sodium bicarbonate is essential, but its effectiveness depends on amelioration of hypoxia, hypercarbia, and anemia. Sodium bicarbonate is contraindicated if CO_2 retention is not alleviated. In the presence of cardiac failure or hypotension, an inotropic agent such as dopamine should be administered.

B. Once stabilized, the infant requires assiduous long-term monitoring of several parameters. Tissue hypoperfusion is clinically recognizable by delayed capillary filling, mottling, and pallor or cyanosis, often associated with metabolic acidosis. Respiratory status is assessed with frequent blood gas determinations and displays of carbon dioxide and oxygen partial pressures plus oxygen saturations by transcutaneous monitors. The dynamics of an adequate response to ventilator pressures must be considered. As pulmonary edema is relieved and lung compliance improves, appropriate pressure settings one day may cause pneumothorax the next day. Diuretics (furosemide preferred) are effective in promoting egress of lung fluid. Universal accumulation of water requires a restricted volume of intravenous fluid in which 50 to 60 ml/kg/day is appropriate. Serial determinations of serum electrolytes, serum and urine osmolalities, and urine output indicate the need for subsequent increments of fluid input. Hypoalbuminemia is common, particularly when the underlying disorder is Rh disease or some other isoimmune blood incompatibility. Alleviation of hypoalbuminemia by use of pure albumin preparations is not advisable when capillary permeability is abnormal. Seepage of albumin into the extravascular space is especially hazardous in the lungs, where resultant enhancement of interstitial edema lessens the probability of successful ventilatory support. Tachyarrhythmias are an indication for digoxin therapy or for cardioversion. Digitalization should entail minimal dosage. Disseminated intravascular coagulation (DIC) or thrombocytopenia alone requires platelet transfusions when the count is <50,000/mm^3. DIC may also require exchange transfusions. Rh disease and other isoimmune incompatibilities are treated with exchange transfusions. Fetal transfusions must usually be followed by postnatal exchange transfusions. Cultures and other data for diagnosis of bacterial infection should be collected soon after birth, before antibiotics are administered.

SBK

References

Davis CL. Diagnosis and management of nonimmune hydrops fetalis. J Reprod Med 1982; 27:594.

Etches PC. Part V: Hydrops fetalis. In: Roberton NRC, ed. Textbook of neonatology. New York: Churchill Livingstone, 1986.

Giacoia GP. Hydrops fetalis (fetal edema). Clin Pediatr 1980; 19:334.

Holzgreve W, Holzgreve B, Curry CJR. Nonimmune hydrops fetalis: Diagnosis and management, Semin Perinatol 1985; 9:52.

Hutchinson AA, Drew JH, Yu VYH, et al. Nonimmunologic hydrops fetalis: A review of 61 cases. Obstet Gynecol 1982; 59:347.

Turkel SB. Conditions associated with nonimmune hydrops fetalis. Clin Perinatol 1982; 9:613.

HYDROPS FETALIS: POSTNATAL MANAGEMENT

(A) Stabilize at birth:

Intrauterine asphyxia	→ Resuscitation
Fixed diaphragm due to ascites	→ Abdominal Paracentesis
Lungs compressed by pleural effusion	→ Thoracentesis
Severe anemia, hypovolemia	→ Simple Transfusion, Packed Cells
Severe anemia, normovolemia	→ Partial Exchange Transfusion with Packed Cells
Metabolic acidosis	→ Correct Anemia, Give Sodium Bicarbonate
Heart failure, hypotension	→ Inotropic Agent, e.g., Dopamine

(B) After stabilization:

Tissue hypoperfusion	→ Volume Expansion
Respiratory insufficiency	→ Appropriate Ventilator Settings
Pulmonary edema	→ Appropriate Ventilator Settings, Diuretics
General edema	→ Fluid Restriction
Low oncotic pressure (hypoalbuminemia)	→ Fresh Frozen Plasma
Tachyarrhythmia	→ Digoxin, Cardioversion, Platelet Transfusion
DIC	→ Exchange Transfusion, Fresh
Thrombocytopenia	→ Platelet Transfusion
Isoimmune hemolysis	→ Exchange Transfusion
Bacterial infection	→ Antibiotics

Cautions:
Avoid blood letting unless hypervolemia is documented
Avoid pure albumin preparations

LABOR AND DELIVERY

Management in the Delivery Room: Apgar
    Score 0–3 (Severe Asphyxia)
Management in the Delivery Room: Apgar
    Scores 4–6 and 7–10
Breech Birth

Abruptio Placentae/Placenta Previa
Prolapsed Cord and Cord Compression
Trauma: Peripheral Nerves
Birth Injury: Viscera and Soft Tissue
Trauma: Bones

MANAGEMENT IN THE DELIVERY ROOM: APGAR SCORE 0–3 (SEVERE ASPHYXIA)

A. Upper and lower airway clearance is applied by modulated wall suction (set at 80–100 torr) rather than by mouth through the traditional DeLee trap. The laryngoscope should have a size 0 blade attached; large babies may sometimes require size 1. The endotracheal tube (ETT) size is 2.5 mm for infants judged to weigh <1300 g, 3.0 mm for infants >1300 g and 3.5 mm for those >3000 g. A manometer and a valve for maintaining PEEP should be attached to the breathing bag.

Clear the larynx of fluid and/or meconium. Ascertain the absence of anomalies such as oral masses or laryngeal web. Adequate peak pressure is indicated by significant chest wall excursion during insufflation and by equal breath sounds clearly audible in each lung with stethoscope at the lateral chest wall close to the axilla. Use the least possible peak pressure to produce these findings. A need for >30 cm H_2O at peak is not unusual, depending on the severity of noncompliance of lungs. The ultimate measure of effective assisted ventilation is an increased heart rate within minutes, followed very shortly thereafter by disappearing cyanosis.

B. If proper function of all components of the apparatus and appropriate ETT placement are assured, and if the heart rate remains <80/min, apply cardiac massage immediately. The most effective method is placement of the thumbs over the sternum at or slightly below the middle of the long axis while the hands envelop the chest to brace the infant's spine during compressions. To avoid interference with the individual who is insufflating and for ease of application, stand at the foot of the bed. The sternum is compressed approximately halfway to the vertebrae at a minimum rate of 100/min. Avoid compression while the lung is maximally expanded. Attempt synchrony with two rapid compressions that alternate with one insufflation. The best indication of blood flow is palpability of femoral or umbilical cord pulses.

C. If the heart rate is <100/min after 2 minutes of resuscitation, epinephrine 1:10,000, in dosage of 0.1–0.2 ml, is diluted with an equal volume of sterile water and instilled into the ETT. Do not interrupt chest compressions. A second operator inserts an umbilical vein catheter, filled with saline and fitted with a syringe at the distal end, for administration of alkali and other preparations that may be required later. Insert the catheter only 2–4 cm past the abdominal wall to avoid its diversion into hepatic vessels, which occurs in at least 30% of catheter insertions. Give sodium bicarbonate through the catheter in an initial dose of 3 mEq/kg of body weight. If the preparation contains 1.0 mEq/ml (44.7 mEq in 50 ml), the osmolality is 1400. Dilution with no less than equal parts of sterile water or 10% glucose is essential. Follow slow (≥3 min) administration of the mixture with a flush with half normal saline. Continued bradycardia after 2 minutes requires repetition of epinephrine instillation at twice the initial dose. Calcium gluconate (10%) should be slowly infused at a dose of 1 mg/kg. Withdraw blood from the umbilical vein for pH determination and for calculation of a second infusion of sodium bicarbonate. If heart rate is <100 and blood pressure is low, and provided that the pH has risen to ≥7.25, a continuous drip of dopamine may be initiated through the venous catheter or a peripheral vein. Dopamine is administered at 7–10 μg/min.

D. Acute hemorrhage is a common cause of failed response to resuscitative measures. Hemorrhage is strongly suggested by presence of placenta previa or abruptio placentae, by multiple gestation associated with cord compression, by cesarean section with retrograde blood flow back to the placenta while the baby is brought up from the uterus prior to cord clamping, and by incision into the placenta during cesarean section. In these circumstances, hypovolemia is also suggested by the presence of poor perfusion, cyanosis or pallor, hypotension, and tachycardia (not always present) or persistent bradycardia. Volume expansion is indicated. Give fresh frozen plasma, 5% albumin, or whole blood, each in a volume of 15–20 ml/kg, slowly to minimize abrupt circulatory overload and its effect on a hypoxic myocardium.

SBK

References

Apgar V. A proposal for new method of evaluation of the newborn infant. Anesth Analg 1953; 32:260.

Bloom RS. Delivery room resuscitation of the newborn. In: Fanaroff AA, Martin RJ, eds. Neonatal-perinatal medicine: Diseases of the fetus and infant. 5th ed. St Louis: Mosby–Year Book, 1992:301.

Corbet AJ, Adams JM, Kenny JD, et al. Controlled trial of bicarbonate therapy in high-risk premature newborn infants. J Pediatr 1977; 91:771.

David R. Closed chest cardiac massage in the newborn infant. Pediatrics 1988; 81:552.

Lindermann R. Resuscitation of newborn with endotracheal administration of epinephrine. Acta Paediatr Scand 1984; 73:210.

Rogers, MC. New developments in cardiopulmonary resuscitation. Pediatrics 1983; 71:655.

Simmons MA, Adcock EW, Bard H, Battaglia FC. Hypernatremia and intracranial hemorrhage in neonates. N Engl J Med 1974; 291:6.

Versmold HT, Kitterman JA, Phibbs RH, et al. Aortic blood pressure during the first 12 hours of life in infants with birth weight 610 to 4,220 grams. Pediatrics 1981; 67:607.

SEVERE ASPHYXIA: APGAR SCORE 0–3

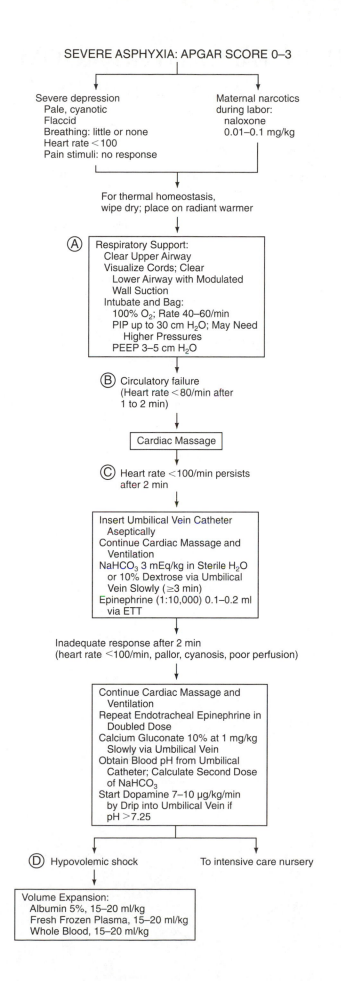

Severe depression
  Pale, cyanotic
  Flaccid
  Breathing: little or none
  Heart rate <100
  Pain stimuli: no response

Maternal narcotics
during labor:
  naloxone
  0.01–0.1 mg/kg

For thermal homeostasis,
wipe dry; place on radiant warmer

Ⓐ Respiratory Support:
  Clear Upper Airway
  Visualize Cords; Clear
    Lower Airway with Modulated
    Wall Suction
  Intubate and Bag:
    100% O_2; Rate 40–60/min
    PIP up to 30 cm H_2O; May Need
      Higher Pressures
    PEEP 3–5 cm H_2O

Ⓑ Circulatory failure
  (Heart rate <80/min after
  1 to 2 min)

Cardiac Massage

Ⓒ Heart rate <100/min persists
  after 2 min

Insert Umbilical Vein Catheter
  Aseptically
Continue Cardiac Massage and
  Ventilation
$NaHCO_3$ 3 mEq/kg in Sterile H_2O
  or 10% Dextrose via Umbilical
  Vein Slowly (≥3 min)
Epinephrine (1:10,000) 0.1–0.2 ml
  via ETT

Inadequate response after 2 min
(heart rate <100/min, pallor, cyanosis, poor perfusion)

Continue Cardiac Massage and
  Ventilation
Repeat Endotracheal Epinephrine in
  Doubled Dose
Calcium Gluconate 10% at 1 mg/kg
  Slowly via Umbilical Vein
Obtain Blood pH from Umbilical
  Catheter; Calculate Second Dose
  of $NaHCO_3$
Start Dopamine 7–10 µg/kg/min
  by Drip into Umbilical Vein if
  pH >7.25

Ⓓ Hypovolemic shock

To intensive care nursery

Volume Expansion:
  Albumin 5%, 15–20 ml/kg
  Fresh Frozen Plasma, 15–20 ml/kg
  Whole Blood, 15–20 ml/kg

MANAGEMENT IN THE DELIVERY ROOM: APGAR SCORES 4–6 AND 7–10

A. Painful stimuli often induce gasping and at least a feeble cry. One or more flicks of the sole with the fingernail seem to be more effective than any other stimulus. A mask through which oxygen flows should be held over the face in anticipation of the gasps in response to pain.

B. If stimulation fails, oxygen is administered by a closely fitting face mask. Position of the head is critical to passage of oxygen to the lower airway. Flexion or extension of the neck precludes an adequate flow. Satisfactory insufflation is indicated by chest excursions and by breath sounds that are audible over both lungs near the axillae. Successful assistance to the moderately asphyxiated infant is ultimately indicated by increase in heart rate within 1 minute and by spontaneous breathing soon thereafter.

C. Failure to respond is indicated by a declining heart rate and increased cyanosis. Immediate intubation and bag-assisted breathing should be applied as outlined for Apgar scores 0–3 (p 22).

SBK

References

Apgar V. A proposal for new method of evaluation of the newborn infant. Anesth Analg 1953; 32:260.

Bloom RS. Delivery room resuscitation of the newborn. In: Fanaroff AA, Martin RJ, eds. Neonatal-perinatal medicine: Diseases of the fetus and infant, 5th ed. St Louis: Mosby–Year Book, 1992:301.

Corbet AJ, Adams JM, Kenny JD, et al. Controlled trial of bicarbonate therapy in high-risk premature newborn infants. J Pediatr 1977; 91:771.

David R. Closed chest cardiac massage in the newborn infant. Pediatrics 1988; 81:552.

Lindermann R. Resuscitation of newborn with endotracheal administration of epinephrine. Acta Paediatr Scand 1984; 73:210.

Rogers MC. New developments in cardiopulmonary resuscitation. Pediatrics 1983; 71:655.

Simmons MA, Adcock EW, Bard H, Battaglia FC. Hypernatremia and intracranial hemorrhage in neonates. N Engl J Med 1974; 291:6.

Versmold HT, Kitterman JA, Phibbs RH, et al. Aortic blood pressure during the first 12 hours of life in infants with birth weight 610 to 4220 grams. Pediatrics 1981; 67:607.

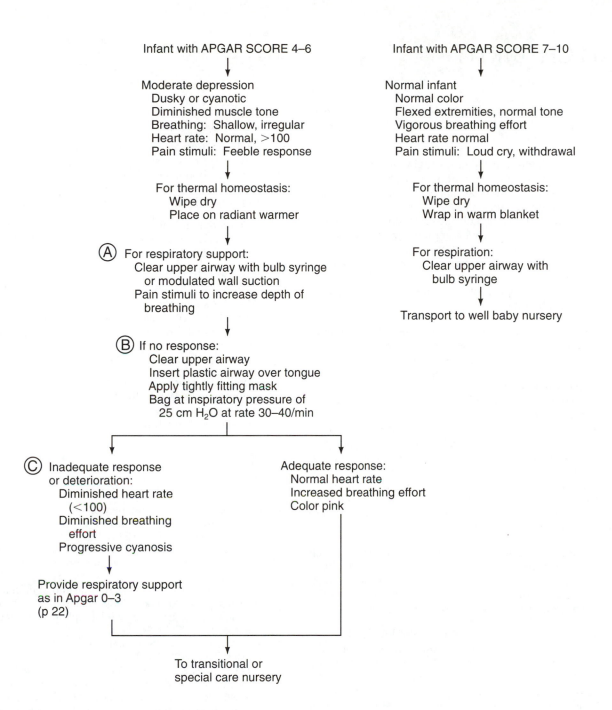

Infant with APGAR SCORE 4–6

Moderate depression
  Dusky or cyanotic
  Diminished muscle tone
  Breathing: Shallow, irregular
  Heart rate: Normal, >100
  Pain stimuli: Feeble response

For thermal homeostasis:
  Wipe dry
  Place on radiant warmer

Ⓐ For respiratory support:
  Clear upper airway with bulb syringe
    or modulated wall suction
  Pain stimuli to increase depth of
    breathing

Ⓑ If no response:
  Clear upper airway
  Insert plastic airway over tongue
  Apply tightly fitting mask
  Bag at inspiratory pressure of
    25 cm H_2O at rate 30–40/min

Ⓒ Inadequate response
  or deterioration:
  Diminished heart rate
    (<100)
  Diminished breathing
    effort
  Progressive cyanosis

Provide respiratory support
as in Apgar 0–3
(p 22)

Adequate response:
  Normal heart rate
  Increased breathing effort
  Color pink

To transitional or
special care nursery

Infant with APGAR SCORE 7–10

Normal infant
  Normal color
  Flexed extremities, normal tone
  Vigorous breathing effort
  Heart rate normal
  Pain stimuli: Loud cry, withdrawal

For thermal homeostasis:
  Wipe dry
  Wrap in warm blanket

For respiration:
  Clear upper airway with
    bulb syringe

Transport to well baby nursery

BREECH BIRTH

A. The incidence of breech birth is higher with earlier gestation: 24% at <24 weeks, 8% at 28–30 weeks, and 3% at term.

B. Aberrant shape of the uterine cavity occurs in uterine abnormalities: e.g., bicornuate uterus, double or septate uterus, abnormal placental implantation (fundal-cornual implantation), with the fetus assuming the more comfortable breech presentation. Constraint in uterine space occurs with multiple gestation and in oligohydramnios (e.g., Potter anomaly), limiting the turning of the fetus as term approaches. In polyhydramnios or low birthweight fetuses, less uterine space constraint may prevent the fetus from settling in a vertex presentation.

C. Fetal abnormalities tend to favor breech presentation. Megacephaly is less compatible with vertex presentation. Either joint dislocations/contractures or neuromuscular dysfunction (hypotonia, hypertonia, or aberrant function) limit fetal activity in utero. Breech presentation is reported with congenital hip dislocation and in Larsen syndrome. Disorders associated with fetal hypotonia include Prader-Willi syndrome, trisomy 21, and Zellweger syndrome. Hypertonia occurs in trisomy 13 and 18 syndromes and in Smith-Lemli-Opitz syndrome. Aberrant muscular function is reported with fetal alcohol syndrome, myotonic dystrophy, Werdnig-Hoffmann syndrome, and familial dysautonomia. Joint contractures are noted in de Lange syndrome.

D. Traumatic injuries are common in vaginal breech births. Soft tissue trauma is manifested as petechiae, ecchymosis, abrasions, or subcutaneous fat necrosis. Although benign in themselves, soft tissue injuries suggest other more severe existing injuries.

E. Spinal cord injury, commonly at the level of C5–T1, results from excessive traction applied during the vaginal birth process. Injury has been reported as a result of hyperextension of the head in utero before cesarian section delivery. Extent of injury varies. Lesions include edema, congestion, neuronal injury, necrosis laceration, and transsection. Clinical manifestations depend on the extent and type of lesions. Skeletal fractures, e.g., clavicular and humeral are not unusual. Brachial plexus injury such as Erb's palsy (C5–C6) and Klumpke's palsy (C8–T1) results from stretching or avulsion of nerve fibers of the brachial plexus. Phrenic nerve injury accompanies 5%–9% of brachial plexus injury of the Erb type. Complete cord transsection results in paraplegia or quadriplegia with respiratory depression, with associated urologic and orthopedic complications.

F. Skull fracture or occipital osteodiastasis, i.e., the separation of the squamous or lateral portion of the occipital bone, could be associated with traumatic intracranial hemorrhage, e.g., posterior fossa hemorrhage, subdural hemorrhage, or dural rupture.

G. Hematomas in the liver, spleen, adrenal gland, and kidney can occur with associated abdominal trauma during difficult breech extraction.

H. The breech fetus is more likely to develop fetal distress—7.8% versus 2.9% in nonbreech fetuses. Also, mean Apgar scores in breech births are lower. Percentages of lower scores are higher in every gestation with breech deliveries. Prolapse cord occurs in 5.2% of breech deliveries versus 0.3% in nonbreech deliveries and is a major cause of asphyxia.

I. Continued traumatic injury and asphyxia are relatively common in breech birth. It is often difficult to separate the effects of asphyxia from trauma when considering outcome of breech births.

HSB

References

Alexopoulos KA. The importance of breech delivery in the pathogenesis of brain damage: End results of a long-term follow-up, Clin Pediatr 1973; 12(4):248.

Axelrod FB, Leistner HL, Porges RF. Breech presentation among infants with familial dysautonomia. J Pediatr 1974; 84(1):107.

Bowes WA Jr. Clinical aspects of normal and abnormal labor. In: Creasy RK, Resnik R, eds. Maternal fetal medicine: Principles and practice. Philadelphia: WB Saunders, 1984:449.

Brans YW, Cassady G. Neonatal spinal cord injuries. Am J Obstet Gynecol 1975; 123(8):918.

Braun FHT, Jones KL, Smith DW. Breech presentation as an indicator of fetal abnormality. J Pediatr 1975; 86(3):419.

Brenner WE, Bruce RD, Hendricks CH. The characteristics and perils of breech presentation. Am J Obstet Gynecol 1974; 118(5):700.

Donn SM, Faix RG: Long-term prognosis for the infant with severe birth trauma. Clin Perinatol 1983; 10(2):507.

Towbin A. Latent spinal cord and brain stem injury in newborn infants. Dev Med Child Neurol 1969; 11:54.

Wigglesworth JS, Husemeyer RP. Intracranial birth trauma in vaginal breech delivery: The continued importance of injury to the occipital bone. Br J Obstet Gynaecol 1977; 84:684.

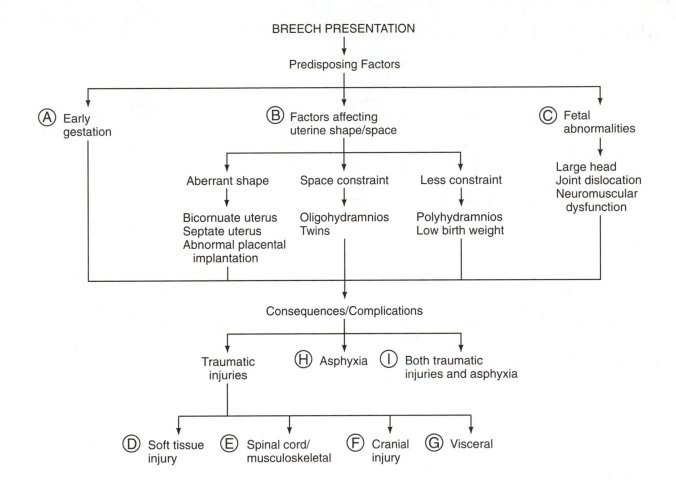

BREECH PRESENTATION

Predisposing Factors

Ⓐ Early gestation

Ⓑ Factors affecting uterine shape/space

Ⓒ Fetal abnormalities

Aberrant shape

Space constraint

Less constraint

Large head
Joint dislocation
Neuromuscular dysfunction

Bicornuate uterus
Septate uterus
Abnormal placental implantation

Oligohydramnios
Twins

Polyhydramnios
Low birth weight

Consequences/Complications

Traumatic injuries

Ⓗ Asphyxia

Ⓘ Both traumatic injuries and asphyxia

Ⓓ Soft tissue injury

Ⓔ Spinal cord/ musculoskeletal

Ⓕ Cranial injury

Ⓖ Visceral

ABRUPTIO PLACENTAE/PLACENTA PREVIA

A. Abruptio placentae is the separation of the normally implanted placenta before birth of the fetus, occurring in 0.5%–1.2% of all pregnancies and accounting for 31% of antepartum hemorrhages. Few cases of abruption may be explained by trauma, uterine tumors, and short umbilical cord. Cocaine addiction is a prominent cause. The role of hypertension is not clear, but 47% of severe abruptio cases with fetal death are associated with maternal hypertension. Associated toxemia occurs in 14% of mild abruption cases and 52% of severe cases; maternal vascular disease appears to be an etiological factor in both hypertension and abruption. Incidence of abruption is also increased among smokers, perhaps related to the vasoconstrictive effect of nicotine. Increased incidence of abruption with advanced maternal age may be explained by increased parity, i.e., endometrial damage with multiparity. The risk of recurrence of placental abruption with fetal death is 30 times higher than the risk in the general population. Pathological placental abnormalities reported with abruptio placentae include necrosis of the decidua basalis at the margin or central areas of the placenta, gross and microscopic infarcts, and stromal fibrosis of the terminal villi.

B. Placenta previa occurs in 1 of 250 births (0.6%) and in 1 of 20 grand multiparas. Previous gestation or induced abortions may damage the endometrium at the underlying placental site, and thus the endometrium becomes unsuitable for subsequent implantation. With low implantation, placental growth tends to proceed centripetally (complete placenta previa) or toward the fundus. When implantation occurs relative to the internal cervical os at the onset of labor, placenta previa may be classified as total or complete, partial, marginal, or lateral. Because delivery by cesarean section is universally favored for all degrees of placenta previa, the influence of the type of previa on outcome is difficult to evaluate.

C. Perinatal mortality ranges from 30% to 50% in abruptio placentae; 11% to 57% of deaths occur in utero. In placenta previa perinatal mortality is seven times higher than in nonprevia cases (21% versus 3%). Among placenta previa cases, perinatal mortality is higher in vaginal deliveries than cesarean section deliveries for all gestational ages and regardless of the type of previa.

D. In abruption or placenta previa, fetal blood loss may be as severe as in fetal exsanguination. Blood loss is more likely when placenta accreta or vasa previa complicates placenta previa.

E. Asphyxia may be related to hypoxia/ischemia resulting from fetal anemia, either chronic or acute. Of placenta previa, 30% is associated with fetal malpresentation; cord prolapse is likely, resulting in severe fetal anoxia. Mean Apgar scores of babies in deliveries complicated by placenta previa are lower than those babies born in the absence of placenta previa.

F. Approximately 20% of placental abruptions terminate in preterm delivery. A similar frequency of preterm birth is reported with placenta previa. Significant perinatal mortality and morbidity in these conditions may be related to the complications of prematurity.

G. Of preterm babies born after placental abruption, 81% have birthweights lower than the mean for their gestational ages; long-standing placental dysfunction may have occurred even before abruption. Fetal growth retardation is common in pregnancy complicated by placenta previa. A good correlation exists between growth retardation and multiple antepartum bleeding episodes. Incidence of congenital malformation is more than doubled with placenta previa, 7% versus 3.2% without placenta previa.

HSB

References

Breen JL, Neubecker R, Gregori CA, Franklin JE Jr. Placenta accreta, increta, and percreta. Obstet Gynecol 1977; 49:43.

Brenner WE, Edelman DA, Hendricks CH. Characteristics of patients with placenta previa and results of "expectant management." Am J Obstet Gynecol 1978; 132:180.

Cotton DB, Read JA, Paul JH, Quilligan EJ. The conservative aggressive management of placenta previa. Am J Obstet Gynecol 1980; 137:687.

Golditch IM, Boyce NE Jr: Management of abruptio placentae. JAMA 1970; 212:288.

Green JR. Placental abnormalities: Placenta previa and abruptio placentae. In: Creasy RK, Resnik R, eds. Maternal fetal medicine: Principles and practice. Philadelphia: WB Saunders, 1989: 592.

Hibbard LT. Placenta previa. Am J Obstet Gynecol 1969; 104:172.

Hibbard BM, Jeffcoate TNA. Abruptio placentae. Obstet Gynecol 1966; 27:155.

Naeye RL, Harness WL, Utts J. Abruptio placentae and perinatal death: A prospective study. Am J Obstet Gynecol 1977; 128:740.

Pritchard JA, Mason R, Corley M, Pritchard S. Genesis of severe placental abruption. Am J Obstet Gynecol 1970; 108:22.

Varma TR. Fetal growth and placental function in patients with placenta praevia. J Obstet Gynaecol Br Commonw 1973; 80:311.

ABRUPTIO PLACENTAE/PLACENTA PREVIA

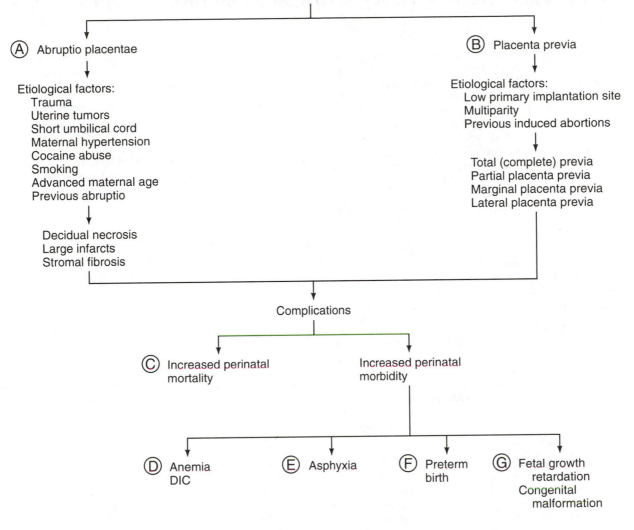

A ─ Abruptio placentae

Etiological factors:
  Trauma
  Uterine tumors
  Short umbilical cord
  Maternal hypertension
  Cocaine abuse
  Smoking
  Advanced maternal age
  Previous abruptio

Decidual necrosis
Large infarcts
Stromal fibrosis

B ─ Placenta previa

Etiological factors:
  Low primary implantation site
  Multiparity
  Previous induced abortions

Total (complete) previa
Partial placenta previa
Marginal placenta previa
Lateral placenta previa

Complications

C ─ Increased perinatal
      mortality

      Increased perinatal
      morbidity

D ─ Anemia
      DIC

E ─ Asphyxia

F ─ Preterm
      birth

G ─ Fetal growth
      retardation
      Congenital
      malformation

PROLAPSED CORD AND CORD COMPRESSION

A. Prolapse of the umbilical cord refers to the descent or protrusion of a segment of the cord between the presenting part and the maternal cervix or pelvis. This may be associated with compression leading to a decreased umbilical blood flow. Cord prolapse is likely when the presenting part at engagement does not completely fit the pelvic cavity. In abnormal presentations the incidence of cord prolapse is high, i.e., 6.6% in breech deliveries and 7.1% in transverse lie. Associated perinatal mortality with cord prolapse is reported to be as high as 49%. Multiple gestation predisposes to cord prolapse because of the associated frequent abnormalities in presentation. When membranes rupture prematurely before the presenting part becomes engaged, the gush of amniotic fluid may carry a segment of the umbilical cord downward, i.e., prolapse. Ultrasound diagnosis of cord presentation also should alert the physician to the possibility of cord prolapse.

B. When cord prolapse with compression occurs, abnormal fetal heart rate, i.e., variable decelerations with or without reduced baseline variability, may be observed on fetal monitoring. With significant decrease in umbilical blood flow, fetal asphyxia is a consequence, and thus scalp blood pH determination may reveal a pH of ≤ 7.20. Obstetrical interventions take into account these indicators of fetal compromise because of cord prolapse.

C. Occult prolapse can occur by similar mechanism as visible cord prolapse and could be as dangerous. With obvious cord prolapse, a segment of the cord is seen at the cervical opening by speculum examination, or the prolapsed cord is palpated during vaginal examination. Compression of the umbilical cord may either be partial or complete and either transient or prolonged. Partial or complete occlusion without depletion of fetal oxygen is likely without consequence, whereas depletion of fetal oxygen results with prolonged occlusion.

D. No consequences occur when cord prolapse is transient, particularly when there are no abnormalities in placental function and perfusion.

E. During umbilical venous occlusion, particularly without arterial occlusion, umbilical blood flow to the fetus ceases while arterial blood flow into the placenta may continue. Neonatal clinical manifestations are consistent with acute blood loss (p 178).

F. Perinatal asphyxia is a severe consequence of prolonged umbilical compression. Both hypoxia and fetal acidosis are associated with increased incidence of respiratory distress syndrome as well as neurological abnormalities. Postnatal manifestations relate to the multiple organ systems that may have been affected by oxygen deprivation and/or decreased organ blood flow.

G. Stillbirths account for half of the total perinatal mortality in cord prolapse cases.

HSB

References

Katz Z, Lancet M, Borenstein R. Management of labor with umbilical cord prolapse, Am J Obstet Gynecol 1982; 142:239.

Korones SB. High-risk newborn infants: The basis for intensive care nursing. St Louis: Mosby—Year Book, 1983:57.

Lange IR, Manning FA, Morrison I, et al. Cord prolapse: Is antenatal diagnosis possible? Am J Obstet Gynecol 1985; 151:1083.

Manning FA, Morrison I, Lange IR, et al. Fetal assessment based on fetal biophysical profile scoring: Experience in 12,620 referred high-risk pregnancies. I. Perinatal mortality by frequency and etiology. Am J Obstet Gynecol 1985; 151:343.

Martin CB, Siassi B, Hon EH. Fetal heart rate patterns and neonatal death in low birthweight infants. Obstet Gynecol 1974; 44:503.

Savage EW, Kohn SG, Wynn RM. Prolapse of the umbilical cord. Obstet Gynecol 1970; 36:502.

Vago T. Prolapse of the umbilical cord: A method of management. Am J Obstet Gynecol 1970; 107:967.

Westgren M, Hormquist P, Ingemarsson I, Svenningsen N. Intrapartum fetal acidosis in preterm infants: Fetal monitoring and long-term morbidity. Obstet Gynecol 1984; 63:355.

PROLAPSED CORD AND CORD COMPRESSION

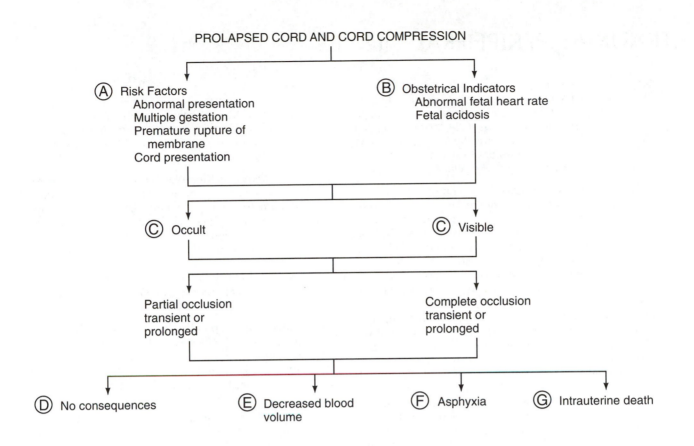

TRAUMA: PERIPHERAL NERVES

A. Peripheral nerve injuries are usually seen after difficult deliveries (e.g., difficult forceps deliveries; prolonged labor; breech deliveries, especially those associated with arrest of the aftercoming head; cephalopelvic disproportion; and in shoulder dystocia, which is not unusual in vaginal delivery of macrosomic infants).

B. Facial nerve palsy results from compression of the peripheral portion of the nerve by forceps or prolonged pressure on the nerve by the maternal sacral promontory. Pressure on the ramus of the mandible may be sustained in utero from a tumor or a persistently positioned fetal foot against the mandible. Peripheral nerve palsy should be differentiated from central nerve paralysis, which results from contralateral CNS injury (temporal bone fracture and/or posterior fossa hemorrhage or tissue destruction) and involves the lower half or two thirds of the face; the forehead and eyelids are not affected. Peripheral paralysis is unilateral; the forehead is smooth on the affected side, and the eye is persistently open. With both forms of paralysis, the mouth is drawn to the normal side when crying, and the nasolabial fold is obliterated on the affected side. Differential diagnoses include Möbius' syndrome, in which the face is expressionless, and congenital absence or hypoplasia of the depressor anguli muscle of the mouth.

C. Optic nerve injury may be preceded by a difficult forceps delivery; the optic nerve is injured by fracture at the region of the optic canal with associated hemorrhage into the nerve sheath. Callus formation from a fracture through the optic foramen may compress the nerve, resulting in optic atrophy (bluewhite optic disk). Prompt surgical intervention may prevent irreversible nerve damage.

D. Isolated vocal cord paralysis is rare, but the recurrent laryngeal branch of the vagus nerve may be injured from excessive traction on the head during breech delivery or from lateral traction of the head with forceps in vertex delivery. Unilateral paralysis may manifest with hoarseness and stridor during crying. Bilateral paralysis is more severe and may present with respiratory difficulty, retractions, cyanosis, stridor, and aphonia.

E. Isolated phrenic nerve injury is rare. Diaphragmatic paralysis is often observed with the ipsilateral brachial nerve injury. Chest radiograph shows elevation of the diaphragm on the affected side. Fluoroscopy reveals seesaw motion of two hemidiaphragms (elevation of the affected side and descent of the normal side on inspiration; opposite movements occur with expiration). Mediastinal shift to the normal side is observed on inspiration. Elective stimulation of the phrenic nerve helps make a diagnosis in questionable cases. Signs of respiratory difficulty are more severe with bilateral phrenic nerve injury.

F. Brachial nerve palsy is seen in three forms: Duchenne-Erb's palsy, Klumpke's palsy, and entire arm paralysis. In Duchenne-Erb's palsy, the fifth and sixth cervical roots (C5 and C6) are injured. Physical examination reveals paralysis of the upper arm.

G. Less common is Klumpke's palsy, in which the eighth cervical and first thoracic roots (C8-T1) are injured. In addition to lower arm paralysis, sensation may be impaired along the ulnar side of the forearm and hand. Dependent edema, cyanosis, and atrophy of hand muscles may develop. Horner's syndrome (ptosis, miosis, and enophthalmos) may be observed with associated injury to the cervical sympathetic fibers of the first thoracic root. Delayed pigmentation of the iris may be an associated finding.

H. With entire arm paralysis, the whole arm is flaccid and motionless. All reflexes are absent; sensory loss is from the shoulder to the fingers. Radiographs of shoulder, cervical spine, and humerus will rule out shoulder joint capsule tear, clavicular fracture, shoulder dislocation, or humeral fracture.

I. Partial immobilization and appropriate positioning are helpful in the first 2 weeks, after which range-of-motion (ROM) exercises may be initiated. Avoid initial active physical therapy; pain from traumatic neuritis occurs with brachial plexus injury.

J. In spinal cord injury, the lower cervical and upper thoracic areas usually are involved after breech deliveries, while upper and mid-cervical levels are involved with difficult vertex deliveries. A pop or snap due to rupture of the dura mater, the supporting structure of the spinal cord, heard during delivery signals severe spinal cord trauma. Manifestations vary according to severity, extent, and level of injury. Lesions above C3 and C4 are associated with diaphragmatic paralysis and are fatal. With respiratory support, infants may survive for only days to a few weeks (neonatal death). Lower cervical and upper thoracic lesions result in flaccidity of the legs and portions of the arm. If the spinal sympathetic pathways are involved, Horner's syndrome may be observed. Outcome is usually devastating; delayed mortality is common among survivors. Partial cord injuries are associated with subtle signs. X-ray films of the spine may demonstrate subluxation or fracture. Myelography may show a block secondary to adhesions in the subarachnoid space. CT may help to demonstrate the level of the lesions. Differential diagnoses include amyotonia congenita, spina bifida occulta, transverse myelitis, and spinal cord tumor.

HSB

PERIPHERAL NERVE TRAUMA

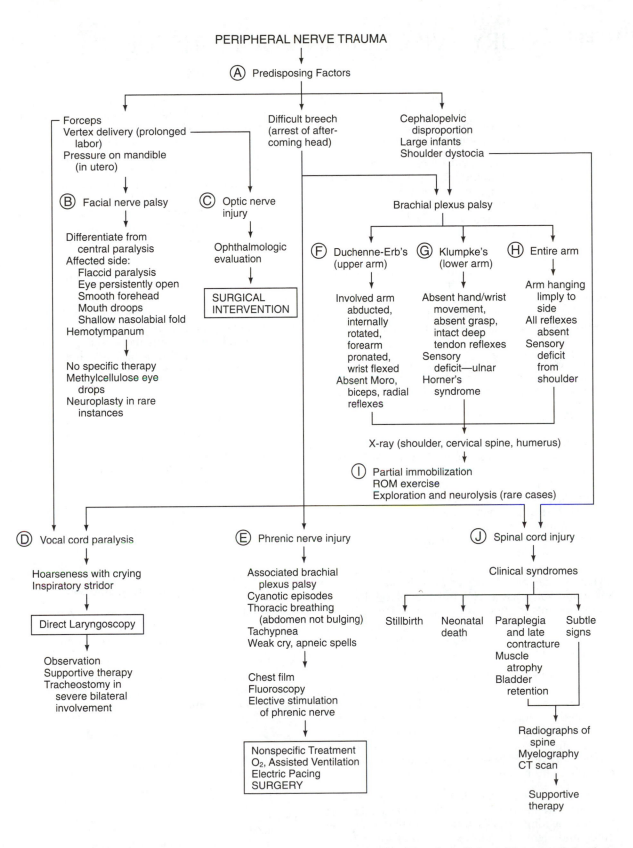

(A) Predisposing Factors

Forceps
Vertex delivery (prolonged labor)
Pressure on mandible (in utero)

Difficult breech (arrest of after-coming head)

Cephalopelvic disproportion
Large infants
Shoulder dystocia

(B) Facial nerve palsy

Differentiate from central paralysis
Affected side:
  Flaccid paralysis
  Eye persistently open
  Smooth forehead
  Mouth droops
  Shallow nasolabial fold
Hemotympanum

No specific therapy
Methylcellulose eye drops
Neuroplasty in rare instances

(C) Optic nerve injury

Ophthalmologic evaluation

SURGICAL INTERVENTION

Brachial plexus palsy

(F) Duchenne-Erb's (upper arm)

Involved arm abducted, internally rotated, forearm pronated, wrist flexed
Absent Moro, biceps, radial reflexes

(G) Klumpke's (lower arm)

Absent hand/wrist movement, absent grasp, intact deep tendon reflexes
Sensory deficit—ulnar
Horner's syndrome

(H) Entire arm

Arm hanging limply to side
All reflexes absent
Sensory deficit from shoulder

X-ray (shoulder, cervical spine, humerus)

(I) Partial immobilization
ROM exercise
Exploration and neurolysis (rare cases)

(D) Vocal cord paralysis

Hoarseness with crying
Inspiratory stridor

Direct Laryngoscopy

Observation
Supportive therapy
Tracheostomy in severe bilateral involvement

(E) Phrenic nerve injury

Associated brachial plexus palsy
Cyanotic episodes
Thoracic breathing (abdomen not bulging)
Tachypnea
Weak cry, apneic spells

Chest film
Fluoroscopy
Elective stimulation of phrenic nerve

Nonspecific Treatment
O$_2$, Assisted Ventilation
Electric Pacing
SURGERY

(J) Spinal cord injury

Clinical syndromes

Stillbirth

Neonatal death

Paraplegia and late contracture
Muscle atrophy
Bladder retention

Subtle signs

Radiographs of spine
Myelography
CT scan

Supportive therapy

References

Korones SB. High-risk newborn infants: The basis for intensive nursing care. St Louis, Times Mirror Mosby College Publishing, 1986:38.

Mangurten HH. Birth injuries. In: Fanaroff AA, Martin RJ, eds. Neonatal-perinatal medicine: Diseases of the fetus and infant. 5th ed. St Louis: Mosby–Year Book, 1992:346.

Painter MJ, Bergman I. Obstetrical trauma to the neonatal central and peripheral nervous system. Semin Perinatol 1982; 6:89.

BIRTH INJURY: VISCERA AND SOFT TISSUE

Visceral and soft tissue injuries may result from difficult deliveries, as in prolonged labor, difficult forceps extraction, breech deliveries, or shoulder dystocia. Injury is usually sustained by the presenting body parts.

A. In prolonged labor with vertex presentation, the head is compressed continuously against the bony maternal pelvis, and scalp injuries and intracranial hemorrhages are likely. When forceps are applied for either head rotation or extraction, facial, eye, and ear injuries may result.

B. Facial and/or periorbital bruising after difficult forceps delivery may herald eye injuries. Subconjunctival and retinal hemorrhages are common and usually resolve spontaneously. Rarely hyphema and vitreous hemorrhages result with associated rupture of Descemet's membrane. Surgical removal of blood may be necessary.

C. Injuries to the ear after forceps extraction may be severe enough to result in external hematoma (cauliflower ear). Associated fracture of the temporal bone may result in inner ear hemorrhage, which requires otolaryngologic evaluation.

D. In extracranial injuries, in addition to visible bruises, the head is usually misshapen. In *cephalhematoma,* bleeding results from disruption of blood vessels passing from the skull to the periosteum. Blood accumulates subperiosteally so that the area of hemorrhage is sharply demarcated (i.e., limited to a cranial bone); the boundaries are easily palpable. Spontaneous resolution occurs in a few weeks to 3 months. Calcium may deposit in the area of the cephalhematoma which persists for several months to a year. *Subgaleal hemorrhage* refers to bleeding in the subaponeurotic tissue. With large blood loss, the infant presents in shock with a rapidly falling hematocrit. This may be associated with a coagulopathy. Treat with blood transfusion, plasma transfusion, and vitamin K administration.

E. In breech deliveries with difficult extraction, excessive mechanical pressure may be applied to the abdomen, or injuries to the neck and head may result from excessive traction in an attempt to deliver the aftercoming head. A difficult vaginal vertex delivery may occur with macrosomic infants (e.g., infant of diabetic mother [IDM], erythroblastosis fetalis), resulting in multiple birth injuries.

F. Subarachnoid, epidural, and subdural hemorrhages are intracranial. *Subarachnoid hemorrhage* represents venous bleeding and is usually asymptomatic. Seizures and signs of brainstem compression are rare. Spontaneous resolution usually occurs in the absence of complications. *Epidural hemorrhage* is rare and difficult to diagnose, and its clinical signs are often delayed because of the expansibility of the neonatal skull. Establish diagnosis by CT. Circulatory and ventilatory support are indicated in cases of rapidly deteriorating condition. *Subdural hemorrhage* results from tentorial laceration with rupture of the lateral sinus, vein of Galen, or straight sinus; from laceration of the falx with rupture of the inferior sagittal sinus; or from rupture of the superficial cerebral veins. Clinical manifestations include stupor or coma, unequal and unresponsive pupils, ataxic respirations, seizures, and full fontanelle. Bloody fluid is aspirated by subdural tap. Establish diagnosis by CT. Treat by subdural tap or burr hole placement to drain the hematoma. Associated coagulopathy also needs correction.

G. Abdominal injuries may be intraperitoneal or retroperitoneal and are often life-threatening.

H. Liver hematoma, which may ultimately rupture, results from abnormal traction at delivery (disruption of peritoneal support ligaments) or from excessive mechanical pressure on the costal margin at delivery (injury to anterior liver surface). Clinical signs include pallor, shock, abdominal distention, and discoloration. Paracentesis reveals bloody fluid. Replace volume loss. Exploratory laparotomy is indicated.

I. Splenic hemorrhage is rare and has a clinical picture similar to liver hemorrhage.

J. Intestinal intramural hematoma is rare. Treatment includes GI tract decompression, parenteral nutrition, and correction of coagulopathy, if present.

K. Renal or adrenal hemorrhage is retroperitoneal in location. Bleeding may be so severe that the infant presents with pallor and shock; paracentesis reveals clear peritoneal fluid. Diagnostic studies include ultrasonography and CT. Radionuclide scans and angiography also may be needed. Signs of adrenal insufficiency may require steroid supplementation.

L. In shoulder dystocia, in either vertex or breech presentation, excessive pull on the neck at delivery may result in cervical spinal cord injuries.

M. Consider hemorrhage into the cervical spine joint capsule or spinal cord bruising after shoulder dystocia and/or with signs of brachial plexus palsy or spinal cord involvement (see p 32).

HSB

References

Donn SM, Faix RG. Long-term prognosis for the infant with severe birth trauma. Clin Perinatol 1983; 10:507.

Faix RG, Donn SM. Immediate management of the traumatized infant. Clin Perinatol 1983; 10:487.

Korones SB. Fetal and neonatal consequences of abnormal labor and delivery. In: High-risk newborn infants: The basis for intensive nursing care. 4th ed. St. Louis: Times Mirror/Mosby College Publishing 1986:38.

Mangurten HH. Birth injuries. In: Fanaroff AA, Martin RJ, eds. Neonatal-perinatal medicine: Diseases of the fetus and infant. 5th ed. St Louis: Mosby—Year Book, 1992:346.

BIRTH INJURY: VISCERA AND SOFT TISSUE

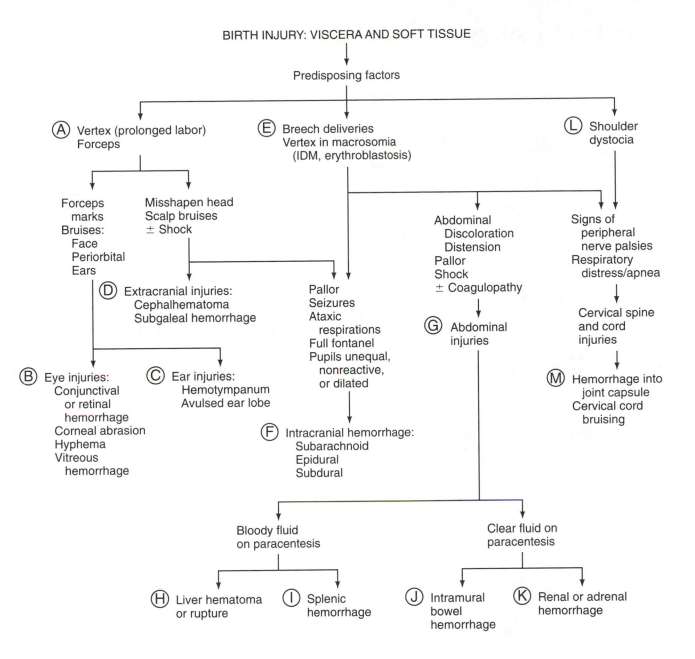

Predisposing factors

(A) Vertex (prolonged labor)
Forceps

(E) Breech deliveries
Vertex in macrosomia
(IDM, erythroblastosis)

(L) Shoulder
dystocia

Forceps
marks
Bruises:
Face
Periorbital
Ears

Misshapen head
Scalp bruises
± Shock

Abdominal
Discoloration
Distension
Pallor
Shock
± Coagulopathy

Signs of
peripheral
nerve palsies
Respiratory
distress/apnea

(D) Extracranial injuries:
Cephalhematoma
Subgaleal hemorrhage

Pallor
Seizures
Ataxic
respirations
Full fontanel
Pupils unequal,
nonreactive,
or dilated

(G) Abdominal
injuries

Cervical spine
and cord
injuries

(B) Eye injuries:
Conjunctival
or retinal
hemorrhage
Corneal abrasion
Hyphema
Vitreous
hemorrhage

(C) Ear injuries:
Hemotympanum
Avulsed ear lobe

(M) Hemorrhage into
joint capsule
Cervical cord
bruising

(F) Intracranial hemorrhage:
Subarachnoid
Epidural
Subdural

Bloody fluid
on paracentesis

Clear fluid on
paracentesis

(H) Liver hematoma
or rupture

(I) Splenic
hemorrhage

(J) Intramural
bowel
hemorrhage

(K) Renal or adrenal
hemorrhage

TRAUMA: BONES

A. Skull fracture is suspected following a difficult vertex delivery, particularly after a misapplied forceps extraction. The infant usually has signs of soft tissue injury such as scalp bruises or cephalhematoma. An indentation or depression on the skull heralds a depressed skull fracture. Linear skull fractures may be observed with a cephalhematoma. The infant usually is asymptomatic. Rarely shock, seizures, or drainage of bloody CSF from ears may be observed when there is associated concussion or hemorrhage from disruption of the venous sinuses. Diagnosis of skull fracture is made by x-ray study. Often no treatment is necessary. Surgical elevation of the depressed fracture may be helpful in extreme cases.

B. Mandibular, maxillary, orbital, or temporal bone fracture may occur as a result of traumatic forceps delivery. Soft tissue swelling, ecchymoses, and abrasions overlying the bone fracture are usually observed. Detailed evaluation by an otolaryngologist and/or ophthalmologist may be required for immediate surgical intervention.

C. Femoral fractures occur usually in the middle third of the shaft and are transverse fractures. Injury results from torsion of the leg during breech extraction. Infrequently, traumatic separation of the upper femoral epiphysis is observed. Diagnosis is made by x-ray study. Traction-suspension may be needed for shaft fracture. Closed reduction and immobilization may be required for epiphyseal separation.

D. Clavicular fracture is the most common bone injury in the newborn. Aside from localized crepitus or swelling, absent ipsilateral Moro reflex is observed. Clavicular fracture does not require specific therapy if the clavicular segments are undisplaced. Displaced fracture requires immobilization for rapid healing and recovery.

E. Humeral fractures are usually located in the diaphysis and are greenstick. Occasionally the fracture is complete. Absent ipsilateral Moro reflex is observed. X-ray examination confirms the diagnosis. Treatment is by immobilization in triangular splint or Velpeau bandage. Adduction is employed for 2–4 weeks. Upper humeral epiphyseal separation occurs rarely. Shoulder dislocation as a result of trauma is rare. A fracture occurring adjacent to an unmineralized epiphysis gives an x-ray picture simulating a dislocation of a neighboring joint (e.g., pseudodislocation of the shoulder, elbow, or hip). True dislocation involving the radial head may result from birth trauma.

F. Injuries to the spine and spinal cord follow overstretching of the vertebral axis or over-rotating the body in relation to the head, usually during breech deliveries or in shoulder dystocias. Cervical spine radiograph will demonstrate vertebral dislocation or fracture. Other possible injuries should be ruled out. Reduction of dislocation, relief of cord compression, and appropriate immobilization are instituted by the neurosurgical consultants. Management should also take into consideration associated nerve injuries (p 32).

HSB

References

Donn SM, Faix RG. Long-term prognosis for the infant with severe birth trauma. Clin Perinatol 1983; 10:507.

Faix RG, Donn SM: Immediate management of the traumatized infant. Clin Perinatol 1983; 10:487.

Korones SB. Fetal and neonatal consequences of abnormal labor and delivery. In: High-risk newborn infants: The basis for intensive nursing care, 4th ed. St Louis, Mosby–Year Book, 1986:38.

Mangurten HH. Birth injuries. In: Fanaroff AA, Martin RJ, eds. Neonatal-perinatal medicine: Diseases of the fetus and infant. 5th ed. St Louis, Mosby–Year Book, 1992:346.

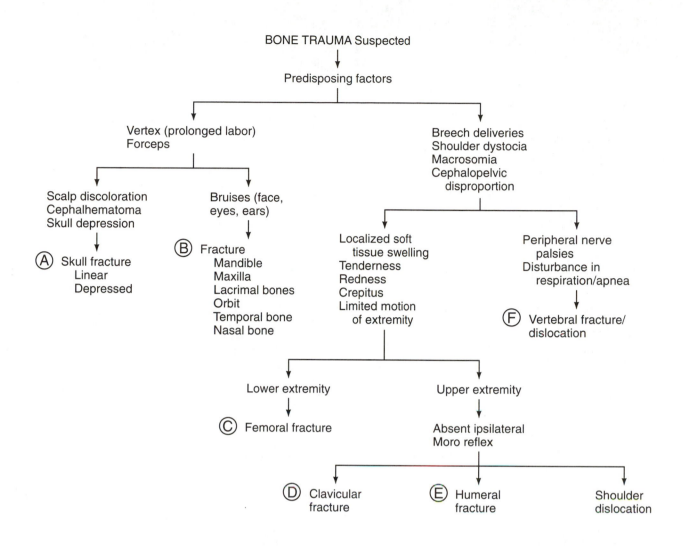

BONE TRAUMA Suspected

Predisposing factors

Vertex (prolonged labor)
Forceps

Breech deliveries
Shoulder dystocia
Macrosomia
Cephalopelvic
  disproportion

Scalp discoloration
Cephalhematoma
Skull depression

Ⓐ Skull fracture
  Linear
  Depressed

Bruises (face,
eyes, ears)

Ⓑ Fracture
  Mandible
  Maxilla
  Lacrimal bones
  Orbit
  Temporal bone
  Nasal bone

Localized soft
  tissue swelling
Tenderness
Redness
Crepitus
Limited motion
  of extremity

Peripheral nerve
  palsies
Disturbance in
  respiration/apnea

Ⓕ Vertebral fracture/
  dislocation

Lower extremity

Ⓒ Femoral fracture

Upper extremity

Absent ipsilateral
Moro reflex

Ⓓ Clavicular
  fracture

Ⓔ Humeral
  fracture

Shoulder
dislocation

HEAT AND WATER BALANCE

Hypothermia
Hyperthermia
Maintenance of Fluid Balance
Oliguria

Oliguria: Management
Polyuria

HYPOTHERMIA

The principal difficulties that befall a cold-stressed, hypothermic infant are increased oxygen consumption (and ultimately hypoxia), metabolic acidosis (lactic acidemia) as a consequence of anaerobic glycolysis, and depletion of glycogen stores with hypoglycemia. Ongoing low-grade cold stress does not cause hypothermia, but it nevertheless entails increased oxygen consumption. The loss of calories to thermogenesis results in diminished weight gain. The energy diverted from growth to thermogenesis can be compensated by increasing calorie intake.

A. Vulnerability to heat loss increases at lower weights and shorter gestational ages. The neonate's surface area is large in relation to body (metabolic) mass, thereby increasing exposure to a hostile thermal environment and predisposing the infant to rates of heat loss that exceed thermogenic capacity. The propensity to heat loss is also greater because there is little or no subcutaneous fat in the smallest infants. Gestational age is the major determinant of the extent of fat deposition; most fat is deposited during the last half of the third trimester. Blood vessels that supply the relatively large surface area lie immediately subjacent to epidermis with little or no heat-retarding fatty tissue as a mantle. Furthermore, the epidermis is thin and porous; its water content is high. Transepidermal water losses are correspondingly high, thereby promoting greater heat loss by evaporation.

B. Negative heat balance is potentially lethal without meticulous provision of a microenvironment that minimizes heat loss. Dissipation of heat is a function of the thermal gradient from baby to environment, which can be manipulated to promote homeostasis. Heat is transferred by convection, conduction, evaporation, and radiation. These modalities, singly and in combination, require control of several environmental factors. Incubators primarily control convective losses by generating a warm ambience. Evaporative losses can be reduced by increasing humidity in the incubator, but most facilities make no such provision in deference to potential infection from contamination of water reservoirs. Radiant heat losses are virtually independent of ambient temperature within the incubator. Heat is transferred from the baby to the incubator wall. The lower wall temperature is approximately midway between ambient temperatures within the incubator and in the nursery itself. Radiant losses can be minimized by surrounding the infant with a plastic shield to provide a primary radiant surface that is warmer than the incubator wall. The shield within the incubator is little affected by nursery

temperatures. This Plexiglas heat shield is inappropriate for radiant warmers. It is virtually opaque to infrared heat. On a radiant warmer, a baby in this shield can be warmed only by the gradual development of a greenhouse effect. In the smallest infants, particularly those below 1000 g, the delay may produce serious cold stress. The appropriate heat shield for a radiant warmer may have Plexiglas side walls, but the top should be covered with only a thin, disposable plastic film. Plexiglas transmits approximately 15% of the warmer's radiance; the thin film transmits 85%. The most important salutary effect of the shield is the protection it provides from airflow, thereby minimizing convective loss. Use of radiant warmers without a proper heat shield entails approximately twice the transepidermal water loss that occurs in the incubator. Continuous care on the radiant warmer requires ongoing surveillance of fluid and electrolyte status. The smaller the body, the more critical the effect of infrared energy on the unshielded infant.

SBK

References

Adamsons K Jr, Gandy GM, James LS. The influence of thermal factors upon oxygen consumption of the newborn human infant. J Pediatr 1965; 66:495.

Baumgart S. Radiant energy and insensible water loss in the premature newborn infant nursed under a radiant warmer. Clin Perinatol 1982; 9:483.

Dahm LS, James LS. Newborn temperature and calculated heat loss in the delivery room. Pediatrics 1972; 49:504.

Fitch CW, Korones SB. Heat shield reduces water loss. Arch Dis Child 1984; 59:886.

Hey EN, Mount LE. Heat losses from babies in incubators. Arch Dis Child 1967; 42:75.

Schwartz RH, Hey EN, Baum JD. Management of the newborn's thermal environment. In Sinclair JC, ed. Temperature regulation and energy metabolism in the newborn. New York: Grune & Stratton, 1978.

Stephenson JM, Du JN, Oliver TK Jr. The effect of cooling on blood gas tensions in newborn infants. J Pediatr 1970; 76:848.

Wheldon AE, Hull D. Incubation of very immature infants. Arch Dis Child 1983; 58:504.

Wu PYK, Hodgman JE. Insensible water loss in preterm infants: Changes with postnatal development and non-ionizing radiant energy. Pediatrics 1974; 54:704.

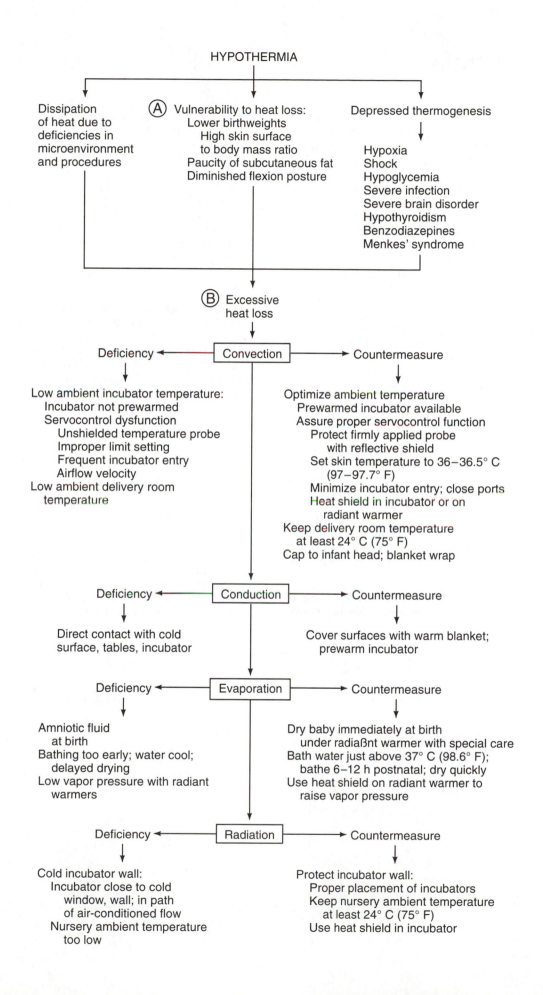

HYPOTHERMIA

Dissipation of heat due to deficiencies in microenvironment and procedures

(A) Vulnerability to heat loss:
  Lower birthweights
  High skin surface to body mass ratio
  Paucity of subcutaneous fat
  Diminished flexion posture

Depressed thermogenesis
  Hypoxia
  Shock
  Hypoglycemia
  Severe infection
  Severe brain disorder
  Hypothyroidism
  Benzodiazepines
  Menkes' syndrome

(B) Excessive heat loss

Deficiency ← Convection → Countermeasure

Low ambient incubator temperature:
  Incubator not prewarmed
  Servocontrol dysfunction
    Unshielded temperature probe
    Improper limit setting
    Frequent incubator entry
    Airflow velocity
Low ambient delivery room temperature

Optimize ambient temperature
  Prewarmed incubator available
  Assure proper servocontrol function
    Protect firmly applied probe with reflective shield
    Set skin temperature to 36−36.5° C (97−97.7° F)
    Minimize incubator entry; close ports
  Heat shield in incubator or on radiant warmer
  Keep delivery room temperature at least 24° C (75° F)
  Cap to infant head; blanket wrap

Deficiency ← Conduction → Countermeasure

Direct contact with cold surface, tables, incubator

Cover surfaces with warm blanket; prewarm incubator

Deficiency ← Evaporation → Countermeasure

Amniotic fluid at birth
Bathing too early; water cool; delayed drying
Low vapor pressure with radiant warmers

Dry baby immediately at birth under radiaßnt warmer with special care
Bath water just above 37° C (98.6° F); bathe 6−12 h postnatal; dry quickly
Use heat shield on radiant warmer to raise vapor pressure

Deficiency ← Radiation → Countermeasure

Cold incubator wall:
  Incubator close to cold window, wall; in path of air-conditioned flow
  Nursery ambient temperature too low

Protect incubator wall:
  Proper placement of incubators
  Keep nursery ambient temperature at least 24° C (75° F)
  Use heat shield in incubator

HYPERTHERMIA

A. In the small infant, heat is gained as readily as it is lost. Hyperthermia is either imposed by environmental factors that tend to overheat, or it is generated by the infant in response to a disorder such as infection. High ambient temperatures in the nursery as well as excessive clothing and blankets generally produce mild elevation in body temperature that is not usually troublesome. Placement of an incubator in the sunlight for protracted time periods may produce serious hyperthermia because of the warming of incubator walls that precludes radiant losses. Furthermore, warming within the incubator is unremittent as a result of the infrared wavelengths that are transmissible through Plexiglas walls. The most dangerous elevations of body temperature have been observed when a thermistor probe loses contact with the skin. The apparatus responds to a continuous low temperature signal to generate heat continuously. This occurs in the incubator; it is more dangerous on the radiant bed. Dehydration, acidosis, hyperelectrolytemia, brain damage, and death are the more extreme consequences of hyperthermia depending on the duration of inadvertent overheating.

B. A thermal gradient from fetus to mother is constantly operative in utero. If the mother is febrile, fetal heat loss, which occurs principally across the placenta, is impeded. The infant's temperature may be elevated at birth, but the predisposition to rapid heat loss precludes detection in most cases. Fever from infection is considerably less frequent in neonates than in older infants and children. In the intensive care nursery, servocontrolled thermal management diminishes the chances of detection when fever occurs.

C. Identification of a few clinical factors is often helpful in determining whether hyperthermia has been environmentally imposed or if it represents a response to infection. The overheated baby does not appear ill; the trunk and extremities seem equally warm to palpation. With a thermometer the extremities register <2° below the abdomen. The infected infant appears ill, and the extremities are palpably cooler than the trunk. By thermometer the temperature of extremities is >2° cooler than abdominal skin. When the baby is environmentally overheated, skin temperature is usually higher at first. Ultimately, core and skin temperatures reach equal and ominous high levels. The infected infant's rectal temperature is higher than the skin.

D. The most serious mishap in thermal management is the loosened skin probe. Hyperthermia develops more rapidly on a radiant bed than in an incubator. Partial loss of skin contact with the probe may be hidden from view by its silvery shield. Although overheating the infant may be more gradual, it is ultimately no less threatening than the loosened probe.

SBK

References

Korones SB. Thermoregulation. In: Korones SB. High-risk newborn infants: The basis for intensive nursing care. 4th ed. St Louis: Mosby—Year Book, 1986.

Schwartz RH, Hey EN, Baum JD. Management of the newborn's thermal environment. In: Sinclair JC, ed. Temperature regulation and energy metabolism in the newborn. New York: Grune and Stratton, 1978.

Swyer PR. Heat loss after birth. In: Sinclair JC, ed. Temperature regulation and energy metabolism in the newborn. New York: Grune and Stratton, 1978.

RISK FACTORS FOR HYPERTHERMIA

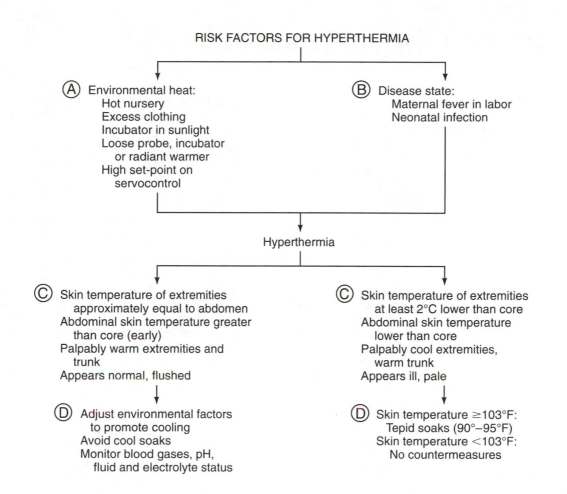

(A) Environmental heat:
    Hot nursery
    Excess clothing
    Incubator in sunlight
    Loose probe, incubator
      or radiant warmer
    High set-point on
      servocontrol

(B) Disease state:
    Maternal fever in labor
    Neonatal infection

Hyperthermia

(C) Skin temperature of extremities
    approximately equal to abdomen
Abdominal skin temperature greater
    than core (early)
Palpably warm extremities and
    trunk
Appears normal, flushed

(C) Skin temperature of extremities
    at least 2°C lower than core
Abdominal skin temperature
    lower than core
Palpably cool extremities,
    warm trunk
Appears ill, pale

(D) Adjust environmental factors
    to promote cooling
Avoid cool soaks
Monitor blood gases, pH,
    fluid and electrolyte status

(D) Skin temperature ≥103°F:
    Tepid soaks (90°–95°F)
Skin temperature <103°F:
    No countermeasures

MAINTENANCE OF FLUID BALANCE

A. The initial fluid volumes are based on our experience with infants who are on radiant warmers and are covered completely with specifically designed heat shields that provide relatively small ambience while avoiding skin contact. Among shielded infants, IWL is thus reduced by a mean of 50%, and radiant energy requirement by 60%, compared with unshielded infants. Realistically, during daily care a shield does not remain in place with the constancy of rigidly controlled experiments. The volumes recommended are influenced by the unavoidable and sometimes protracted time intervals of shield removal.

B. For extremely low birthweight infants (<800 g), the initial fluid volumes recommended here are somewhat higher than have been generally published. Most authors have recognized the need to increase fluids to similar levels but only during the second or third postnatal days. Transcutaneous water losses, sometimes >200 ml/kg/day, occur with awesome rapidity. A hyperosmolar syndrome frequently develops within 24 hours. Once established it is extremely difficult to rectify. The prevention of hyperosmolarity and its rapid development depend on (1) measures taken to minimize transcutaneous water loss (effective shielding and an optimal thermal environment) and (2) administration of water in sufficient volume to compensate for transepidermal losses. The hyperosmolar state in its fullest expression consists of oliguria, inordinately rapid weight loss, hypernatremia, and hyperkalemia. Early on, elevated serum sodium and potassium may be evident in the absence of diminished urine output. If inadequately managed, the dehydration progresses to hypovolemia, shock, renal failure, and death. In the presence of other complications, particularly intraventricular hemorrhage (grades III and IV), the process is more fulminant. Our experience has shown that administration of large fluid volumes on admission (during day of birth) has remarkably diminished the incidence of hyperosmolarity and renal failure in infants whose birthweight is <800 g.

C. Although various aspects of immature renal function have been implicated, the hyperosmolar state is largely attributable to water loss through an immature epidermis of high water content, is extremely porous, and has yet to generate keratin. However, the skin of small for gestational age babies who are <800 g is more mature, and the presence of keratin diminishes the water loss expected of appropriate for gestational age infants of similar birthweight. In recognition of this variation the quantity of IV fluid should be reduced. Furthermore, the stratum corneum begins to be elaborated between 1 and 2 weeks after birth so that transcutaneous fluid loss may be diminished significantly. Parameters of overhydration become evident in these circumstances, indicating a need to reduce fluid load.

SBK

References

Bell EF, Weinstein MR, Oh W. Heat balance in premature infants: Comparative effects of convectively heated incubator and radiant warmer with and without plastic heat shield. J Pediatr 1980; 96:460.

Costarino AT, Baumgart S. Controversies in fluid and electrolyte therapy for the premature infant. Clin Perinatol 1988; 15:863−878.

Costarino AT, Baumgart S. Modern fluid and electrolyte management of the critically ill premature infant. Pediatr Clin North Am 1986; 33:153−178.

Doyle LW, Sinclair JC. Insensible water loss in newborn infants. Clin Perinatol 1982; 9:453−482.

Fitch CW, Korones SB. Heat shield reduces water loss. Arch Dis Child 1984; 59:886−888.

MAINTENANCE OF FLUID BALANCE

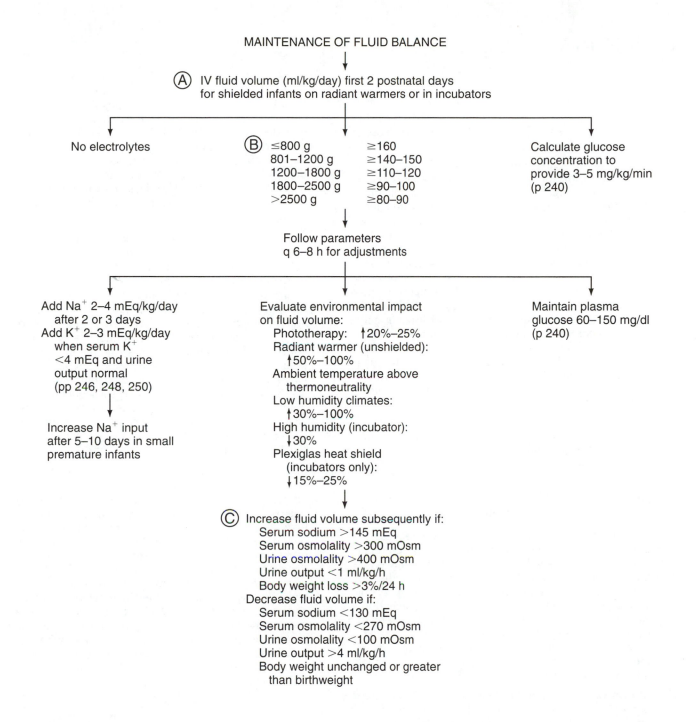

Ⓐ IV fluid volume (ml/kg/day) first 2 postnatal days
for shielded infants on radiant warmers or in incubators

No electrolytes

Ⓑ ≤800 g   ≥160
    801–1200 g   ≥140–150
    1200–1800 g   ≥110–120
    1800–2500 g   ≥90–100
    >2500 g   ≥80–90

Calculate glucose
concentration to
provide 3–5 mg/kg/min
(p 240)

Follow parameters
q 6–8 h for adjustments

Add Na⁺ 2–4 mEq/kg/day
    after 2 or 3 days
Add K⁺ 2–3 mEq/kg/day
    when serum K⁺
    <4 mEq and urine
    output normal
    (pp 246, 248, 250)

Increase Na⁺ input
after 5–10 days in small
premature infants

Evaluate environmental impact
on fluid volume:
    Phototherapy: ↑20%–25%
    Radiant warmer (unshielded):
        ↑50%–100%
    Ambient temperature above
        thermoneutrality
    Low humidity climates:
        ↑30%–100%
    High humidity (incubator):
        ↓30%
    Plexiglas heat shield
        (incubators only):
        ↓15%–25%

Maintain plasma
glucose 60–150 mg/dl
(p 240)

Ⓒ Increase fluid volume subsequently if:
    Serum sodium >145 mEq
    Serum osmolality >300 mOsm
    Urine osmolality >400 mOsm
    Urine output <1 ml/kg/h
    Body weight loss >3%/24 h
Decrease fluid volume if:
    Serum sodium <130 mEq
    Serum osmolality <270 mOsm
    Urine osmolality <100 mOsm
    Urine output >4 ml/kg/h
    Body weight unchanged or greater
        than birthweight

OLIGURIA

Oliguria is defined as a urine output of less than 1.0 ml/kg/hr. Etiological factors are numerous but may be categorized into prerenal disorders, intrinsic renal diseases, and postrenal conditions.

A. In evaluation of an infant with renal insufficiency or failure, a history of cystic kidneys in the family may indicate autosomal or recessive disorders. Oligohydramnios during pregnancy suggests impaired fetal urine excretion. In perinatal asphyxia, cardiovascular instability may be associated with renal insufficiency or failure. Congenital malformations may provide clues to certain syndromes that are associated with renal malformation. Renal hypoplasia or agenesis is commonly found with pulmonary hypoplasia. Palpable abdominal masses may indicate renal enlargement, cysts, or other tumors that may obstruct urinary flow. Inappropriate antidiuretic hormone secretion must be suspected when an infant has seizures. The infant's state of hydration must be evaluated through physical examination, assessment of fluid-electrolyte intake and output, and analysis of serum and urine chemistries.

B. Electrolytes, BUN, creatinine, and osmolalities from the serum and urine also aid evaluation of renal function. The fraction of sodium excretion (Fe_{Na}) is calculated by the formula:

$$Fe_{Na}(\%) = \frac{Urine\ Na^+ \times Serum\ creatinine}{Serum\ Na^+ \times Urine\ creatinine} \times 100$$

The mean Fe_{Na} reported in renal failure is 4.25 ± 2.18% compared with less than 1% in prerenal failure; Fe_{Na} is usually high in the low birthweight infant. Hematuria with RBC casts in the urine indicates renal parenchymal injury or disease. High numbers of WBCs in the urine suggest urinary tract infection. Abnormal CBC and metabolic acidosis may be seen in neonatal sepsis with associated cardiovascular dysfunction. Metabolic acidosis may indicate inability of the kidneys in conserving bicarbonate (e.g., renal tubular disorders).

C. Most neonates void at the delivery room. Ninety-two percent of healthy neonates void by 24 hours of age and 99% by 48 hours. The frequency of micturition varies from two to six times in the first and second days of life to five to twenty-five times on the succeeding days.

D. To determine the etiology of oliguria, urinary catheterization may be necessary to differentiate between decreased urine production and normal urine production but inadequate urine excretion. If the problem is in urine excretion an enlarged bladder is usually palpable. If urine production is diminished, abdominal ultrasound may demonstrate renal enlargement, cystic changes, or other masses or tumors. Doppler insonation of the renal arteries may detect abnormal hemodynamics. Radioisotope studies (renal scan, renogram) indicate location and size of the kidneys, blood flow distribution, and overall renal function.

Obstructive uropathy is a major possibility when an enlarged bladder is palpated or when there is a laxed, wrinkled, soft, flabby abdominal wall. Most of these conditions are relieved surgically and renal function could be preserved. Urinary retention without disturbance in normal urine production may also be observed in lower spinal cord lesions (myelomeningocoele) or when an infant is heavily sedated or paralyzed.

E. Prerenal causes include disorders associated with decreased renal perfusion. Inadequate fluid intake or dehydration from increased fluid losses (diarrhea, increased evaporative losses in a tiny premature infant, or vomiting) results in hypovolemia and consequently renal insufficiency. Renal perfusion may be compromised by hypotension from blood loss or myocardial dysfunction as in perinatal asphyxia or congestive heart failure. In the syndrome of inappropriate antidiuretic hormone secretion (SIADH), intravascular volume may be adequate but high ADH levels promote water retention and consequently urine output is decreased. Vasodilators, especially those given to mothers before delivery (e.g., beta-agonists, captopril), could result in neonatal hypotension and renal insufficiency.

F. Intrinsic renal diseases include congenital abnormalities, infection, vascular occlusion of the renal vein or artery, other vascular disorders, and acute tubular necrosis from hypovolemia, hypoxemia, or nephrotoxic drugs. Indomethacin is commonly used for the pharmacological closure of the ductus. The mechanisms for its renal effects are not clear. The associated decreased glomerular filtration rate may be due to decreased renal blood flow from inhibition of prostaglandin synthesis, a change in renal permeability and/or augmentation of ADH action. Tolazoline is a potent vasodilator but causes profound renal arterial vasoconstriction especially in association with hypokalemia and hypoxia. Hypertonic contrast agents may cause renal vein thrombosis, ischemia, and renal insufficiency.

HSB

References

Baliga R, Lewy JE. Pathogenesis and treatment of edema. Pediatr Clin North Am 1987; 34:639.

Engle WD. Evaluation of renal function and acute renal failure in the neonate. Pediatr Clin North Am 1986; 33:129.

Guignard J-P, John EG. Renal function in the tiny, premature infant. Clin Perinatol 1986; 13:377.

Karlowicz MG, Adelman RD. Acute renal failure in the neonate. Clin Perinatol 1992; 19(1):139.

Spitzer A, Bernstein J, Boichis H, Edelmann CM Jr. Kidney and urinary tract. In: Fanaroff AA, Martin RJ, eds. Neonatal-perinatal medicine: Diseases of the fetus and infant. 5th ed. St Louis: Mosby—Year Book, 1992:1293.

Stapleton FB, Jones DP, Green RS. Acute renal failure in neonates: Incidence, etiology, and outcome. Pediatr Nephrol 1987; 1:314.

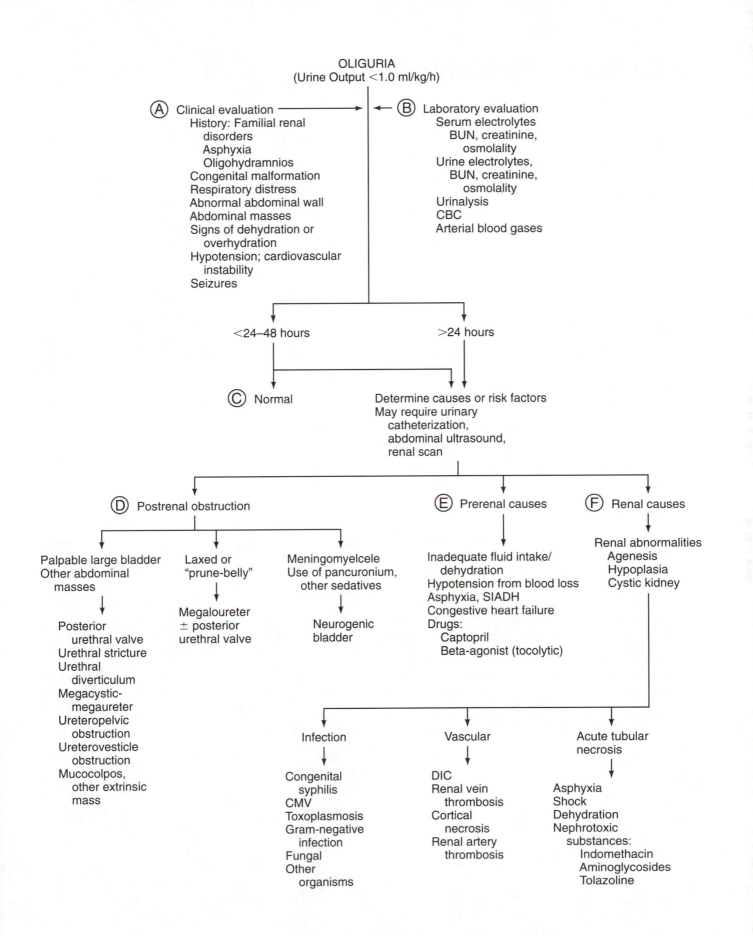

OLIGURIA
(Urine Output <1.0 ml/kg/h)

Ⓐ Clinical evaluation ⟶ ⟵ Ⓑ Laboratory evaluation
History: Familial renal
disorders
Asphyxia
Oligohydramnios
Congenital malformation
Respiratory distress
Abnormal abdominal wall
Abdominal masses
Signs of dehydration or
overhydration
Hypotension; cardiovascular
instability
Seizures

Serum electrolytes
BUN, creatinine,
osmolality
Urine electrolytes,
BUN, creatinine,
osmolality
Urinalysis
CBC
Arterial blood gases

<24–48 hours   >24 hours

Ⓒ Normal   Determine causes or risk factors
May require urinary
catheterization,
abdominal ultrasound,
renal scan

Ⓓ Postrenal obstruction   Ⓔ Prerenal causes   Ⓕ Renal causes

Palpable large bladder
Other abdominal
masses
↓
Posterior
urethral valve
Urethral stricture
Urethral
diverticulum
Megacystic-
megaureter
Ureteropelvic
obstruction
Ureterovesticle
obstruction
Mucocolpos,
other extrinsic
mass

Laxed or
"prune-belly"
↓
Megaloureter
± posterior
urethral valve

Meningomyelcele
Use of pancuronium,
other sedatives
↓
Neurogenic
bladder

Inadequate fluid intake/
dehydration
Hypotension from blood loss
Asphyxia, SIADH
Congestive heart failure
Drugs:
Captopril
Beta-agonist (tocolytic)

Renal abnormalities
Agenesis
Hypoplasia
Cystic kidney

Infection
↓
Congenital
syphilis
CMV
Toxoplasmosis
Gram-negative
infection
Fungal
Other
organisms

Vascular
↓
DIC
Renal vein
thrombosis
Cortical
necrosis
Renal artery
thrombosis

Acute tubular
necrosis
↓
Asphyxia
Shock
Dehydration
Nephrotoxic
substances:
Indomethacin
Aminoglycosides
Tolazoline

OLIGURIA: MANAGEMENT

A. The management of oliguria depends primarily on the establishment of its etiology. In postrenal causes whenever urine production is maintained but excretion is impaired by obstructive uropathy, temporary measures such as the Crede's method and urinary catheter insertion promote drainage. However if obstruction is proximal to the bladder, surgical intervention is indicated. Impairment of bladder function from use of muscle relaxants and sedatives resolves spontaneously after discontinuation of these drugs. Neurogenic bladder from spinal cord lesions requires indwelling catheterization or a vesicostomy procedure.

B. In prerenal failure, a fluid challenge of 10–15 ml/kg of plasma expander results in immediate and sustained increase in urine output. A diuretic may be given (e.g., furosemide 1–2 mg/kg) intravenously as an adjunctive therapy to promote diuresis. If the infant is hypovolemic, volume loss needs to be replaced and normal blood volume must be maintained. When the systemic vascular resistance is low because of vasodilator therapy, additional volume infusion maintains adequate circulating blood volume and systemic blood pressure. However, if blood pressure remains low after adequate volume expansion, the use of ionotropic agents or vasopressors is indicated. Inappropriate antidiuretic hormone secretion may occur with various neonatal disorders; blood pressure and blood volume are normal or even high, which is also associated with weight gain. The syndrome of inappropriate ADH secretion is managed by fluid restriction (see section **D**) with or without diuretic administration and treatment of the condition that led to SIADH.

C. In some cases of intrinsic renal disease, hypovolemia may be an associated finding. If this is in consideration, intravascular volume expansion may be indicated. Supportive measures (maintenance of normal blood pressure and correction of acid-base imbalance and electrolyte abnormalities) have to be instituted. Hyperkalemia is a common manifestation in renal insufficiency/failure, and prompt treatment prevents arrhythmias (see p 250). Adequate nutrition and calories also need to be provided. An appropriate serum albumin level maintains adequate oncotic pressure.

D. Fluid restriction refers to limiting fluid intake to insensible loss (50–55 ml/kg in a term infant, and 80–120 ml/kg in the premature infant with a higher insensible water loss in those who are smaller and have lower birthweight). Once urine output is established, fluid intake is increased by an amount equal to the urine output. Decreasing serum creatinine and BUN levels are indicative of successful management.

E. The etiology of the renal failure needs to be treated. Some congenital conditions such as renal hypoplasia or agenesis are lethal. Renal function usually improves when nephrotoxic drugs are discontinued. Some disorders such as renal vascular thrombosis or stenosis may require surgical correction. Lesions limited to one kidney may be treated by nephrectomy.

F. In irreversible renal failure, peritoneal dialysis serves as a temporary measure. Hemodialysis is an alternative therapy.

HSB

References

Engle WD. Evaluation of renal function and acute renal failure in the neonate. Pediatr Clin North Am 1986; 33:129.

Feld LG, Kaskel FJ, Schoeneman MJ. The approach to fluid and electrolyte therapy in pediatrics. In: Barness LA, ed. Advances in pediatrics. vol 35. Chicago: Mosby–Year Book, 1988:497.

Guignard J-P, John EG. Renal function in the tiny, premature infant. Clin Perinatol 1986; 12:377.

Linshaw MA. Potassium homeostasis and hypokalemia. Pediatr Clin North Am 1987; 34:649.

Spitzer A, Bernstein J, Boichis H, Edelmann CM Jr. Kidney and urinary tract. In: Fanaroff AA, Martin RJ, eds. Neonatal-perinatal medicine: Diseases of the fetus and infant. 5th ed. St Louis: Mosby–Year Book, 1992:1293.

OLIGURIA: MANAGEMENT

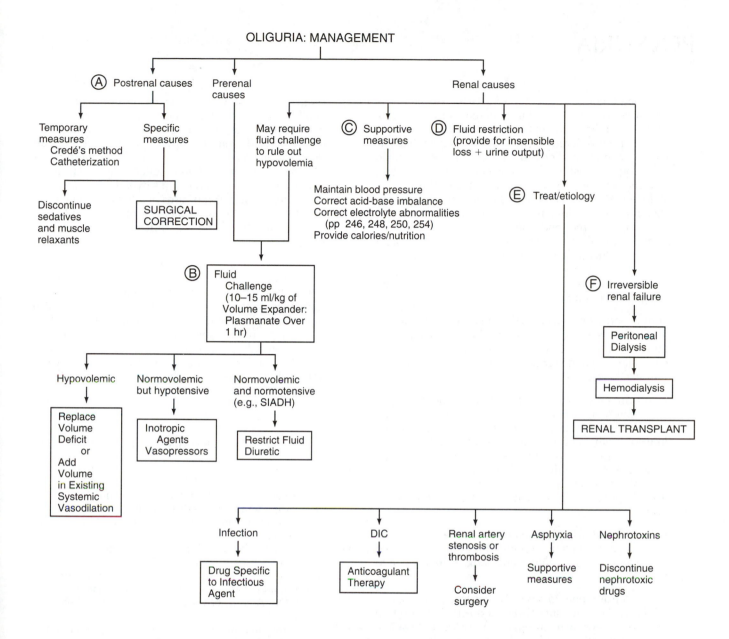

(A) Postrenal causes   Prerenal causes   Renal causes

Temporary measures
Credé's method
Catheterization

Specific measures

Discontinue sedatives and muscle relaxants

SURGICAL CORRECTION

May require fluid challenge to rule out hypovolemia

(C) Supportive measures

(D) Fluid restriction (provide for insensible loss + urine output)

Maintain blood pressure
Correct acid-base imbalance
Correct electrolyte abnormalities
    (pp 246, 248, 250, 254)
Provide calories/nutrition

(E) Treat/etiology

(B) Fluid Challenge (10–15 ml/kg of Volume Expander: Plasmanate Over 1 hr)

Hypovolemic   Normovolemic but hypotensive   Normovolemic and normotensive (e.g., SIADH)

Replace Volume Deficit or Add Volume in Existing Systemic Vasodilation

Inotropic Agents Vasopressors

Restrict Fluid Diuretic

(F) Irreversible renal failure

Peritoneal Dialysis

Hemodialysis

RENAL TRANSPLANT

Infection   DIC   Renal artery stenosis or thrombosis   Asphyxia   Nephrotoxins

Drug Specific to Infectious Agent

Anticoagulant Therapy

Consider surgery

Supportive measures

Discontinue nephrotoxic drugs

POLYURIA

A. A neonate voids an average of 20–60 ml/day in the first week of life; this volume increases to a range of 100–320 ml/day thereafter. A urine output of 1–3 ml/kg/h is considered normal. An output >5 ml/kg/h is extremely high, and possibilities of renal or extrarenal pathologies have to be considered. Urine output reflects not only renal function but also the infant's state of hydration. Particular attention must be paid to determination of fluid intake, electrolyte intake as well as urine volume and electrolyte losses. Signs of dehydration in the presence of high urine output suggest induced diuresis or inability of the kidney to conserve water. On the other hand, rapid weight gain or edema may result with excessive fluid load despite adequate renal function.

B. Serum and urine electrolytes, glucose, osmolalities, and urine specific gravity aid in determining the etiology of polyuria. Fraction of sodium excretion is calculated from the serum and urine sodium and urea nitrogen (see p 46).

C. If an infant's state of hydration is normal with hyponatremia, and urine Na^+, $FeNa^+$, urine osmolality, and specific gravity are decreased, rapid volume infusion with salt-free isotonic solution (5% dextrose or intralipid) is a possible etiology. However if an infant appears slightly dehydrated and voiding a large volume of concentrated urine, diuresis is suspected from hyperglycemia or infusion of hypertonic solutions.

D. In an edematous infant with hypernatremia, sodium overload is a strong possibility. This is easily corrected by decreasing or discontinuing sodium supplementation.

E. Polyuria from renal losses of Na^+ is treated specific to etiology. Sodium supplementation is increased in cases of salt-losing nephropathy. Very low birthweight infants normally have high fraction of sodium excretion, and sodium losses need to be replaced. Diuretics are discontinued if appropriate. Some infants with bronchopulmonary dysplasia require diuretics; Na^+ and K^+ supplementation correct the electrolyte imbalance, but increased urine output is observed within one hour of diuretic therapy. Theophylline and caffeine are given for apnea of prematurity; these drugs may have associated diuretic effect. Particular attention must be given to an infant's hydration when these drugs are given. In some cases of adrenal insufficiency that are nonsalt losing, sodium is retained and hypernatremia results; therapy is directed to specific hormone replacement.

F. In diabetes insipidus arginine vasopression is deficient. Water is thus excreted inappropriately. Therefore serum sodium is high but urine osmolality and specific gravity are low. Diabetes insipidus may also be of the nephrogenic type wherein the renal tubule is insensitive to the antidiuretic hormone. Therapy should provide sufficient fluid volume to maintain hydration. Indomethacin may improve renal concentrating ability, especially when given with diuretics.

HSB

References

Engle WD. Evaluation of renal function and acute renal failure in the neonate. Pediatr Clin North Am 1986; 33:129.

Feld LG, Kaskel FJ, Schoeneman MJ. The approach to fluid and electrolyte therapy in pediatrics. In: Barness LA, ed. Advances in pediatrics. vol 35. Chicago: Mosby–Year Book, 1988:497.

Guignard J-P, John EG. Renal function in the tiny, premature infant. Clin Perinatol 1986; 13:377.

Meites S, ed. Pediatric clinical chemistry: A survey of normals, methods, and instrumentation, with commentary. Washington, DC: American Association for Clinical Chemistry, 1977:259.

Spitzer A, Bernstein J, Boichis H, Edelmann CM Jr. Kidney and urinary tract. In: Fanaroff AA, Martin RJ, eds. Neonatal-perinatal medicine: Diseases of the fetus and infant. 5th ed. St Louis: Mosby–Year Book, 1992:1293.

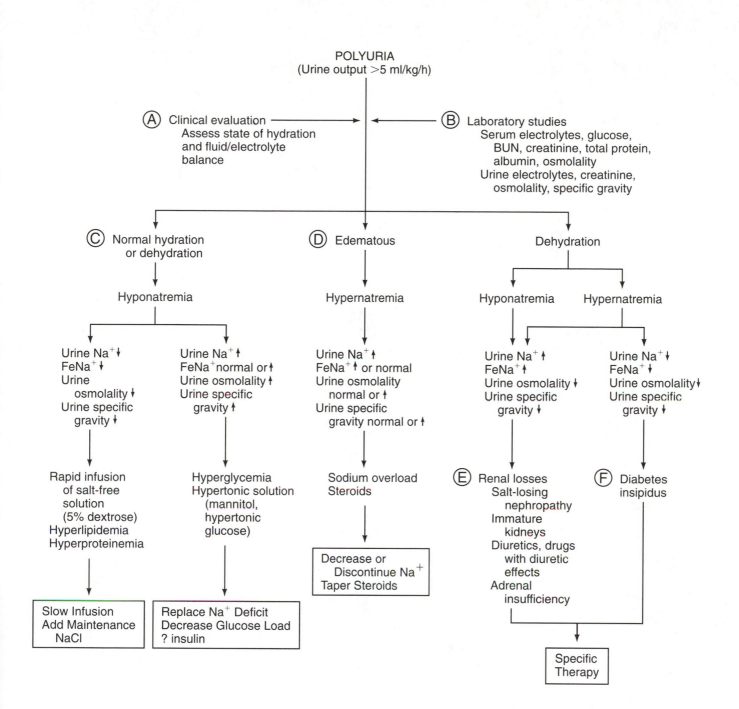

POLYURIA
(Urine output >5 ml/kg/h)

Ⓐ Clinical evaluation
Assess state of hydration
and fluid/electrolyte
balance

Ⓑ Laboratory studies
Serum electrolytes, glucose,
BUN, creatinine, total protein,
albumin, osmolality
Urine electrolytes, creatinine,
osmolality, specific gravity

Ⓒ Normal hydration
or dehydration

Ⓓ Edematous

Dehydration

Hyponatremia

Hypernatremia

Hyponatremia

Hypernatremia

Urine Na^+ ↓
$FeNa^+$ ↓
Urine
osmolality ↓
Urine specific
gravity ↓

Urine Na^+ ↑
$FeNa^+$ normal or ↑
Urine osmolality ↑
Urine specific
gravity ↑

Urine Na^+ ↑
$FeNa^+$ ↑ or normal
Urine osmolality
normal or ↑
Urine specific
gravity normal or ↑

Urine Na^+ ↑
$FeNa^+$ ↑
Urine osmolality ↓
Urine specific
gravity ↓

Urine Na^+ ↓
$FeNa^+$ ↓
Urine osmolality ↓
Urine specific
gravity ↓

Rapid infusion
of salt-free
solution
(5% dextrose)
Hyperlipidemia
Hyperproteinemia

Hyperglycemia
Hypertonic solution
(mannitol,
hypertonic
glucose)

Sodium overload
Steroids

Ⓔ Renal losses
Salt-losing
nephropathy
Immature
kidneys
Diuretics, drugs
with diuretic
effects
Adrenal
insufficiency

Ⓕ Diabetes
insipidus

Slow Infusion
Add Maintenance
NaCl

Replace Na^+ Deficit
Decrease Glucose Load
? insulin

Decrease or
Discontinue Na^+
Taper Steroids

Specific
Therapy

PHYSICAL SIGNS

COLOR
Jaundice: Diagnosis
Jaundice: Management
Cyanosis
Pallor

BREATHING
Apnea
Tachypnea
Stridor

THE HEAD
Large Head
Small Head
Misshaped Head
Wide Sutures
Bulging Fontanelles

THE CHEST
Abnormal Contour of Chest
Retractions and Respiratory Distress

THE ABDOMEN
Vomiting/Excessive Gastric Aspirate:
    Differential Diagnosis
Bloody Stools: Differential Diagnosis
Abdominal Enlargement Due to Gaseous
    Distention
Abdominal Masses
Abdominal Enlargement Due to Isolated
    Ascites (Intraperitoneal Fluid Accumulation)
Hepatomegaly
Splenomegaly
Enlarged Kidneys and Bladder

JAUNDICE: DIAGNOSIS

A. Jaundice is a yellow skin discoloration resulting from increased circulating unconjugated and conjugated bilirubin. Bilirubin is formed from the catabolism of heme from hemoglobin. Through oxidation catalyzed by microsomal heme oxygenase, iron, carbon monoxide, and biliverdin are produced from heme. Biliverdin is further reduced by biliverdin reductase (NADPH-dependent) and bilirubin is formed. Bilirubin in the serum is predominantly indirect or unconjugated; direct bilirubin is ≤15% of total bilirubin. Jaundice is noted in 50% of term neonates and in a higher percentage of preterm babies.

B. Although jaundice in the newborn is often physiologic, direct the workup toward excluding disorders that may require immediate therapy. Onset of jaundice at <24 hours of age suggests increased bilirubin production from excessive RBC breakdown (e.g., hemolysis). Thus hematocrit is low, reticulocyte count is increased, and peripheral blood smear may show an increased number of nucleated RBCs, fragmented cells, abnormal erythrocytes, spherocytes, and poikilocytes. A positive Coombs' test indicates isoimmune disorder.

C. Isoimmune disorder or isoimmune hemolysis results from maternal antibodies (IgG) directed against fetal RBC antigens. Commonly involved antigens include Rh (D), A, and B. Less common are Kell, C, E, and Duffy. Hallmarks of severe disease include generalized edema (hydrops fetalis), severe congestive heart failure, severe anemia, hepatosplenomegaly, high reticulocyte count, and increasing levels of indirect bilirubin. Peripheral smear shows increased nucleated RBCs in Rh disease and increased spherocytes in ABO disease. Direct Coombs' test may be negative in ABO disease.

D. In nonimmune disorders Coombs' test is negative. In severe congenital infection, indirect hyperbilirubinemia at <24 hours of age is not unusual. Associated malformations (e.g., microcephaly, hydrocephalus, hepatosplenomegaly, heart defects) are usually observed with severe congenital viral, protozoal, or spirochetal infections. Anemia and reticulocytosis may be severe in congenital syphilis. Because bacterial infection requires immediate, appropriate antimicrobial coverage, do a septicemia workup. Also, consider both infection and isoimmune disorders of mild to moderate degree in evaluating jaundice with onset after 24 hours of age.

E. Drugs such as antimalarials, sulfonamides, nitrofurans, antipyretics, analgesics, and naphthalene may induce hemolysis in a neonate with glucose-6-phosphate dehydrogenase (G-6-PD) deficiency. With hemolysis, hematocrit is low, reticulocyte count is high, and peripheral smear demonstrates a varying number of nucleated RBCs, spherocytes, poikilocytes, and crenated and fragmented cells. Heinz bodies may be observed with supravital staining techniques.

F. Hyperbilirubinemia from hemolysis may be attributed to defect in RBC enzyme, membrane, or hemoglobin. Examples of RBC enzyme disorders are G-6-PD deficiency and pyruvate kinase deficiency.

G. Congenital spherocytosis, a hereditary disorder, is characterized by abnormally fragile erythrocytes, because of a primary membrane disturbance.

H. α-Thalassemia and β-thalassemia are examples of hemoglobinopathies.

I. Respiratory distress, infants of diabetic mothers (IDM), or other conditions with prolonged acidosis may be associated with hyperbilirubinemia, with or without significant hemolysis.

J. Physiologic jaundice is jaundice observed after 24 hours of age, with a total serum bilirubin concentration not exceeding 12 mg/dl in a term infant and 15 mg/dl in a premature infant. Peak levels occur at 3 days and 5 days, respectively, for term and preterm infants. One possible mechanism is increased bilirubin load because of increased RBC volume, decreased RBC survival, increase in early labeled bilirubin, and increased enterohepatic circulation. Other mechanisms include (1) defective hepatic uptake of bilirubin from plasma, (2) defective bilirubin conjugation and excretion, and (3) decreased hepatic oxygenation.

K. In breast milk jaundice syndromes, the unsaturated fatty acids (NEFAs) content inhibits bilirubin conjugation. Breast milk may also contain an inhibitor of glucuronyl transferase activity and may be responsible for the earlier onset breast milk jaundice. Studies also allude to increased enterohepatic circulation of bilirubin with breast feeding.

L. Examples of metabolic and endocrine disorders include Crigler-Najjar syndrome, Gilbert's disorder, hypothyroidism, tyrosinosis, IDM, hypermethionemia, hypopituitarism, and anencephaly.

M. Other causes of jaundice include disorders associated with extravascular blood collection (petechiae, hematoma, occult hemorrhage), swallowed blood syndrome, and increased enterohepatic circulation (pyloric stenosis and bowel obstruction).

N. In the presence of high hematocrit, consider polycythemia/hyperviscosity syndrome.

O. When direct bilirubin levels are >1.5 mg/dl or >15% of total bilirubin level, consider infection (congenital viral, protozoal, bacterial), hepatitis, biliary atresia, cholestasis from amino acid infusion, and α-1-antitrypsin deficiency, cystic fibrosis, tyrosinosis, and galactosemia. Liver biopsy and operative cholangiography may be needed to establish etiology of direct hyperbilirubinemia.

HSB

Reference

AAP Committee on Fetus and Newborn and ACOG Committee on Obstetrics: Maternal fetal medicine: Guidelines for perinatal care, Elk Grove Village, Ill: American Academy of Pediatrics, 1992:204.

For additional references see p 56.

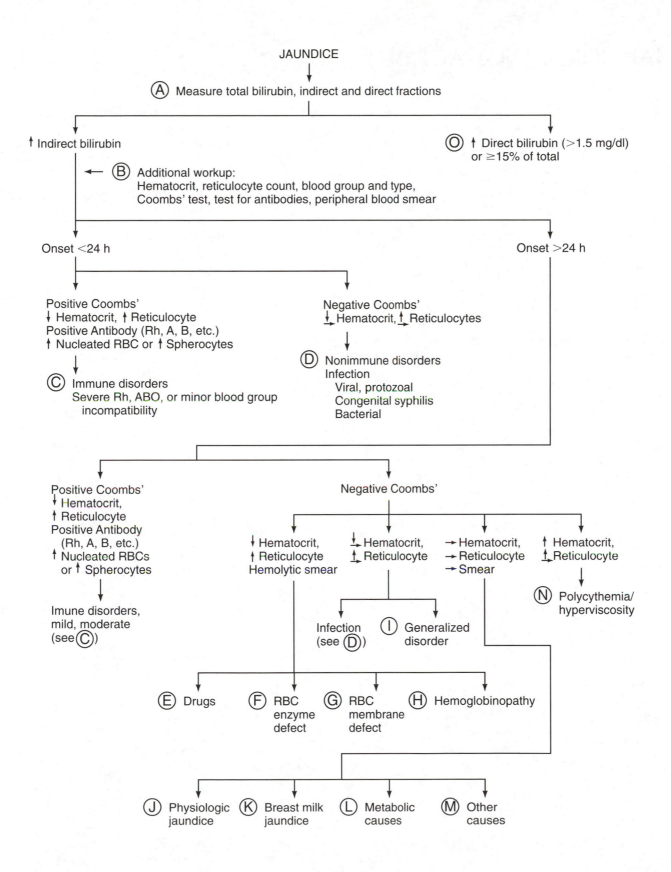

JAUNDICE
↓
Ⓐ Measure total bilirubin, indirect and direct fractions

↑ Indirect bilirubin

Ⓞ ↑ Direct bilirubin (>1.5 mg/dl)
or ≥15% of total

← Ⓑ Additional workup:
Hematocrit, reticulocyte count, blood group and type,
Coombs' test, test for antibodies, peripheral blood smear

Onset <24 h

Onset >24 h

Positive Coombs'
↓ Hematocrit, ↑ Reticulocyte
Positive Antibody (Rh, A, B, etc.)
↑ Nucleated RBC or ↑ Spherocytes
↓
Ⓒ Immune disorders
Severe Rh, ABO, or minor blood group
incompatibility

Negative Coombs'
↕ Hematocrit, ↕ Reticulocytes
↓
Ⓓ Nonimmune disorders
Infection
Viral, protozoal
Congenital syphilis
Bacterial

Positive Coombs'
↓ Hematocrit,
↑ Reticulocyte
Positive Antibody
(Rh, A, B, etc.)
↑ Nucleated RBCs
or ↑ Spherocytes
↓
Imune disorders,
mild, moderate
(see Ⓒ)

Negative Coombs'

↓ Hematocrit,
↑ Reticulocyte
Hemolytic smear

↕ Hematocrit,
↕ Reticulocyte

→ Hematocrit,
→ Reticulocyte
→ Smear

↑ Hematocrit,
↕ Reticulocyte
↓
Ⓝ Polycythemia/
hyperviscosity

Infection
(see Ⓓ)

Ⓘ Generalized
disorder

Ⓔ Drugs   Ⓕ RBC
enzyme
defect

Ⓖ RBC
membrane
defect

Ⓗ Hemoglobinopathy

Ⓙ Physiologic
jaundice

Ⓚ Breast milk
jaundice

Ⓛ Metabolic
causes

Ⓜ Other
causes

JAUNDICE: MANAGEMENT

A. An aggressive approach is appropriate when the etiology of the jaundice is associated with pathological disorders, e.g., severe hemolysis, or in conditions when bilirubin binding is diminished by acidosis or hypoalbuminemia.

B. Exchange transfusion is done either to correct severe anemia by removing antibody-coated fetal red cells or to remove bilirubin. Approximately 85% of the baby's blood volume is replaced by a double volume exchange transfusion. Mortality from exchange transfusion is <1%. Potential hazards include vascular, cardiac, metabolic, bleeding, and infectious complications; necrotizing enterocolitis, perforation of the umbilical vein, and hypothermia are other complications.

C. By using phototherapy, unconjugated bilirubin in the skin is converted to photoisomers that are water soluble and excreted in the bile without conjugation. Phototherapy is less effective in hemolytic disease. Some of the side effects are rash, loose stools, lethargy, increased insensible water loss, and dehydration.

D. Lack of properly designed studies or observational data on which to base clinical guidelines for treatment of neonates with bilirubin ≤20 mg/dl allows the American Academy of Pediatrics to consider both aggressive and conservative management as rational approaches. Thus it is acceptable to allow serum bilirubin concentration to approach 15–20 mg/dl before considering exchange transfusion.

E. Phenobarbital enhances both conjugation and excretion of bilirubin. Antenatal or postnatal administration is associated with reduced bilirubin level. It takes several days, however, to attain significant blood phenobarbital levels.

F. New therapies using metalloporphyrins (heme oxygenase inhibitors) and a hepatic enzyme-inducing drug like zixoryn are now under investigation primarily for treatment of prolonged jaundice.

G. Portoenterostomy and liver transplantation are surgical treatments considered for biliary atresia.

HSB

References

American Academy of Pediatrics. Guidelines for perinatal care. Elk Grove Village, IL: American Academy of Pediatrics, 1992:204.

Landaw SA, Drummond GS, Kappas A. Targeting of heme oxygenase inhibitors to the spleen markedly increases their ability to diminish bilirubin production. Pediatrics 1989; 84:1091.

Maisels MJ. Neonatal jaundice. In: Avery GB, ed. Neonatology pathophysiology and management of the newborn. 3rd ed. Philadelphia: JB Lippincott, 1987:534.

Oski FA, Naiman JL. Hematologic problems in the newborn. 3rd ed. Philadelphia: WB Saunders, 1982: 97, 245, 283.

Stevenson DK, Rodgers PA, Vreman HJ. The use of metalloporphyrins for the chemoprevention of neonatal jaundice. Am J Dis Child 1989; 143:353.

JAUNDICE: MANAGEMENT

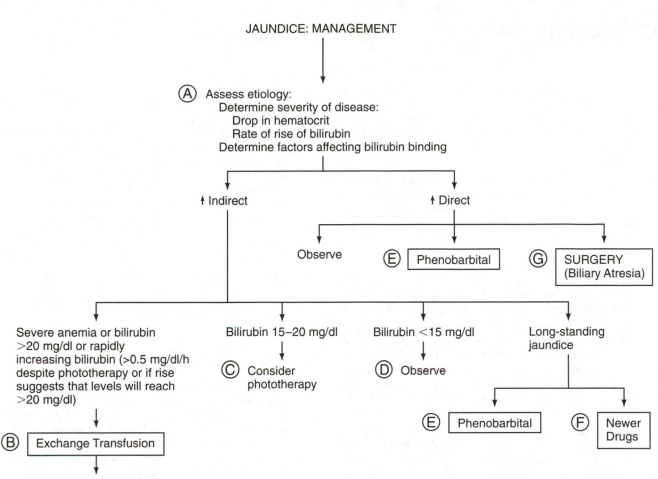

(A) Assess etiology:
    Determine severity of disease:
        Drop in hematocrit
        Rate of rise of bilirubin
    Determine factors affecting bilirubin binding

↑ Indirect

↑ Direct

Observe

(E) Phenobarbital

(G) SURGERY (Biliary Atresia)

Severe anemia or bilirubin >20 mg/dl or rapidly increasing bilirubin (>0.5 mg/dl/h despite phototherapy or if rise suggests that levels will reach >20 mg/dl)

Bilirubin 15–20 mg/dl

(C) Consider phototherapy

Bilirubin <15 mg/dl

(D) Observe

Long-standing jaundice

(E) Phenobarbital

(F) Newer Drugs

(B) Exchange Transfusion

Interval determination of bilirubin and hematocrit to decide on retreatment

CYANOSIS

A. Peripheral cyanosis occurs in an otherwise well infant. It is limited to the extremities, usually hands and feet and occasionally the circumoral area as well. Peripheral cyanosis may be a sign of impending shock or infection, but babies so affected are not otherwise well.

B. Central cyanosis implies hypoxemia (Pa_{O_2} <50 torr), but not all hypoxemic babies are cyanotic. At a given Pa_{O_2}, the neonate's oxygen saturation is higher than the adult's because the neonatal oxygen-hemoglobin dissociation curve is shifted to the left of the adult's. Neonatal erythrocytes release less oxygen to tissues at any given Pa_{O_2} than adult erythrocytes. Thus while Pa_{O_2} declines to levels as low as 32 torr, the neonatal erythrocyte may retain enough oxygen to produce the apparent paradox of a hypoxemic infant who is pink.

C. Breathing pattern is the most informative of all physical signs for discerning pulmonary from nonpulmonary disorders. Cyanotic nonpulmonary disorders are usually associated with an abnormal rate and/or depth of breathing, but without significant retractions. Whether affected infants breath rapidly or slowly, the absence of retractions indicates unimpaired airflow.

D. Rapid retraction-free breathing suggests cardiac abnormality, persistent fetal circulation (PFC), blood disease (methemoglobinemia), metabolic disorder (hypoglycemia, adrenal insufficiency, hypothermia), early shock, early infection (septicemia, meningitis), or an abdominal catastrophe such as necrotizing enterocolitis, volvulus, or spontaneous gastric perforation. Slow, retraction-free breathing suggests CNS depression, as in perinatal asphyxia, periventricular-intraventricular hemorrhage (PV-IVH), and hypoxic-ischemic encephalopathy. Slow breathing occurs in neuromuscular dysfunction caused either by disease (congenital myotonic dystrophy, transient myasthenia gravis) or by pharmacotoxicity (hypermagnesemia from maternal $MgSO_4$ therapy). Also, in severe shock, the overwhelmed infant's breathing is usually slowed.

E. Retractions indicate involvement of lungs or muscles of respiration. In any clinical entity, retractions are the result of incomplete lung expansion while breathing against a significant impedance to airflow. Upper airway obstruction is uncommon; it includes choanal atresia, laryngeal web, tracheal stenosis, cystic hygroma, Pierre Robin syndrome, and goiter. By contrast, kinking or plugging of an endotracheal tube is a common event.

Air leak (extraneous air) syndromes most often begin with alveolar rupture followed by injection of air into the pulmonary interstitium. The clinical syndromes that result depend on migration of extraneous air to other locations, or its retention in the pulmonary interstitium (see p 142).

Parenchymal lung disease is the most frequent cause of retractions with cyanosis. Of these disorders, respiratory distress syndrome and transient tachypnea of the newborn are most common. Others are pulmo-nary hypoplasia, meconium aspiration, pneumonia, cystic adenomatoid malformation of the lung, and lobar emphysema.

Ineffective diaphragmatic contraction is actually a peripheral nerve disorder when it is caused by phrenic nerve trauma, which is usually a component of brachial plexus injury. Congenital diaphragmatic hernia produces retractions and cyanosis because of space-occupying intrathoracic abdominal viscera and pulmonary hypoplasia. Neuromuscular disorders such as Werdnig-Hoffmann disease and congenital myotonic dystrophy produce retractions when diaphragm activity is sufficiently vigorous to initiate some inspiratory effort while muscles of the chest wall are severely hypotonic. The polycythemia-hyperviscosity syndrome diminishes lung compliance by hyperperfusion and distention of pulmonary vessels.

F. Cyanotic congenital heart disease is unlikely if the Pa_{O_2} is $\geq$ 150 torr after the infant has been placed in 100% O_2 for at least 10 minutes.

G. Simultaneously drawn samples for blood gas determination from the right radial artery (preductal) and the descending aorta (postductal) are useful for estimating the clinical significance of a right-to-left ductal shunt. In babies suspected of PFC we have often observed that the ductal shunt is clinically significant if preductal Pa_{O_2} is <50 torr and postductal Pa_{O_2} is 15% lower.

H. The Pa_{O_2} is often normal even though the infant is cyanotic. A drop of normal venous blood placed on filter paper turns bright red when exposed to room air; the dark brown blood of methemoglobinemia does not change. Therapy with 1% methylene blue solution (1.0 mg/kg) is shortly followed by disappearance of cyanosis, suggesting a toxic etiology (benzocaine, phenacetin, some older sulfonamides such as sulfathiazole and sulfapyridine, and nitrates-nitrites in well water and in carrots) or a deficiency of methemoglobin reductase. If cyanosis is not diminished after therapy, hemoglobin M or an associated G-6-PD deficiency is probable. Spectrophotometry confirms the diagnosis of methemoglobinemia.

SBK

References

Fletcher BD. The radiology of respiratory distress syndrome and its sequelae in hyaline membrane disease. In: Stern L, ed. Hyaline membrane disease: Pathogenesis and pathophysiology. Orlando: Grune and Stratton, 1984:119.

Goldman HI, Maralit A, Sun S, et al. Neonatal cyanosis and arterial oxygen saturation. J Pediatr 1973; 82:319.

Hohn AR, Stanton RE. The cardiovascular system. In: Fanaroff AA, Martin RJ, eds. Neonatal-perinatal medicine. 5th ed. St Louis: Mosby—Year Book, 1992:883.

Mullett MD, Bucciarelli RL. Non-cardiac causes of cyanosis. In: Moller JH, Neal WA, eds. Fetal, neonatal and infant cardiac disorders. Norwalk, Conn: Appleton and Lange, 1990:797.

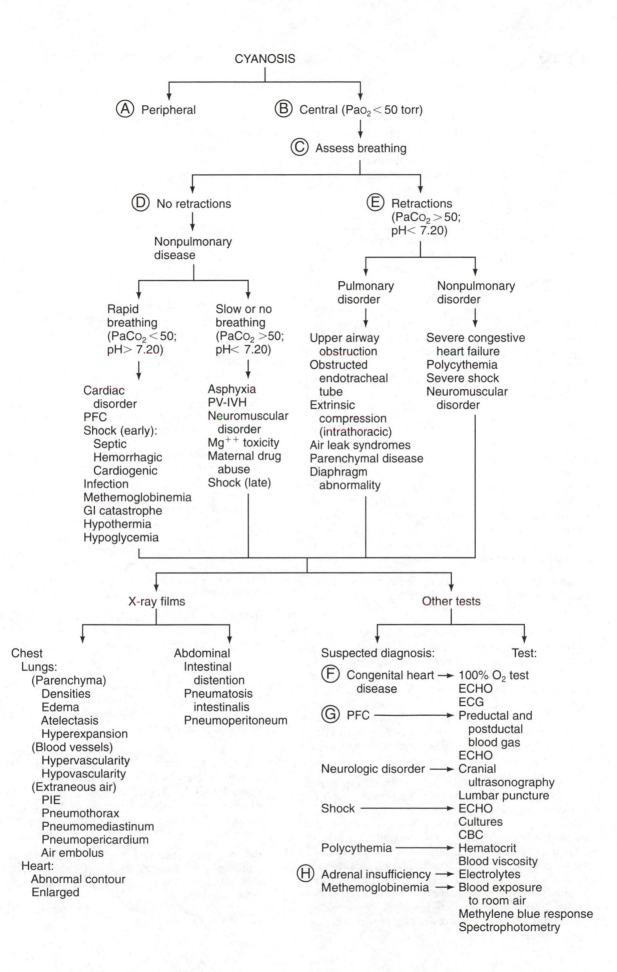

CYANOSIS

(A) Peripheral   (B) Central (Pao$_2$ < 50 torr)

(C) Assess breathing

(D) No retractions

Nonpulmonary disease

Rapid breathing (PaCo$_2$ < 50; pH > 7.20)

Cardiac disorder
PFC
Shock (early):
  Septic
  Hemorrhagic
  Cardiogenic
Infection
Methemoglobinemia
GI catastrophe
Hypothermia
Hypoglycemia

Slow or no breathing (PaCo$_2$ > 50; pH < 7.20)

Asphyxia
PV-IVH
Neuromuscular disorder
Mg^{++} toxicity
Maternal drug abuse
Shock (late)

(E) Retractions (PaCo$_2$ > 50; pH < 7.20)

Pulmonary disorder

Upper airway obstruction
Obstructed endotracheal tube
Extrinsic compression (intrathoracic)
Air leak syndromes
Parenchymal disease
Diaphragm abnormality

Nonpulmonary disorder

Severe congestive heart failure
Polycythemia
Severe shock
Neuromuscular disorder

X-ray films

Chest
Lungs:
  (Parenchyma)
    Densities
    Edema
    Atelectasis
    Hyperexpansion
  (Blood vessels)
    Hypervascularity
    Hypovascularity
  (Extraneous air)
    PIE
    Pneumothorax
    Pneumomediastinum
    Pneumopericardium
    Air embolus
Heart:
  Abnormal contour
  Enlarged

Abdominal
Intestinal distention
Pneumatosis intestinalis
Pneumoperitoneum

Other tests

Suspected diagnosis:

(F) Congenital heart disease
(G) PFC

Neurologic disorder

Shock

Polycythemia

(H) Adrenal insufficiency
Methemoglobinemia

Test:

100% O$_2$ test
ECHO
ECG
Preductal and postductal blood gas
ECHO
Cranial ultrasonography
Lumbar puncture
ECHO
Cultures
CBC
Hematocrit
Blood viscosity
Electrolytes
Blood exposure to room air
Methylene blue response
Spectrophotometry

PALLOR

A. Assessment of pallor in the newborn should include careful physical examination and determination of hematocrit, peripheral smear, and reticulocyte count. Clinical manifestations may help distinguish acute from chronic blood loss. Hematocrit indicates severity of blood loss; reticulocyte count is increased in long-standing anemia.

B. In chronic blood loss or anemia, the pallor is disproportionately marked compared with the cardiorespiratory signs, i.e., minimal cardiorespiratory decompensation. Hepatosplenomegaly suggests extramedullary hematopoiesis. Hematocrit is low, reticulocyte count is high. RBC morphology reveals hypochromic cells and microcytes. Chronic anemia is observed in fetomaternal, fetoplacental, or fetofetal transfusion. In fetomaternal transfusions the Kleihauer-Betke technique demonstrates RBCs containing fetal hemoglobin in maternal blood. Fetal hemorrhage into a chorioangioma of the placenta may be associated also with thrombocytopenia. In chronic twin-to-twin transfusion, the donor twin is anemic and smaller than the recipient twin; weight difference is >20% of the larger twin's weight.

C. Because of the chronicity of the anemia, intravascular volume is often normal. Volume expansion is rarely necessary. Treatment of chronic blood loss is by slow packed cell transfusion or preferably partial exchange transfusion with packed cells that raise hematocrit to a desired level. Packed cells 3 ml/kg will raise hemoglobin level by 1 g/dl. Also, iron stores may be depleted and iron therapy may be necessary.

D. In a jaundiced infant, chronic in utero hemolytic disease and other causes of hemolysis need to be considered (see p 54).

E. In vitamin E deficiency, hemolysis occurs as a consequence of peroxidation of lipid components of the RBC membrane. The syndrome is usually observed in premature infants with ≤1500 g birthweight at 4−6 weeks of age. This is preventable with vitamin E supplementation of 10−15 mg/day during the first 6−8 weeks of life. Vitamin E deficiency may be corrected by administration of 50−200 units of vitamin E daily for 2 weeks. Monitoring of plasma vitamin E level is recommended.

F. In acute blood loss physical examination reveals pallor, tachycardia, hypotension, i.e., cardiorespiratory decompensation. Hematocrit is low with normal reticulocyte count. Peripheral smear shows macrocytes and normochromic cells. Acute blood loss results from obstetrical causes (abruptio placentae, placenta previa, umbilical cord rupture, accidental laceration of the placenta during cesarean section, cord prolapse); acute fetomaternal, fetofetal, or fetoplacental transfusion; obvious bleeding in the newborn (cephalhematoma, subgaleal hemorrhage); occult hemorrhage (intracranial hemorrhage, retroperitoneal hemorrhage, liver or spleen rupture); or from iatrogenic causes (blood sampling and disconnected arterial catheters).

G. Therapy of acute blood/volume loss should be directed toward immediate volume expansion with plasma, albumin, or whole blood. Also, packed cell transfusion may be necessary to boost hemoglobin and hematocrit.

H. Anemia of prematurity results from the decline of hemoglobin concentration at a rate of 1 g/dl per week in premature infants of <1500 g birthweight between the second and eighth weeks of life to a mean hemoglobin ≤9 g/dl. Reticulocyte count is normal or slightly increased. Often no treatment is required. However, with decompensation (persistent tachycardia and tachypnea, lethargy, poor feeding, and increasing oxygen requirement), packed RBC transfusion may be indicated. Vitamin E deficiency needs to be considered in the differential diagnosis when low hematocrit persists despite increasing reticulocyte count. (See section E.)

I. Diamond-Blackfan syndrome (congenital hypoplastic anemia, congenital pure red cell aplasia, or erythrogenesis imperfecta) is characterized by impaired RBC production, normochromic anemia, macrocytic RBCs, and persistent reticulocyte count <2%, with normal platelet and leukocyte production. Physical anomalies (short stature, thumb abnormalities, cleft palate, blue sclerae, microphthalmia, cataracts, short neck, and congenital heart disease) are reported in 30% of cases. Steroid therapy results in increased hematocrit and reticulocytes.

J. In vitamin B_{12} transport protein transcobalamin II deficiency, a possibly autosomal recessive trait, infants are not anemic at birth but become anemic at a later age. Reticulocytopenia, thrombocytopenia, and leukopenia are associated findings. Profound megaloblastic changes are seen on bone marrow examination. For therapy, intramuscular injection of 1000 μg of vitamin B_{12} is repeated weekly until the infant is hematologically normal.

K. Refractory sideroblastic anemia is characterized by macrocytic anemia, reticulocytopenia, neutropenia, and thrombocytopenia. Bone marrow studies show normal cellularity, vacuolization of erythroid and myeloid precursors, hemosiderosis, and ringed sideroblasts. Pancreatic exocrine dysfunction may be present.

L. Pallor may be observed in infants with cardiovascular collapse, i.e., severe perinatal asphyxia or septic shock. Pallor is the result of hypoperfusion rather than a low hematocrit.

HSB

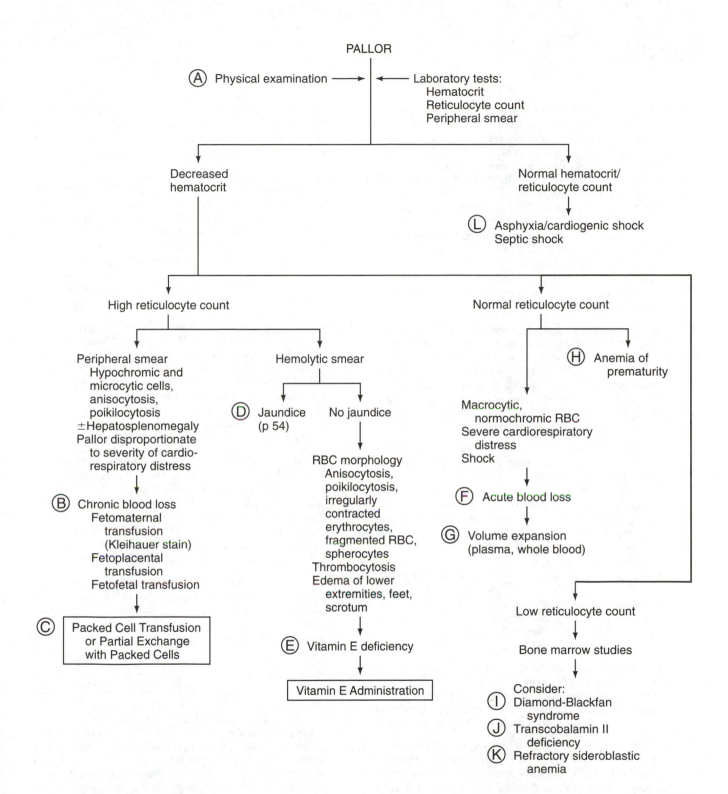

References

Mollison PL. Blood transfusion in clinical medicine, 3rd ed. Oxford: Blackwell Scientific Publications, 1961:614.

Oski FA, Barness LA. Vitamin E deficiency: a previously unrecognized cause of hemolytic anemia in premature infants. J Pediatr 1976; 79:569.

Oski FA, Naiman JL, eds.: Hematologic problems in the newborn. 3rd ed. Philadelphia: WB Saunders, 1982:56.

Pachedly C, Musiker S. Twin-to-twin transfusion syndrome. Postgrad Med 1970; 47:172.

Schulman I. The anemia of prematurity. J Pediatr 1959; 54:633.

Shepherd MK, Weatherall DJ, Conley CL. Semi-quantitative estimation of distribution of fetal hemoglobin in red cell populations. Johns Hopkins Hosp 1962; 110:293.

Zipursky A, Pollock J, Neelands P, et al. The transplacental passage of foetal red blood cells and the pathogenesis of Rh immunisation during pregnancy. Lancet 1963; 2:489.

APNEA

A. Apnea is cessation of respiration >20 seconds, usually accompanied by bradycardia (heart rate <100/min). History, with particular attention to the infant's previous well-being (e.g., respiratory status before the apneic episode), may provide a clue to possible etiologies. Apneic episodes may result from diseases unique to the premature infant or from diseases common to neonates of all gestational ages. Moreover, some disorders cause apnea within minutes or hours of birth; others may result in apneic episodes at varying postnatal ages. The presence of other clinical signs such as jaundice, pallor, a shocklike picture, cyanosis, bradycardia, tachycardia, or abdominal distention needs to be assessed in making a working clinical diagnosis.

B. Because apnea is a manifestation of various conditions, multiple diagnostic studies are recommended. Evaluation of acid-base status, oxygenation, and ventilation establishes the severity of the disease. Serum or plasma chemistries rule out associated biochemical abnormalities. Chest film helps establish a pulmonary etiology. Results of the CBC and septicemia workup support clinical suspicion of infection.

C. Apnea of prematurity refers to recurrent apneic episodes that begin at 1–2 days of age (before 1 week of age) in premature infants (≤34 weeks' gestation) and without identifiable cause. Proposed mechanisms include unstable or depressed respiratory control system, decreased responsiveness of chemoreceptors, rapid-eye-movement sleep, active pharyngeal or laryngeal reflexes, and spontaneous airway obstruction. Methylxanthine therapy (theophylline or caffeine) increases levels of cyclic AMP by inhibiting phosphodiesterase, increases ventilatory response to CO_2, and improves diaphragmatic contractility. Other treatment modes include oxygen therapy, CPAP, oscillating water beds, and mechanical ventilation if other interventions have failed.

D. In sepsis and/or meningitis or neonatal infection in general, appropriate workup supports the diagnosis. Infants with infection may show rapid deterioration with a shocklike picture; some may have abdominal signs consistent with ileus or necrotizing enterocolitis.

E. Consider aspiration in an infant who has been doing well and feeding. Formula is aspirated with tracheal suctioning, and chest radiograph confirms aspiration pneumonitis. Apnea occurring during or shortly after feeding suggests gastroesophageal (GE) reflux.

F. Cardiac disorders (e.g., transposition of the great vessels, hypoplastic left heart syndrome, congenital heart block) should be suspected in an apneic neonate who apparently had been doing well in the first few hours or days of life.

G. Preterm babies with periventricular-intraventricular hemorrhage (PV-IVH) after 1 week of age may develop progressive ventricular dilation, which may be severe enough to result in depressed respiratory effort and then apnea. Associated brain injury without ventricular dilation may cause seizures and apnea.

H. Neonates may be depressed at birth and become apneic because of a perinatal asphyxia or oversedation from maternal drugs (magnesium sulfate, naloxone, opiates, general anesthesia). Those with perinatal asphyxia also may develop seizures with associated apnea. Congenital neuromuscular disorders (e.g., arthrogryposis multiplex congenita, congenital myotonias), chest wall deformities, and diaphragmatic disorders may be associated with asphyxia leading to apnea.

I. Various diseases associated with pulmonary insufficiency or respiratory distress may become severe enough to result in respiratory failure and apnea. Hyaline membrane disease (HMD) or respiratory distress syndrome type I refers to surfactant deficiency syndrome resulting in end-expiratory alveolar atelectasis, which leads to increasing oxygen requirement, retractions, increased work of breathing, respiratory failure, and apnea (see p 120).

J. Respiratory insufficiency of prematurity (RIP, immature lung syndrome) occurs in very premature, low-birth-weight infants. The lungs appear clear and well aerated on radiograph (p 120). Oxygen and ventilator requirements are minimal. Babies who are weaned off the ventilator prematurely or not mechanically ventilated have increasing respiratory distress and ultimately respiratory failure and apnea.

K. PV-IVH is a common complication in premature babies, particularly those with respiratory distress. It usually develops in the first 4–5 days of life with further evolution or progression to larger lesions by 1 week of age. Apnea is one of the presenting signs of PV-IVH.

L. With improvement in respiratory status, especially in preterm babies with HMD or RIP, left-to-right shunt through the anatomically patent ductus is likely. Increased pulmonary blood flow results in interstitial edema or pulmonary edema. A clinically decompensated patent ductus arteriosus (PDA) is manifested as increased respiratory effort, bounding pulses, rales on auscultation, cardiomegaly, cyanosis and bradycardia with handling, and apneic spells. Although left-to-right shunt through the PDA may become evident during the first week of life, a decompensated state may not result until after 1 week of age in many patients.

M. Anemia of prematurity is often asymptomatic unless severe cardiorespiratory decompensation develops.

N. Cold stress should be considered in apneic infants, particularly when onset is soon after birth, during or

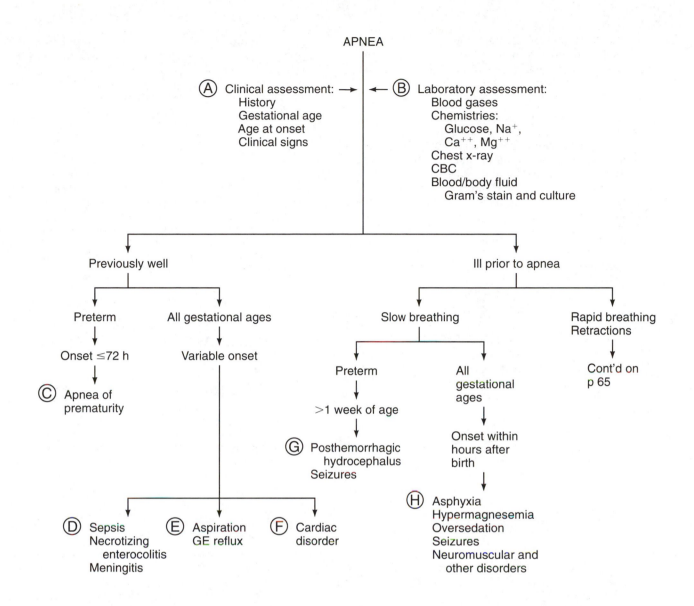

APNEA

(A) Clinical assessment: →   ← (B) Laboratory assessment:
    History   Blood gases
    Gestational age   Chemistries:
    Age at onset   Glucose, Na^+,
    Clinical signs Ca^{++}, Mg^{++}
                                     Chest x-ray
                                     CBC
                                     Blood/body fluid
                                         Gram's stain and culture

Previously well   Ill prior to apnea

Preterm   All gestational ages   Slow breathing   Rapid breathing
                                                                        Retractions

Onset ≤72 h   Variable onset   Preterm   All   Cont'd on
                                                         gestational   p 65
                                                         ages

(C) Apnea of   >1 week of age Onset within
    prematurity   hours after
                                                         birth

                                         (G) Posthemorrhagic
                                             hydrocephalus
                                             Seizures   (H) Asphyxia
                                                                             Hypermagnesemia
                                                                             Oversedation
                                                                             Seizures
(D) Sepsis   (E) Aspiration (F) Cardiac   Neuromuscular and
    Necrotizing   GE reflux   disorder   other disorders
    enterocolitis
    Meningitis

after a procedure, or during or after transport. With cold stress, responses include hypoxemia, metabolic acidosis, hypoglycemia, and apnea. Hyperthermia, rapid rewarming, or rapid fluctuation of temperature to either direction may be associated with apnea.

O. Airway obstruction (e.g., choanal atresia, meconium aspiration, mucous plugs as in postextubation atelectasis) is usually manifested clinically as severe and progressive respiratory difficulty leading to respiratory failure and apnea. "Air hunger" suggests upper airway obstruction. With choanal atresia and meconium aspiration, respiratory difficulty occurs soon after birth.

P. Pneumonia, sepsis, or meningitis may be manifested first as tachypnea with or without chest retractions and may be followed by apneic spells. Other clinical signs such as mottling, poor perfusion, abdominal distention, bloody stools, and temperature instability may be observed. Generalized conditions such as hypoglycemia, hyponatremia, hypernatremia, and hyperammonemia are other causes of apnea in the newborn.

HSB

References

Brazy JE, Kinney HC, Oakes WJ. Central nervous system structural lesions causing apnea at birth. J Pediatr 1987; 111:163.

Lagercrantz H. Neuromodulators and respiratory control in the infant. Clin Perinatol 1987; 14:683.

Marchal F, Bairam A, Vert P. Neonatal apnea and apneic syndromes. Clin Perinatol 1987; 14:509.

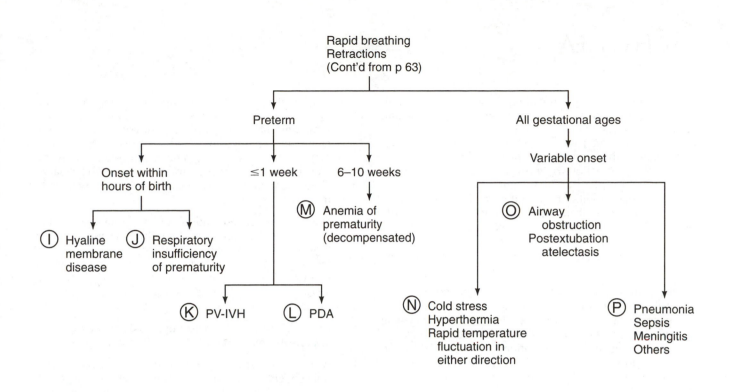

Rapid breathing
Retractions
(Cont'd from p 63)

Preterm

All gestational ages

Onset within
hours of birth

≤1 week

6–10 weeks

Variable onset

Ⓘ Hyaline
membrane
disease

Ⓙ Respiratory
insufficiency
of prematurity

Ⓜ Anemia of
prematurity
(decompensated)

Ⓞ Airway
obstruction
Postextubation
atelectasis

Ⓚ PV-IVH

Ⓛ PDA

Ⓝ Cold stress
Hyperthermia
Rapid temperature
fluctuation in
either direction

Ⓟ Pneumonia
Sepsis
Meningitis
Others

TACHYPNEA

Tachypnea refers to rapid breathing (≥ 60/min) and may be observed with chest retractions (intercostal, subcostal, xiphoid, or sternal retractions) and/or cyanosis. Retractions are usually observed with existing pulmonary/airway abnormalities, which often are demonstrated with chest radiograph examination. Cyanosis indicates abnormality in oxygenation, i.e., PaO_2 <50 torr, and may be observed in tachypneic babies with or without retractions. Abnormally increased $PaCO_2$ indicates inadequate ventilation primarily resulting from pulmonary lesions. Normal or low $PaCO_2$ suggests that tachypnea is likely due to nonpulmonary causes (e.g., congenital heart disease, metabolic disorders, and CNS disease).

A. Lung abnormalities categorized as generalized diminution of aeration or hypoaeration are usually seen in hyaline membrane disease (HMD) and congenital pneumonia. Diffuse atelectasis or parenchymal disease results in poor ventilation, decreased PaO_2, and respiratory acidosis, and when severe is also associated with metabolic acidosis.

B. Hyperaeration of both lungs is not an unusual finding in the very immature infant, i.e., respiratory insufficiency of prematurity (RIP) (p 122), or when air trapping results as in meconium aspiration, upper airway obstruction (ball-valve effect), or in pulmonary interstitial emphysema (PIE), usually as a result of ventilator use.

C. Segmental or lobar lung involvement may be in the form of atelectasis, emphysema, consolidation, and rarely as a sequestered lung segment.

D. Abnormalities of pulmonary vessels, e.g., hypovascularity as in severe dehydration, persistent pulmonary hypertension, or persistent fetal circulation, and hypervascularity as in polycythemia/hyperviscosity syndrome, may be clinically evident as tachypnea, with or without cyanosis and retractions.

E. Heart abnormalities may be evident by chest radiograph. An enlarged heart as in heart failure, myocarditis, and pericardial effusion may be a finding in a tachypneic neonate. Retractions, however, may be minimal, but the infant is often cyanotic with normal $PaCO_2$ or ventilation.

F. Another clue to a cardiac pathology is an abnormality in shape or position.

G. Abnormalities of other structures from lungs and heart may be evident on the chest radiograph. Usual symptoms of diaphragmatic paralysis or hernia are tachypnea, retractions, and cyanosis. With large diaphragmatic hernia, respiratory distress is so severe that immediate surgical intervention is necessary. Diaphragmatic hernia is usually associated with pulmonary hypoplasia.

H. Extrapleural accumulation of air (pneumothorax, pneumomediastinum) or fluid (hydrothorax, hemothorax) results in severe tachypnea, retractions, and cyanosis. These abnormalities are easily diagnosed by chest radiograph. Definitive treatment is aspiration of air or fluid or continuous drainage with a chest tube (p 142).

I. Chest deformities, as in arthrogryposis or osteogenesis imperfecta, may compromise ventilation.

J. A normal chest radiograph does not necessarily rule out congenital heart disease. Transposition of the great vessel and hypoplastic left heart syndrome may present initially with tachypnea as an early sign of decompensation with a normal cardiac size by chest radiograph.

K. CNS lesions such as meningitis or hypoxic-ischemic insults may result in overstimulation of the respiratory center, resulting in tachypnea. In the absence of lung pathology, hyperventilation results, and thus $PaCO_2$ is low resulting in respiratory alkalosis.

L. Babies with metabolic disorders, e.g., hypothermia, hyperthermia, or hypoglycemia, may have tachypnea.

HSB

References

Avery ME, Fletcher BD, Williams RG. The lung and its disorders in the newborn infant. 4th ed. Philadelphia: WB Saunders, 1981.

Korones SB. High risk newborn infants: The basis for intensive nursing care. 4th ed. St Louis, Mosby–Year Book, 1986: 204.

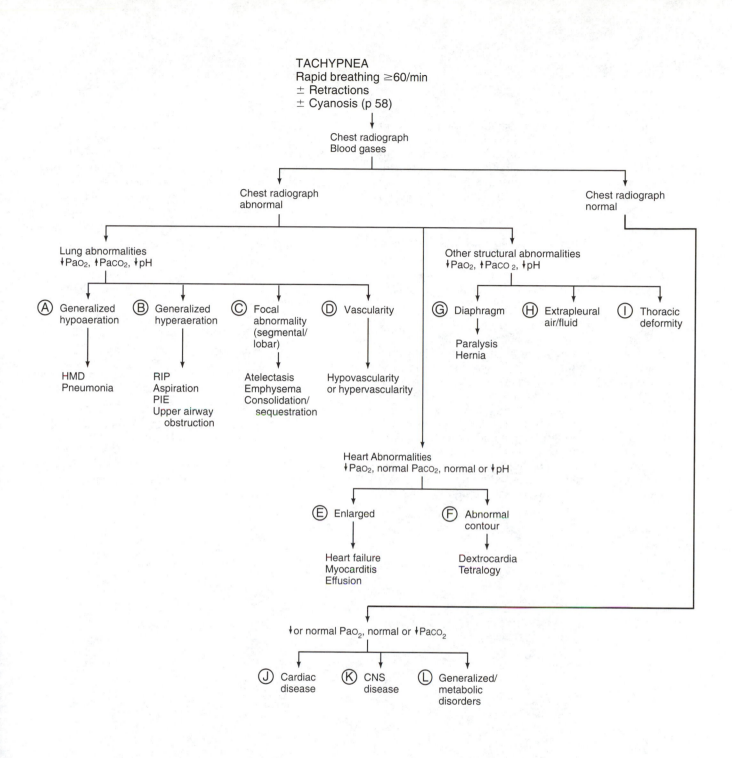

TACHYPNEA
Rapid breathing ≥60/min
± Retractions
± Cyanosis (p 58)

Chest radiograph
Blood gases

Chest radiograph
abnormal

Chest radiograph
normal

Lung abnormalities
↓PaO_2, ↑$PaCO_2$, ↓pH

(A) Generalized
hypoaeration

(B) Generalized
hyperaeration

(C) Focal
abnormality
(segmental/
lobar)

(D) Vascularity

HMD
Pneumonia

RIP
Aspiration
PIE
Upper airway
obstruction

Atelectasis
Emphysema
Consolidation/
sequestration

Hypovascularity
or hypervascularity

Other structural abnormalities
↓PaO_2, ↑$PaCO_2$, ↓pH

(G) Diaphragm

Paralysis
Hernia

(H) Extrapleural
air/fluid

(I) Thoracic
deformity

Heart Abnormalities
↓PaO_2, normal $PaCO_2$, normal or ↓pH

(E) Enlarged

Heart failure
Myocarditis
Effusion

(F) Abnormal
contour

Dextrocardia
Tetralogy

↓or normal PaO_2, normal or ↓$PaCO_2$

(J) Cardiac
disease

(K) CNS
disease

(L) Generalized/
metabolic
disorders

STRIDOR

Stridor refers to noisy breathing, usually inspiratory and of laryngeal or tracheal origin. Stridor must be differentiated from noisy breathing of nasal or bronchial origin. Differential diagnosis is approached by careful clinical assessment and determination of age of onset, whether stridor is intermittent or constant, and whether there is associated respiratory difficulty.

A. Abnormal facies are observed in syndromes with micrognathia and/or large tongue (macroglossia). Stridor has been described with Down's syndrome. Neck masses could cause upper airway obstruction so that stridor with respiratory difficulty is then observed.

B. In the presence of normal facies and normal neck examination, the age at onset, associated respiratory difficulty or distress, and history of intubation or resuscitation are helpful in assessing etiology. In the presence of respiratory distress or worsening respiratory difficulty, causes of laryngeal obstruction, congenital or acquired, and intrinsic or extrinsic, are considered. Intrinsic congenital laryngeal disorders manifest from birth (e.g., laryngeal web, hemangioma, cysts, and stenosis). Acquired intrinsic laryngeal lesions include laryngeal edema, stenosis, and vocal cord injury; these complications are considered after tracheal intubation for resuscitation or assisted ventilation. Vocal cord paralysis may result from damaged recurrent laryngeal nerve during traumatic deliveries. Extrinsic laryngeal obstruction may be due to a vascular ring or rarely to a mediastinal thyroid tumor. Stridor from laryngitis or laryngeal infection (bacterial or viral) is not common in the newborn period. In endemic areas diphtheria and tetanus neonatorum are important considerations.

C. Stridor without respiratory distress is observed in congenital laryngeal stridor. Onset of stridor at birth is rare; it is usually toward the first week of life. Stridor occurs because of the easy collapsibility of the aryepiglottic folds or the epiglottis itself. Stridor is intermittent, is influenced by position, and is induced by crying, feeding, or sleeping. Expected course is spontaneous resolution.

HSB

References

Davies PA, Robinson RJ, Scopes JW, et al. Stridor. In: Medical care of newborn babies. Philadelphia: JB Lippincott, 1972:145.

Illingworth RS: Stridor. In: Common symptoms of disease in children. 5th ed. Oxford: Blackwell Scientific Publications, 1975:159.

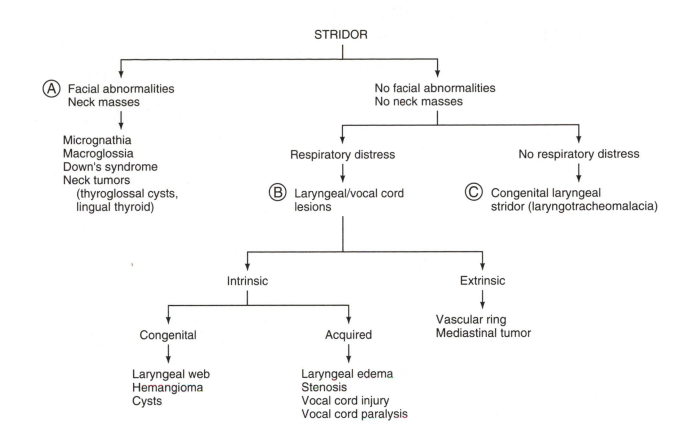

STRIDOR

A Facial abnormalities
Neck masses

No facial abnormalities
No neck masses

Micrognathia
Macroglossia
Down's syndrome
Neck tumors
(thyroglossal cysts,
lingual thyroid)

Respiratory distress

No respiratory distress

B Laryngeal/vocal cord
lesions

C Congenital laryngeal
stridor (laryngotracheomalacia)

Intrinsic

Extrinsic

Congenital

Acquired

Vascular ring
Mediastinal tumor

Laryngeal web
Hemangioma
Cysts

Laryngeal edema
Stenosis
Vocal cord injury
Vocal cord paralysis

LARGE HEAD

A. Head size (head circumference) must be evaluated in proportion to other body measurements such as length, birthweight, and chest circumference. Normally, head circumference, birth weight, and length plot out at about the same percentile on the growth chart at a given gestational age. Head circumference at term ranges from 33–35 cm (13–14 inches), and chest circumference ranges from 30–33 cm (12–13 inches). The head is also examined for its shape, sutures, and fontanelles. Sutures normally are overriding at birth because of molding and become slightly separated within a few days when the head achieves its normal contour. Both anterior and posterior fontanelles are open (the anterior fontanelle is larger than the posterior fontanelle) and are soft, flat, and not tense or bulging on palpation.

B. A large head, the circumference plotting out at ≥90th percentile as the birthweight and length, is typical in a large for gestational age (LGA) infant. Sutures and fontanelles are normal. In Beckwith-Wiedemann syndrome, the infant is macrosomic or a giant with macroglossia, large kidneys, pancreatic hyperplasia, and adrenocortical cytomegaly; hypoglycemia is the syndrome's common metabolic feature.

C. Head circumference may be disproportionately large in relation to weight and length. Then birthweight and length need to be assessed as to whether they fall within the average range for a given gestational age. At normal weight and length, examination of the suture lines and fontanelles may give a clue to the underlying disorder. With normal sutures and fontanelles, a large head may represent a normal variant. Normal sutures and fontanelles are also observed in familial macrencephaly, an autosomal dominant disorder without apparent neurological deficit. The cases of isolated autosomal recessive macrencephaly are likely to be associated with mental retardation. Mucopolysaccharidosis and osteopetrosis are some examples of disorders with macrocephaly.

D. A large head, usually misshaped, with ill-defined suture lines and fontanelles and fluctuant soft tissue on palpation, especially after traumatic vertex deliveries, should alert one to a possibility of a subgaleal hemorrhage. A rapidly increasing head size, falling hematocrit, pallor, and hypotension are common associated manifestations. Blood volume replacement is definitive treatment. Resorption of the hemorrhage occurs over several days.

E. Congenital hypothyroidism is considered when the sutures and fontanelles are wide but with no evidence of increased intracranial pressure (ICP) on palpation, especially with associated hypotonia, macroglossia, umbilical hernia, and prolonged hyperbilirubinemia.

F. Sutures that are widely separated and tense, full, and bulging fontanelles strongly indicate increased ICP, i.e., ventriculomegaly or hydrocephalus. Hydrocephalus may be an isolated congenital malformation, an associated abnormality in spina bifida, associated with chromosome aberration or intrauterine infection, or acquired after postnatal intracranial hemorrhage or meningitis. Increased ICP is also suggested by "sunsetting" eyes.

G. When weight is below normal but length is normal, chromosomal aberrations and intrauterine infections with associated hydrocephalus need to be considered. Often other abnormalities are also present.

H. Cerebral edema from asphyxia, intracranial hemorrhage, space occupying lesions, or infectious etiology is associated with increased ICP. Sutures become widely separated, and head size increases with increasing ICP.

I. When birthweight and length are below normal and sutures and fontanelle may be wide but soft, dysmaturity, severe intrauterine growth retardation (asymmetric, small for gestational age [SGA] infants), and various types of dwarfism are possibilities. If signs of increased ICP are present among asymmetric SGA babies, hydrocephalus and cerebral edema should be ruled out.

J. Babies with dwarfism (thanatophoric, achondroplasia, or achondrogenesis syndrome) have macrocephaly but with soft sutures and fontanelles.

HSB

References

Jones KL. Smith's recognizable patterns of human malformation. 4th ed. Philadelphia: WB Saunders, 1988.

Roach A. Macrocrania, microcrania, and craniosynostosis. In: Coleman M, ed. Neonatal neurology. Baltimore: University Park Press, 1981: 167.

Volpe JJ. Neurology of the newborn. 2nd ed. Philadelphia: WB Saunders, 1987: 33.

LARGE HEAD

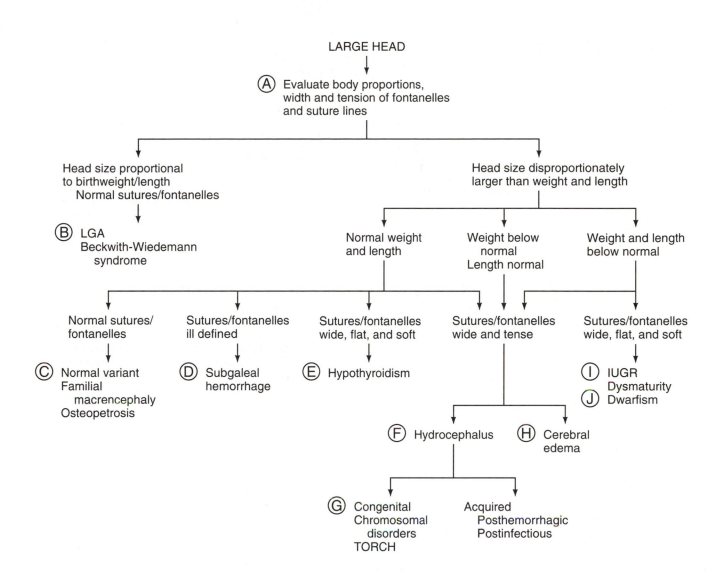

(A) Evaluate body proportions,
width and tension of fontanelles
and suture lines

Head size proportional
to birthweight/length
Normal sutures/fontanelles

Head size disproportionately
larger than weight and length

(B) LGA
Beckwith-Wiedemann
syndrome

Normal weight
and length

Weight below
normal
Length normal

Weight and length
below normal

Normal sutures/
fontanelles

Sutures/fontanelles
ill defined

Sutures/fontanelles
wide, flat, and soft

Sutures/fontanelles
wide and tense

Sutures/fontanelles
wide, flat, and soft

(C) Normal variant
Familial
macrencephaly
Osteopetrosis

(D) Subgaleal
hemorrhage

(E) Hypothyroidism

(I) IUGR
Dysmaturity
(J) Dwarfism

(F) Hydrocephalus

(H) Cerebral
edema

(G) Congenital
Chromosomal
disorders
TORCH

Acquired
Posthemorrhagic
Postinfectious

SMALL HEAD

A. Evaluate head circumference relative to body weight and length. Sutures and fontanelles are both likely to be normal, if not narrowed and small, respectively; that is, signs of increased intracranial pressure are unlikely. Other physical findings (abnormal facies, other malformations, hepatomegaly) may give a clue to the possibility of chromosomal aberrations or infection.

B. Small head in an infant whose weight and length are also below normal for a given gestational age is a finding in a severe intrauterinely growth-retarded infant (symmetric IUGR). Thus head circumference, birth weight, and length are below the 10th percentile of the growth curve. A proportionately small head is also seen in those who are familially or constitutionally small. Twins with congenital hyperthyroidism may present with physical measurements consistent with symmetric IUGR. However, subsequent follow-up may reveal asymmetric head with craniostenosis, cerebral atrophy, and ventriculomegaly.

C. When the head size is small in an infant with appropriate birth weight and length for a given gestational age, consider chromosomal disorders, teratogenic disorders, congenital infections, metabolic causes, and micrencephaly vera. Infants with chromosomal disorders, teratogenic disorders, or congenital infection (TORCH syndrome) often have signs of dysmaturity. They are asymmetric, small for gestational age (SGA) babies. In the absence of signs of dysmaturity or wasting, a small head may be a variation of normal and thus no other abnormality observed. Microcephaly is a common finding in infants born to mothers with phenylketonuria (PKU). In micrencephaly vera a small brain results from a derangement of neuronal proliferation. The condition

is familial, and inheritance may be autosomal recessive or X-linked recessive. Ocular abnormalities are reported with X-linked recessive micrencephaly.

D. An infant born with normal head, weight, and length may fail to achieve normal brain growth because of postnatal brain insults, such as neonatal asphyxia (hypoxia-ischemia), intracranial hemorrhage, meningitis, conditions associated with hypoxia and/or hypotension (e.g., sepsis, necrotizing enterocolitis and malnutrition). Brain growth, and therefore head growth, is arrested. In severe insult, brain tissue destruction leads to atrophy, porencephaly, or hydranencephaly.

E. Some babies with small head are macrosomic. Infants of diabetic mothers (IDMs) who are large for gestational age have weights and lengths plotting at or over the ninetieth percentile but normal head circumference. Thus they appear microcephalic relative to their other body measurements. Microcephaly is an occasional finding in Beckwith-Wiedemann Syndrome.

HSB

References

Jones KL. Smith's recognizable patterns of human malformation. 4th ed. Philadelphia: WB Saunders, 1988.

Kopelman AE. Delayed cerebral development in twins with congenital hyperthyroidism. Am J Dis Child 1983; 137:842.

Roach A. Macrocrania, microcrania, and craniosynostosis. In: Coleman M, ed. Neonatal neurology. Baltimore: University Park Press, 1981:167.

Volpe JJ. Neurology of the newborn. 2nd ed. Philadelphia: WB Saunders, 1987:33.

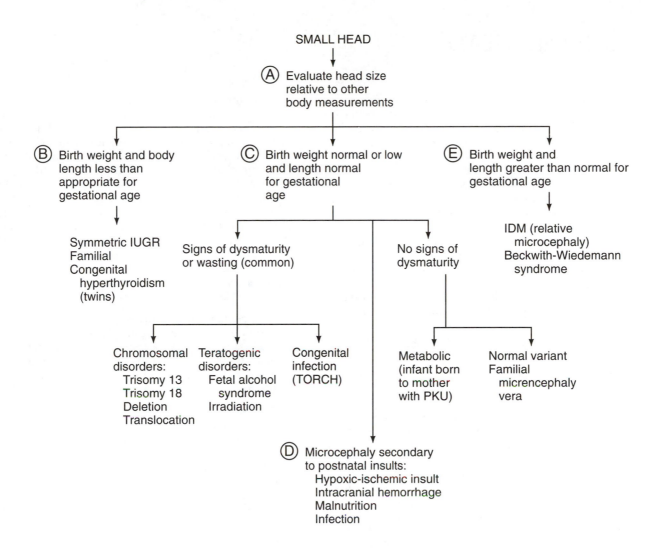

SMALL HEAD

(A) Evaluate head size relative to other body measurements

(B) Birth weight and body length less than appropriate for gestational age

Symmetric IUGR
Familial
Congenital hyperthyroidism (twins)

(C) Birth weight normal or low and length normal for gestational age

Signs of dysmaturity or wasting (common)

Chromosomal disorders:
  Trisomy 13
  Trisomy 18
  Deletion
  Translocation

Teratogenic disorders:
  Fetal alcohol syndrome
  Irradiation

Congenital infection (TORCH)

No signs of dysmaturity

Metabolic (infant born to mother with PKU)

Normal variant
Familial
micrencephaly vera

(D) Microcephaly secondary to postnatal insults:
  Hypoxic-ischemic insult
  Intracranial hemorrhage
  Malnutrition
  Infection

(E) Birth weight and length greater than normal for gestational age

IDM (relative microcephaly)
Beckwith-Wiedemann syndrome

MISSHAPED HEAD

A. In the evaluation of a misshaped head, one must carefully examine the scalp or soft tissue; palpate the surfaces of the cranial bones, the suture lines, and edges; and palpate the sutures and fontanelles for indications of increased intracranial pressure (increased width or wide separation of sutures; wide fontanelles; tense, bulging, or full fontanelles). In addition, the head shape should be evaluated in relation to facial size, shape, and abnormalities. In the newborn, the facial structures are diminutive compared with the calvarium, thus the unduly large appearance of the skull. Normal face-to-skull ratio ranges from 3:1 to 5:1. Certain facial abnormalities are unique to specific syndromes or chromosomal aberrations. One must also be familiar with unusual head shapes that are variants of normal; these findings have no pathological significance. Cranial bone abnormalities (e.g., fracture, synostosis) are verified by skull radiographs.

B. Scalp or soft tissue abnormalities may explain a finding of a misshaped head in the newly born. Babies born vaginally from vertex presentation have prominent occiput because of soft tissue edema or swelling, i.e., *caput succedaneum*. The sutures are overriding as a result of molding, and the normal head shape becomes evident in a few days when the caput is resolved and the sutures become normally separate. Traumatic vertex delivery may be associated with *cephalhematoma*, usually involving a parietal bone and at times bilateral. In the presence of *subgaleal* hemorrhage, the head appears large in which the dependent side is more prominent (blood tends to accumulate on dependent areas). The scalp is fluctuant on palpation. Because subgaleal hemorrhage is likely of traumatic origin, bruising of scalp or face may be seen.

C. Encephalocele results from a disorder of anterior neural tube closure. The lesion (protrusion or mass) is located in the occipital region in 75%–80% of cases. Associated malformations are not uncommon.

D. Abnormalities of the cranial bone may result from trauma, abnormal intrauterine development, premature suture closures, chromosomal aberrations (e.g., suture lines may be normal but cranial shape is unusual), or from disorders associated with either small or unusually large cranium. A depressed traumatic skull fracture may result in a misshaped head.

E. Early in the embryonic life, total failure of neurulation and failure of anterior neural tube closure result in craniorachischisis totalis and anencephaly, respectively.

F. Abnormalities in the suture lines such as loss of mobility, prominent bony ridges, and absent fontanelles suggest premature closure or fusion of the sutures. The various sutures involved in misshaped heads are indicated in parentheses in the algorithmn.

One or more suture lines may be involved; synostosis is demonstrable by skull radiographs. Variation in head shape results from limited brain growth in areas of the cranium with prematurely fused sutures while brain growth continues in areas of unfused sutures. Determination of the horizontal cephalic index (CI) calculated as maximum breadth/maximum length ×100 helps the categorization of the craniosynostosis. Premature fusion of single or multiple sutures is observed in certain syndromes. Immediate neurosurgical intervention is indicated to relieve increased intracranial pressure and minimize abnormal brain growth. Scaphocephaly is at times referred to as dolichocephaly. Triphyllocephaly is described as the cloverleaf skull (kleeblattschadel anomaly).

G. Dolichocephaly in the absence of synostosis is observed in pathological conditions such as trisomy 18, Hurler's syndrome, lissencephaly, and Bloom's syndrome. Brachycephaly in the absence of synostosis is a feature of trisomy 21, achondroplasia, and deLange syndrome.

H. The unusual shape of the cranium may represent a normal variation or it may be related to a definite cranial abnormality. Brachycephaly refers to a cranial configuration wherein the occipitofrontal diameter is narrow and the biparietal diameter is wide. In dolichocephaly, the occipitofrontal diameter is long and the biparietal diameter is narrow. Breech babies delivered vaginally have a long skull (dolichocephalic) as a result of molding of the head by the fundus of the uterus. Babies delivered by cesarean section with the head unengaged or in breech presentation tend to have a spherical head, somewhat brachycephalic. In Asians, brachycephaly represents a normal variation. In growing premature infants, biparietal diameter of the skull is narrow compared to the anteroposterior diameter, giving a dolichocephalic appearance.

HSB

References

Coleman M, ed. Neonatal neurology. Baltimore: University Park Press, 1981:21.

Jones KL. Smith's recognizable patterns of human malformation. 4th ed. Philadelphia: WB Saunders, 1988.

Roach A. Macrocrania, microcrania, and craniosynostosis. In: Coleman M, ed. Neonatal neurology. Baltimore: University Park Press, 1981:167.

Simpson DA, David JD. Craniosynostosis. In: Hoffman HJ, Epstein F, eds. Disorders of the developing nervous system: Diagnosis and treatment. Boston: Blackwell Scientific Publications, 1986:323.

Swischuck LE. Radiology of the newborn and young infant. 2nd ed. Baltimore: Williams & Wilkins, 1980:736.

Volpe JJ. Neurology of the newborn. 2nd ed. Philadelphia: WB Saunders, 1987:2.

MISSHAPED HEAD

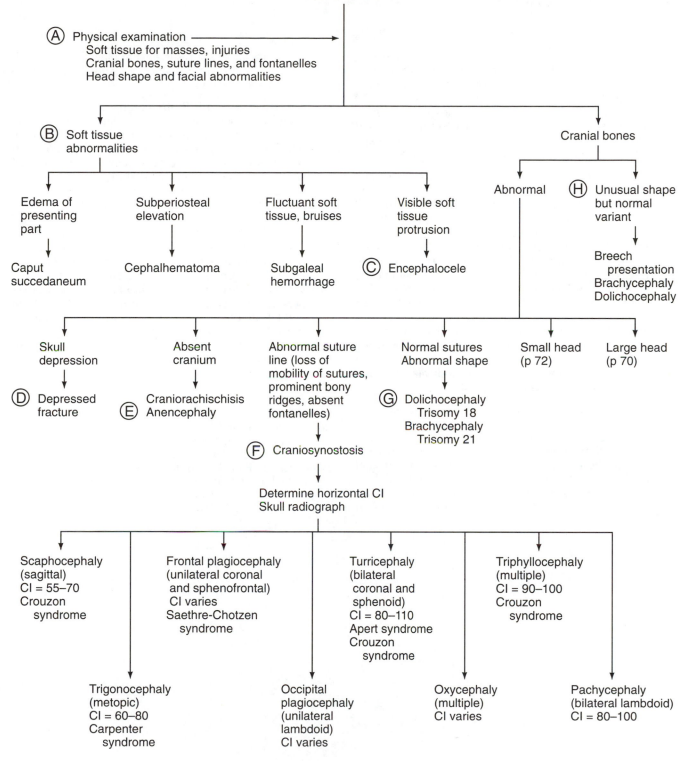

A Physical examination
 Soft tissue for masses, injuries
 Cranial bones, suture lines, and fontanelles
 Head shape and facial abnormalities

B Soft tissue abnormalities

Cranial bones

Edema of presenting part

Subperiosteal elevation

Fluctuant soft tissue, bruises

Visible soft tissue protrusion

Abnormal

H Unusual shape but normal variant

Caput succedaneum

Cephalhematoma

Subgaleal hemorrhage

C Encephalocele

Breech presentation
Brachycephaly
Dolichocephaly

Skull depression

Absent cranium

Abnormal suture line (loss of mobility of sutures, prominent bony ridges, absent fontanelles)

Normal sutures Abnormal shape

Small head (p 72)

Large head (p 70)

D Depressed fracture

E Craniorachischisis Anencephaly

G Dolichocephaly Trisomy 18 Brachycephaly Trisomy 21

F Craniosynostosis

Determine horizontal CI
Skull radiograph

Scaphocephaly (sagittal)
CI = 55–70
Crouzon syndrome

Frontal plagiocephaly (unilateral coronal and sphenofrontal)
CI varies
Saethre-Chotzen syndrome

Turricephaly (bilateral coronal and sphenoid)
CI = 80–110
Apert syndrome
Crouzon syndrome

Triphyllocephaly (multiple)
CI = 90–100
Crouzon syndrome

Trigonocephaly (metopic)
CI = 60–80
Carpenter syndrome

Occipital plagiocephaly (unilateral lambdoid)
CI varies

Oxycephaly (multiple)
CI varies

Pachycephaly (bilateral lambdoid)
CI = 80–100

WIDE SUTURES

A. Head size, shape, and the size and tension of fontanelles must be examined in the evaluation of an infant with wide sutures. Although increased intracranial pressure is always suspected in the presence of widened sutures, several possibilities exist wherein spread sutures occur without necessarily increased intracranial pressure (ICP). Both head size and shape aid in differential diagnosis (pp 70, 72, 74).

B. When signs of increased ICP are absent, especially when head size and shape are normal, the following normal anatomical/physiological variations need to be considered: presence of wormian bones, dysmaturity, and growth spurt in a premature or a previously ill infant. *Wormian bones* are intercalated bones present in the posteroparietal and occipital areas and often have no clinical significance. Wormian bones may be seen in cleidocranial dysostosis, in osteogenesis imperfecta, and rarely in congenital hypothyroidism (see section **C**). In dysmaturity and/or intrauterine growth retardation, diminished bone mineralization may explain the widened sutures. Similarly, in growing premature infants or in those infants who have been chronically ill, the spread sutures indicate "rebound brain growth" or "catch-up growth."

C. Wide sutures and large fontanelles (not tense or bulging) are seen in congenital hypothyroidism. Pseudospread sutures are also observed in conditions associated with poor mineralization or under ossification of the cranial bones, e.g., hypothyroidism and dwarfism, such as osteogenesis imperfecta, hypophosphatasia, progeria, achondrogenesis, and thanatophoric dysplasia. Wide sutures are also seen in cleidocranial dysostosis (defect of clavicle, late ossification of cranial sutures, autosomal dominant with no mental abnormality).

D. In early increased ICP, the coronal suture is the first suture to widen; the anterior fontanel enlarges and bulging is observed (p 78). Then the sagittal suture becomes involved next, and finally the lambdoid and squamosal sutures become widened. However, all sutures may become involved at the same time if the marked increase in intracranial pressure is acute or abrupt. With spreading of the sutures, head circumference increases at an abnormal rate. "Sun-setting" irises are observed. Etiologies for increased ICP include hydrocephalus, cerebral edema, intracranial hemorrhage, masses or tumors, and noncranial systemic disorders such as congestive heart failure, vitamin A intoxication, and chronic pulmonary disorders. Specialized studies such as ultrasound head scan and CT are often necessary diagnostic procedures.

HSB

References

Roach A. Macrocrania, microcrania, and craniosynostosis. In: Coleman M, ed. Neonatal neurology. Baltimore: University Park Press, 1981:167.

Swischuck LE. Radiology of the newborn and young infant. 2nd ed. Baltimore: Williams & Wilkins, 1980:736.

Volpe JJ. Neurology of the newborn. 2nd ed. Philadelphia: WB Saunders, 1987:2.

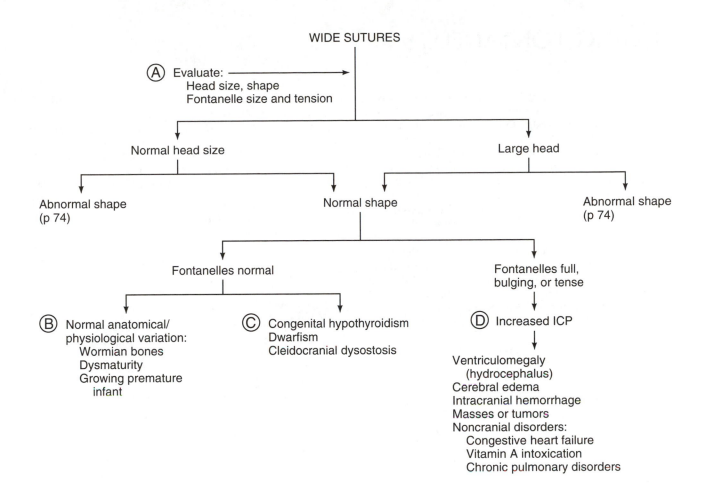

WIDE SUTURES

Ⓐ Evaluate:
　　Head size, shape
　　Fontanelle size and tension

Normal head size

Large head

Abnormal shape
(p 74)

Normal shape

Abnormal shape
(p 74)

Fontanelles normal

Fontanelles full,
bulging, or tense

Ⓑ Normal anatomical/
physiological variation:
　　Wormian bones
　　Dysmaturity
　　Growing premature
　　　infant

Ⓒ Congenital hypothyroidism
Dwarfism
Cleidocranial dysostosis

Ⓓ Increased ICP

Ventriculomegaly
　　(hydrocephalus)
Cerebral edema
Intracranial hemorrhage
Masses or tumors
Noncranial disorders:
　　Congestive heart failure
　　Vitamin A intoxication
　　Chronic pulmonary disorders

BULGING FONTANELLES

A. For all practical purposes, bulging fontanelles are a sign of increased intracranial pressure (ICP), and the etiology must be investigated. In the evaluation of an infant with a bulging fontanelle, consider the age of onset; associated abnormalities in head size, shape, and sutures; and any associated facial dysmorphism. Also evaluate the infant for other signs of increased ICP, such as split sutures, "setting-sun" irises, apnea or ataxic respirations, bradycardia, hypotension or hypertension, seizures, dilated and/or fixed pupils, loss of consciousness or irritability, and biochemical changes that may be consistent with inappropriate ADH secretion. Other physical examination findings may give a clue to the etiology of increased ICP. Bruit auscultated over the fontanelles suggests arteriovenous malformation (AVM). Skull radiographs may show split sutures, wide fontanelles, fractures, and/or calcifications. A positive transillumination suggests hydrocephalus. Ventriculomegaly and periventricular-intraventricular hemorrhage (PV-IVH) are easily demonstrable by head ultrasound scan.

B. With a bulging fontanelle, obvious at birth in a misshaped head, consider traumatic injuries and various types of craniostenosis (except for the universal craniostenosis). Subdural hemorrhage and rarely subarachnoid and epidural hemorrhage are associated with increased ICP and cerebral edema. A history of difficult delivery; scalp or soft tissue bruises; seizures; hypotension; marked pallor; dilated, unequal, or nonreacting pupils; and rapid clinical deterioration suggest traumatic intracranial hemorrhage. Depressed skull fracture following difficult forceps delivery may cause cerebral contusion and increased ICP. A subdural hemorrhage may be demonstrated by a head ultrasound scan. CT scan is diagnostic for intracranial hemorrhages, but transporting a clinically unstable infant for the procedure may not be feasible. A subdural tap should aid in diagnosis of a subdural hemorrhage and relief of the increased ICP.

C. Skull films of the abnormally shaped head show fusion of the sutures; the sutures involved depend on the category of craniostenosis. Examination of the head reveals bony ridge in the involved suture lines and compensatory wide sutures and bulging fontanelles in the uninvolved areas.

D. In congenital hydrocephalus, the head is usually large at birth, sutures are wide, eyes demonstrate the "setting-sun" sign, the head transilluminates, the skull x-rays show wide sutures with or without a lacunar skull, and head ultrasound shows ventriculomegaly. When calcifications are not seen on skull films and/or head ultrasound, the congenital hydrocephalus may be due to isolated aqueductal stenosis, Arnold-Chiari malformation, or Dandy-Walker syndrome. Congenital hydrocephalus is commonly seen with neural tube defects or a malformation in various chromosomal aberrations or syndromes. Certain facies are unique to specific syndromes.

E. In the presence of skull calcifications (periventricular calcifications), congenital infection, TORCH (toxoplasmosis, rubella, cytomegalovirus, herpes), must be ruled out. Findings often associated may include hepatosplenomegaly, jaundice (both direct and indirect hyperbilirubinemia), thrombocytopenia, skin petechiae or ecchymoses, and cardiac malformations.

F. When a large head does not transilluminate but increased ICP is evident from the skull films and head ultrasound shows no ventriculomegaly, consider a space-occupying mass or AVM. A head scan usually demonstrates a space-occupying mass or a large, pulsating AVM; a CT scan may be necessary for definitive diagnosis. A bruit is audible over the fontanelle in AVM.

G. In conditions associated with diminished bone ossification, wherein the head is of normal size but sutures are spread, the wide fontanelles may seem tense by palpation. Examples of such disorders include dysmaturity or asymmetric intrauterine growth retardation and the various types of dwarfism.

H. When the head is normal at birth but signs of increased ICP become evident several hours or a few days later, consider cerebral edema caused by either asphyxia, neonatal meningitis, or, in a premature infant, the possibility of a large periventricular intracranial hemorrhage either at onset or at evolution.

I. In a premature infant, a rapidly increasing head size and tense fontanelle after 1 week of age suggest development of posthemorrhagic hydrocephalus, which may be related to diminished CSF absorption by the intraventricular blood or to obliterative arachnoiditis in the posterior fossa. Progressive ventricular dilation is demonstrated by serial head ultrasound. Meningitis, encephalitis, or brain abscess is associated with increased ICP and may occur at any time in the neonatal period. Pleocytosis, elevated CSF protein, and hypoglycorrhachia are suggestive, and a positive CSF culture is diagnostic of CNS infection. Conditions such as congestive heart failure (CHF), vitamin A intoxication, and disorders with chronic pulmonary insufficiency may present with bulging fontanelles with neither ventriculomegaly nor intracranial hemorrhage as an associated finding. In CHF, digitalization results in the disappearance of the bulging fontanelle. In a growing premature infant or in a previously chronically ill infant, the head size may increase rapidly as part of a "growth spurt" or "catch-up" growth. Sutures become separated, and the wide fontanelles may seem tense or bulging.

HSB

References

Haller JS. Skull transillumination. In: Coleman M, ed. Neonatal neurology. Baltimore: University Park Press, 1981:41.

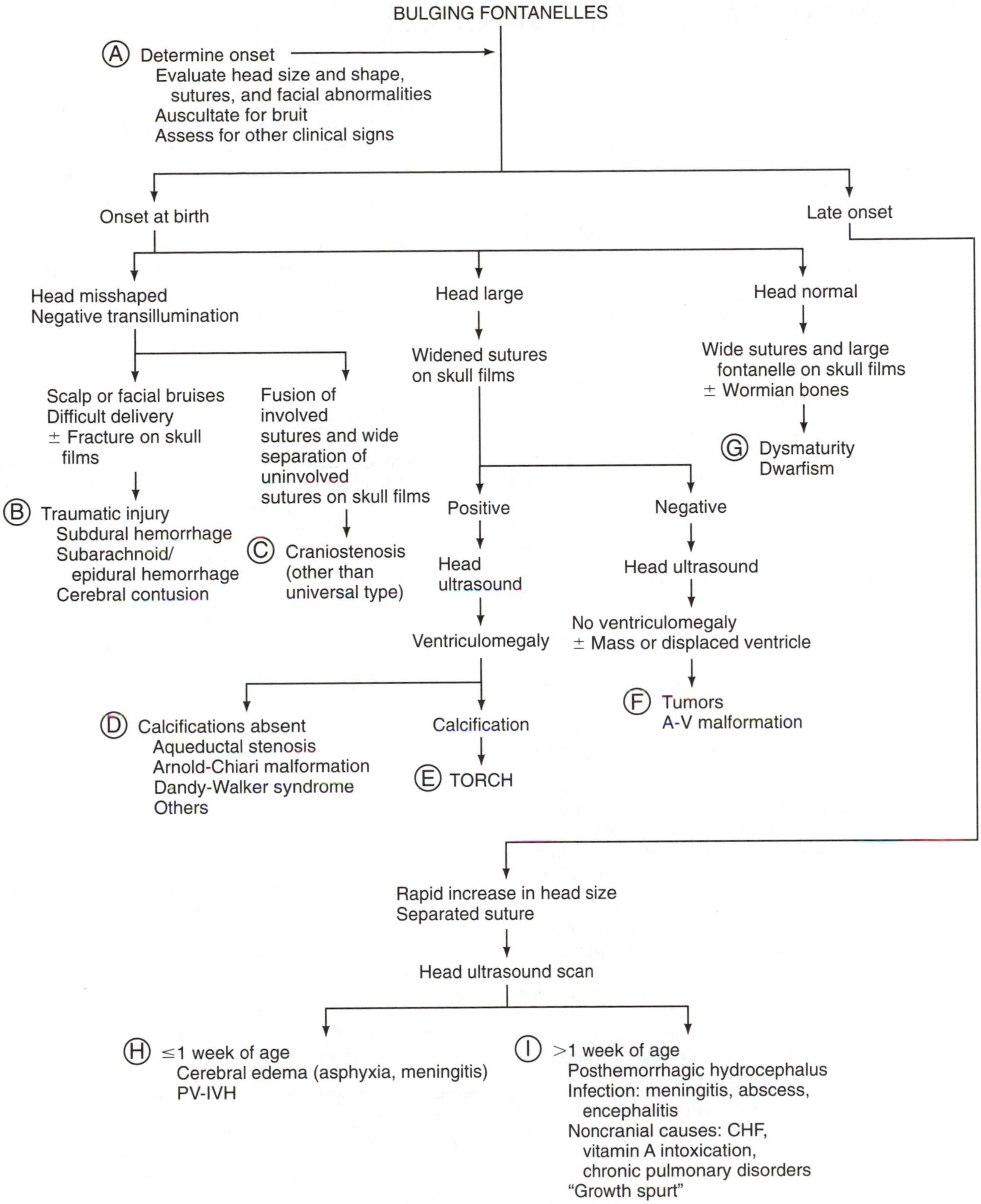
BULGING FONTANELLES
Ⓐ Determine onset
Evaluate head size and shape, sutures, and facial abnormalities
Auscultate for bruit
Assess for other clinical signs
Onset at birth
Late onset
Head misshaped
Negative transillumination
Head large
Head normal
Scalp or facial bruises
Difficult delivery
± Fracture on skull films
Fusion of involved sutures and wide separation of uninvolved sutures on skull films
Widened sutures on skull films
Wide sutures and large fontanelle on skull films
± Wormian bones
Ⓑ Traumatic injury
Subdural hemorrhage
Subarachnoid/ epidural hemorrhage
Cerebral contusion
Ⓒ Craniostenosis (other than universal type)
Ⓖ Dysmaturity
Dwarfism
Positive
Negative
Head ultrasound
Head ultrasound
Ventriculomegaly
No ventriculomegaly
± Mass or displaced ventricle
Ⓓ Calcifications absent
Aqueductal stenosis
Arnold-Chiari malformation
Dandy-Walker syndrome
Others
Calcification
Ⓔ TORCH
Ⓕ Tumors
A-V malformation
Rapid increase in head size
Separated suture
Head ultrasound scan
Ⓗ ≤1 week of age
Cerebral edema (asphyxia, meningitis)
PV-IVH
Ⓘ >1 week of age
Posthemorrhagic hydrocephalus
Infection: meningitis, abscess, encephalitis
Noncranial causes: CHF, vitamin A intoxication, chronic pulmonary disorders
"Growth spurt"

Roach A. Neuroradiological evaluation. In: Coleman M, ed. Neonatal neurology. Baltimore: University Park Press, 1981:81.

Roach A. Macrocrania, microcrania, and craniosynostosis. In: Coleman M, ed. Neonatal neurology. Baltimore: University Park Press, 1981:167.

Swischuck LE. Radiology of the newborn and young infant. 2nd ed. Baltimore: Williams & Wilkins, 1980.

Volpe JJ. Neurology of the newborn. 2nd ed. Philadelphia: WB Saunders, 1987.

ABNORMAL CONTOUR OF CHEST

A. In the examination of a neonate, particular attention is focused not only on the presence or absence of retractions but also on the symmetry of the chest, the presence of abnormal protrusions or defects, as well as the relationship of the chest circumference to the head and abdominal girth. Symmetry does not necessarily rule out pathology. A chest wall may "balloon out" (barrel chest) as a result of overdistension of the lungs from interstitial air accumulation or overdistended alveoli (ball-valve mechanism in upper airway obstruction); the diaphragms are pushed down and flattened on chest radiograph. The lungs may be compressed but the chest wall anteroposterior diameter is increased with bilateral pneumothoraces; rapid clinical deterioration accompanies this complication.

B. A symmetrical chest may appear flattened with increase in the transverse diameter. Physical examination easily detects the presence of subcutaneous edema. Intercostal retractions may be visible anteriorly but none along the lateral thorax since edema fluid tends to settle along the sides and back when an infant is in supine position. Subcutaneous edema suggests anasarca particularly from hydrops fetalis (see p 14, 16, 18).

C. When the thorax is small, especially when narrow (decreased transverse diameter), the normal abdomen becomes very prominent, i.e. the normal size abdomen is disproportionately larger than the small thorax. The ribs are often short and the costochondral junction flared and irregular; thus the narrow chest cavity is bell-shaped in appearance. Shortened limbs suggest dwarfism; some of these conditions such as the achondroplasia, achondrogenesis, and thanatophoric dwarfism are lethal. Vertebral anomalies and polydactyly are associated findings in Majewski syndrome, Saldino-Noonan syndrome, Ellis-van Creveld syndrome, and Jeune syndrome.

D. The most common sternal defect is pectus excavation. The sternum dips posteriorly toward the vertebrae and is maximally depressed above the xiphoid. This is of sporadic occurrence and is often an isolated deformity. Pectus excavation is an associated finding in various syndromes, e.g., Marfan's syndrome and osteogenesis imperfecta I. Surgery may be necessary to relieve respiratory difficulty.

E. Other malformations of the sternum include short sternum, partial or complete defect in sternal fusion, and protrusion deformity. Complete sternal separation is usually associated with other malformations, often lethal such as ectopia cordis. Sternal protrusion (pigeon breast) is a less common abnormality.

F. When asymmetry is evident, one needs to rule out conditions that are not associated with rib cage anomalies. Chest asymmetry may indicate unilateral pneumothorax, diaphragmatic paralysis, or hydrothorax. In diaphragmatic hernia, an important clinical sign is a scaphoid abdomen (abdominal contents are in one of the thoracic cavities).

G. Vertebral anomalies particularly in misaligned vertebrae may manifest as chest asymmetry. Some disorders with small thorax may be associated with vertebral anomalies.

H. Absence of ribs could result in an asymmetrical chest. In Poland syndrome there is unilateral defect of the pectoralis muscle; nipple, areola, and scapula may be absent.

I. Abnormal protrusions from the chest wall include tumors, cysts, and bony prominences from calcified rib fractures. Commonly tumors or masses protrude from external structures of thorax, i.e., skin, cartilage, or bone. However large internal tumors (congenital mesenchymoma or hamartoma) may cause complete destruction of the ribs or thoracic deformity.

HSB

References

Avery ME, Fletcher BD, Williams RG. Abnormalities of the diaphragm, chest wall, and pleura. In: Avery ME, Fletcher BD, Williams RG. The lung and its disorders in the newborn infant. 4th ed. Philadelphia: WB Saunders, 1981:182.

Davis GM, Bureau MA. Pulmonary and chest wall mechanics in the control of respiration in the newborn. Clin Perinatol 1987; 14:551.

Jones KL. Smith's recognizable patterns of human malformation. 4th ed. Philadelphia: WB Saunders, 1988.

Swischuk LE. Skeletal system and soft tissues. In: Swischuk LE. Radiology of the newborn and young infant. 2nd ed. Baltimore: Williams & Wilkins, 1980:611.

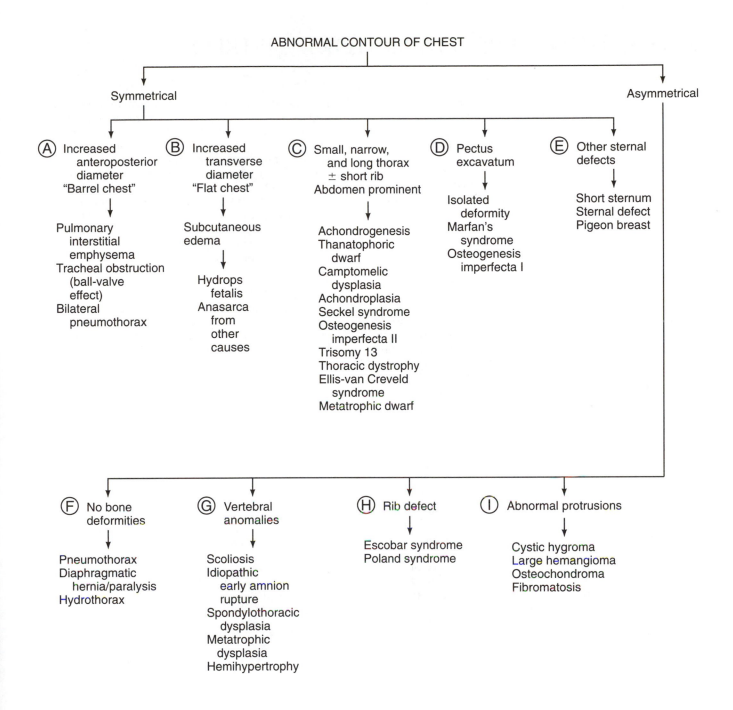

ABNORMAL CONTOUR OF CHEST

Symmetrical

Asymmetrical

(A) Increased
anteroposterior
diameter
"Barrel chest"

Pulmonary
interstitial
emphysema
Tracheal obstruction
(ball-valve
effect)
Bilateral
pneumothorax

(B) Increased
transverse
diameter
"Flat chest"

Subcutaneous
edema

Hydrops
fetalis
Anasarca
from
other
causes

(C) Small, narrow,
and long thorax
± short rib
Abdomen prominent

Achondrogenesis
Thanatophoric
dwarf
Camptomelic
dysplasia
Achondroplasia
Seckel syndrome
Osteogenesis
imperfecta II
Trisomy 13
Thoracic dystrophy
Ellis-van Creveld
syndrome
Metatrophic dwarf

(D) Pectus
excavatum

Isolated
deformity
Marfan's
syndrome
Osteogenesis
imperfecta I

(E) Other sternal
defects

Short sternum
Sternal defect
Pigeon breast

(F) No bone
deformities

Pneumothorax
Diaphragmatic
hernia/paralysis
Hydrothorax

(G) Vertebral
anomalies

Scoliosis
Idiopathic
early amnion
rupture
Spondylothoracic
dysplasia
Metatrophic
dysplasia
Hemihypertrophy

(H) Rib defect

Escobar syndrome
Poland syndrome

(I) Abnormal protrusions

Cystic hygroma
Large hemangioma
Osteochondroma
Fibromatosis

RETRACTIONS AND RESPIRATORY DISTRESS

A. Retractions are one of the primary signs of respiratory distress in the neonate. Their presence indicates interference in the normal entry of air into the respiratory tract. However, their absence does not necessarily denote normalcy; retractions may not be evident in a feeble infant with severe lung disease or in an infant unable to have diaphragmatic excursions because of bilateral phrenic nerve paralysis. These conditions result in apnea and bradycardia serving as a warning of poor air exchange.

B. Minimal intercostal and subcostal retractions in the presence of a disproportionately marked tachypnea suggest nonpulmonary etiology. Examples are cardiac disorders, severe anemia, central nervous system diseases, and metabolic acidosis from various causes. Rapid breathing with minimal-to-absent retractions may result from the CNS respiratory center dysfunction as in perinatal asphyxia, meningitis, or brain hemorrhage. In metabolic acidosis, respiratory compensation is evident by tachypnea with minimal-to-absent retractions; arterial blood gases demonstrate low $Paco_2$ and a large base deficit. Severe anemia, especially from acute blood loss, may be associated with tachypnea with only minimal retractions.

C. When intercostal, subcostal, and sternal/xiphoid retractions are marked with associated moderate-to-severe tachypnea, parenchymal lung involvement is a primary consideration. Commonly found in the neonate are respiratory distress syndrome, atelectasis, pneumonia, and interstitial emphysema. Retractions are observed bilaterally, with a decrease in anteroposterior diameter in most instances except in the pulmonary interstitial emphysema or in respiratory distress syndrome II. Generalized edema may mask intercostal retractions whereas xiphoid or sternal retraction often remains evident.

D. In extrapulmonary disorder involvement is more often unilateral than bilateral, and the retractions are observed in the hemithorax with the better air exchange or where air exchange is possible. Thus in diaphragmatic hernia, hemothorax, pneumothorax, hydrothorax, or lobar emphysema the chest bulges out with minimal retractions on the involved side but with marked compensatory retractions on the opposite side. Asymmetry is a clinical hallmark of most of these disorders. Other air leaks, e.g., pneumopericardium or pneumoperitoneum, may be an associated finding with pneumothorax or pneumomediastinum.

E. When retractions are severe, especially when involving the suprasternal/supraclavicular area, obstruction of the upper airway should be suspected. The infant appears to have "air hunger," has "violent respiratory effort," and yet air exchange is absent or minimal. Wheezing or stridor may be heard (see p 68).

HSB

References

Carlo WA. Assessment of pulmonary function. In: Fanaroff AA, Martin RJ, eds. Neonatal-perinatal medicine: Diseases of the fetus and infant. 5th ed. St Louis: Mosby–Year Book, 1992:801.

Korones SB. High-risk newborn infants: The basis for intensive nursing care. 4th ed. St Louis: Mosby–Year Book, 1986: 151, 204.

Miller MJ, Fanaroff AA, Martin RJ. Other aspiration syndromes. In: Fanaroff AA, Martin RJ, eds. Neonatal-perinatal medicine: Diseases of the fetus and infant. 5th ed. St Louis: Mosby–Year Book, 1992:837.

RETRACTIONS AND RESPIRATORY DISTRESS

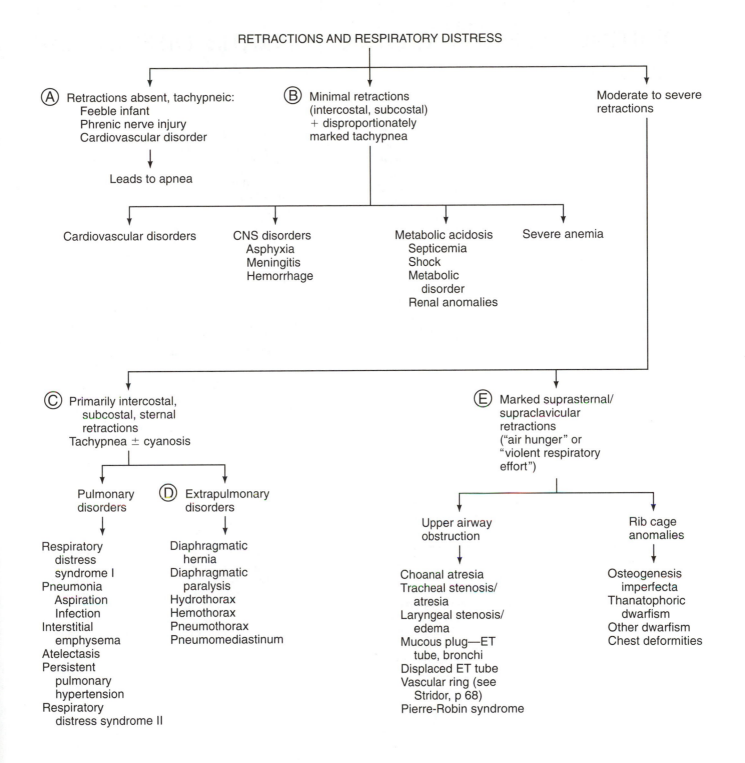

(A) Retractions absent, tachypneic:
    Feeble infant
    Phrenic nerve injury
    Cardiovascular disorder

Leads to apnea

(B) Minimal retractions
(intercostal, subcostal)
+ disproportionately
marked tachypnea

Moderate to severe
retractions

Cardiovascular disorders

CNS disorders
    Asphyxia
    Meningitis
    Hemorrhage

Metabolic acidosis
    Septicemia
    Shock
    Metabolic
       disorder
    Renal anomalies

Severe anemia

(C) Primarily intercostal,
subcostal, sternal
retractions
Tachypnea ± cyanosis

(E) Marked suprasternal/
supraclavicular
retractions
("air hunger" or
"violent respiratory
effort")

Pulmonary
disorders

(D) Extrapulmonary
disorders

Upper airway
obstruction

Rib cage
anomalies

Respiratory
   distress
   syndrome I
Pneumonia
   Aspiration
   Infection
Interstitial
   emphysema
Atelectasis
Persistent
   pulmonary
   hypertension
Respiratory
   distress syndrome II

Diaphragmatic
   hernia
Diaphragmatic
   paralysis
Hydrothorax
Hemothorax
Pneumothorax
Pneumomediastinum

Choanal atresia
Tracheal stenosis/
   atresia
Laryngeal stenosis/
   edema
Mucous plug—ET
   tube, bronchi
Displaced ET tube
Vascular ring (see
   Stridor, p 68)
Pierre-Robin syndrome

Osteogenesis
   imperfecta
Thanatophoric
   dwarfism
Other dwarfism
Chest deformities

VOMITING/EXCESSIVE GASTRIC ASPIRATE: DIFFERENTIAL DIAGNOSIS

A. Vomiting and excessive gastric aspirate (>10 or 15 ml) may be bilious or nonbilious. With some exceptions, bilious vomiting indicates an obstructive lesion distal to the ampulla of Vater. Duodenal obstruction is quite likely if abdominal distention is either absent or limited to the epigastric area. As the site of an obstructive lesion descends, the onset of vomiting is later, and abdominal distention more pronounced. Bilious vomiting and distention are also produced by such generalized processes as necrotizing enterocolitis (NEC) and severe ileus associated with septicemia. Whereas vomiting is often a presenting (or at least an early) sign of localized intestinal lesions, septicemia is usually apparent from other signs by the time bilious vomiting appears. Bile-tinged gastric aspirate in small quantities is not unusual in otherwise well infants <800 g and in any infant whose nasogastric tube has been propelled through the gastric antrum. Duodenal atresia may be accompanied by other major anomalies such as congenital cardiac malformations, tracheoesophageal fistulas, renal malformations, and occasionally the VATER syndrome. Duodenal atresia is a well-known component of trisomy 21. Contrast studies rule out extrinsic duodenal obstruction caused by malrotation (Ladd's bands) with or without volvulus.

B. The most frequent cause of nonbilious vomiting or gastric retention is NEC. Both vomiting and abdominal distention are most often the earliest signs of disease. Other surgical diseases that cause consistent nonbilious vomiting (preampullary duodenal obstruction, obstructive gastric lesions) are less common and usually indicated by typical gas patterns on a plain film of the abdomen. Vomiting or excessive gastric aspirate often occurs as a result of overfeeding smaller infants by increasing intake with inappropriate rapidity. Infections, particularly septicemia, cause generalized intestinal dilation (ileus) as well as vomiting. Inborn errors of metabolism may cause recurrent vomiting, but these disorders are associated with an array of signs that are considerably more significant as clinical indicators.

C. Hematemesis (bloody gastric aspirate) indicates a serious underlying disorder, except for the syndrome of swallowed maternal blood, which may be identified by the Apt test. Mix one part gastric aspirate (or stool) and five parts tap water. Add 4 ml of the centrifuged pink supernatant to 1 ml of 1% sodium hydroxide. Alkali-resistant fetal hemoglobin remains pink; maternal hemoglobin A turns yellow-brown in 1 to 2 minutes. Except for NEC the surgical disorders that cause bloody vomitus are rare. Bloody gastric content associated with NEC is a sinister sign of extensive disease that may involve the stomach. Proper administration of vitamin K has virtually eliminated hemorrhagic disease of the newborn. Tolazoline therapy requires a nasogastric tube that is aspirated periodically because diffuse and massive gastric hemorrhage may occur during tolazoline administration, particularly when the drug is given by continuous drip. Bloody gastric content is rare with theophylline therapy.

SBK

References

Flake AW, Ryckman FC. The neonatal gastrointestinal tract: Selected anomalies and intestinal obstruction. In: Fanaroff AA, Martin RJ, eds. Neonatal-perinatal medicine: Diseases of the fetus and infant. St Louis: Mosby—Year Book, 1992:1038.

Touloukian RJ. Intestinal atresia. Clin Perinatol 1978; 5:3.

Young DG. Gastroenterology: Congenital defects and surgical problems. In: Roberton NRC, ed. Textbook of neonatology. New York: Churchill Livingstone, 1986:407.

VOMITING OR GASTRIC ASPIRATE >10 ml

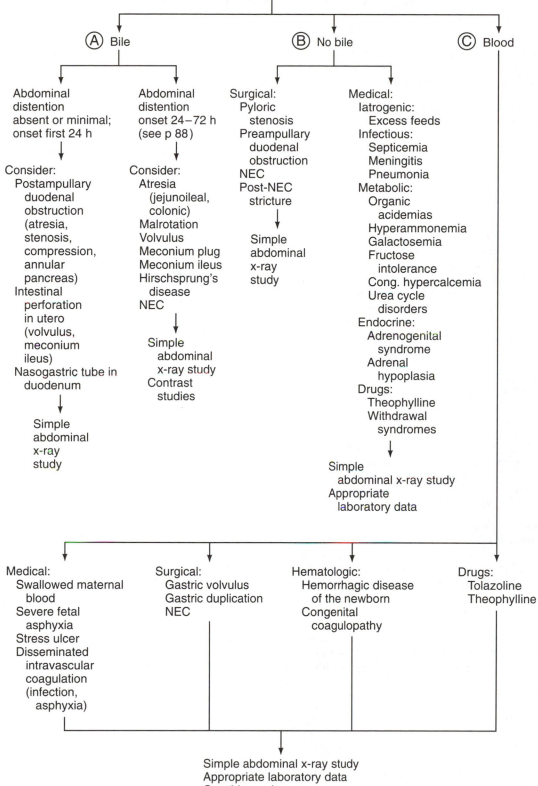

Ⓐ Bile

Abdominal
distention
absent or minimal;
onset first 24 h

Consider:
Postampullary
duodenal
obstruction
(atresia,
stenosis,
compression,
annular
pancreas)
Intestinal
perforation
in utero
(volvulus,
meconium
ileus)
Nasogastric tube in
duodenum

Simple
abdominal
x-ray
study

Abdominal
distention
onset 24–72 h
(see p 88)

Consider:
Atresia
(jejunoileal,
colonic)
Malrotation
Volvulus
Meconium plug
Meconium ileus
Hirschsprung's
disease
NEC

Simple
abdominal
x-ray study
Contrast
studies

Ⓑ No bile

Surgical:
Pyloric
stenosis
Preampullary
duodenal
obstruction
NEC
Post-NEC
stricture

Simple
abdominal
x-ray
study

Medical:
Iatrogenic:
Excess feeds
Infectious:
Septicemia
Meningitis
Pneumonia
Metabolic:
Organic
acidemias
Hyperammonemia
Galactosemia
Fructose
intolerance
Cong. hypercalcemia
Urea cycle
disorders
Endocrine:
Adrenogenital
syndrome
Adrenal
hypoplasia
Drugs:
Theophylline
Withdrawal
syndromes

Simple
abdominal x-ray study
Appropriate
laboratory data

Ⓒ Blood

Medical:
Swallowed maternal
blood
Severe fetal
asphyxia
Stress ulcer
Disseminated
intravascular
coagulation
(infection,
asphyxia)

Surgical:
Gastric volvulus
Gastric duplication
NEC

Hematologic:
Hemorrhagic disease
of the newborn
Congenital
coagulopathy

Drugs:
Tolazoline
Theophylline

Simple abdominal x-ray study
Appropriate laboratory data
Consider endoscopy

85

BLOODY STOOLS: DIFFERENTIAL DIAGNOSIS

A. Gross blood is bright red when it originates from lower levels of the intestine, but with copious bleeding bright red blood may originate from higher levels. Intestinal bleeding is rarely a cause of hemorrhagic shock, although a diminished hematocrit may sometimes result.

B. Color tests (Hematest, guaiac) for stool blood are sometimes so sensitive that they are positive if a rectal temperature is taken. In an otherwise well infant the isolated finding of microscopic blood in stool is rarely significant.

C. Necrotizing enterocolitis (NEC) is a frequent cause of bloody stools. Blood is rarely observed in an infant who is otherwise asymptomatic; other signs of NEC predominate. The quantity of blood lost is not in itself a problem. Anal fissures are also common; they usually cause bloody streaks or sometimes more impressive quantities of blood. Stress ulcers in the duodenum and stomach, as well as hemorrhagic gastritis, may also give rise to an impressive quantity of blood. They are usually associated with severe illness of any type and prolonged steroid therapy. The gastric bleeding associated with tolazoline therapy is thought to originate from hemorrhagic gastritis. Although rare in the neonate, theophylline therapy also causes hemorrhagic gastritis. Ischemic and gangrenous lesions of the intestine are regularly associated with obvious abdominal signs that suggest their presence. Bleeding from Meckel's diverticulum is rare during the neonatal period. Milk protein sensitivity is due to cow's milk or soy bean formula; bloody stools first appear during the second or third weeks of life.

D. A number of diseases, largely extrinsic to the gastrointestinal tract, may be associated with blood in stools. Disseminated intravascular coagulation (DIC) produces dramatic signs everywhere else. Bleeding is evident at numerous sites, and the underlying disease is a preoccupying feature of the total clinical situation. Hemorrhagic disease of the newborn resulting from vitamin K deficiency is prevented by vitamin K administration at birth. If vitamin K is not administered, bloody stools appear on the second or third day, in infants who have no other clinical signs or little else besides bruising. Malabsorption of vitamin K and intestinal bleeding may accompany conjugated hyperbilirubinemia caused by severe hepatocellular disease of various etiologies. Severe liver disease additionally impairs generation of other clotting factors, giving rise to generalized bleeding. Infections such as cytomegalovirus, toxoplasmosis, syphilis, and bacterial septicemia may precipitate bowel bleeding associated with bleeding elsewhere, as manifestations of DIC and severely impaired liver function. Diffuse (miliary) hemangiomatosis is rare. Multiple hemangiomata are distributed throughout the body; although bloody stools occur, they are of minor importance in the spectrum of life-threatening difficulties caused by hemangiomata elsewhere.

E. A relatively small amount of stool blood in an otherwise well infant usually remains unexplained. In the absence of other signs, investigational procedures are advisedly postponed. An Apt test may differentiate between the melena caused by fetal or adult blood. Presence of adult blood indicates swallowed maternal blood. A negative test however (no adult blood) does not rule out the syndrome. Cracked bleeding nipples of nursing mothers are also sources of swallowed blood.

SBK

References

Ament ME. Diagnosis and management of upper gastrointestinal tract bleeding in the pediatric patient. Pediatr Rev 1990; 12:107–116.

Oldham KT, Lobe TE. Gastrointestinal hemorrhage in children: A pragmatic update. Pediatr Clin North Am 1985; 32:1247–1263.

Sherman NJ, Clatworthy HW, Jr. Gastrointestinal bleeding in neonates: A study of 94 cases. Surgery 1967; 62:614–619.

Silber G. Lower gastrointestinal bleeding. Pediatr Rev 1990; 12:85–93.

Silber GH, Klish WJ. Hematochezia in infants less than 6 months of age. Am J Dis Child 1986; 140:1097–1098.

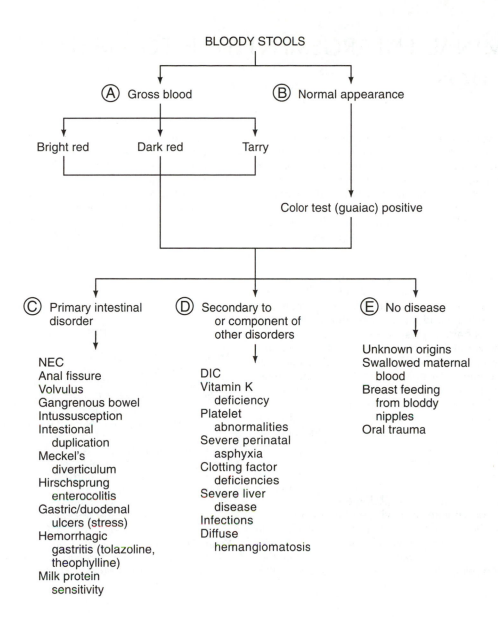

BLOODY STOOLS

Ⓐ Gross blood   Ⓑ Normal appearance

Bright red   Dark red   Tarry

Color test (guaiac) positive

Ⓒ Primary intestinal disorder

Ⓓ Secondary to or component of other disorders

Ⓔ No disease

NEC
Anal fissure
Volvulus
Gangrenous bowel
Intussusception
Intestional
   duplication
Meckel's
   diverticulum
Hirschsprung
   enterocolitis
Gastric/duodenal
   ulcers (stress)
Hemorrhagic
   gastritis (tolazoline,
   theophylline)
Milk protein
   sensitivity

DIC
Vitamin K
   deficiency
Platelet
   abnormalities
Severe perinatal
   asphyxia
Clotting factor
   deficiencies
Severe liver
   disease
Infections
Diffuse
   hemangiomatosis

Unknown origins
Swallowed maternal
   blood
Breast feeding
   from bloddy
   nipples
Oral trauma

ABDOMINAL ENLARGEMENT DUE TO GASEOUS DISTENTION

A. Unless a prenatal diagnosis was made by ultrasound, evaluation of an enlarged abdomen entails a number of initial observations. A tightly distended abdomen precludes palpation of enlarged organs or masses. Differentiation of distending gas from fluid accumulation is occasionally surmised by a percussed hollow sound or by eliciting a fluid wave. Bluish black discoloration of abdominal skin suggests blood or meconium in the peritoneal space.

B. Temporally related circumstances indicate the unfolding of any disease process. Therefore, it is essential to determine whether maternal polyhydramnios occurred, when abdominal distention appeared, whether meconium was passed, when excessive aspirate or vomiting appeared, and if it was bilious. Iatrogenic factors must also be considered in this temporal context. Mechanical ventilation may have caused pneumothorax, nasal CPAP or endotracheal (ET) tube displacement into the esophagus may have produced gastric and intestinal distention, and indomethacin therapy may have caused intestinal perforations.

C. Intraperitoneal air originates either from the thorax or from gastrointestinal perforations. Severe tension pneumothorax distends the abdomen by forcing the diaphragm downward or by virtue of a pulmonary air leak into the posterior mediastinum, which then migrates through diaphragmatic apertures into the peritoneal space. Necrotizing enterocolitis, spontaneous isolated perforations of the stomach and intestine, and malrotation with volvulus are the major intraabdominal sources of free peritoneal air. Rarely perforations follow exchange transfusion. Isolated spontaneous rupture at any level of the GI tract has been reported repeatedly in association with oral or intravenous administration of indomethacin, which was given for closure of a patent ductus arteriosus. Regardless of the source of intraperitoneal air, large accumulations that preclude diaphragmatic excursion must be evacuated by abdominal paracentesis.

SBK

References

Aschner JL, Deluga KS, Metlay LA, et al. Spontaneous focal gastrointestinal perforation in very low birth weight infants. J Pediatr 1988; 113:364.

Ryckman FC, Balistreri WF. The neonatal gastrointestinal tract: Selected anomalies and intestinal obstruction. In: Fanaroff AA, Martin RJ, eds. Neonatal-perinatal medicine: Diseases of the fetus and infant. St Louis: Times Mirror/Mosby College Publishing, 1987.

Tan CEL, Kiely EM, Agrawal M, et al. Neonatal gastrointestinal perforation. J Pediatr Surg 1989; 24:888.

Touloukian RJ. Intestinal atresia. Clin Perinatol 1978; 5:3.

Wolf WM, Snover DC, Leonard AS. Localized intestinal perforation following intravenous indomethacin in premature infants. J Pediatr Surg 1989; 24:409.

Young DG. Gastroenterology: Congenital defects and surgical problems. In: Roberton NRC, ed. Textbook of neonatology. New York: Churchill Livingstone, 1986.

ABDOMINAL ENLARGEMENT DUE TO GASEOUS DISTENTION

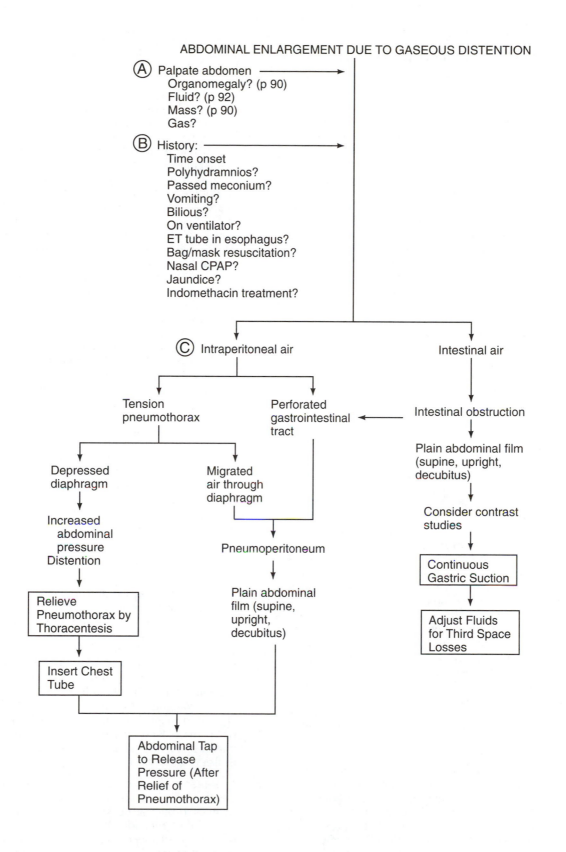

Ⓐ Palpate abdomen
   Organomegaly? (p 90)
   Fluid? (p 92)
   Mass? (p 90)
   Gas?

Ⓑ History:
   Time onset
   Polyhydramnios?
   Passed meconium?
   Vomiting?
   Bilious?
   On ventilator?
   ET tube in esophagus?
   Bag/mask resuscitation?
   Nasal CPAP?
   Jaundice?
   Indomethacin treatment?

Ⓒ Intraperitoneal air

Intestinal air

Tension pneumothorax

Perforated gastrointestinal tract

Intestinal obstruction

Depressed diaphragm

Migrated air through diaphragm

Plain abdominal film (supine, upright, decubitus)

Increased abdominal pressure Distention

Pneumoperitoneum

Consider contrast studies

Relieve Pneumothorax by Thoracentesis

Plain abdominal film (supine, upright, decubitus)

Continuous Gastric Suction

Insert Chest Tube

Adjust Fluids for Third Space Losses

Abdominal Tap to Release Pressure (After Relief of Pneumothorax)

ABDOMINAL MASSES

A. Abdominal masses are relatively rare in the newborn, occurring in fewer than 1% in published surveillance reports. Masses may represent enlargement of otherwise normal organs (severe gastric distention, hepatomegaly, bladder distention, hydronephrosis); nonneoplastic anomalies such as intestinal duplication, ovarian cysts; and tumors both benign and malignant such as Wilms' tumor, neuroblastoma, and teratoma. The most freely movable masses are intestinal, intraperitoneal, or ovarian. The location of any mass is a general indication of diagnostic possibilities, but ultimately radiograph, ultrasound, in some instances CT imaging, and pertinent laboratory data are all essential for diagnosis and therapy.

B. Besides gaseous distention of the stomach due to causes listed previously, masses in the upper abdominal quadrants most often tend to be hepatic or adrenal. Extensive hepatomegaly, particularly when accompanied by splenomegaly, enlarges the upper abdomen impressively. Herpes, cytomegalovirus, syphilis, and erythroblastosis may cause severe hepatosplenomegaly (p 96, 98). Subcapsular hematoma of the liver usually follows trauma during delivery, particularly in breech presentation of large infants. Retention of accumulating blood beneath the liver capsule produces a sizable mass that may not become evident for three or more days while the baby's hematocrit declines steadily. Rupture of the capsule is catastrophic, resulting in circulatory collapse and perhaps death. Rupture of the spleen is considerably less frequent. It is virtually limited to traumatized infants whose spleens are considerably enlarged. A mass is sometimes palpable in the left upper quadrant. As in rupture of the liver, a catastrophic course is characteristic. Adrenal hemorrhage is also a consequence of trauma during delivery, occurring most often in breech presentations and in larger infants. The resultant mass may be palpable in the upper abdomen, but frequently blood from the adrenal gland accumulates in the perinephric areas to simulate renal enlargement. Massive liver enlargement resulting from metastatic neuroblastoma produces an impressive mass. In the neonate, the liver and sometimes the skin are the most frequent sites of metastatic neuroblastoma.

C. Palpable midabdominal masses in the neonate most frequently arise from the urinary tract. Normal kidneys are most easily palpated during the first few hours after birth. The lower pole of a normal kidney can be palpated above the umbilical level. In the presence of enlargement or displacement of the kidney, the lower pole is distinctly inferior to the level of the umbilicus. A unilateral renal mass is due to hydronephrosis, multicystic kidney disease, mesoblastic nephroma, Wilms' tumor, or renal vein thrombosis. Bilateral masses are produced by hydronephrosis or polycystic kidney disease. Hydronephrosis and renal vein thrombosis have smooth surfaces. A multicystic kidney is grossly and irregularly nodular. The surfaces of polycystic kidneys are not nearly as rough and irregular as those of a multicystic kidney. Multicystic malformation of the kidney is rarely bilateral. It tends to cause impressive abdominal distention. A horseshoe kidney often appears as an abdominal mass. At first impression it feels like an enlarged kidney, but the isthmus is palpable across the midline and continuous with the contralateral kidney. Neuroblastoma is the most frequent of neonatal malignancies. It is more often recognized because of its metastases than as a primary mass. Although the tumor may arise from any sympathetic ganglion, in over half of affected neonates it is an abdominal mass. The liver may be dramatically enlarged because it is riddled with metastases. A urachal cyst is the result of failed obliteration of the urachus at its middle segment. The cyst is palpable in the midline somewhere between the umbilicus and the symphysis pubis. It varies in size and is situated just beneath the anterior abdominal wall. Urachal cysts are often unidentifiable during the newborn period. Vitelline (omphalomesenteric) cysts are the product of failed middle segment obliteration of the omphalomesenteric duct. The mass is immediately caudal to the umbilicus and is situated just beneath the skin. It is often associated with a Meckel's diverticulum, which is situated at the proximal (intestinal) end of an omphalomesenteric duct that has not become obliterated.

D. The most frequently encountered mass in the lower abdomen is a distended normal bladder. In males if distention is excessive and if it persists after voiding (especially with a meager stream), posterior urethral valves are likely to be the obstructive factor. A neurogenic bladder may function similarly but its presence is usually perceived after the more prominent signs of CNS dysfunction (perinatal asphyxia) or spinal cord disorder (trauma, meningomyelocele) are recognized. Hydrometrocolpos comes to the attention of the examiner as a protruding cystlike mass at the vaginal introitus. The enlarged uterus is palpable as a pelvic mass. Neuroblastoma may produce a presacral mass when it originates from the organ of Zuckerkandl or from other sympathetic ganglia.

E. Mesenteric and omental cysts are sometimes sufficiently indistinct to mimic ascites. When clearly delineated they are easily movable. Both the cyst of intestinal duplication and the rigid intestinal segment of inspissated meconium (meconium ileus) may appear anywhere in the abdomen. They are freely movable and relatively superficial.

SBK

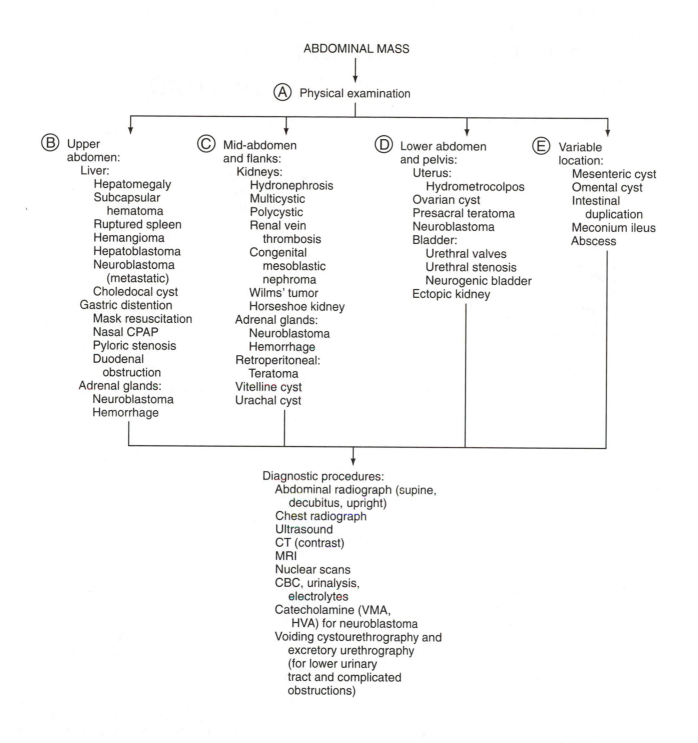

ABDOMINAL MASS

(A) Physical examination

(B) Upper abdomen:
   Liver:
      Hepatomegaly
      Subcapsular
         hematoma
      Ruptured spleen
      Hemangioma
      Hepatoblastoma
      Neuroblastoma
         (metastatic)
      Choledocal cyst
   Gastric distention
      Mask resuscitation
      Nasal CPAP
      Pyloric stenosis
      Duodenal
         obstruction
   Adrenal glands:
      Neuroblastoma
      Hemorrhage

(C) Mid-abdomen and flanks:
   Kidneys:
      Hydronephrosis
      Multicystic
      Polycystic
      Renal vein
         thrombosis
      Congenital
         mesoblastic
         nephroma
      Wilms' tumor
      Horseshoe kidney
   Adrenal glands:
      Neuroblastoma
      Hemorrhage
   Retroperitoneal:
      Teratoma
   Vitelline cyst
   Urachal cyst

(D) Lower abdomen and pelvis:
   Uterus:
      Hydrometrocolpos
   Ovarian cyst
   Presacral teratoma
   Neuroblastoma
   Bladder:
      Urethral valves
      Urethral stenosis
      Neurogenic bladder
   Ectopic kidney

(E) Variable location:
   Mesenteric cyst
   Omental cyst
   Intestinal
      duplication
   Meconium ileus
   Abscess

Diagnostic procedures:
   Abdominal radiograph (supine,
      decubitus, upright)
   Chest radiograph
   Ultrasound
   CT (contrast)
   MRI
   Nuclear scans
   CBC, urinalysis,
      electrolytes
   Catecholamine (VMA,
      HVA) for neuroblastoma
   Voiding cystourethrography and
      excretory urethrography
      (for lower urinary
      tract and complicated
      obstructions)

References

Allen RG. Tumor masses of the neonate. Clin Perinatol 1978; 5:115–134.

Hartman GE, Shochat SJ. Abdominal mass lesions in the newborn: Diagnosis and treatment. Clin Perinatol 1989; 16:123–135.

Henderson KC, Torch EM. Differential diagnosis of abdominal masses in the neonate. Pediatr Clin North Am 1977; 24:557–578.

Schwartz MZ, Shaul DB. Abdominal masses in the newborn. Pediatr Rev 1989; 11:172–179.

Swischuk LE, Hayden CK, Jr. Abdominal masses in children. Pediatr Clin North Am 1985; 32:1281–1297.

ABDOMINAL ENLARGEMENT DUE TO ISOLATED ASCITES (INTRAPERITONEAL FLUID ACCUMULATION)

A. "Isolated" ascites is an intraperitoneal accumulation of fluid, excluding fluid accumulations in other serous cavities and subcutaneous edema that characterize hydrops fetalis. With some exceptions, isolated ascites is usually due to a number of intraabdominal abnormalities, whereas the disorders that produce hydrops fetalis are considerably more diverse and numerous. Typical postnatal physical signs include prominent abdominal skin vessels, uniform abdominal distention, and sometimes the elicitation of a fluid wave. Occasionally ascitic fluid can be recognized only by x-ray or ultrasonography. Abdominal x-ray indicates homogeneous density throughout. When large amounts of fluid have accumulated, intestinal gas, if present, is usually clustered at the midabdomen. Ultrasonography demonstrates fluid and associated intraabdominal abnormalities. Ascites is often diagnosed in utero by ultrasound examination. A considerable amount of diagnostic data is often available before birth. Sequential ultrasound examinations in utero have revealed that isolated ascites may be a prelude to hydrops fetalis or may disappear spontaneously. When it disappears, the neonate's abdominal skin is lax and diastasis recti is obvious.

B. Abdominal paracentesis is not necessary in all cases. The pediatric surgical literature repeatedly asserts that complications are very unlikely if the procedure is properly performed and that the perforation of intestine with a small needle is self-sealing. Nevertheless, if noninvasive imaging establishes the diagnosis of small bowel obstruction or perforation, urinary tract obstruction, or meconium peritonitis, the indications for surgery preclude any need for paracentesis. Furthermore, it is difficult to envision self-sealing punctures in a tightly distended gut with an overstretched wall. However, in the absence of conclusive indications, examination of ascitic fluid is indispensable. When necrotizing enterocolitis (NEC) is progressive, fluid accumulation may require paracentesis because bowel rupture of any size may produce a significant amount of fluid (usually sanguinopurulent or dark brown) in the absence of a telltale accumulation of free peritoneal air. Dark brown fluid may also accumulate from gangrenous unperforated gut. Paracentesis is advisable when liver and spleen are enlarged, liver dysfunction has been demonstrated, and a diagnosis has not been established. Congenital nonbacterial and syphilitic infections are diagnosed by multiple modalities other than examination of ascitic fluid, but when ascites is a component of hydrops, evaluating the fluid is preferable. Ascitic fluid of CMV, toxoplasmosis, and syphilis is sometimes serosanguineous. When liver disease is present with direct hyperbilirubinemia, the fluid is deep yellow. Jaundice

and acholic stool associated with ascites suggest a ruptured extrahepatic biliary duct, most often at the junction of the cystic and common ducts.

C. Electrolytes, glucose, BUN, and creatinine determinations are not usually useful. These concentrations tend to be similar to serum concentrations because of equilibration of ascitic fluid with plasma.

D. Clear, pale yellow fluid is the least specific of all the gross appearances. Urinary ascites is reportedly the most common diagnosis. In such instances, urinary tract obstruction occurs at any level but most often below the ureteropelvic junction. Advanced obstructions are readily demonstrated, if not already diagnosed in utero or surmised from physical signs at birth. Generally, urea and creatinine contents are similar to serum, but a number of reports have described values higher than serum but lower than urine. An unsuccessful attempt to insert an umbilical artery catheter resulted in avulsion of the urachus from the bladder dome, direct communication of the bladder with the peritoneal space, and then massive urinary ascites. Nonpurulent infections cause isolated ascites as well as hydrops fetalis. Variable WBC counts have in common a preponderance of lymphocytes, and total protein may be elevated. Syphilis, CMV, toxoplasmosis, and hepatitis of unknown etiology have all been implicated. The mechanisms of ascites produced by lysosomal storage diseases are unknown. α-1-Antitrypsin deficiency has been described to cause severe neonatal cirrhosis, portal hypertension, and isolated ascites.

E. Distinctly bilious ascitic fluid, in the absence of free peritoneal air, indicates a ruptured extrahepatic biliary duct. Affected infants are moderately jaundiced and their stools are acholic.

F. Either serosanguineous or dark brown fluid may be associated with gangrenous intestine, most commonly as a consequence of NEC and less often from small bowel obstruction, volvulus, or meconium peritonitis. Fluid from the last disorder contains meconium particles unless intrauterine bowel rupture had healed after occurring well before birth. In that circumstance, fluid is clear and green.

G. Purulent fluid is produced by ruptured bowel from any cause, most frequently from NEC and rarely in association with septicemia. Cell counts, smear for organisms, and cultures identify the etiologic agents.

H. Milky fluid is specific for chylous ascites, which is believed to be caused by abdominal lymphatic anomalies that obstruct lymph flow from the intestine. Before feeding, ascitic fluid is clear, contains a

ABDOMINAL ENLARGEMENT DUE TO INTRAPERITONEAL FLUID

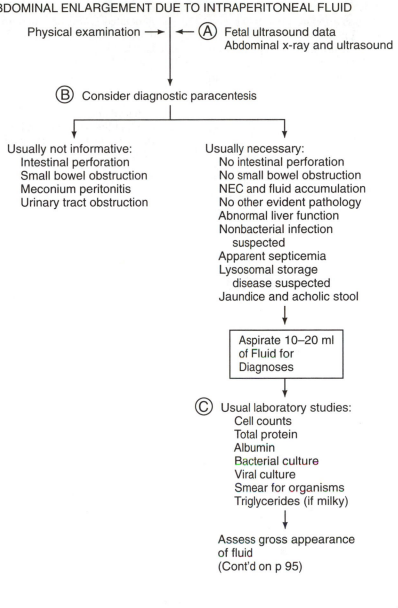

Physical examination ⟶ | ← (A) Fetal ultrasound data
Abdominal x-ray and ultrasound

(B) Consider diagnostic paracentesis

Usually not informative:
Intestinal perforation
Small bowel obstruction
Meconium peritonitis
Urinary tract obstruction

Usually necessary:
No intestinal perforation
No small bowel obstruction
NEC and fluid accumulation
No other evident pathology
Abnormal liver function
Nonbacterial infection
suspected
Apparent septicemia
Lysosomal storage
disease suspected
Jaundice and acholic stool

Aspirate 10–20 ml
of Fluid for
Diagnoses

(C) Usual laboratory studies:
Cell counts
Total protein
Albumin
Bacterial culture
Viral culture
Smear for organisms
Triglycerides (if milky)

Assess gross appearance
of fluid
(Cont'd on p 95)

moderate number of lymphocytes, and is low in protein. The typical chylous appearance follows feedings and subsequently clears when feedings are discontinued. Chylous fluid contains higher concentrations of triglyceride than serum. If fluid was aspirated during intravenous lipid administration, serum and fluid triglyceride concentrations are virtually equal.

SBK

References

Griscom NT, Colodny AH, Rosenberg HK, et al. Diagnostic aspects of neonatal ascites: Report of 27 cases. Am J Roentgenol 1977; 128:961.

Hadlock FP, Deter RL, Garcia-Pratt J, et al. Fetal ascites not associated with Rh incompatibility: Recognition and management with sonography. Am J Roentgenol 1980; 134:1225.

Kosloske AM, Goldthorn JF. Paracentesis as an aid to the diagnosis of intestinal gangrene. Arch Surg 1982; 117:571.

Machin GA. Diseases causing fetal and neonatal ascites. Pediatr Pathol 1985; 4:195.

Winn HN, Stiller R, Grannum PAT, et al. Isolated fetal ascites: Prenatal diagnosis and management. Am J Perinatol 1990; 7:370.

Assess gross appearance of fluid

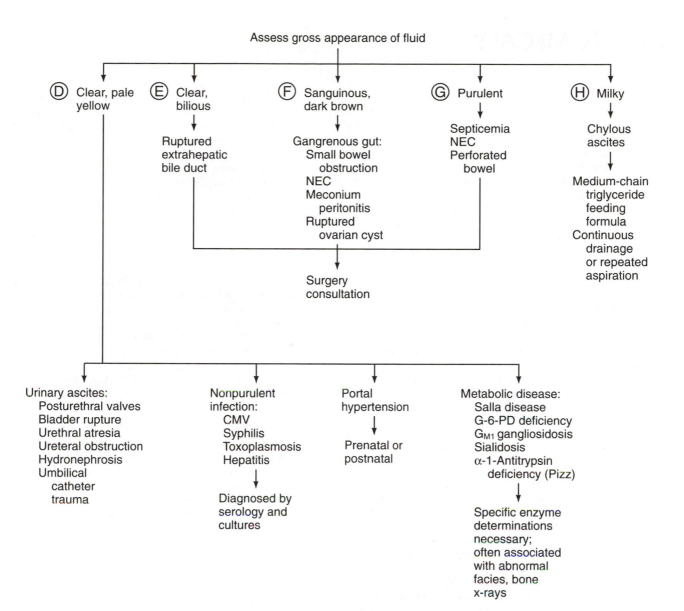

Ⓓ Clear, pale
yellow

Ⓔ Clear,
bilious

Ruptured
extrahepatic
bile duct

Ⓕ Sanguinous,
dark brown

Gangrenous gut:
Small bowel
obstruction
NEC
Meconium
peritonitis
Ruptured
ovarian cyst

Surgery
consultation

Ⓖ Purulent

Septicemia
NEC
Perforated
bowel

Ⓗ Milky

Chylous
ascites

Medium-chain
triglyceride
feeding
formula
Continuous
drainage
or repeated
aspiration

Urinary ascites:
Posturethral valves
Bladder rupture
Urethral atresia
Ureteral obstruction
Hydronephrosis
Umbilical
catheter
trauma

Nonpurulent
infection:
CMV
Syphilis
Toxoplasmosis
Hepatitis

Diagnosed by
serology and
cultures

Portal
hypertension

Prenatal or
postnatal

Metabolic disease:
Salla disease
G-6-PD deficiency
G_{M1} gangliosidosis
Sialidosis
α-1-Antitrypsin
deficiency (Pizz)

Specific enzyme
determinations
necessary;
often associated
with abnormal
facies, bone
x-rays

HEPATOMEGALY

A. There is usually little doubt that a liver is enlarged when its edge is palpated at a level below the umbilicus, but there should be, because location of a liver edge does not reliably indicate enlargement. Enlargement should be ascertained by additionally defining the location of the liver's most superior surface (dome). A tension pneumothorax, for example, displaces an unenlarged liver downward. Although one is not particularly intent on liver size when dealing with a life-threatening pneumothorax, the concept of displacement versus enlargement is well illustrated. The role of pleural fluid and, more frequently, overexpanded lungs must be evaluated to identify hepatomegaly accurately. When these intrathoracic disorders are bilateral, the left lobe is also displaced into the abdomen. The literature stresses percussion of dullness as a dependable method for locating the liver dome, but this is actually not feasible in most of the small babies in an NICU. X-ray of the chest and abdomen is quite useful, and if there is lingering doubt, ultrasound clarifies the issue. Imaging is particularly worthwhile in circumstances that spuriously indicate liver enlargement. Thus subcapsular hematomas and choledochal cysts are particularly misleading in this respect. Evaluation of an enlarged liver should also include auscultation for bruit, which may indicate hemangiomatosis.

B. Liver enlargement can be clearly categorized according to the structural constituents that are disrupted, but in reality several categories usually coexist. The major intrahepatic components that undergo alteration are the sinusoids (the intrahepatic vascular supply), the bile ducts and canaliculi (conduits of secreted bile), hepatocytes, Kupffer cells (phagocytes that line the sinusoids), and connective tissue throughout the liver but particularly in the portal areas and the periphery of lobules. Extrahepatic structures include the portal and hepatic veins, extrahepatic bile ducts, and the gallbladder. Hepatomegaly is produced by a number of disease processes that alter these structural components. Sinusoids and venules are distended by congestive heart failure or, rarely, by postsinusoidal obstruction in the hepatic vein (Budd-Chiari syndrome). Intrahepatic and extrahepatic biliary obstruction gives rise to bile duct proliferation within the liver and to inflammatory changes that evolve to chronicity, involve hepatocytes, and culminate in biliary cirrhosis. Connective tissue may be stuffed with a variety of cellular elements that contribute substantially to hepatic enlargement. These cells may be inflammatory as in hepatitis due to bacterial, viral, and parasitic agents or to toxic drugs, or they may be "infiltrative."

The infiltrates are most often erythrocyte precursors that are normally present in small quantities as remnants of earlier normal fetal erythropoiesis in the liver. These erythrocyte precursors proliferate in response to fetal and neonatal anemia (extramedullary hematopoiesis), most commonly in Rh and ABO blood incompatibilities and in other hemolytic processes as well. Hepatocytes become enlarged by abnormal storage of lipids, glycogen, or mucopolysaccharides and other substance accumulations. They also enlarge in response to infectious agents, bacterial endotoxin, and hepatotoxic drugs. Kupffer cells constitute approximately 10% of all cells in the liver. They are virtual sentinels that line hepatic sinusoids, and their primary function is to phagocytize bacterial endotoxin, abnormal erythrocytes, antigen-antibody complexes, toxic drugs, and numerous other substances. Proliferation and hypertrophy of Kupffer cells significantly contribute to hepatomegaly. Extrahepatic biliary obstruction (atresia, choledochal cysts) causes intrahepatic inspissation of bile, bile duct proliferation, chronic inflammation at bile duct sites, and ultimately biliary cirrhosis.

C. Liver enlargement is attributable to disruption of several structural components by processes of metabolic, inflammatory, hematologic, and neoplastic origin. The clinical entities most often associated with hepatomegaly in the newborn are infections (intrauterine and postnatally acquired), maternal-fetal blood incompatibilities, obstruction to bile flow, and congestive heart failure.

SBK

References

Andres JM, Mathis RK, Walker WA. Liver disease in infants, part I: Developmental hepatology and mechanisms of liver dysfunction. J Pediatr 1977; 90:686.

Gryboski J, Walker WA. Development and evaluation of liver function. In: Gastrointestinal problems in the infant. 2nd ed. Philadelphia: WB Saunders, 1983.

Gryboski J, Walker WA. The liver and biliary tree. In: Gastrointestinal problems in the infant. 2nd ed. Philadelphia: WB Saunders, 1983.

Mathis RK, Andres JM, Walker WA. Liver disease in infants, part II: Hepatic disease states. J Pediatr 1977; 90:864.

Reiff MI, Osborn LM. Clinical estimation of liver size in newborn infants. Pediatrics 1983; 71:46.

Walker WA, Mathis RK. Hepatomegaly: An approach to differential diagnosis. Pediatr Clin North Am 1975; 22:929.

HEPATOMEGALY

(A) Physical signs:
   Liver edge >3 cm
      below right
      costal margin;
      dome of liver at
      fifth intercostal
      space
   Consistency normal or
      firm; surface smooth,
      nodular, or irregular
   Bruits

Imaging:
   Ultrasound
   X-ray abdomen

(B) Jaundice — Other signs

→ Blood disorder (p 54) → Anemia, polycythemia, thrombocytopenia

→ Intrinsic liver and/or biliary tract disease → Abnormal liver function tests

→ Nonbacterial intrauterine infection (p 112) → Splenomegaly, petechiae, ecchymoses, abnormal CNS signs

→ Bacterial infection (p 104) → Clinical course and laboratory findings of septicemia, meningitis, pneumonia

→ Metabolic disorders:
   α-1-Antitrypsin → Ascites

   Galactosemia → Hypoglycemia, cataracts, septicemia

   Hereditary fructose intolerance → Vomiting, seizures, splenomegaly

   Cerebrohepatorenal disease (Zellweger) → Dysmorphic features, hypotonia

→ Infantile Gaucher's disease → Hydrops, spasticity, strabismus, splenomegaly

No jaundice — Other signs

→ Congestive heart failure → Typical cardiopulmonary signs

→ Glycogen storage disease → Cardiac failure, hypotonia, hypoglycemia

→ Tumors:
   Hepatoblastoma → Hemihypertrophy, thrombocytosis

   Hemangioma → Skin hemangiomas, cardiac failure

   Neuroblastoma (metastatic) → Abdominal flank mass, "blueberry muffin" skin lesions

   Wilms' tumor (metastatic) → Hemihypertrophy, kidney mass

→ Hepatic vein thrombosis (Budd-Chiari) → Ascites

→ Subcapsular hematoma → Increasing anemia, intraperitoneal blood, shock

(C) Most frequent causes:
   Infection (intrauterine, postnatal)
   Maternal-fetal blood incompatibility
   Congestive heart failure
   Perinatal asphyxia
   Bile duct obstruction

SPLENOMEGALY

A. Detection of a large spleen by physical examination is important because splenomegaly indicates several disease processes, all of which are serious and often life-threatening. The splenic tip is palpable in up to 10% of normal term infants and, with considerably less frequency, in small prematures. When palpable as an abdominal mass, the spleen is already at least twice its usual size. In the extreme, the lower pole may extend into the left lower quadrant, and the splenic notch can be palpated. In differentiating the spleen from other masses, regardless of size the superior surface is never palpable because it is covered by the lower rib cage. An enlarged spleen is usually first discerned as an anterior abdominal mass, easily felt through the neonate's thin abdominal wall. Kidney masses are usually more medial and inferior; their superior surfaces are often palpable. The mass in question can be identified reliably by abdominal ultrasound.

B. Splenomegaly in the absence of liver enlargement is unusual because the disease processes that produce enlargement of one generally involve both organs. Splenic cysts and obstruction of the splenic and portal veins are the exceptions. Tension pneumothorax on the left may displace the spleen downward, spuriously suggesting enlargement.

C. Splenomegaly with hepatomegaly is produced by generalized disease processes such as infections, hemolytic anemias, and inborn errors of metabolism. Enlargement of both organs is mainly attributable to reticuloendothelial proliferation, extramedullary hematopoiesis, and proliferation of cells storing abnormal substances. Intrahepatic disorders that interfere with blood flow through the liver may cause portal hypertension and splenomegaly as a consequence. The list of inborn errors of metabolism includes storage diseases in which cellular responses that are prominent in both organs cause enlargement. Splenomegaly is not a sign of congestive heart failure in the neonate, presumably because of extreme hepatic distensibility and the rarity of chronic heart failure.

SBK

References

Pearson HA. The spleen and disturbances of splenic function. In: Nathan DG, Oski FA, eds. Hematology of infancy and childhood. 3rd ed. Philadelphia: WB Saunders, 1987:900.

Pearson HA. Diseases of the blood: Development of the hematopoietic system. In: Behrman RE, Vaughan VC III, Nelson WE, eds. Nelson textbook of pediatrics. 13th ed. Philadelphia: WB Saunders, 1987:1033.

PALPABLE SPLEEN

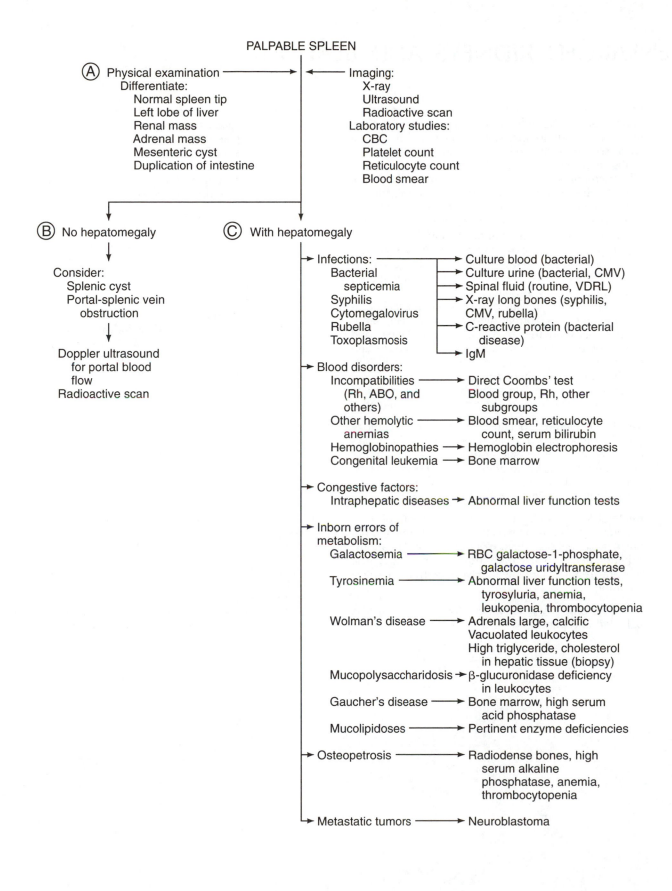

(A) Physical examination
Differentiate:
  Normal spleen tip
  Left lobe of liver
  Renal mass
  Adrenal mass
  Mesenteric cyst
  Duplication of intestine

Imaging:
  X-ray
  Ultrasound
  Radioactive scan
Laboratory studies:
  CBC
  Platelet count
  Reticulocyte count
  Blood smear

(B) No hepatomegaly

Consider:
  Splenic cyst
  Portal-splenic vein
    obstruction

Doppler ultrasound
  for portal blood
  flow
Radioactive scan

(C) With hepatomegaly

Infections: ⟶ Culture blood (bacterial)
  Bacterial ⟶ Culture urine (bacterial, CMV)
    septicemia ⟶ Spinal fluid (routine, VDRL)
  Syphilis ⟶ X-ray long bones (syphilis,
  Cytomegalovirus   CMV, rubella)
  Rubella ⟶ C-reactive protein (bacterial
  Toxoplasmosis   disease)
  ⟶ IgM

Blood disorders:
  Incompatibilities ⟶ Direct Coombs' test
    (Rh, ABO, and   Blood group, Rh, other
    others)   subgroups
  Other hemolytic ⟶ Blood smear, reticulocyte
    anemias   count, serum bilirubin
  Hemoglobinopathies ⟶ Hemoglobin electrophoresis
  Congenital leukemia ⟶ Bone marrow

Congestive factors:
  Intraphepatic diseases ⟶ Abnormal liver function tests

Inborn errors of
metabolism:
  Galactosemia ⟶ RBC galactose-1-phosphate,
      galactose uridyltransferase
  Tyrosinemia ⟶ Abnormal liver function tests,
      tyrosyluria, anemia,
      leukopenia, thrombocytopenia
  Wolman's disease ⟶ Adrenals large, calcific
    Vacuolated leukocytes
    High triglyceride, cholesterol
      in hepatic tissue (biopsy)
  Mucopolysaccharidosis ⟶ β-glucuronidase deficiency
      in leukocytes
  Gaucher's disease ⟶ Bone marrow, high serum
      acid phosphatase
  Mucolipidoses ⟶ Pertinent enzyme deficiencies

Osteopetrosis ⟶ Radiodense bones, high
      serum alkaline
      phosphatase, anemia,
      thrombocytopenia

Metastatic tumors ⟶ Neuroblastoma

ENLARGED KIDNEYS AND BLADDER

A. Specific assessment of the kidneys is an important component of the initial postnatal physical examination and repeatedly thereafter. Abdominal masses of some sort are estimated to occur in 0.5% of all live births (approximately 18,000–20,000 infants annually); two-thirds of these are renal masses. Palpation of the abdomen during routine physical examination is not sufficient for evaluation of the kidneys. Several specific techniques have been described. An effective technique entails placement of one hand beneath the supine infant while slowly palpating more deeply with the other hand placed on the abdomen. Fingers of the dorsally placed hand are positioned caudal to the rib cage to exert upward pressure in the area of the costovertebral angle with gradually deepened abdominal palpation. A normal kidney is identified, sandwiched between the examining hands. Upper and lower poles, lateral margins, size, contour, and consistency are all perceptible. In skilled hands 70% of the suspected abnormalities found on physical examination are documented by other appropriate procedures, usually as determined by a consultant.

B. Renal enlargement because of intrinsic pathology (multicystic kidney disease, tumors) is usually unilateral. However, polycystic disease is always bilateral. Hydronephrosis is bilateral in 10% of affected infants. Renal vein thrombosis, metastatic neoplasm, and Wilms' tumor are less frequently bilateral.

C. Bilateral kidney enlargement may be the result of a generalized disorder in which renal involvement is but one component of a broad spectrum of manifestations. Additionally, urinary tract obstruction may cause bilateral renal enlargement. Hydronephrosis is most common.

D. When renomegaly is identified, the bladder must be palpated and percussed for distention. The neonate's bladder is situated somewhat higher in the abdomen than in the older child. Abnormal bladder distention may be palpated as high as the umbilicus. Associated megaureters may feel like an abdominal mass. Initial visualization by ultrasound confirms the impression of bladder enlargement. Cystourethography is necessary to visualize the urethra and bladder.

E. Several modalities of diagnostic imaging provide specific diagnoses. Ultrasound shows absence or enlargement of kidneys, size and contour, and the solid or fluid nature of masses. Intravenous pyelography (IVP) is sometimes required, but with considerably less frequency than in the past. Unless the ureters are considerably dilated, ultrasound will not depict ureteral abnormalities such as misinsertions. Voiding cystourethrography (VCUG) is indispensable for visualizing the bladder and urethra. Radioactive (radionuclide) scans are excellent indicators of size, shape, sites of obstruction, and the status of renal blood flow.

SBK

References

Clarke NW, Gough DCS, Cohen SH. Neonatal urological ultrasound: diagnostic inaccuracies and pitfalls. Arch Dis Child 1989; 64:578–580.

Gilli G, Berry AC, Chantler C. Syndromes with a renal component. In: Holliday MA, Barratt TM, Vernier RL., eds. Pediatric nephrology. 2nd ed. Baltimore: Williams & Wilkins, 1987: 384–404.

Guignard J-P. Neonatal nephrology. In: Holliday MA, Barratt TM, Vernier RL, eds. Pediatric nephrology. 2nd ed. Baltimore: Williams & Wilkins, 1987:921–944.

Wilson DA. Ultrasound screening for abdominal masses in the neonatal period. Am J Dis Child 1982; 136:147–151.

ENLARGED KIDNEYS and BLADDER

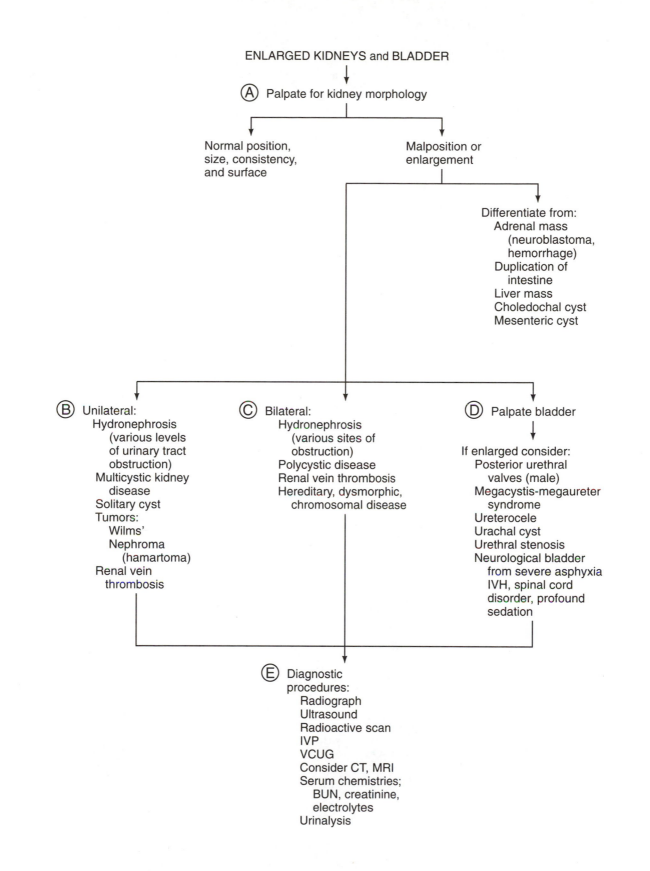

Ⓐ Palpate for kidney morphology

Normal position, size, consistency, and surface

Malposition or enlargement

Differentiate from:
    Adrenal mass
      (neuroblastoma,
      hemorrhage)
    Duplication of
      intestine
    Liver mass
    Choledochal cyst
    Mesenteric cyst

Ⓑ Unilateral:
    Hydronephrosis
      (various levels
      of urinary tract
      obstruction)
    Multicystic kidney
      disease
    Solitary cyst
    Tumors:
      Wilms'
      Nephroma
        (hamartoma)
    Renal vein
      thrombosis

Ⓒ Bilateral:
    Hydronephrosis
      (various sites of
      obstruction)
    Polycystic disease
    Renal vein thrombosis
    Hereditary, dysmorphic,
      chromosomal disease

Ⓓ Palpate bladder

If enlarged consider:
    Posterior urethral
      valves (male)
    Megacystis-megaureter
      syndrome
    Ureterocele
    Urachal cyst
    Urethral stenosis
    Neurological bladder
      from severe asphyxia
      IVH, spinal cord
      disorder, profound
      sedation

Ⓔ Diagnostic
    procedures:
      Radiograph
      Ultrasound
      Radioactive scan
      IVP
      VCUG
      Consider CT, MRI
      Serum chemistries;
        BUN, creatinine,
        electrolytes
      Urinalysis

INFECTION

Maternal-Fetal Transmission of Bacterial
  Infection (Vertical Transmission)
Bacterial Infection: Risks, Clinical Signs, and
  Etiology

Bacterial Infection: Diagnosis and
  Management
Congenital Syphilis
Nonbacterial Infection: Viruses and
  Toxoplasma
Fungus Infection: *Candida*

MATERNAL-FETAL TRANSMISSION OF BACTERIAL INFECTION (VERTICAL TRANSMISSION)

A. Ascent of vaginal and cervical organisms into the amniotic cavity is the most frequent route by which the mother transmits fetal infection. Organisms are derived from a colonized or diseased birth canal. The usual fetal outcome is colonization with no active disease, even in the presence of chorioamnionitis. Less frequently the ascending process leads to neonatal disease. Maternal factors that enhance the possibility of neonatal disease include early membrane rupture, protracted labor, active infection of birth canal tissues, and previous placement of a cerclage for cervical incompetence. Fetal vulnerabilities that increase the possibility of neonatal disease are the virulence of organisms, inoculum size, immaturity of host defense, and premature birth. Any of the clinical entities of bacterial infection in the neonate may result from fetal aspiration and swallowing of organisms that have proliferated in the amniotic fluid. Vertically transmitted bacterial infections are clinically recognizable within approximately 72 hours after birth, often earlier in premature infants. Bacterial diseases that occur later are nosocomial infections. The most common vertically transmitted bacterial infections are neonatal pneumonia (from fetal aspiration of organisms in amniotic fluid) and septicemia, which is presumably the result of bacterial invasion of the bloodstream from respiratory or GI tract inocula. Otitis media is rarely diagnosed in neonates, but its identification at autopsies of septicemic infants is not unusual. Bacteria probably gain access to the middle ear from the nasopharynx through the eustachian tubes. The bacteria that cause perinatal infection constitute the normal flora of the vagina. Of the numerous vaginal strains of bacteria, those most frequently involved in ascending transmission are Group B streptococci, *Escherichia coli* and other gram-negative enteric bacilli, and *Listeria monocytogenes*. Several nonbacterial organisms are also involved in the ascending route (p 112).

B. During the second stage of labor, the fetus comes in direct contact with organisms in the cervix and vagina and with strains that originate in the intestine. These bacteria are aspirated and swallowed; they also colonize mucous membranes and skin. Gonorrheal ophthalmia is acquired during birth by this direct contact. The neonatal sequelae of this process do not differ from those associated with the ascending route of transmission.

C. Transmission of bacterial infection across the placenta is rare except for *Treponema pallidum*. Placental transmission requires maternal bacteremia or a localized infectious lesion within the placenta itself. Transplacental infection is characteristic of vertically transmitted nonbacterial infections (p 112).

SBK

References

Benirschke K. Routes and types of infection in the fetus and the newborn. Am J Dis Child 1960; 99:714.

Blanc WA. Pathways of fetal and early neonatal infection: Viral placentitis, bacterial and fungal chorioamnionitis. J Pediatr 1961; 59:473.

Davies PA, Gothefors LA. Prenatal infection. In: Bacterial infections in the fetus and newborn infant. Philadelphia: WB Saunders, 1984:98.

Davies PA, Gothefors LA. Characteristics of intrapartum and postnatal infection. In: Bacterial infections in the fetus and newborn infant. Philadelphia: WB Saunders, 1984:112.

Klein JO, Remington JS. Current concepts of infections of the fetus and newborn infant. In: Infectious disease of the fetus and newborn infant. 3rd ed. Philadelphia: WB Saunders, 1990:1.

MATERNAL-FETAL TRANSMISSION OF BACTERIAL INFECTION (VERTICAL TRANSMISSION)

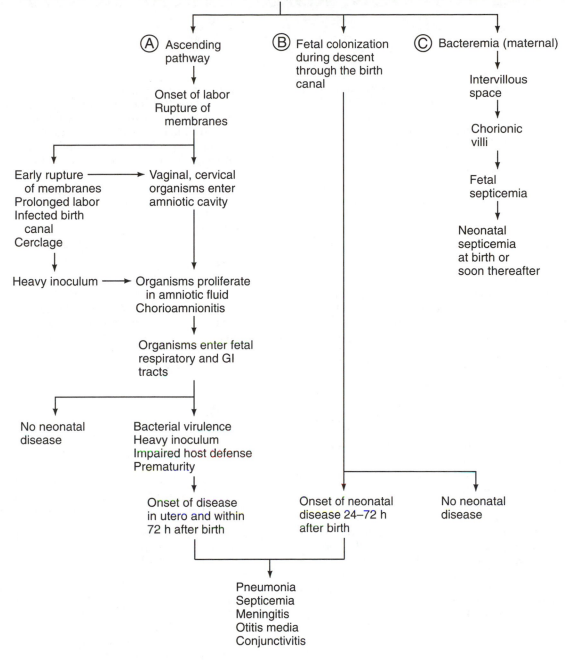

Ⓐ Ascending pathway

Ⓑ Fetal colonization during descent through the birth canal

Ⓒ Bacteremia (maternal)

Onset of labor
Rupture of membranes

Intervillous space

Chorionic villi

Fetal septicemia

Neonatal septicemia at birth or soon thereafter

Early rupture of membranes
Prolonged labor
Infected birth canal
Cerclage

Vaginal, cervical organisms enter amniotic cavity

Heavy inoculum ⟶ Organisms proliferate in amniotic fluid
Chorioamnionitis

Organisms enter fetal respiratory and GI tracts

No neonatal disease

Bacterial virulence
Heavy inoculum
Impaired host defense
Prematurity

Onset of disease in utero and within 72 h after birth

Onset of neonatal disease 24–72 h after birth

No neonatal disease

Pneumonia
Septicemia
Meningitis
Otitis media
Conjunctivitis

BACTERIAL INFECTION: RISKS, CLINICAL SIGNS, AND ETIOLOGY

A. The neonatal sequelae of prenatal risks are evident within the first 3 or 4 postnatal days, but clinical disease often occurs without adverse prenatal antecedents. Most chorioamnionitis does not cause maternal fever and uterine tenderness. The amniotic cavity is normally sterile until the onset of labor. As labor progresses, infecting organisms are more likely to enter amniotic fluid. Prolonged labor is apparently associated with a higher incidence of amniotic infection. Sustained fetal tachycardia (>160 beats/min), with no other identifiable cause, has been associated with a significantly higher incidence of neonatal clinical infection.

B. For at least the first 2 or 3 days, infections are caused by organisms derived from maternal vaginal and intestinal flora. With increasing frequency after the first 3 postnatal days, infection is due to bacteria from the nursery environment. Bacterial infections acquired in the hospital are considered to be "horizontally transmitted," preponderantly from personnel but also as complications of invasive procedures. In recent years coagulase-negative staphylococci have emerged as the predominant organisms involved in nosocomial infection, presumably by the same modes of transmission attributed to other organisms. Several circumstances enhance the risk of horizontal transmission. Increased patient-nurse ratios place a burden on nursing that precludes consistent handwashing and sometimes give rise to negligent aseptic technique. Infection is transmitted rarely by contaminated equipment, intravenous fluids, breast milk (banked), and contaminated blood. By far the most common modality of organism spread is the unwashed hands of personnel that became contaminated by previous contact with an infant's colonized skin, secretions, or stool. The organisms so acquired have developed resistance to therapy by virtue of protracted and pervasive use of antibiotics in most intensive care nurseries.

C. Host susceptibility is a common denominator of both vertically and horizontally transmitted infections. Of all neonatal risks, low birth weight is the most hazardous. The propensity for males to be affected more frequently than females, and to survive less often, is well known. This phenomenon has been observed in infections that are acquired prenatally or postnatally, particularly in septicemia caused by gram-negative enteric organisms. Invasive procedures, mechanical respiratory support, multiple sites of intravenous therapy, indwelling catheters and nasogastric tubes, and multiple skin punctures for samples of blood are all fixed components of care in the NICU. The longer the nursery stay, the more likely it is that a baby acquires a nosocomial infection.

D. Most lists of clinical signs do not consider the variables associated with time of onset, degree of prematurity, support by mechanical ventilation, or management in a servocontrolled incubator. Clinical indicators of neonatal infection are often said to be subtle, but actually they are not as subtle as they are nonspecific, which gives rise to the familiar complexities of differential diagnosis.

SBK

References

Baker CJ, Edwards MV. Group B streptococcal infections. In: Remington JS, Klein JO, eds. Infectious diseases of the fetus and newborn infant. 3rd ed. Philadelphia: WB Saunders, 1990:742.

Davies PA, Gothefors LA. Prenatal infection. In: Bacterial infections in the fetus and newborn infant. Philadelphia: WB Saunders, 1984:98.

Davies PA, Gothefors LA. Characteristics of intrapartum and postnatal infection. In: Bacterial infections in the fetus and newborn infant. Philadelphia: WB Saunders, 1984:112.

Graves GR, Rhodes PG. Tachycardia as a sign of early onset neonatal sepsis. Pediatr Infect Dis J 1984; 3:404.

Klein JO, Marcy SM. Bacterial sepsis and meningitis. In: Remington JS, Klein JO. Infectious diseases of the fetus and newborn infant. 3rd ed. Philadelphia: WB Saunders, 1990:601.

Neonate at Risk of BACTERIAL INFECTION

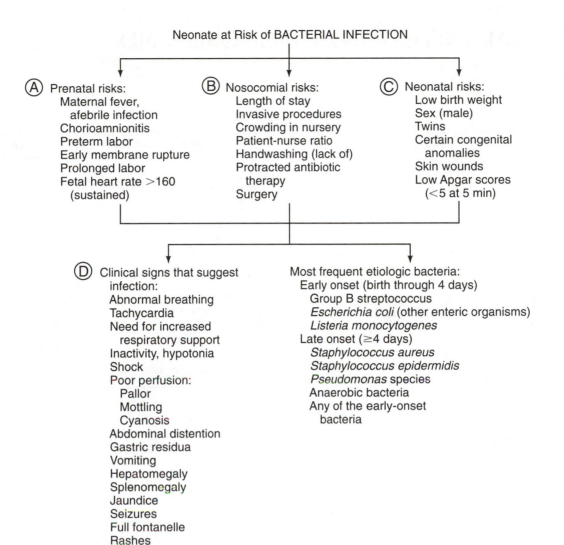

(A) Prenatal risks:
   Maternal fever,
      afebrile infection
   Chorioamnionitis
   Preterm labor
   Early membrane rupture
   Prolonged labor
   Fetal heart rate >160
      (sustained)

(B) Nosocomial risks:
   Length of stay
   Invasive procedures
   Crowding in nursery
   Patient-nurse ratio
   Handwashing (lack of)
   Protracted antibiotic
      therapy
   Surgery

(C) Neonatal risks:
   Low birth weight
   Sex (male)
   Twins
   Certain congenital
      anomalies
   Skin wounds
   Low Apgar scores
      (<5 at 5 min)

(D) Clinical signs that suggest
   infection:
   Abnormal breathing
   Tachycardia
   Need for increased
      respiratory support
   Inactivity, hypotonia
   Shock
   Poor perfusion:
      Pallor
      Mottling
      Cyanosis
   Abdominal distention
   Gastric residua
   Vomiting
   Hepatomegaly
   Splenomegaly
   Jaundice
   Seizures
   Full fontanelle
   Rashes

Most frequent etiologic bacteria:
   Early onset (birth through 4 days)
      Group B streptococcus
      Escherichia coli (other enteric organisms)
      Listeria monocytogenes
   Late onset (≥4 days)
      Staphylococcus aureus
      Staphylococcus epidermidis
      Pseudomonas species
      Anaerobic bacteria
      Any of the early-onset
         bacteria

BACTERIAL INFECTION: DIAGNOSIS AND MANAGEMENT

No known test or panel of tests exonerates the clinician from rational artfulness in deciding whether treatment for infection is appropriate. Rational artfulness entails placing in perspective the pertinent prenatal factors, clinical manifestations, and results of laboratory tests. Even the blood culture, a universal reference standard, may have serious disadvantages. Contaminated cultures are not uncommon (although infrequently cited in published studies), particularly when inexperienced trainees draw samples for blood culture. Conversely, the finding of negative blood cultures during illness, followed by proved septicemia at autopsy, is not rare. The decision to treat a baby whose status is equivocal ultimately depends on the clinician's well-informed judgment, published scores and statistically derived risks notwithstanding.

A. Asymptomatic babies at risk are usually 34 gestational weeks or more. Any one of the significant risks in the algorithm requires investigation and initiation of antibiotics. Early membrane rupture refers to occurrence 24–48 hours before delivery. The listed significant risks are greater if associated with the listed secondary risks, which in themselves do not require investigation or treatment if the infant is asymptomatic.

B. Values in parentheses are abnormal. The literature is not in agreement with the clinical significance of abnormal results, except for the blood culture. The white cell indexes should be included in total assessment. A number of reports have cited their low level of sensitivity and specificity, whereas other reports have demonstrated rather impressive results. At our institution the most frequent causes of leukopenia and abnormal I : T ratios during the first 24 postnatal hours are maternal hypertension, perinatal asphyxia, and intraventricular hemorrhage, in which the abnormal values ordinarily approach normality within 24 hours. Follow-up assessment usually provides the basis for discontinuing treatment within 72 hours. In our experience with asymptomatic infants, three normal C-reactive protein (CRP) values, taken at 12-hour intervals, are a reliable indication of the absence of infection, especially when reinforced by normal white cell indexes.

C. Initial choice of antibiotics is based on the etiologic organisms expected (Table 1). Early infection presumes vertical transmission. The recommended antibiotics are effective against the majority of infections derived from maternal vaginal and cervical flora.

D. The symptomatic baby requires prompt decisions. Any one of the clinical signs listed in the algorithm is an indication for investigation and treatment, unless one is confident that a noninfectious process is in progress. A lumbar puncture may be ill advised in profoundly ill babies who cannot withstand the procedure. It should

TABLE 1   Most Frequent Etiologic Bacteria and Appropriate Antibiotics in Current Use

Bacteria	Antibiotic
Group B streptococcus	Penicillin or ampicillin + aminoglycoside
E. coli, other enteric gram negative	Gentamicin, amikacin, tobramycin
Listeria monocytogenes	Ampicillin + gentamicin or cefotaxime
Staphylococcus epidermidis	Vancomycin or nafcillin
Staphylococcus aureus	Vancomycin or nafcillin
Enterococcus	Ampicillin or vancomycin
Haemophilus species	Ampicillin or cefotaxime
Pseudomonas species	Gentamicin or tobramycin or amikacin + ceftazidime or ticarcillin
Anaerobic bacteria	Clindamycin
Chlamydia (conjunctivitis)	Erythromycin

be performed later if the infant's status improves. In many instances a lumbar puncture is not necesary for adequate evaluation. Serum glucose is often elevated or sometimes depressed at the onset of an infection. If a lumbar puncture is performed, the CSF glucose level must be compared with a serum level drawn simultaneously. By itself the CSF glucose concentration is too often uninformative. Normal CSF glucose in the neonate is at least two thirds of the serum level. Spinal fluid cell counts are frequently confounded by unavoidable erythrocyte content; a ratio formula for red cells to white cells is useless. Organisms seen on Gram's stain of spinal fluid are unequivocally diagnostic. Serious infections usually cause metabolic acidosis; blood gas and/or pH determinations are thus essential.

E. Later onset of disease may yet involve the same organisms, but one must also reckon with other nosocomial bacteria as well. These organisms vary with time and place. In the 1950s and early 1960s, Staphylococcus aureus predominated. Since the early 1970s group B streptococci have been preponderant. For the past few years, we have been preoccupied with coagulase-negative staphylococci; vancomycin or nafcillin is thus added to the aminoglycoside-ampicillin combination for initial treatment of infection with onset past 3 postnatal days. However, nosocomial infections due to gram-negative enteric bacteria have been consistently common through the years. Information regarding prevalence of organisms in the nursery at any given time should be constantly available. If Serratia or Pseudomonas species abound, additional antibiotics for these organisms should be given for late-onset disease. Changes in initial therapy

BACTERIAL INFECTION Suspected

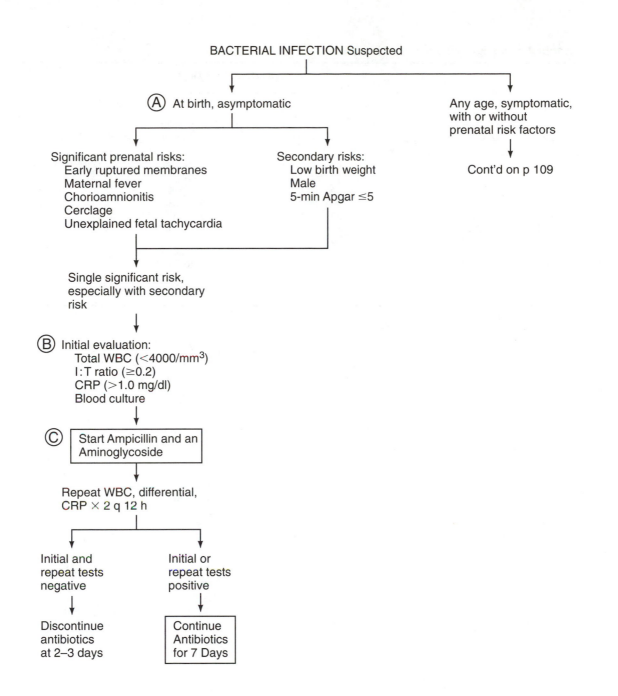

Ⓐ At birth, asymptomatic

Any age, symptomatic, with or without prenatal risk factors

Cont'd on p 109

Significant prenatal risks:
  Early ruptured membranes
  Maternal fever
  Chorioamnionitis
  Cerclage
  Unexplained fetal tachycardia

Secondary risks:
  Low birth weight
  Male
  5-min Apgar ≤5

Single significant risk, especially with secondary risk

Ⓑ Initial evaluation:
  Total WBC ($<4000/mm^3$)
  I:T ratio ($≥0.2$)
  CRP (>1.0 mg/dl)
  Blood culture

Ⓒ Start Ampicillin and an Aminoglycoside

Repeat WBC, differential, CRP × 2 q 12 h

Initial and repeat tests negative

Initial or repeat tests positive

Discontinue antibiotics at 2–3 days

Continue Antibiotics for 7 Days

TABLE 2 Antibiotic Dosage Schedules in Neonates

Drug	Route	Single Doses in mg/kg BW ≤2000 g Age ≤1 wk mg/kg/dose	Single Doses in mg/kg BW ≤2000 g Age >1 wk mg/kg/dose	Single Doses in mg/kg BW >2000 g Age ≤1 wk mg/kg/dose	Single Doses in mg/kg BW >2000 g Age >1 wk mg/kg/dose
Amikacin	IV,IM	7.5 q 12 h	10 q 8 h	10 q 12 h	10 q 8 h
Ampicillin*	IV,IM	100 q 12 h	50–75 q 8 h	75 q 8 h	50 q 6 h
Carbenicillin	IV,IM	100 q 12 h	100 q 8 h	100 q 8 h	100 q 6 h
Cefotaxime	IV,IM	50 q 12 h	50 q 8 h	50 q 12 h	50 q 8 h
Ceftazidime	IV,IM	30–50 q 12 h	30–50 q 12 h	30–50 q 12 h	30–50 q 12 h
Gentamicin	IV,IM	2.5 q 12 h	2.5 q 8 h	2.5 q 12 h	2.5 q 8 h
Nafcillin*	IV	25 q 12 h	50 q 8 h	25 q 8 h	25 q 6 h
Penicillin G*	IV,IM	25,000 U q 12 h	25,000 U q 8 h	25,000 U q 8 h	25,000 U q 6 h
Ticarcillin	IV,IM	75 q 12 h	75 q 8 h	75 q 8 h	75 q 6 h
Tobramycin	IV,IM	2.5 q 12 h	2.5 q 8 h	2 q 12 h	2 q 8 h
Vancomycin	IV	10 q 12 h	10 q 8 h	10 q 12 h	10 q 8 h

*For meningitis, double the recommended dosage.

may be necessary as indicated by cultures and sensitivity results or by failure to respond. Table 2 lists dosage schedules for frequently used antibiotics.

SBK

References

Ainbender E, Cabatu EE, Guzman DM, Sweet AY. Serum C-reactive protein and problems of newborn infants. J Pediatr 1982; 101:438.

Goldman DA, Durbin WA Jr, Freeman J Nosocomial infections in a neonatal intensive care unit. J Infect Dis 1981; 144:449.

Klein JO, Marcy SM. Bacterial sepsis and meningitis. In: Remington JS, Klein JO, eds. Infectious disease of the fetus and newborn infant. 3rd ed. Philadelphia; WB Saunders, 1990:601.

Philip AGS. Response of C-reactive protein in neonatal group B streptococcal infection. Pediatr Infect Dis J 1985; 4:145.

Pierce JR, Merenstein GB, Stocker JT. Immediate postmortem cultures in an intensive care nursery. Pediatr Infect Dis J 1984; 3:510.

Speer CH, Bruns A, Gahr M. Sequential determination of CRP, α_1-antitrypsin and haptoglobin in neonatal septicaemia. Acta Paediatr Scand 1983; 72:679.

(D) Infant of any age,
symptomatic,
with or without prenatal
risk factors
(cont'd from p 108)

Respiratory distress,
new or worsened
Poor perfusion, pallor,
mottling
Cyanosis
Increased ventilator support,
or FIo$_2$ if in oxygen hood
Abdominal distention
Inactivity, hypotonia
Fever, hypothermia
Seizures (see pp 194 and 196)

Initial evaluation:
Total WBC, differential
I:T ratio
CRP
CSF (chemistries, cell content,
Gram's stain, culture)
Serum glucose
Blood gas/pH
Blood culture
X-ray chest
X-ray abdomen (if distended)
Other appropriate cultures

(E) Start Antibiotics
Birth through 3 days
Ampicillin
Aminoglycoside
At >3 Days
Ampicillin
Aminoglycoside
Vancomycin or
Nafcillin

Subsequent evaluations:
Clinical signs
CRP q 12 h × 2; thereafter
q 24–48 h to assess
response to antibiotic
therapy
Total leukocytes
I:T ratio
CSF 48–72 h after onset
of therapy for meningitis
Serum chemistries:
Electrolytes
BUN, creatinine
Glucose
X-ray chest; abdomen
if distended

All CRPs normal
Apparent noninfectious
disorder
Aggregate of
initial and
subsequent tests
not supportive of
infection

CRP remains abnormal
Aggregate of results
support infection
No apparent noninfectious
disorder
Infection documented by
blood and other cultures

Stop antibiotics at
3–5 days

Continue Antibiotics
7–14 Days (Sepsis)
21 Days (Meningitis)

CONGENITAL SYPHILIS

A. The incidence of congenital syphilis has increased significantly over recent years. Not only is a high index of suspicion for this disease necessary but also in most institutions routine serologic screening is in place for all mothers and babies. The major challenge for the clinician is in the evaluation of an asymptomatic infant born to a mother with a positive serologic test. Pertinent information on the mother's history, therapy, and serologic titers is important in determining whether an infant should have a workup, be treated, or be observed. Infants born to mothers who have not been treated, who have had inadequate treatment, whose treatment is undocumented, or who have been treated within 1 month of delivery must be considered as having the disease, even if asymptomatic, and must be treated appropriately. Screening is necessary for infants born to mothers who have had poor or no prenatal care or who have not had serologic screening after 28 weeks' gestation.

B. The clinical spectrum of congenital syphilis includes intrauterine fetal death, symptomatic disease, and asymptomatic disease. Most infants (60–70%) are asymptomatic at birth. Clinical manifestations in the neonate are variable. The neonate with congenital syphilis may have hydrops fetalis, bone lesions, or nephrotic syndrome or may present with only severe hemolytic anemia. An unexplained large placenta should make one suspicious of congenital syphilis.

C. In most infants with congenital syphilis, a presumptive diagnosis is made by one of two types of serologic tests: (1) the nontreponemal tests for anticardiolipin antibody titer determination (Venereal Disease Research Laboratories [VDRL] test and rapid plasma reagin [RPR] test) or (2) treponemal antibody titers (fluorescent treponemal antibody absorbed [FTA-ABS] and microhemagglutination assay for antibody to *Treponema pallidum* [MHATP]). Antibody titers from either of the nontreponemal tests correlate well with disease activity; that is, titer increases with active infection and decreases with treatment. The VDRL may be positive in autoimmune disorders; pregnancy per se does not give a positive VDRL. Once positive, treponemal antibody titers remain positive for life and do not correlate with treatment or disease activity.

D. In infants suspected of having congenital syphilis, regardless of symptoms, a lumbar puncture should be done for CSF analysis to rule out neurosyphilis. Increased WBC count and high protein concentration in the CSF suggest CNS involvement. A positive CSF VDRL is diagnostic of neurosyphilis. However, blood contamination of CSF (e.g., traumatic tap) may yield false-positive results, and a negative CSF VDRL does not rule out neurosyphilis. A negative FTA-ABS strongly indicates absence of neurosyphilis. CSF FTA-ABS and RPR yield high false-positive results; they are not recommended for CSF analysis.

E. Because congenital syphilis often involves multiple organ systems, certain laboratory tests help to establish the extent of the disease. White blood cell count may show leukemoid reaction. Platelet count may be low. In the presence of hemolytic anemia, hematocrit is low while reticulocyte count is high. Liver function tests demonstrate increase in liver enzymes (AST, ALT, GGTP); bilirubin level may be elevated. Chest x-ray in cases of "pneumonia alba" shows extensive radiopacities. Radiographs of the long bones may demonstrate periosteal reaction and metaphyseal dystrophy (osteochondritis). Urinalysis, when there is associated renal involvement, shows proteinuria.

F. Symptomatic congenital syphilis needs to be treated with aqueous penicillin G, 50,000 units/kg/dose IV q 12 hours in the first week of life and q 8 hours thereafter during the first month. The duration of therapy is 10–14 days; this regimen is also adequate in treatment of neurosyphilis. Infants with neurosyphilis should be reevaluated every 6 months for the first 3 years of life. A positive CSF VDRL in 6 months requires retreatment. Others have proposed as an alternative therapy procaine penicillin G, 50,000 units/kg IM daily for 10–14 days for congenital syphilis without associated CNS involvement. If a mother was treated adequately over a month before delivery, an infant is merely followed up with repeated serologic testing, provided adequate follow-up is assured. If noncompliance to follow-up is likely, benzathine penicillin G, 50,000 units/kg is administered IM.

HSB

References

Hernandez JA. Congenital syphilis: the great imitator (lecture outline), Feb 1992.

Ikeda MK, Jenson HB. Evaluation and treatment of congenital syphilis. J Pediatr 1990; 117:843.

US Department of Health and Human Services (PHS). Sexually transmitted diseases: Treatment guidelines. Atlanta: US Government Printing Office, 1989.

Wendel GD. Gestational and congenital syphilis. Clin Perinatol 1988; 15:287.

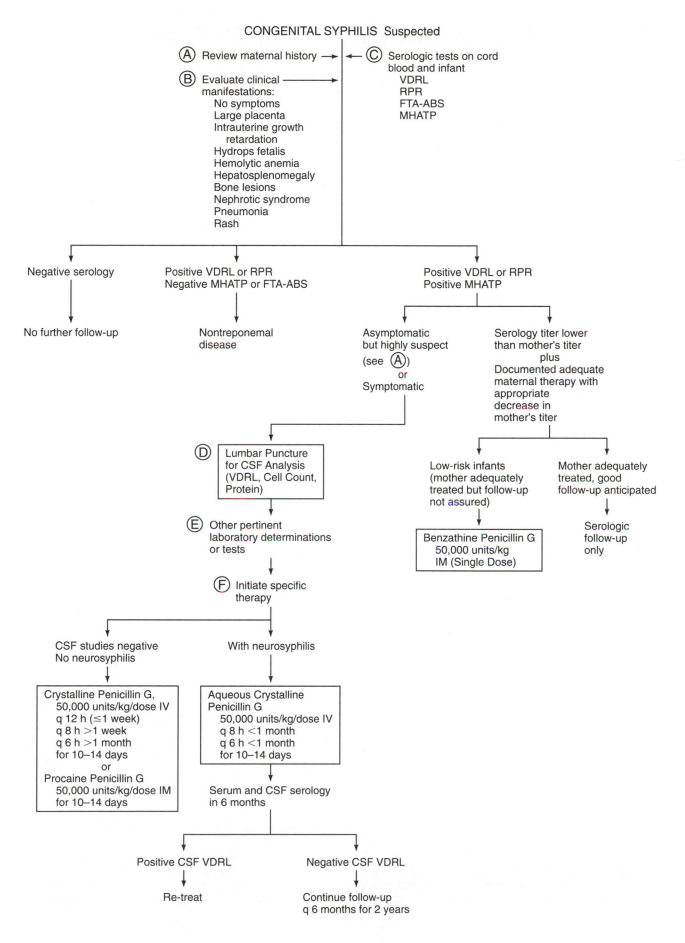

CONGENITAL SYPHILIS Suspected

Ⓐ Review maternal history →   ← Ⓒ Serologic tests on cord
                                         blood and infant
Ⓑ Evaluate clinical →   VDRL
   manifestations: RPR
      No symptoms   FTA-ABS
      Large placenta   MHATP
      Intrauterine growth
         retardation
      Hydrops fetalis
      Hemolytic anemia
      Hepatosplenomegaly
      Bone lesions
      Nephrotic syndrome
      Pneumonia
      Rash

Negative serology   Positive VDRL or RPR   Positive VDRL or RPR
                         Negative MHATP or FTA-ABS   Positive MHATP

No further follow-up   Nontreponemal   Asymptomatic   Serology titer lower
                              disease   but highly suspect   than mother's titer
                                                    (see Ⓐ)   plus
                                                         or   Documented adequate
                                                    Symptomatic   maternal therapy with
                                                                          appropriate
                                                                          decrease in
                                                                          mother's titer

                                          Ⓓ Lumbar Puncture   Low-risk infants   Mother adequately
                                             for CSF Analysis   (mother adequately   treated, good
                                             (VDRL, Cell Count,   treated but follow-up   follow-up anticipated
                                             Protein)   not assured)

                                          Ⓔ Other pertinent   Serologic
                                             laboratory determinations   Benzathine Penicillin G   follow-up
                                             or tests   50,000 units/kg   only
                                                                         IM (Single Dose)

                                             Ⓕ Initiate specific
                                                therapy

CSF studies negative   With neurosyphilis
No neurosyphilis

Crystalline Penicillin G,   Aqueous Crystalline
   50,000 units/kg/dose IV   Penicillin G
   q 12 h (≤1 week)   50,000 units/kg/dose IV
   q 8 h >1 week   q 8 h <1 month
   q 6 h >1 month   q 6 h <1 month
   for 10–14 days   for 10–14 days
      or
Procaine Penicillin G   Serum and CSF serology
   50,000 units/kg/dose IM   in 6 months
   for 10–14 days

                 Positive CSF VDRL   Negative CSF VDRL

                 Re-treat   Continue follow-up
                                           q 6 months for 2 years

NONBACTERIAL INFECTIONS: VIRUSES AND TOXOPLASMOSIS

A. Abnormal signs appear in unpredictable combinations and in more than one entity. These infections may be acquired in utero, during labor, or postnatally in the nursery. Congenital toxoplasmosis and rubella are virtually always acquired by the transplacental route. Herpes simplex infection is usually acquired intrapartum and rarely by earlier placental passage. Cytomegalovirus (CMV) infection is most often transplacentally acquired, causing lesions that are evident at birth, but occasional instances of intrapartum transmission are associated with onset of disease several weeks later. Enteroviral disease is usually acquired as a nosocomial infection. The diagnosis of *Enterovirus* infection transmitted before birth is substantially aided by information regarding maternal infection. Evidence of maternal involvement is of particular importance in the diagnosis of neonatal herpes infection.

B. There are three clinically distinguishable categories of herpes simplex infection: disseminated disease, CNS disease, and disease restricted to skin, eye, and mouth. Disseminated infection entails high mortality, formerly >90% but now reduced to 60% by antiviral drug therapy. In varying combinations, the disease involves vesicles in the skin (absent in 20% of affected infants), eye, mouth, lung, liver, adrenals, CNS, and virtually every other organ of the body. Encephalitis occurs in 90% of affected infants. In the absence of vesicles, bacterial sepsis is a leading cause of confusion, and congenital syphilis is not far behind. Disseminated disease occurs in approximately one third to one half of herpes-infected infants. The category of CNS disease implies absence of generalized manifestations, save for skin, eye, and mucous membrane lesions in some infants. In the absence of other suggestive signs of herpes infection, encephalitis is identified with great difficulty. Maternal history of infection is pivotal. Serial CSF samples demonstrate progressively increased protein (>1000 mg) and cell content. Viral culture is positive in only 25–40% of cases. The third clinical category involves lesions localized to the skin, mouth, and eyes. Later recurrence of skin lesions is common. Approximately one third of these infants develop neurologic abnormalities during the first year of life, despite initially inapparent CNS involvement. No mortality is associated with this form of the disease. Diagnosis of herpes depends upon culture of virus. Serologic findings are infrequently useful. Vesicles are the most reliable source of virus, but multiple sites should be simultaneously cultured. The current drug of choice for therapy is acyclovir IV every 8–12 h in a total daily dose of 30 mg/kg for 10–14 days.

C. Most severe CMV infections are acquired in utero, resulting in multiple organ involvement and a mortality of approximately 33%. Intrapartum infection does not often cause severe disease; most often these infants are asymptomatic, but developmental disabilities and hearing deficit may appear later. The current infrequency of congenital rubella has made CMV a leading perinatal cause of hearing impairment. Interstitial pneumonitis caused by intrapartum CMV infection is indistinguishable from other infectious etiologies. Onset occurs several weeks after birth. Mortality is approximately 20%; in survivors of pneumonitis the disease disappears in 2–3 weeks. CMV may also be transmitted by blood transfusion, resulting in enlargement of liver and spleen, a gray shocklike appearance, absolute lymphocytosis, thrombocytopenia, and hemolytic anemia. Use of blood that is seronegative for CMV avoids infection. Serologic tests are not useful for the diagnosis of congenital disease. Isolation of the virus is definitive in symptomatic babies. There is no available specific treatment for CMV infection.

D. Toxoplasmosis is acquired in utero; the majority of infected infants are asymptomatic in the neonatal period, but some develop mental retardation, CNS abnormalities, and ocular disorders in later infancy and childhood. Maternal disease is often asymptomatic. The earlier in pregnancy infection is transmitted, the more severe the neonatal disease. Neither intrapartum nor postnatal transmission plays a role in neonatal disease. Symptomatic disease is severe, usually involving CNS and other generalized signs of infection. The intracranial calcifications of toxoplasmosis are diffusely distributed, often in the basal ganglia and periventricular regions as well. Brain calcifications of CMV infection are more likely to be restricted to the periventricular area. Differentiation of the two diseases according to distribution of intracranial calcifications is not accurate. Pyrimethamine and sulfadiazine in combination are recommended for treatment of infants with overt congenital disease or proved subclinical infection. Duration of treatment is 1 year. Spiramycin is alternated with the pyrimethamine-sulfadiazine combination during the year of therapy. Folinic acid is added to counteract the marrow depression caused by pyrimethamine. See reference list for details of schedules and dosages.

E. Congenital rubella infection is now a rare occurrence because of widespread administration of an effective vaccine. Rubella virus is transplacentally transmitted throughout pregnancy. The earlier the transmission, the more devastating the fetal consequences. Serologic testing of neonates involves demonstration of specific IgM antibodies, which at present are diagnostic. False-positive results may occur. An alternative method entails blood samples at 3, 5, and 6 months of age for specific IgG antibody titers by hemagglutination-inhibition (HI). Maternally derived antibodies decrease steadily; persistent or increased titers indi-

NONBACTERIAL INFECTION Suspected

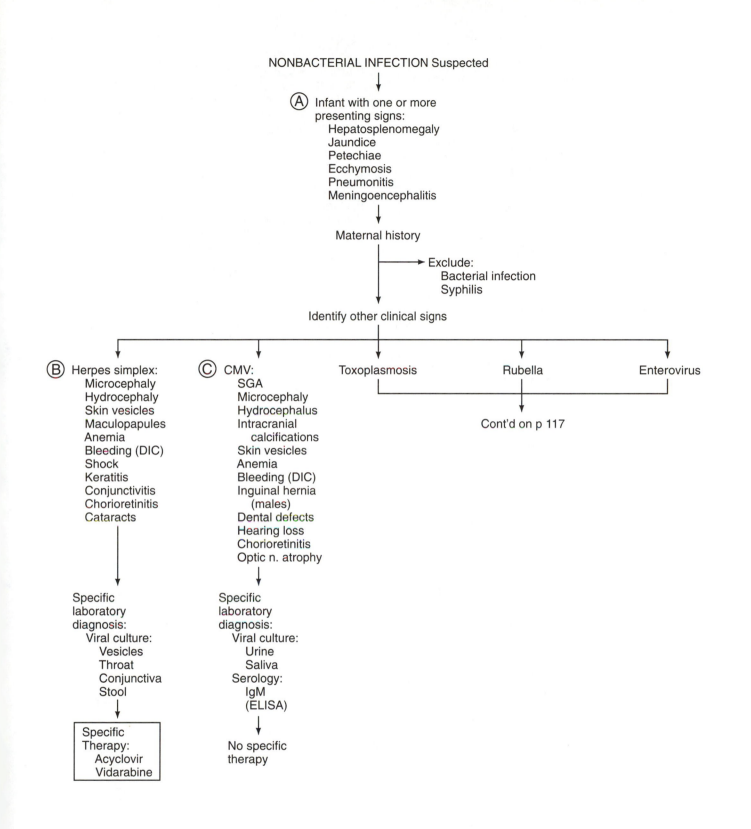

Ⓐ Infant with one or more
presenting signs:
　　Hepatosplenomegaly
　　Jaundice
　　Petechiae
　　Ecchymosis
　　Pneumonitis
　　Meningoencephalitis

Maternal history

→ Exclude:
　　Bacterial infection
　　Syphilis

Identify other clinical signs

Ⓑ Herpes simplex:
　　Microcephaly
　　Hydrocephaly
　　Skin vesicles
　　Maculopapules
　　Anemia
　　Bleeding (DIC)
　　Shock
　　Keratitis
　　Conjunctivitis
　　Chorioretinitis
　　Cataracts

Ⓒ CMV:
　　SGA
　　Microcephaly
　　Hydrocephalus
　　Intracranial
　　　calcifications
　　Skin vesicles
　　Anemia
　　Bleeding (DIC)
　　Inguinal hernia
　　　(males)
　　Dental defects
　　Hearing loss
　　Chorioretinitis
　　Optic n. atrophy

Toxoplasmosis

Rubella

Enterovirus

Cont'd on p 117

Specific
laboratory
diagnosis:
　Viral culture:
　　Vesicles
　　Throat
　　Conjunctiva
　　Stool

Specific
laboratory
diagnosis:
　Viral culture:
　　Urine
　　Saliva
　Serology:
　　IgM
　　(ELISA)

Specific
Therapy:
　Acyclovir
　Vidarabine

No specific
therapy

cate congenital disease. The most reliable method for diagnosis is culture of the virus. The most lucrative site for culture is the nasopharynx.

F. The enteroviruses include Coxsackieviruses, ECHO viruses, and poliomyelitis viruses. Poliomyelitis virus is rare; *Enterovirus* disease in neonates is caused by Coxsackievirus and ECHO virus. The vast majority of infections are acquired postnatally. A number of ECHO virus nursery epidemics have been described. Placental and intrapartum transmission are well documented in several reports. Intrauterine ascending infection is unproved. Postnatal transmission is by person-to-person contact, as in older individuals. Illness may be febrile with no specific symptoms, or perhaps with associated mild aseptic meningitis. A severe type of illness that mimics bacterial sepsis is common and sometimes fatal. Signs of hepatitis, encephalitis, myocarditis, respiratory disease, diarrhea, and fever are the usual manifestations of severe infection. Diagnosis can only be established by culturing the virus. There is no specific therapy available, although it is advisable to administer intravenous immunoglobulin (IVIG) for severe illness, and it may be equally advisable in nursery epidemics of *Enterovirus* disease.

SBK

References

Cherry JD. Enteroviruses. In: Remington JS, Klein JO, eds. Infectious diseases of the fetus and newborn infant. 3rd ed. Philadelphia: WB Saunders, 1990:325.

Hanshaw JB, Dudgeon JA, Marshall WC. Differential diagnosis on the basis of physical findings. In: Viral diseases of the fetus and newborn. 2nd ed. Philadelphia: WB Saunders, 1985: 243.

Preblud SR, Alford CA Jr. Rubella. In: Remington JS, Klein JO, eds. Infectious diseases of the fetus and newborn infant. 3rd ed. Philadelphia: WB Saunders, 1990:196.

Remington JS, Desmonts G. Toxoplasmosis. In: Remington JS, Klein JO, eds. Infectious diseases of the fetus and newborn infant. 3rd ed. Philadelphia: WB Saunders, 1990:89.

Stagno S. Cytomegalovirus. In: Remington JS, Klein JO, eds. Infectious diseases of the fetus and newborn infant. 3rd ed. Philadelphia: WB Saunders, 1990:241.

Whitley RJ. Herpes simplex virus infections. In: Remington JS, Klein JO, eds. Infectious diseases of the fetus and newborn infant. 3rd ed. Philadelphia: WB Saunders, 1990:282.

Identify other clinical signs
(cont'd from p 115)

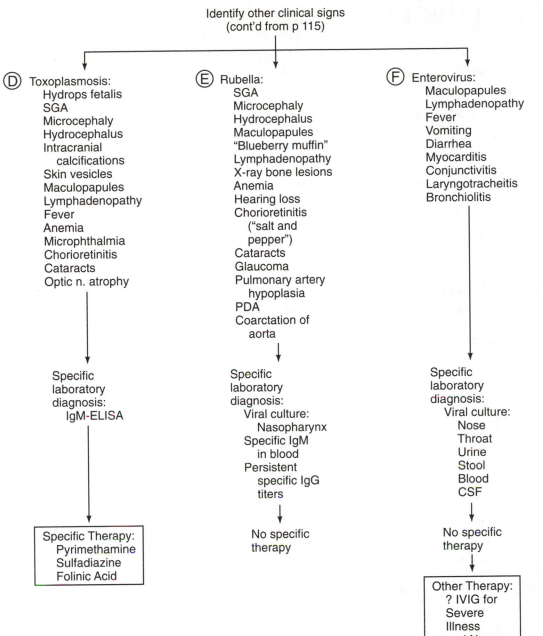

(D) Toxoplasmosis:
    Hydrops fetalis
    SGA
    Microcephaly
    Hydrocephalus
    Intracranial
        calcifications
    Skin vesicles
    Maculopapules
    Lymphadenopathy
    Fever
    Anemia
    Microphthalmia
    Chorioretinitis
    Cataracts
    Optic n. atrophy

Specific
laboratory
diagnosis:
    IgM-ELISA

Specific Therapy:
    Pyrimethamine
    Sulfadiazine
    Folinic Acid

(E) Rubella:
    SGA
    Microcephaly
    Hydrocephalus
    Maculopapules
    "Blueberry muffin"
    Lymphadenopathy
    X-ray bone lesions
    Anemia
    Hearing loss
    Chorioretinitis
        ("salt and
        pepper")
    Cataracts
    Glaucoma
    Pulmonary artery
        hypoplasia
    PDA
    Coarctation of
        aorta

Specific
laboratory
diagnosis:
    Viral culture:
        Nasopharynx
    Specific IgM
        in blood
    Persistent
        specific IgG
        titers

No specific
therapy

(F) Enterovirus:
    Maculopapules
    Lymphadenopathy
    Fever
    Vomiting
    Diarrhea
    Myocarditis
    Conjunctivitis
    Laryngotracheitis
    Bronchiolitis

Specific
laboratory
diagnosis:
    Viral culture:
        Nose
        Throat
        Urine
        Stool
        Blood
        CSF

No specific
therapy

Other Therapy:
    ? IVIG for
    Severe
    Illness
    and Nursery
    Epidemics

FUNGUS INFECTION: *CANDIDA*

A. The risk of candidiasis has expanded extensively in only the past few years. There has been insufficient time for description of the current experience to appear in periodic literature and texts. The risks have grown as smaller babies survive in greater numbers in the NICU. These survivals imply protracted and multiple courses of antibiotics, invasive procedures in greater number and over longer time intervals, prolonged administration of hyperalimentation fluid to more babies and most recently, the widespread use of corticosteroids for bronchopulmonary dysplasia.

B. Intrauterine and intrapartum infections occur infrequently. These exposures generally result in mucocutaneous lesions; on fewer occasions pulmonary disease follows aspiration of organisms. Contamination from amniocentesis is rare but real.

C. Mortality from disseminated candidiasis is high. The clinical signs mimic bacterial sepsis or herpes simplex disease. Apparently no part of the body has been spared from tissue destruction by the organism. A fungus mass is unique to candidiasis. It has been identified most often in the heart and various blood vessels and in the kidney at the ureteropelvic junction where urine flow may be impeded. Another sign unique to candidiasis and common in affected infants is endophthalmitis. This is characterized by cloudy vitreous and "cotton balls" representing fungal masses. Asymptomatic fungemia is a common phenomenon, particularly in babies who receive hyperalimentation through a deep centrally placed catheter. A few reports describe spontaneous recovery from untreated symptomatic *Candida* septicemia.

D. Laboratory diagnosis depends on culture and visualization of the organism. Often positive results are difficult to interpret because the organism is ubiquitous and therefore may be a mere contaminant, especially in urine. Meningitis and brain abscess do not always produce abnormal findings in spinal fluid. Blood cultures may be negative when candidemia is present. Multiple cultures are essential.

E. Ultrasound of the kidney and echocardiography are valuable for a demonstration of fungal masses. X-ray studies may initially suggest the presence of a mass. Ophthalmoscopy may be diagnostic if a fungus mass is identified.

F. Amphotericin is the treatment of choice. A number of infants seem to respond remarkably to initial small doses of the drug. Treatment should begin with 0.1 mg/kg daily, given intravenously over a period of 4–6 hours. The daily dose may require increments up to a final dose of 1.0 mg/kg. Treatment should be maintained for 10–14 days. Assiduous monitoring is mandatory. Complications include cardiac arrhythmias and hypokalemia as a result of urinary potassium losses. BUN and creatinine also should be determined regularly to identify impaired renal function.

SBK

References

Eckstein CW, Kass EJ. Anuria in a newborn secondary to bilateral ureteropelvic fungus balls. J Urol 1982; 127:109.

Faix RG. Systemic *Candida* infections in infants in intensive care nurseries: High incidence of central nervous system involvement. J Pediatr 1984; 105:616.

Foker JE, Bass JL, Thompson T et al. Management of intracardiac fungal masses in premature infants. J Thorac Cardiovasc Surg 1984; 87:244.

Johnson EE, Bass JL, Thompson TR, et al. *Candida* septicemia and right atrial mass secondary to umbilical vein catheterization. Am J Dis Child 1981; 135:275.

Johnson EE, Thompson TR, Green TP, et al. Systemic candidiasis in very low-birth-weight infants (1,500 grams), Pediatrics 1984; 73:138.

Kirpekar M, Abiri MM, Hilfer C, et al. Ultrasound in the diagnosis of systemic candidiasis (renal and cranial) in very low birth weight premature infants. Pediatr Radiol 1986; 16:17.

Michelson PE, Rupp R, Efthimiadis B. Endogenous *Candida* endophthalmitis leading to bilateral corneal perforation. Am J Ophthalmol 1975; 80:800.

Miller MJ. Fungal infections. In: Remington JS, Klein JO, eds. Infectious diseases of the fetus and newborn infant. 3rd ed. Philadelphia: WB Saunders, 1990:475.

FUNGUS INFECTION: CANDIDA

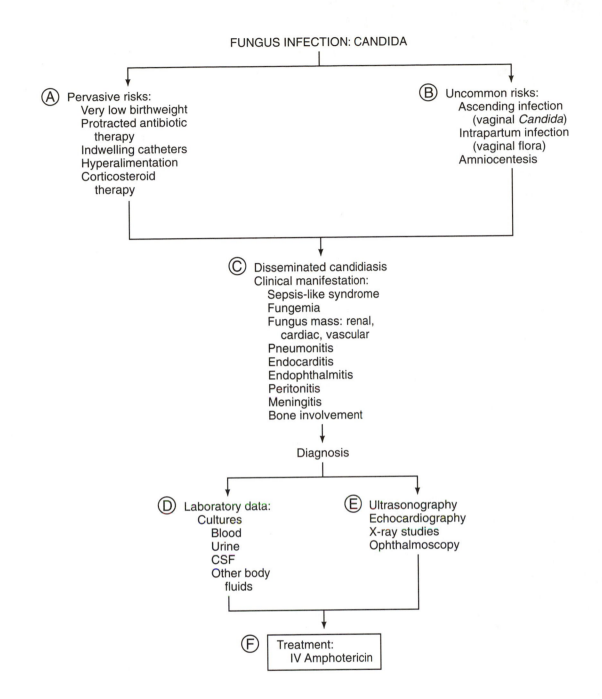

Ⓐ Pervasive risks:
  Very low birthweight
  Protracted antibiotic
    therapy
  Indwelling catheters
  Hyperalimentation
  Corticosteroid
    therapy

Ⓑ Uncommon risks:
  Ascending infection
    (vaginal *Candida*)
  Intrapartum infection
    (vaginal flora)
  Amniocentesis

Ⓒ Disseminated candidiasis
  Clinical manifestation:
    Sepsis-like syndrome
    Fungemia
    Fungus mass: renal,
      cardiac, vascular
    Pneumonitis
    Endocarditis
    Endophthalmitis
    Peritonitis
    Meningitis
    Bone involvement

Diagnosis

Ⓓ Laboratory data:
  Cultures
    Blood
    Urine
    CSF
    Other body
      fluids

Ⓔ Ultrasonography
  Echocardiography
  X-ray studies
  Ophthalmoscopy

Ⓕ Treatment:
  IV Amphotericin

DISORDERS BY ORGAN SYSTEM

PULMONARY DISORDERS
Respiratory Distress Syndrome:
  Pathogenesis and Diagnosis
Respiratory Distress Syndrome:
  Management
Respiratory Distress Syndrome:
  Specific Therapy
Meconium Aspiration
Transient Tachypnea of the Newborn
  (RDS Type II)
Bronchopulmonary Dysplasia
Pleural Effusion (Hydrothorax and
  Chylothorax)
Massive Pulmonary Hemorrhage
Diaphragmatic Hernia
Complications of Mechanical
  Ventilation
Pulmonary Air Leak

CARDIOVASCULAR DISORDERS
Bradycardia
Tachycardia
Diminished Heart Sounds
Mediastinal Shift
Hypertension
Hypertension: Therapy
Abnormal Central Venous Pressure
Shock
Patent Ductus Arteriosus
Persistent Fetal Circulation
Myocardial Ischemia

GASTROINTESTINAL DISORDERS
Necrotizing Enterocolitis:
  Diagnosis
Necrotizing Enterocolitis:
  Management
Intestinal Obstruction
Esophageal Atresia and
  Tracheoesophageal Fistulas
Ineffective Suck and/or Swallow

HEMATOLOGIC DISORDERS
Anemia Due to Blood Loss
Anemia Due to Hemolysis
Polycythemia/Hyperviscosity
Platelet Disorders:
  Thrombocytopenia
Platelet Disorders:
  Thrombocytosis
Neutropenia
Disseminated Intravascular
  Coagulation
Bleeding Infants

NEUROLOGIC DISORDERS
Seizures
Seizures: Therapy
Jitteriness
Hypotonia
Hypoxic-Ischemic
  Encephalopathy
Hypoxic-Ischemic
  Encephalopathy: Therapy
Periventricular-
  Intraventricular Hemorrhage:
  Pathophysiology
Periventricular-
  Intraventricular Hemorrhage:
  Therapy

OCULAR ABNORMALITIES
Pupillary Opacities (White Pupils)
Retinopathy of Prematurity

SKIN AND SUBCUTANEOUS TISSUES
Purpura
Blisters
Edema and Sclerema
Hemangiomas
Lymphangiomas
Pigmented Lesions

RESPIRATORY DISTRESS SYNDROME: PATHOGENESIS AND DIAGNOSIS

A. Diminished severity of respiratory distress syndrome (RDS) is apparently associated with a number of prenatal conditions characterized by fetal distress and an enhanced release of fetal endogenous steroids. Maternal disorders include toxemia, advanced diabetes (types D, F, and R), drug abuse, and chronic retroplacental abruptio. Prolonged membrane rupture is also associated with attenuation or absence of RDS; the longer the interval between rupture and birth, the lower the incidence of neonatal disease. Maternal steroid therapy between 7 days and 24 hours before birth has a similar effect that has been observed preponderantly in females. Fetal undergrowth is the result of ongoing fetal distress of some type (nonbacterial infection, placental insufficiency), and these infants are also less frequently affected. Even in the absence of other factors, simply being female or black entails a lessened likelihood of severe RDS.

B. The fundamental life-threatening pulmonary disorder is atelectasis and deflation instability. The other facets of pulmonary dysfunction are a by-product of failure to expand the lungs at peak inspiration and inability to sustain partial expansion (distention stability) at end expiration. The latter abnormality is the basis for the success of positive end-expiratory pressure (PEEP, CPAP) in improving gas exchange, particularly oxygenation. The role of the hyaline membrane is not considered to be significant.

C. Prenatal assessment depends upon determination of lecithin-sphingomyelin (L/S) ratios and, in some instances, the presence of phosphatidylglycerol (PG). A number of variations of the L/S ratio procedure have been reported since its original description by Gluck and Kulovich in 1973. Generally, L/S ratios >2 are virtually certain predictions that RDS will not occur. At ratios between 1.5 and 2 approximately 40% of infants are affected. Below a ratio of 1, 75% of neonates have RDS. PG is elaborated late in pregnancy, at 35 weeks or later. It may appear at considerably younger gestational ages in conditions that produce fetal chronic distress and early maturation of surfactant production. At any gestational age, PG is an important indication of lung maturity.

D. Two different sets of clinical signs are identifiable within the diagnostic designation of RDS: hyaline membrane disease (HMD) and respiratory insufficiency of prematurity (RIP). The latter has often been called "immature lung." Each has a distinctly different course and x-ray appearance when uncomplicated by intraventricular-periventricular hemorrhage or infection. The classic syndrome of HMD entails worsening of respiratory insufficiency during the first 36 hours after birth, followed by a plateau of severity and then improvement. This sequence of events is altered, usually protracted, by the need for mechanical ventilatory support and its resultant pulmonary barotrauma. The x-ray appearance of HMD indicates underaeration, varying degrees of atelectasis, and air bronchograms. The clinical signs of RIP are discernible in babies whose birth weights are <1200–1300 g, but with increasing frequency as birth weight decreases. At <800–1000 g, RIP is the most frequent manifestation of respiratory distress syndrome. It differs considerably from HMD in clinical course and x-ray appearance. Little if any mechanical respiratory support is needed. When it is necessary, considerable diminution in support is possible after 12–72 h. Thereafter the infant can be managed for varying periods of time in an oxygen hood. The radiograph reveals normal or somewhat increased expansion of the lungs with no evidence of atelectasis or air bronchograms. In babies who have been chronically stressed, the thymic shadow is diminished in size or absent. In these infants surfactant maturation is probably accelerated, but in others surfactant maturity is not demonstrable. Tachypnea and chest wall retractions are the rule.

SBK

References

Edwards DK, Jacob J, Gluck L. The immature lung: Radiographic appearance, course, and complications. 1980; Am J Roentgenol 135:659.

Harris TR. Physiological principles. In: Goldsmith JP, Karotkin EH, ed. Assisted ventilation of the neonate. 2nd ed. Philadelphia: WB Saunders, 1988.

Morley CJ. Pulmonary disease of the newborn. Part II. The respiratory distress syndrome. In: Roberton NRC, ed. Textbook of neonatology. London: Churchill Livingstone, 1986.

Stern L, ed. Hyaline membrane disease: Pathogenesis and pathophysiology. Orlando: Grune & Stratton, 1984.

RESPIRATORY DISTRESS SYNDROME

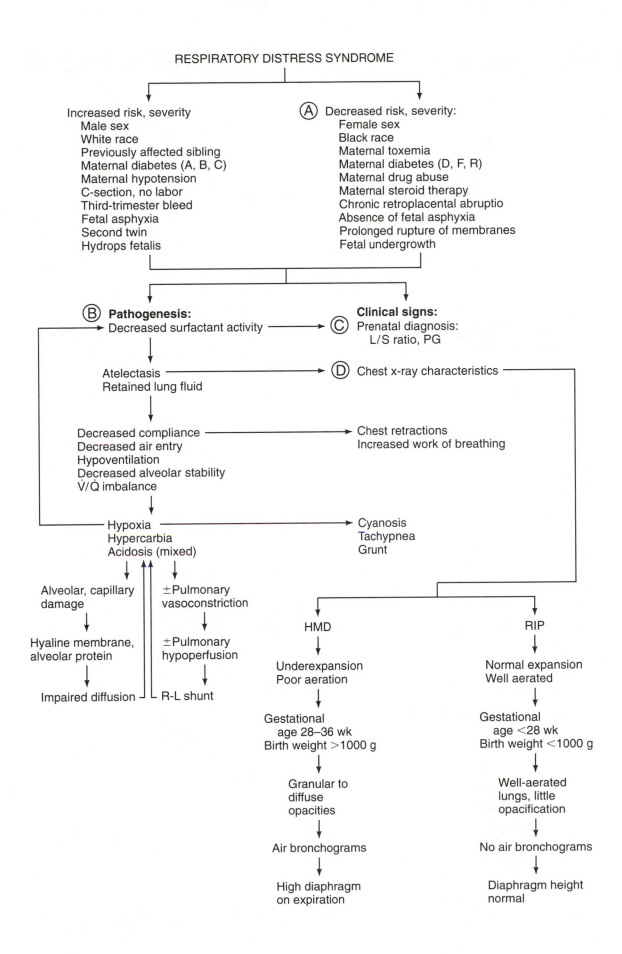

Increased risk, severity
  Male sex
  White race
  Previously affected sibling
  Maternal diabetes (A, B, C)
  Maternal hypotension
  C-section, no labor
  Third-trimester bleed
  Fetal asphyxia
  Second twin
  Hydrops fetalis

(A) Decreased risk, severity:
  Female sex
  Black race
  Maternal toxemia
  Maternal diabetes (D, F, R)
  Maternal drug abuse
  Maternal steroid therapy
  Chronic retroplacental abruptio
  Absence of fetal asphyxia
  Prolonged rupture of membranes
  Fetal undergrowth

(B) **Pathogenesis:**
Decreased surfactant activity ⟶

(C) **Clinical signs:**
Prenatal diagnosis:
  L/S ratio, PG

Atelectasis ⟶
Retained lung fluid

(D) Chest x-ray characteristics

Decreased compliance ⟶
Decreased air entry
Hypoventilation
Decreased alveolar stability
V̇/Q̇ imbalance

Chest retractions
Increased work of breathing

Hypoxia ⟶
Hypercarbia
Acidosis (mixed)

Cyanosis
Tachypnea
Grunt

Alveolar, capillary
damage

±Pulmonary
vasoconstriction

Hyaline membrane,
alveolar protein

±Pulmonary
hypoperfusion

Impaired diffusion ⌐ ⌐ R-L shunt

HMD
  ↓
Underexpansion
Poor aeration
  ↓
Gestational
  age 28–36 wk
Birth weight >1000 g
  ↓
Granular to
diffuse
opacities
  ↓
Air bronchograms
  ↓
High diaphragm
on expiration

RIP
  ↓
Normal expansion
Well aerated
  ↓
Gestational
  age <28 wk
Birth weight <1000 g
  ↓
Well-aerated
lungs, little
opacification
  ↓
No air bronchograms
  ↓
Diaphragm height
normal

123

RESPIRATORY DISTRESS SYNDROME: MANAGEMENT

A. Supportive measures, in contrast to specific therapy, consist primarily of respiratory support and extrapulmonary management. Specific therapy is described on p 124.

B. The vigor of respiratory support is determined by the severity of disease. A minority of affected infants can be adequately treated with oxygen in a hood. The course of the disease often rapidly deteriorates, particularly during the first postnatal hours. Blood gas values that at first indicate the adequacy of a hood may worsen precipitously. Therefore, in many nurseries a chest film characterized by moderate density and air bronchograms in association with prominent chest retractions are indications for immediate application of end-expiratory positive pressure even if blood gas values are initially satisfactory. Early application of CPAP shortens the duration of ventilatory support. Most infants do require early application of some form of end-expiratory pressure. They need CPAP if they can breathe adequately; they need a respirator if they have no such capacity.

CPAP should be attempted tenaciously before proceeding to mechanical support because the incidence of short-term complications (air leak syndromes, pulmonary hemorrhage) and the later sequelae of chronic lung disease (bronchopulmonary dysplasia) are minimized by more passive support. On initial application of CPAP, a high Pa_{CO_2} will decline as oxygenation improves. If satisfactory oxygenation has been achieved, a persistently elevated Pa_{CO_2} will not usually be diminished by enhancing end-expiratory positive pressure. Accumulation of carbon dioxide plus pH <7.25 indicates a need for mechanical support. Occasionally a high Pa_{CO_2} is the result of excessive distending pressure. If the infant fails to maintain an adequate respiratory rate when CPAP is first applied, manually assisted breathing for approximately 5 minutes is often followed by spontaneous respiration, particularly when an endotracheal tube is used for the CPAP. CPAP is most commonly delivered via a nasopharyngeal or endotracheal tube. The advantage of the nasopharyngeal route is its ease of application and avoidance of the complications of endotracheal intubation. Its major disadvantages are restlessness and struggling that often necessitate deep sedation. The complications of end-expiratory positive pressure, whether CPAP or PEEP, are described on p 140.

C. The first settings are approximations. Early, when blood gases have not yet been determined, appropriate pressure settings are most reliably suggested by the extent of chest wall excursion and the audibility of air entry in response to mechanical ventilation. Auscultation is pivotal. It should be done at the axillae because the anterior chest transmits relatively loud sounds from the large airways. At the very least, air entry should be barely audible during rising inspiratory pressures indicated on the respirator gauge. If air entry cannot be heard, raise peak inspiratory pressure by 2 cm, the presence of chest excursions notwithstanding. The grading of hazards associated with changes in settings is ranked from 0 to 4+ to indicate the likelihood of damaging barotrauma, which produces air leak syndromes immediately and BPD later. At any peak inspiratory pressure, the shorter an inspiratory time, the less the hazard of barotrauma. Schemes for weaning vary widely from one NICU to another. Diminution of pressure setting as rapidly as can be tolerated is the overriding concern of the weaning process presented here.

SBK

References

Boros SJ, Reynolds JW. Hyaline membrane disease treated with early end-expiratory pressure: One year's experience. Pediatrics 1975; 56:218.

Brady JP, Gregory GA. Assisted ventilation. In: Klaus MH, Fanaroff AA, eds. Care of the high risk neonate. 3rd ed. Philadelphia: WB Saunders, 1986.

Chatburn RL, Carlo WA, Lough MD. Clinical algorithm for pressure-limited ventilation of neonates with respiratory distress syndrome. Respir Care 1983; 28:1579.

Fox WW, Spitzer AR, Shutack JG. Positive pressure ventilation: Pressure- and time-cycled ventilators. In: Goldsmith JP, Karotkin EH, eds. Assisted ventilation of the neonate. 2nd ed. Philadelphia: WB Saunders, 1988.

RESPIRATORY DISTRESS SYNDROME: MANAGEMENT

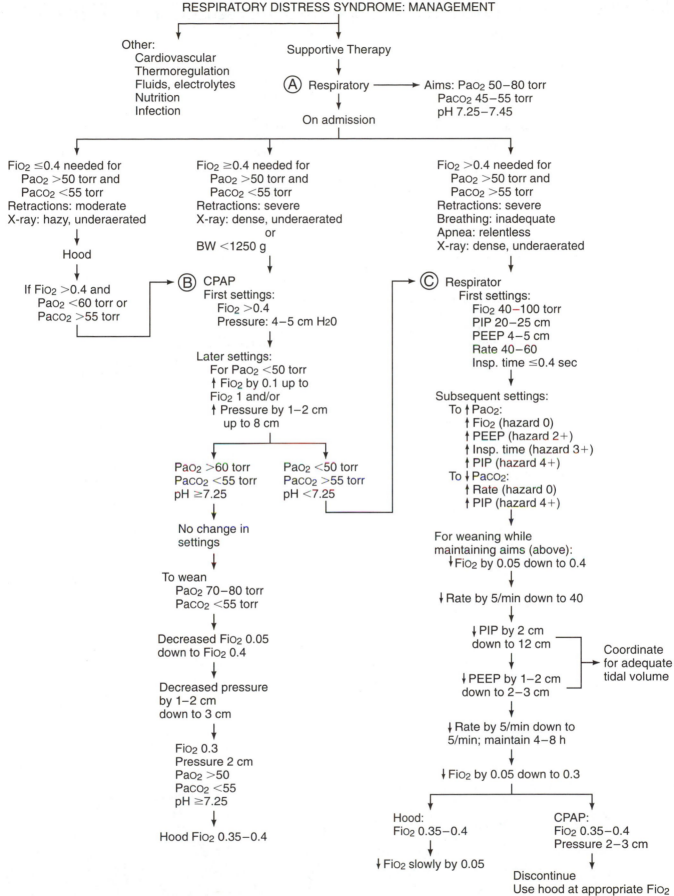

Other:
  Cardiovascular
  Thermoregulation
  Fluids, electrolytes
  Nutrition
  Infection

Supportive Therapy

Ⓐ Respiratory ⟶ Aims: Pa_{O_2} 50–80 torr
                        Pa_{CO_2} 45–55 torr
                        pH 7.25–7.45

On admission

Fi_{O_2} ≤0.4 needed for
  Pa_{O_2} >50 torr and
  Pa_{CO_2} <55 torr
Retractions: moderate
X-ray: hazy, underaerated

Hood

If Fi_{O_2} >0.4 and
  Pa_{O_2} <60 torr or
  Pa_{CO_2} >55 torr

Fi_{O_2} ≥0.4 needed for
  Pa_{O_2} >50 torr and
  Pa_{CO_2} <55 torr
Retractions: severe
X-ray: dense, underaerated
  or
BW <1250 g

Ⓑ CPAP
First settings:
  Fi_{O_2} >0.4
  Pressure: 4–5 cm H_2O

Later settings:
For Pa_{O_2} <50 torr
↑ Fi_{O_2} by 0.1 up to
  Fi_{O_2} 1 and/or
↑ Pressure by 1–2 cm
  up to 8 cm

Pa_{O_2} >60 torr Pa_{O_2} <50 torr
Pa_{CO_2} <55 torr Pa_{CO_2} >55 torr
pH ≥7.25   pH <7.25

No change in
settings

To wean
  Pa_{O_2} 70–80 torr
  Pa_{CO_2} <55 torr

Decreased Fi_{O_2} 0.05
down to Fi_{O_2} 0.4

Decreased pressure
by 1–2 cm
down to 3 cm

Fi_{O_2} 0.3
Pressure 2 cm
Pa_{O_2} >50
Pa_{CO_2} <55
pH ≥7.25

Hood Fi_{O_2} 0.35–0.4

Fi_{O_2} >0.4 needed for
  Pa_{O_2} >50 torr and
  Pa_{CO_2} >55 torr
Retractions: severe
Breathing: inadequate
Apnea: relentless
X-ray: dense, underaerated

Ⓒ Respirator
First settings:
  Fi_{O_2} 40–100 torr
  PIP 20–25 cm
  PEEP 4–5 cm
  Rate 40–60
  Insp. time ≤0.4 sec

Subsequent settings:
To ↑Pa_{O_2}:
  ↑ Fi_{O_2} (hazard 0)
  ↑ PEEP (hazard 2+)
  ↑ Insp. time (hazard 3+)
  ↑ PIP (hazard 4+)
To ↓Pa_{CO_2}:
  ↑ Rate (hazard 0)
  ↑ PIP (hazard 4+)

For weaning while
maintaining aims (above):
  ↓Fi_{O_2} by 0.05 down to 0.4

↓ Rate by 5/min down to 40

↓ PIP by 2 cm
down to 12 cm

↓ PEEP by 1–2 cm
down to 2–3 cm

Coordinate
for adequate
tidal volume

↓ Rate by 5/min down to
5/min; maintain 4–8 h

↓ Fi_{O_2} by 0.05 down to 0.3

Hood: CPAP:
Fi_{O_2} 0.35–0.4 Fi_{O_2} 0.35–0.4
                        Pressure 2–3 cm

↓Fi_{O_2} slowly by 0.05

Discontinue
Use hood at appropriate Fi_{O_2}

RESPIRATORY DISTRESS SYNDROME: SPECIFIC THERAPY

A. The aim of specific therapy is to enhance surfactant activity. It is accomplished by prenatal administration of steroids to mothers and by instillation of surfactant preparations into the airway of the neonate.

B. Betamethasone, dexamethasone, and hydrocortisone have been administered to mothers in premature labor to accelerate maturity of fetal surfactant production. In general, steroids must be administered from 24 hours to 7 days before delivery. Dexamethasone was used in the National Institutes of Health Multicenter Trial, given in four doses of 5 mg each every 12 hours. Maximum effect can be expected when therapy is begun 48 hours before birth. Apparently males are little affected, but a definite ameliorating effect for respiratory distress syndrome (RDS) has been noted in females, especially black females. Benefits are unlikely before 28 gestational weeks or beyond 32 to 34 weeks. There is no effect on RDS among twins, in the presence of premature membrane rupture, or in pregnancy-induced hypertension.

C. Surfactant preparations are administered immediately after birth in the delivery room (preventive) or up to 8 hours later (rescue). Optimal results may follow instillation before the first breath or perhaps very shortly thereafter. Data are incomplete regarding the timing of dosage, the most effective type of preparation (human, bovine, synthetic), and the number of postnatal doses for optimal results. A short-term beneficial response has been reported in virtually every study (increased Pao_2, decreased $PaCo_2$, diminished ventilatory pressure and Fio_2), yet the data concerning survival, incidence of bronchopulmonary dysplasia, duration of ventilator support, and hospital stay are inconsistent. From the first human trial in Japan and in a number of later studies, a heightened incidence of patent ductus arteriosus has been observed. The incidence of intraventricular-periventricular hemorrhage has not diminished with surfactant treatment. In spite of the current paucity of information relating to the long-term effectiveness of surfactant treatment, the current consensus is that its use is warranted.

SBK

References

Charon A, Taeusch HW, Fitzgibbon C, et al. Factors associated with surfactant treatment response in infants with severe respiratory distress syndrome. Pediatrics 1989; 83:348.

Collaborative Group on Antenatal Steroid Therapy. Effect of antenatal dexamethasone administration on the prevention of respiratory distress syndrome. Am J Obstet Gynecol 1981; 141:276.

Hallman M, Merritt TA, Jarvenpaa A-L, et al. Exogenous human surfactant for treatment of severe respiratory distress syndrome: A randomized prospective clinical trial. J Pediatr 1985; 106:963.

Jobe A. Respiratory distress syndrome: Pathologic basis for new therapeutic efforts. In: Emmanouilides GC, Baylen BG, eds. Neonatal cardiopulmonary distress. Chicago: Year Book Medical Publishers, 1988.

Jobe A, Ikegami M. Surfactant treatment of respiratory distress syndrome. Am Rev Respir Dis 1987; 136:1256.

RESPIRATORY DISTRESS SYNDROME: SPECIFIC THERAPY

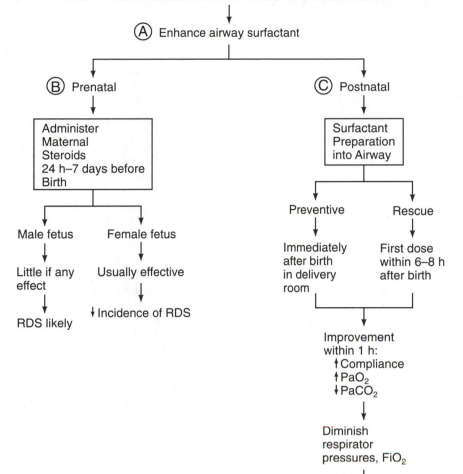

A. Enhance airway surfactant

B. Prenatal

Administer Maternal Steroids 24 h–7 days before Birth

Male fetus → Little if any effect → RDS likely

Female fetus → Usually effective → ↓Incidence of RDS

C. Postnatal

Surfactant Preparation into Airway

Preventive → Immediately after birth in delivery room

Rescue → First dose within 6–8 h after birth

Improvement within 1 h:
↑Compliance
↑PaO₂
↓PaCO₂

Diminish respirator pressures, FiO₂

↓Pneumothorax
?↓BPD
↓Mortality
IVH, no change

MECONIUM ASPIRATION

Approximately 10% of all babies are delivered through meconium-stained amniotic fluid, but only a fraction are symptomatic. In the absence of other abnormalities, meconium-stained amniotic fluid is not in itself an indication for either visualization of cords or tracheal suction. Furthermore, visualization of vocal cords by itself is a futile maneuver because tracheal aspiration of meconium occurs with no supraglottic evidence of it. Meconium passage in utero is probably not always related to asphyxia, but the clinician must act on the assumption that an asphyxiating episode has occurred. Antenatal data such as abnormal fetal heart rate (HR) tracing (late decelerations and loss of beat-to-beat variability) and scalp pH <7.2 are strong indicators of fetal asphyxia and a troublesome outcome. The meconium aspiration syndrome is rare below 34 gestational weeks; it is most frequent in postterm infants.

A. Immediately upon extrusion of the head and before total body delivery, the obstetrician should use a DeLee catheter to suction the mouth, hypopharynx, and nose in an attempt (usually successful) to minimize aspiration of upper airway contents. Subsequent procedures depend upon infant status.

B. The vigorous, pink infant whose breathing is unimpaired and whose HR is >120 needs only routine care. The moderately depressed infant is pale or cyanotic with fair respiratory effort and an HR of 100–120 beats per minute. Immediate tracheal suction is required for removal of meconium beneath the vocal cords. Suction is applied through the endotracheal (ET) tube by means of an adapter that connects the ET tube with a wall suction apparatus that has been set at 90 to 100 torr. The ET tube is slowly withdrawn as suction is applied. Reintubation and suction are repeated to evacuate maximal quantities of aspirated meconium but for no longer than 1 minute after birth. Some authors recommend a 2-minute limit. After suction, some moderately depressed infants respond with spontaneous respiration, retractions, good color, and a HR >120. For them, free-flow oxygen may suffice; in the NICU Pa_{O_2} between 80 and 100 torr can be maintained with an oxygen hood. In many other infants, the HR remains <120, breath sounds are decreased, and respiratory effort is impaired. These infants require assisted ventilation by bag and ET tube or by means of a portable ventilator during transfer to the NICU. In the nursery, mechanical ventilatory support is usually required. Pa_{O_2} is maintained above usual levels at 80 to 100 torr to minimize or prevent constriction of pulmonary vasculature.

C. The severely asphyxiated infant whose HR is <100 will not tolerate protracted tracheal suction, but evacuation of lung aspirate is nevertheless mandatory. Severe bradycardia is the major indication for cessation of suction and the initiation of endotracheal oxygen. If the HR rises >100 following endotracheal oxygen, another attempt at tracheal suction is indicated. In the NICU, mechanical ventilation is necessary. Meconium aspiration occurs in relatively large babies who often effectively resist the ventilator. Neuromuscular blockade (pancuronium) is indicated for such infants. A poor response to ventilator support should arouse suspicion of pneumothorax, severe pneumonitis (which may be chemical or bacterial), cardiogenic shock, or persistent fetal circulation (PFC). Pneumonitis and PFC are the most frequent difficulties. Severe meconium aspiration syndrome is the result of profound fetal asphyxia. Management of these babies requires attention to the several neonatal consequences of fetal asphyxia such as cerebral edema, renal failure (acute tubular necrosis), bleeding diathesis (DIC), metabolic acidosis (lactic acidosis), hypoglycemia, hypocalcemia, and infection. There are few more pressing and complex situations than the severely asphyxiated infant with massive meconium aspiration.

SBK

References

Gregory GA, Gooding CA, Phibbs RH, Tooley WH. Meconium aspiration in infants: A prospective study. J Pediatr 1970; 85:848.

Hudak BB, Jones MD: Meconium aspiration. In: Nelson NM, ed. Current therapy in neonatal-perinatal medicine. 2nd ed. Philadelphia: BC Decker, 1990:299.

Linder N, Aranda JV, Tsur M, et al. Need for endotracheal intubation and suction in meconium-stained neonates. J Pediatr 1988; 112:613.

Ting P, Brady JP. Tracheal suction in meconium aspiration. Am J Obstet Gynecol 1975; 122:767.

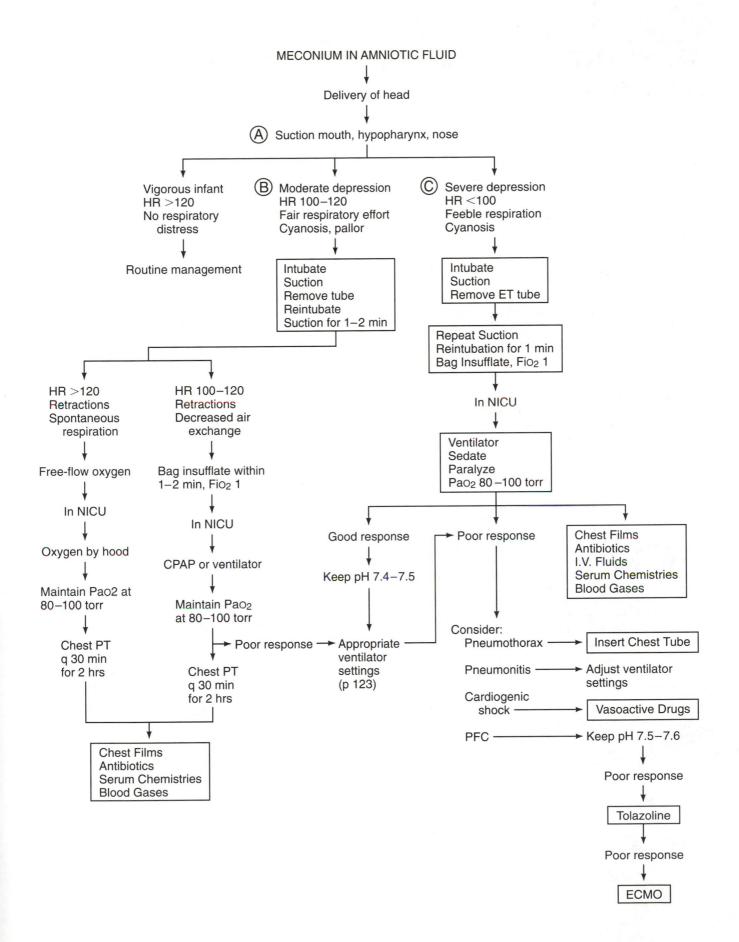

MECONIUM IN AMNIOTIC FLUID

Delivery of head

Ⓐ Suction mouth, hypopharynx, nose

Vigorous infant
HR >120
No respiratory distress

Routine management

Ⓑ **Moderate depression**
HR 100–120
Fair respiratory effort
Cyanosis, pallor

Intubate
Suction
Remove tube
Reintubate
Suction for 1–2 min

Ⓒ **Severe depression**
HR <100
Feeble respiration
Cyanosis

Intubate
Suction
Remove ET tube

Repeat Suction
Reintubation for 1 min
Bag Insufflate, FiO$_2$ 1

In NICU

Ventilator
Sedate
Paralyze
PaO$_2$ 80–100 torr

HR >120
Retractions
Spontaneous respiration

Free-flow oxygen

In NICU

Oxygen by hood

Maintain PaO2 at 80–100 torr

Chest PT q 30 min for 2 hrs

HR 100–120
Retractions
Decreased air exchange

Bag insufflate within 1–2 min, FiO$_2$ 1

In NICU

CPAP or ventilator

Maintain PaO$_2$ at 80–100 torr

Poor response → Appropriate ventilator settings (p 123)

Chest PT q 30 min for 2 hrs

Chest Films
Antibiotics
Serum Chemistries
Blood Gases

Good response

Keep pH 7.4–7.5

Poor response

Chest Films
Antibiotics
I.V. Fluids
Serum Chemistries
Blood Gases

Consider:
Pneumothorax → Insert Chest Tube

Pneumonitis → Adjust ventilator settings

Cardiogenic shock → Vasoactive Drugs

PFC → Keep pH 7.5–7.6

Poor response

Tolazoline

Poor response

ECMO

TRANSIENT TACHYPNEA OF THE NEWBORN (RDS TYPE II)

The syndrome of transient tachypnea of the newborn (TTN) (respiratory distress syndrome [RDS] type II) is presumably caused by incomplete evacuation of fetal lung fluid in infants born at or near term. At birth most infants are vigorous. Respiratory difficulty is evident within 30 minutes following delivery. RDS II is a self-limited disorder that disappears within 24 hours (sometimes not until 48–72 hours), commensurate with clearing of fetal lung fluid.

A. A baby with RDS II is usually vigorous and capable of strong respiratory effort. The more severely affected infants may have suffered a mild asphyxiating episode intrapartum. They are thus relatively inactive, though their effective respiratory effort is sustained. Since the lungs are water-laden, compliance is reduced, airway resistance is increased, and one may therefore expect impressive chest retractions. Rales and rhonchi are usually (not always) absent, and breath sounds are usually undiminished. Hyperexpansion of the lungs increases the anteroposterior diameter of the chest, imparting the classic "barrel chest" appearance. The vast majority of affected infants are cyanotic in room air.

B. The radiologic appearance of the chest is usually clearly distinguishable from the RDS of prematures. The hallmark of TTN is hyperexpansion (or normal expansion) of the lungs; the hallmark of RDS is underexpansion (atelectasis). The chest film appears emphysematous in varying degrees, intercostal bulging is sometimes in evidence, and the diaphragm is distinctly flattened. The flat diaphragm is most impressive in a lateral view of the chest. In severe TTN some pulmonary interstitial edema is evident, sometimes in multiple focal areas. Occasionally pleural fluid is seen at the periphery, more frequently along interlobar fissures and costophrenic angles. There is very little in the chest radiograph of TTN to suggest the diagnostic possibility of hyaline membrane disease (RDS), but pneumonia cannot be excluded.

C. Hypoxemia is the rule; hypercarbia, if it occurs at all, is mild—not higher than 55 torr. Extreme hypercarbia is rare in TTN; if it is present another diagnosis must be seriously considered.

D. The major concern in differential diagnosis is pneumonia, usually caused by Group B *Streptococcus* but also by any other bacterial agent. An antenatal history that suggests a risk of intrauterine bacterial infection may be sufficient to justify antibiotic therapy. Total leukocyte count and differential are also suggestive. Serial CRP determinations are taken three times at 12-hour intervals (pp 106, 108, 109).

E. Treatment of RDS type II entails supplemental oxygen provided in a hood. Most often, relatively little FiO_2 supplementation oxygenates affected babies very effectively. Usually there is no need for repeated, frequent arterial blood gases, if transcutaneous PaO_2 and oxygen saturation monitoring are available. The need for CPAP and mechanical ventilation is sufficiently rare in RDS II to cast serious doubt on the diagnosis. If pneumonia is suspected by virtue of antenatal history or initial leukocyte count and differential, antibiotic therapy is appropriate. Severely affected babies require a high FiO_2, and they are thus clinically suspect for pneumonia regardless of initial laboratory results.

SBK

References

Avery ME, Fletcher BD, Williams RG. The lung and its disorders in the newborn infant. 4th ed. Philadelphia: WB Saunders, 1981:312.

Avery ME, Gatewood, OB, Brumley G. Transient tachypnea of the newborn: Possible delayed resorption of fluid at birth. Am J Dis Child 1966; 111:380–385.

Sundell H, Garrett J, Blankenship WJ, et al. Studies on infants with type II respiratory distress syndrome. J Pediatr 1971; 78:754.

Swischuk LE. Radiology of the newborn and young infant. Baltimore: Williams & Wilkins, 1980:58.

TRANSIENT TACHYPNEA OF THE NEWBORN (RDS TYPE II)

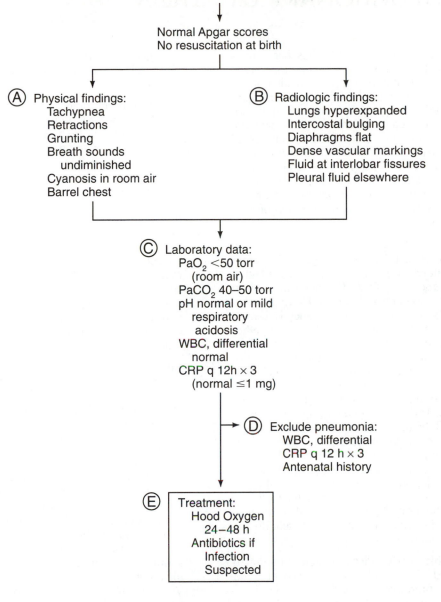

Normal Apgar scores
No resuscitation at birth

Ⓐ Physical findings:
   Tachypnea
   Retractions
   Grunting
   Breath sounds
      undiminished
   Cyanosis in room air
   Barrel chest

Ⓑ Radiologic findings:
   Lungs hyperexpanded
   Intercostal bulging
   Diaphragms flat
   Dense vascular markings
   Fluid at interlobar fissures
   Pleural fluid elsewhere

Ⓒ Laboratory data:
   PaO$_2$ <50 torr
      (room air)
   PaCO$_2$ 40–50 torr
   pH normal or mild
      respiratory
      acidosis
   WBC, differential
      normal
   CRP q 12h × 3
      (normal ≤1 mg)

Ⓓ Exclude pneumonia:
   WBC, differential
   CRP q 12 h × 3
   Antenatal history

Ⓔ Treatment:
   Hood Oxygen
      24–48 h
   Antibiotics if
   Infection
   Suspected

BRONCHOPULMONARY DYSPLASIA

A. Bronchopulmonary dysplasia (BPD) has been traditionally described as a sequela to hyaline membrane disease and the ventilatory support entailed in its management. However, BPD follows an array of pulmonary disorders, and the common denominator for all of them is treatment with positive pressure ventilation (PPV). We have not seen an infant treated solely in an oxygen hood or on CPAP who subsequently developed BPD. The primary source of injury during PPV is barotrauma. The role of oxygen toxicity is very real, but without accompanying barotrauma BPD does not seem to follow administration of high concentrations of oxygen.

B. Although injurious changes are no doubt already in progress, the signs of BPD usually become apparent after approximately 2 postnatal weeks. Most affected babies are still receiving PPV. The need for oxygen does not diminish as expected; indeed Fio_2 must often be increased. $Paco_2$ rises and the tendency is to raise PIP in an attempt to lower the $Paco_2$. The x-ray, rather than improving, now reflects the acute injury, which is primarily alveolar wall and capillary endothelial damage, accumulation of exudate and cellular debris in small airways, and a crippling of mucociliary function that permits accumulation of intraluminal airway detritus. The early radiologic consequences, often seen as patchy and linear densities, are primarily caused by interstitial edema and some alveolar collapse. Small bubbles within the radiodensities represent initial stages of localized air trapping. Elsewhere regional hyperinflation may be evident; it is also the beginning of more extensive air trapping if the disease progresses. At this point be certain that the predominant functional disruption is not due to patent ductus arteriosus or to pneumonia.

C. To manage this early disease state, minimize barotrauma and Fio_2, and ascertain proper fluid volume to avoid fluid overload and enhanced pulmonary edema. To minimize PIPs, we accept $Paco_2$ as high as 65 torr, provided that the pH remains at 7.25. Maintenance of this pH in the face of a high $Paco_2$ requires renal retention of bicarbonate for compensation of respiratory acidosis. This requires several days for full development. The response to diuretics at this stage of the disease is irregular. If the desired response to diuretics ensues, $Paco_2$ diminishes with little or no need to increase barotrauma by raising the PIP. The use of steroids early in the disease is now widespread. Despite several encouraging reports describing short-term effectiveness of steroids, acceptable documentation and elucidation of issues such as long-term outcome and complications have yet to be reported.

D. Onset of the chronic phase of the disease cannot be clearly delineated. Reparative processes proceed as acute destructive ones progress. When repair is the predominant ongoing process, chronic disease is clinically discernible. Acute episodes of bronchospasm appear; some are life-threatening. Ventilator settings must be augmented. The lungs are exquisitely sensitive to fluid excess; inordinate weight gain due to fluid overload usually indicates excess pulmonary fluid. The x-ray continues to reflect densities, which are now augmented and are also caused by areas of atelectasis. Focal and regional hyperexpansion are more prominent. Blebs sometime progress to large, space-occupying cysts. Fibrosis is discernible throughout the lung. The general pattern is bilateral hyperexpansion that often flattens the diaphragm and produces a smaller than usual heart shadow, unless cor pulmonale supersedes to cause cardiac enlargement.

E. Management requires a broad spectrum of activities, discreetly applied. Monitor blood gases with minimum skin pricking for blood samples to avoid hypoxia and spurious laboratory results. Ventilator settings should maintain Pao_2 and $Paco_2$ at levels described above. Pulmonary vasculature is particularly sensitive to marginal hypoxia; resultant vasoconstriction contributes to the ultimate evolution of cor pulmonale. Diuretics (furosemide) is a mainstay, best given periodically at the longest intervals the baby can tolerate while averting abnormal serum electrolytes. Ongoing bronchodilation may be achieved with daily theophylline to maintain blood levels at 12–15 mg/L. Acute bronchospastic episodes are treated with β-adrenergic agonists by nebulization of isoetharine (Bronkosol), metaproterenol (Alupent), or albuterol (Proventil, Ventolin). If Fio_2 is <0.8, approximately half of our acutely bronchospastic babies respond to transient elevation of PIP and an Fio_2 raised to 1. At many centers these nebulizations are ongoing q 6–8 hours. Pharmacologic therapy is detailed and complex (see References for extensive discussion). Adequate nutrition for the baby with chronic lung disease often requires more than the usual 120 kcal/kg/day. Caloric density of formula is usually increased to minimize chances of fluid overload.

SBK

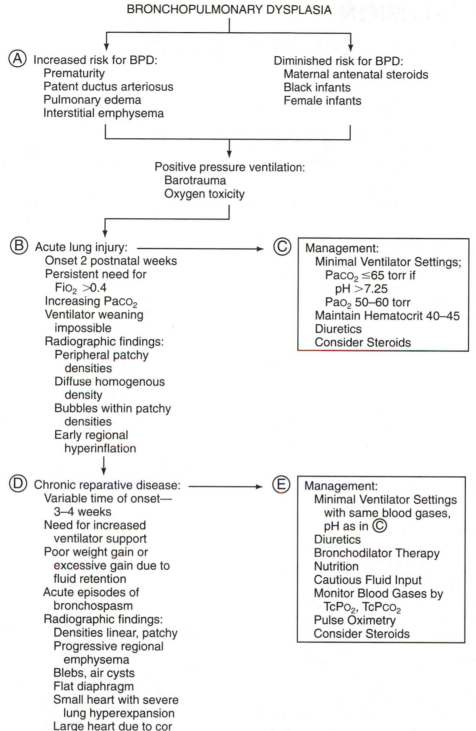

BRONCHOPULMONARY DYSPLASIA

Ⓐ Increased risk for BPD:
   Prematurity
   Patent ductus arteriosus
   Pulmonary edema
   Interstitial emphysema

Diminished risk for BPD:
   Maternal antenatal steroids
   Black infants
   Female infants

Positive pressure ventilation:
   Barotrauma
   Oxygen toxicity

Ⓑ Acute lung injury: ⟶ Ⓒ
   Onset 2 postnatal weeks
   Persistent need for
     FiO_2 >0.4
   Increasing $PaCO_2$
   Ventilator weaning
     impossible
   Radiographic findings:
     Peripheral patchy
       densities
     Diffuse homogenous
       density
     Bubbles within patchy
       densities
     Early regional
       hyperinflation

Ⓒ Management:
   Minimal Ventilator Settings;
     $PaCO_2$ ≤65 torr if
     pH >7.25
   PaO_2 50–60 torr
   Maintain Hematocrit 40–45
   Diuretics
   Consider Steroids

Ⓓ Chronic reparative disease: ⟶ Ⓔ
   Variable time of onset—
     3–4 weeks
   Need for increased
     ventilator support
   Poor weight gain or
     excessive gain due to
     fluid retention
   Acute episodes of
     bronchospasm
   Radiographic findings:
     Densities linear, patchy
     Progressive regional
       emphysema
     Blebs, air cysts
     Flat diaphragm
     Small heart with severe
       lung hyperexpansion
     Large heart due to cor
       pulmonale

Ⓔ Management:
   Minimal Ventilator Settings
     with same blood gases,
     pH as in Ⓒ
   Diuretics
   Bronchodilator Therapy
   Nutrition
   Cautious Fluid Input
   Monitor Blood Gases by
     $TcPO_2$, $TcPCO_2$
   Pulse Oximetry
   Consider Steroids

References

Avery GB. Bronchopulmonary dysplasia. In: Nelson WM, ed. Current therapy in neonatal-perinatal medicine. 2nd ed. Philadelphia: BC Decker, 1990.

Bancalari E, Gerhardt T. Bronchopulmonary dysplasia. Pediatr Clin North Am 1986; 33:1.

Bancalari E, Stocker JT, eds. Bronchopulmonary dysplasia. Washington, DC: Hemisphere, 1988.

Blanchard PW, Brown TM, Coates AL. Pharmacotherapy in bronchopulmonary dysplasia. Clin Perinatol 1987; 14:881.

Korones SB. Complications. In: Goldsmith JP, Karotkin EH, eds. Assisted ventilation of the neonate. 2nd ed. Philadelphia: WB Saunders, 1988:245.

Merritt TA, Northway WH Jr, Boynton BR, eds. Bronchopulmonary dysplasia. Boston: Blackwell Scientific, 1988.

O'Brodovich HM, Mellins RB. State of the art: Bronchopulmonary dysplasia: Unresolved neonatal acute lung injury. Am Rev Respir Dis 1985; 132:694.

PLEURAL EFFUSION
(HYDROTHORAX AND CHYLOTHORAX)

A. This discussion is limited to pleural effusion in the absence of hydrops fetalis or the accumulation of fluid in other serous cavities. Antenatal diagnosis of pleural effusion has increased with use of ultrasound. Primary fetal hydrothorax may involve a negligible quantity of fluid causing no difficulty, or it may be the first indication of a progressive process that culminates in hydrops fetalis. Pleural fluid may accumulate sufficiently to displace the mediastinum and pose a threat to fetal survival. Intrauterine thoracentesis is performed in these circumstances. Placement of a pleuroamniotic shunt has been reported to be successful on several occasions when recurrent reaccumulation of pleural fluid was life-threatening. Intrauterine intervention is not indicated for unilateral effusions that occur late in gestation and do not displace the mediastinum. Mortality among such fetuses is negligible. In numerous instances, serial ultrasound examinations have revealed spontaneous resolution of fluid accumulations. Pleural fluid during the second trimester may lead to pulmonary hypoplasia on the affected side. Polyhydramnios sometimes calls attention to the need for ultrasound evaluation, subsequently revealing the presence of fluid in the pleural space. Bilateral effusion is usually a component of hydrops fetalis.

B. Before the use of ultrasound became pervasive for management of pregnancy, pleural effusion (usually described as chylothorax) was described as a de novo event soon after birth or later by several days. The later diagnoses probably resulted from rapid fluid accumulation following the institution of oral feedings. However, the incidence of intrauterine onset is unknown, and the frequency of prenatal onset in many of these babies is more apparent with the use of ultrasound. In the vast majority of cases fluid accumulation is limited to the right hemithorax. Left-sided involvement is rare. If the effusion begins in the second or perhaps early third trimester, pulmonary hypoplasia may add to the respiratory distress. The x-ray study characteristically indicates fluid density in the pleural space that, in its most severe expression, displaces the mediastinum and depresses the ipsilateral diaphragm. The disease process may be short, requiring but one chest tap. In the extreme case, it may persist for months requiring numerous thoracenteses followed by continuous drainage through a pleural tube. Ultimately, a few babies require surgery to locate a disrupted thoracic duct. Most cases go unexplained. A few are secondary to another event such as chest surgery, thrombosis of the superior vena cava from a centrally placed catheter, lymphangiectasia and, rarely pneumonia in the neonate. Before oral feedings or administration of intravenous lipids, the fluid is clear and pale yellow. The vast majority of cells are lymphocytes. Protein concentration is 2–4 g/dl. Oral feeding imparts a milky or opalescent appearance to the fluid.

C. Treatment is aimed at fluid evacuation and prevention of reaccumulation. After 4 or 5 chest taps, accumulation is probably best controlled by pleural tube placement and continuous drainage. During the course of treatment the aggregate volume of fluid removed has been reported as high as 3000 ml. Monitoring for abnormalities of serum electrolytes and protein and maintenance of fluid balance are obligatory. Oral feeding with standard formulas that contain long-chain fatty acids seems to stimulate greater accumulation of fluid because lymphatic absorption from the gut increases several fold after feedings. Formulas containing medium-chain triglycerides (MCT) are preferred because MCT are not absorbed into the lymphatics and do not stimulate as great a flow of chyle. However, this desirable response to the MCT formulas has not been observed consistently.

SBK

References

Avery ME, Fletcher BD, Williams RG. The lung and its disorders in the newborn infant. 4th ed. Philadelphia: WB Saunders, 1981:197.

Dhande V, Kattwinkel J, Alford B. Recurrent bilateral pleural effusions secondary to superior vena cava obstruction as a complication of central venous catheterization. Pediatrics 1983; 72:109–113.

Longaker MT, Laberge J-M, Dansereau J, et al. Primary fetal hydrothorax: Natural history and management. J Pediatr Surg 1989; 24:573–576.

Swischuk LE. Radiology of the newborn and young infant. 2nd ed. Baltimore: Williams & Wilkins, 1980:152.

Van Aerde J, Campbell AN, Smyth JA, et al. Spontaneous chylothorax in newborns. Am J Dis Child 1984; 138:961–964.

PLEURAL EFFUSION (HYDROTHORAX, CHYLOTHORAX)

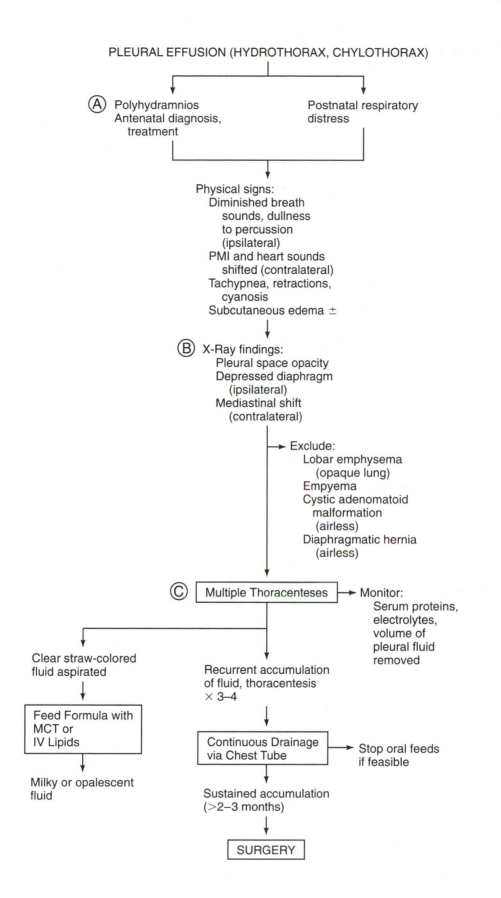

Ⓐ Polyhydramnios
Antenatal diagnosis,
treatment

Postnatal respiratory
distress

Physical signs:
  Diminished breath
    sounds, dullness
    to percussion
    (ipsilateral)
  PMI and heart sounds
    shifted (contralateral)
  Tachypnea, retractions,
    cyanosis
  Subcutaneous edema ±

Ⓑ X-Ray findings:
  Pleural space opacity
  Depressed diaphragm
    (ipsilateral)
  Mediastinal shift
    (contralateral)

→ Exclude:
    Lobar emphysema
      (opaque lung)
    Empyema
    Cystic adenomatoid
      malformation
      (airless)
    Diaphragmatic hernia
      (airless)

Ⓒ Multiple Thoracenteses → Monitor:
    Serum proteins,
    electrolytes,
    volume of
    pleural fluid
    removed

Clear straw-colored
fluid aspirated

Recurrent accumulation
of fluid, thoracentesis
× 3–4

Feed Formula with
MCT or
IV Lipids

Milky or opalescent
fluid

Continuous Drainage
via Chest Tube → Stop oral feeds
                   if feasible

Sustained accumulation
(>2–3 months)

SURGERY

MASSIVE PULMONARY HEMORRHAGE

A. Massive pulmonary hemorrhage is clinically recognizable; interstitial and alveolar hemorrhage are usually recognized only at autopsy. Massive pulmonary hemorrhage is a life-threatening episode that complicates a preexisting disorder. The reported associations with risk factors such as prematurity, intrauterine undergrowth, and maternal toxemia merely indicate risks for the occurrence of these preexisting disorders. We could not find a recent review of massive pulmonary hemorrhage as it is currently encountered in the NICU. Most recently pulmonary hemorrhage has occurred on numerous occasions in association with exogenous surfactant administration. Severe asphyxia, symptomatic patent ductus arteriosus (PDA), hyaline membrane disease (HMD), and pneumonia (particularly that due to gram-negative bacilli) are the most frequent antecedents to massive pulmonary hemorrhage. We have not seen spontaneous hemorrhage in a previously well infant or in one not supported by mechanical ventilation.

B. Laceration of the lung occurs during chest tube insertion with a relatively inflexible plastic tube, particularly one fitted with a stylus or trocar. Routine airway suction may yield impressive quantities of blood if airway mucosa is traumatized. This occurs if the suction catheter is advanced to the point of wedging prior to its withdrawal during applied suction. We have not seen hemorrhage during suction because depth of insertion was limited to the level of the endotracheal tube tip.

C. Babies with pulmonary hemorrhage are virtually always on mechanical ventilatory support. Generally oxygenation has been adequate, and they become abruptly hypoxic, often breathing in opposition to the ventilator with severe retractions. Blood may well up into the endotracheal tube spontaneously or during endotracheal suction instituted to relieve apparent airway obstruction. In a few instances, the vigorous airway support needed for severe asphyxia at birth is followed by a hemorrhagic episode.

D. Appearance of the chest film varies widely from clear lungs to total bilateral homogeneous opacity. The usual pattern is nodular, patchy, or widely linear densities peripheral to the hilar regions.

E. Bloody endotracheal fluid is most often a consequence of hemorrhagic edema. The hematocrit of this fluid has been shown to be considerably lower than blood, usually as low as 4–10%. Left heart failure and PDA are associated with this edematous type of hemorrhage. Hematocrit of circulating blood and blood pressure are unaffected by this type of pulmonary bleed. By contrast, laceration during chest tube insertion causes frank hemorrhage; the consequences of blood loss usually ensue. Pulmonary hemorrhage is rarely an isolated manifestation of a bleeding diathesis.

F. PEEP must be applied to levels as high as 8 cm H_2O, sometimes higher, to control bleeding by tamponade. Although airway suction must be performed initially, periodically repeated suction should be avoided unless hypoxemia or hypercarbia supervenes.

SBK

References

Avery ME, Fletcher BD, Williams RG. Pulmonary hemorrhage. In: The lung and its disorders in the newborn infant. Philadelphia: WB Saunders, 1981:303.

Rowe S, Avery ME. Massive pulmonary hemorrhage in the newborn: II. Clinical considerations. J Pediatr 1966; 69:12.

Trompeter R, Yu VYH, Aynsley-Green A, Roberton NRC. Massive pulmonary haemorrhage in the newborn infant. Arch Dis Child 1975; 50:123.

MASSIVE PULMONARY HEMORRHAGE

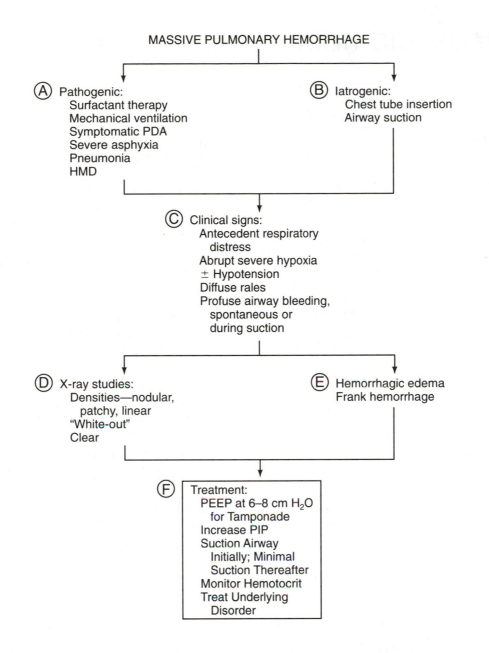

Ⓐ Pathogenic:
  Surfactant therapy
  Mechanical ventilation
  Symptomatic PDA
  Severe asphyxia
  Pneumonia
  HMD

Ⓑ Iatrogenic:
  Chest tube insertion
  Airway suction

Ⓒ Clinical signs:
  Antecedent respiratory
    distress
  Abrupt severe hypoxia
  ± Hypotension
  Diffuse rales
  Profuse airway bleeding,
    spontaneous or
    during suction

Ⓓ X-ray studies:
  Densities—nodular,
    patchy, linear
  "White-out"
  Clear

Ⓔ Hemorrhagic edema
  Frank hemorrhage

Ⓕ Treatment:
  PEEP at 6–8 cm H_2O
    for Tamponade
  Increase PIP
  Suction Airway
    Initially; Minimal
    Suction Thereafter
  Monitor Hemotocrit
  Treat Underlying
    Disorder

DIAPHRAGMATIC HERNIA

A. Antenatal diagnosis is made by ultrasound, which is often performed because of suspected polyhydramnios. In a transverse view, the most reliable sign is a fluid-filled retrocardiac mass. Absence of an abdominal stomach and mediastinal shift also indicate diaphragmatic hernia. Perform continuous prenatal evaluations and delivery at a tertiary-level perinatal center once fetal diaphragmatic hernia is suspected.

B. Mortality has changed little during the past few decades, despite the enhanced effectiveness of neonatal intensive care. Survival rates are particularly poor when there are associated cardiac anomalies. Ninety-nine percent of herniations are unilateral, 90% are on the left side, and 85 to 90% are posterolateral (foramen of Bochdalek). Respiratory distress is the common denominator of all early signs, with an onset that varies from birth to 24 hours later. Severe signs and early onsets are apparently functions of hernia size and therefore the extent of pulmonary hypoplasia. An enlarged chest and diminished abdominal girth (scaphoid) depend on the amount of herniated viscera (stomach, intestine, liver, spleen). Total stomach herniation is associated with high mortality. Breath sounds are usually diminished on the side of the hernia, but displacement of the mediastinum may be so extensive and underexpansion of the contralateral lung so severe as to markedly decrease breath sounds all over the chest. Onset of respiratory distress may be delayed in right-sided hernias; they often primarily involve protrusion of the liver through the diaphragm. This type of hernia sometimes is asymptomatic during mechanical ventilatory support, only to appear when the support is weaned. This phenomenon has been noted on several occasions during management of group B streptococcal infection.

C. Assiduous assessment for associated major anomalies is mandatory. They have been reported in ≥50% of affected infants and are associated with at least twice the mortality of uncomplicated diaphragmatic hernias. The mortality of infants with major cardiac malformation is reportedly as high as 80%.

D. Radiographs should include chest and abdomen and usually suffice for diagnosis. Placement of a nasogastric (NG) tube before the x-ray aids in identifying location of the stomach and in the orientation to other thoracic organs, particularly in early films that are gasless. Be particularly careful to identify right and left sides on the x-ray. Abnormal abdominal gas pattern or absence of gas is characteristic. In a few instances, instillation of a small quantity of air or radiopaque dye may be necessary to ascertain the diagnosis. Ultrasound is helpful in questionable cases.

E. Resuscitation differs little from the advised procedures for any depressed infant, except for mandatory avoidance of distention of the herniated stomach and intestine. Respiratory support must therefore utilize an endotracheal (ET) tube; use of a mask is contraindicated.

F. At the earliest possible moment put in place a large-bore gastric tube (oral) with applied intermittent suction. Prompt placement of arterial and venous lines is also urgent. Respiratory support should entail the lowest possible pressures needed to maintain Pao_2 >80 torr if feasible. Low pressures diminish the high vulnerability to pneumothorax. Maintenance of a Pao_2 at higher levels than usual is intended to heighten the troughs in the fluctuating oxygen level that characterizes the ventilatory course of affected infants. The sensitivity of pulmonary vasculature to marginal oxygenation may exacerbate the difficulty in maintaining oxygenation because of pulmonary vasospasm (persistent fetal circulation, PFC). For the same reason, pH should be as high as is reasonable; serum glucose and calcium should be monitored frequently. An inordinate sensitivity to slight fluid overload superimposes pulmonary edema.

G. Postoperatively, infants are more likely to survive if they experience a "honeymoon" period of 12 to 24 hours. This is often followed by deterioration. To minimize chances of PFC, ventilatory efforts to maintain the highest feasible Pao_2 on an Fio_2 of 1 should continue for approximately 4 days even if oxygenation appears to be generous. Other measures used preoperatively are continued during the postoperative period.

SBK

References

Benjamin DR, Juul S, Siebert JR. Congenital posterolateral diaphragmatic hernia: Associated malformations. J Pediatr Surg 1988; 23:899.

Cunniff C, Jones KL, Jones MC. Patterns of malformation in children with congenital diaphragmatic defects. J Pediatr 1990; 116:258.

Gleeson F. Pitfalls in the diagnosis of congenital diaphragmatic hernia. Arch Dis Child 1991; 66:670.

Levin DL. Congenital diaphragmatic hernia: A persistent problem. J Pediatr 1987; 111:390.

Levy RJ, Rosenthal A, Freed MD, et al. Persistent pulmonary hypertension in a newborn with congenital diaphragmatic hernia: Successful management with tolazoline. Pediatrics 1977; 60:740.

Rogers BM. Congenital diaphragmatic hernia. In: Nelson NM, ed. Current therapy in neonatal-perinatal medicine. 2nd ed. Philadelphia: BC Decker, 1990:206.

DIAPHRAMAGTIC HERNIA

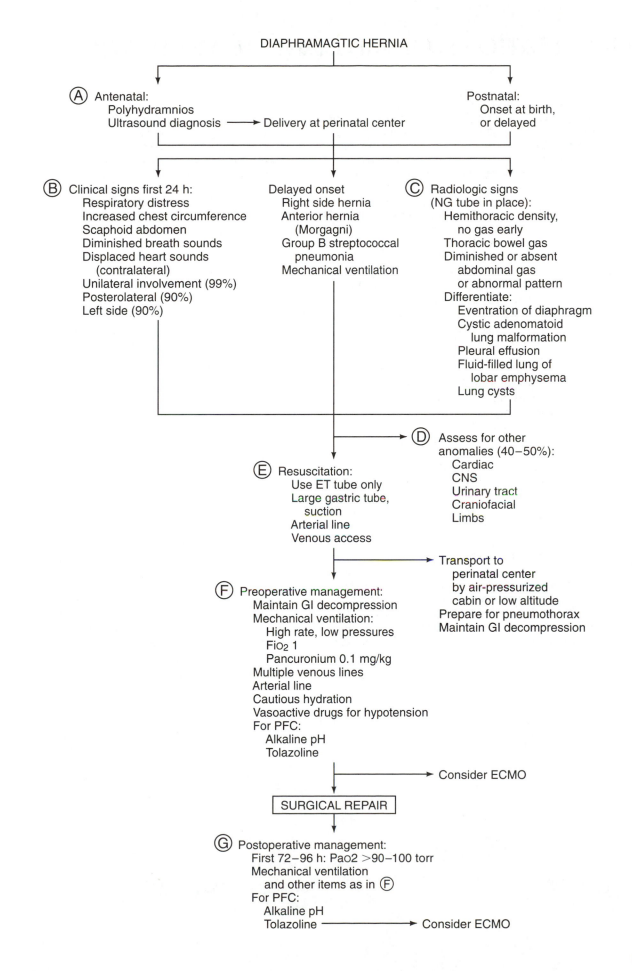

Ⓐ Antenatal:
   Polyhydramnios
   Ultrasound diagnosis ——→ Delivery at perinatal center

Postnatal:
   Onset at birth,
   or delayed

Ⓑ Clinical signs first 24 h:
   Respiratory distress
   Increased chest circumference
   Scaphoid abdomen
   Diminished breath sounds
   Displaced heart sounds
      (contralateral)
   Unilateral involvement (99%)
   Posterolateral (90%)
   Left side (90%)

Delayed onset
   Right side hernia
   Anterior hernia
      (Morgagni)
   Group B streptococcal
      pneumonia
   Mechanical ventilation

Ⓒ Radiologic signs
   (NG tube in place):
      Hemithoracic density,
         no gas early
      Thoracic bowel gas
      Diminished or absent
         abdominal gas
         or abnormal pattern
   Differentiate:
      Eventration of diaphragm
      Cystic adenomatoid
         lung malformation
      Pleural effusion
      Fluid-filled lung of
         lobar emphysema
      Lung cysts

Ⓓ Assess for other
   anomalies (40–50%):
      Cardiac
      CNS
      Urinary tract
      Craniofacial
      Limbs

Ⓔ Resuscitation:
   Use ET tube only
   Large gastric tube,
      suction
   Arterial line
   Venous access

Transport to
   perinatal center
   by air-pressurized
   cabin or low altitude
Prepare for pneumothorax
Maintain GI decompression

Ⓕ Preoperative management:
   Maintain GI decompression
   Mechanical ventilation:
      High rate, low pressures
      Fio₂ 1
      Pancuronium 0.1 mg/kg
   Multiple venous lines
   Arterial line
   Cautious hydration
   Vasoactive drugs for hypotension
   For PFC:
      Alkaline pH
      Tolazoline

→ Consider ECMO

[SURGICAL REPAIR]

Ⓖ Postoperative management:
   First 72–96 h: Pao2 >90–100 torr
   Mechanical ventilation
      and other items as in Ⓕ
   For PFC:
      Alkaline pH
      Tolazoline ——————→ Consider ECMO

COMPLICATIONS OF MECHANICAL VENTILATION

A. Endotrachial tube problems (abrupt onset): deterioration of blood gases is often the result of malposition or occlusion of the endotracheal tube. Differentiation from pneumothorax is urgent (p 142). In the smallest infants, tube dislocation may occur because of infant movement, whether spontaneous or imposed. Downward displacement of but a few millimeters causes serious underventilation of one lung, the function of which is marginal even in circumstances of optimal airflow. In the smallest infants, chest expansion and bilateral intensity of breath sounds usually appear to be adequate, yet the effect on blood gases is similar to initial misplacement of a tube into the right main bronchus. Slight withdrawal of the endotracheal tube rapidly rectifies blood gas abnormalities (indicated on transcutaneous monitors) if the tube is not occluded.

Occlusion by inspissated secretions or clotted blood causes hypoxemia and hypercarbia. In the extreme, chest expansion and breath sounds are virtually absent. Occlusion by viscous fluid, by contrast, is more likely to cause hypercarbia, while oxygenation remains normal. This type of occlusion is often associated with accumulation of secretions at levels below the tip of the tube.

Postextubation atelectasis usually affects the right upper lobe, but multilobar involvement is not unusual. The incidence of atelectasis can be minimized by two or three sessions of assiduous chest percussion and airway suction at 10- to 20-minute intervals before extubation. Chest percussion and oropharyngeal suction should be performed after extubation.

B. Endotracheal tube problems (gradual onset): laryngeal edema is first perceived after extubation, often several hours later. The use of steroids and racemic epinephrine is not consistently successful. If reintubation is necessary, a smaller tube is sometimes helpful. Suction catheter injury and oversized endotracheal tubes may cause tracheal occlusion and subglottic stenosis. Nasal edema and infection occur with the use of nasotracheal tubes. Prolonged intubation is occasionally associated with a midline groove in the hard palate that is unrelated to the position of the orotracheal tube. The palatal groove eventually disappears spontaneously. Necrotic tracheobronchitis is a serious, infrequent complication that causes complete tracheal occlusion by sequestration of necrotic epithelium. The onset of clinical deterioration may be surprisingly abrupt. Bronchoscopy is required to clear the trachea.

Tissue injury to the larynx and trachea is more likely with inappropriately large tubes. A 2.5-mm tube should be used for babies whose birth weights are <1300 g, a 3-mm tube for weights between 1300 and 3500 g, and a 3.5-mm tube for larger infants. These weight intervals are approximate. Judgment must be applied when a tube fits too tightly upon insertion.

C. Extraneous air syndromes (air leaks) are discussed on p 142.

D. For patent ductus arteriosus, see p 162; pulmonary hemorrhage, p 136; and bronchopulmonary dysplasia, p 132.

SBK

References

Joshi V, Mandavia S, Stern L, et al. Acute lesions induced by endotracheal intubation. Am J Dis Child 1972; 124:646.

Kirpalani H, Higa T, Perlman M, et al. Diagnosis and therapy of necrotizing tracheobronchitis in ventilated neonates. Crit Care Med 1985; 13:792.

Papsidero MJ, Pashley NRT. Acquired stenosis of the upper airway in neonates. Ann Otol Rhinol Laryngol 1980; 89:512.

String R, Possy V. Endotracheal intubation: Complications in neonates. Arch Otolaryngol 1977; 103:329.

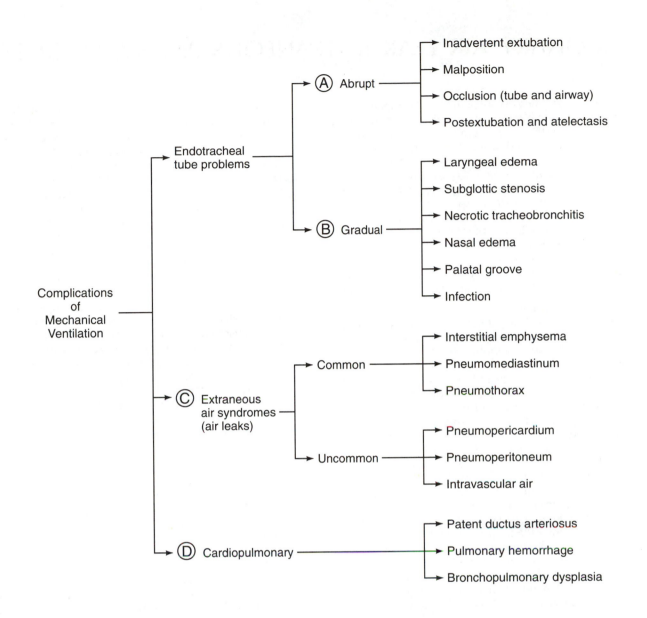

Complications of Mechanical Ventilation

Endotracheal tube problems
- (A) Abrupt
  - Inadvertent extubation
  - Malposition
  - Occlusion (tube and airway)
  - Postextubation and atelectasis
- (B) Gradual
  - Laryngeal edema
  - Subglottic stenosis
  - Necrotic tracheobronchitis
  - Nasal edema
  - Palatal groove
  - Infection

(C) Extraneous air syndromes (air leaks)
- Common
  - Interstitial emphysema
  - Pneumomediastinum
  - Pneumothorax
- Uncommon
  - Pneumopericardium
  - Pneumoperitoneum
  - Intravascular air

(D) Cardiopulmonary
- Patent ductus arteriosus
- Pulmonary hemorrhage
- Bronchopulmonary dysplasia

PULMONARY AIR LEAK (EXTRANEOUS AIR SYNDROMES)

A. Air leak syndromes originate in alveolar rupture, with the exception of puncturing trauma. Air from ruptured alveoli enters the interstitium. When it accumulates within the lungs and without extension, pulmonary interstitial emphysema (PIE) results. When it dissects to the hilum and into the pleural, pericardial, or anterior mediastinal spaces, clinical signs appear, depending on the location of extraneous air accumulation. Air also enters lymphatics and migrates to form subpleural blebs, which may then rupture into the pleural space. Pneumoperitoneum occurs when air dissects through the diaphragm by way of the esophageal aperture. Fatal air emboli are produced by extremely high ventilator pressures, forcing air into lacerated pulmonary vessels.

B. Accumulation of interstitial air imposes diffusion barriers, compresses vessels to diminish perfusion, and diminishes lung compliance. On x-ray the lung is hyperexpanded and generally studded with radiolucencies that vary in size and in contour from cystic to cylindrical. In the extreme, a profusion of air cysts imparts a bubbly appearance on x-ray throughout both lungs. Although increased ventilatory pressures are required for the maintenance of adequate blood gases in these circumstances, the need for the lowest possible pressures is an overriding consideration. The use of high-frequency ventilators is reportedly effective. When PIE is unilateral, selective intubation of the unaffected lung collapses the affected one. If adequate gas exchange is feasible for 6–24 h in the single expanded lung, PIE is usually eliminated from the therapeutically collapsed lung. PIE may progress to other air leak syndromes, most frequently to pneumothorax. A high incidence of PIE during the first 24 hours has been noted in infants who later develop bronchopulmonary dysplasia.

C. Spontaneous pneumomediastinum occurs during the first few breaths, usually in term infants. It also occurs occasionally in babies with respiratory distress syndrome (RDS) II (TTN). Spontaneous pneumomediastinum has been reported in 2.5/1000 live births. It is usually asymptomatic in these circumstances. Pneumomediastinum also occurs during mechanical ventilatory support. In the absence of other air leak syndromes, treatment requires only hood oxygen. Rarely, massive mediastinal air may seriously impede cardiac venous return, requiring evacuation of air by tube insertion into the mediastinum. X-ray of the chest in the anteroposterior view occasionally reveals an uplifted thymus ("sail sign") but more frequently fails to reveal mediastinal air; a lateral projection is diagnostic.

D. Effective management of pneumothorax begins with frequent auscultation of the chest in all infants who are on mechanical ventilatory support. Pneumothorax is often suspected early in its course when distinctly diminished breath sounds are heard unilaterally. In abrupt and severe cases there may not be time for x-ray confirmation. Diminished breath sounds and contralateral shift of heart sounds are indications for relief of a tension pneumothorax by needle aspiration. Transillumination usually confirms these physical findings, but there are pitfalls to be avoided. Large babies with thick chest walls transilluminate poorly, particularly in a partially darkened area of the nursery. Also, the chest often transilluminates impressively in small preterm babies with PIE. Furthermore, edema of the chest wall transmits light extensively in the absence of pneumothorax. Needle aspiration is a temporary therapeutic procedure; it is not advised for diagnosis of pneumothorax that is not suggested by physical signs and transillumination. Pneumothoraces occur most frequently during the first 3 postnatal days and are often associated with periventricular-intraventricular hemorrhage. They occur preponderantly in the sickest infants who require high ventilator pressures. They are also produced by indiscreetly high ventilator pressures. Pneumothorax may also occur spontaneously, mostly in term infants during the first few breaths and occasionally in babies with RDS II (TTN).

E. Pneumopericardium is usually life-threatening, but rarely an asymptomatic baby is serendipitously identified by x-ray. Overall mortality is approximately 50%. The most distinctive clinical features are produced by cardiac tamponade, including abrupt cyanosis, hypotension, and inaudible heart sounds in the presence of electrical cardiac activity reflected on the oscilloscope or ECG. X-ray reveals a radiolucent ring around the entire heart, including its inferior (diaphragmatic) surface. Air at the diaphragmatic cardiac surface is diagnostic. Pneumopericardium is usually accompanied by PIE or pneumothorax. Pericardial tap is urgently indicated to relieve tamponade, but air reaccumulates in approximately 50% of cases. An indwelling catheter for continuous closed drainage is thus required.

F. Pneumoperitoneum occurs when mediastinal air dissects into the peritoneal space through the diaphragmatic esophageal aperture. This manifestation of air leak syndrome must be differentiated from perforation of the GI tract. Presence of PIE or pneumothorax, plus absence of intestinal abnormality on x-ray and by clinical history, strongly suggests alveolar origin of free peritoneal air. Massive air accumulation in the peritoneum often precludes adequate diaphragmatic excursion. In these circumstances paracentesis is necessary for evacuation of the abdominal air.

G. Air emboli cause sudden circulatory collapse. The heart stops or beats only several times per minute. In the presence of even a feeble heartbeat, crepitus is sometimes audible during systole. The baby is pulseless and grossly mottled by randomly distributed

PULMONARY AIR LEAK

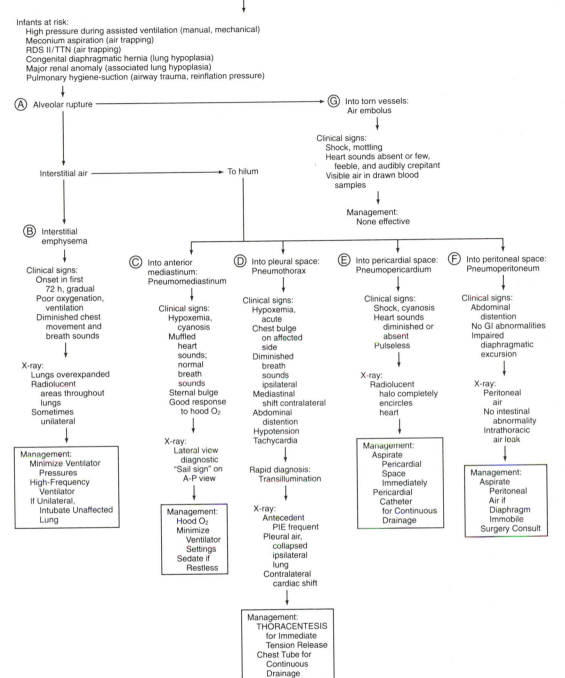

Infants at risk:
High pressure during assisted ventilation (manual, mechanical)
Meconium aspiration (air trapping)
RDS II/TTN (air trapping)
Congenital diaphragmatic hernia (lung hypoplasia)
Major renal anomaly (associated lung hypoplasia)
Pulmonary hygiene-suction (airway trauma, reinflation pressure)

(A) Alveolar rupture ⟶ (G) Into torn vessels:
Air embolus

Clinical signs:
Shock, mottling
Heart sounds absent or few,
feeble, and audibly crepitant
Visible air in drawn blood
samples

Management:
None effective

Interstitial air ⟶ To hilum

(B) Interstitial
emphysema

Clinical signs:
Onset in first
72 h, gradual
Poor oxygenation,
ventilation
Diminished chest
movement and
breath sounds

X-ray:
Lungs overexpanded
Radiolucent
areas throughout
lungs
Sometimes
unilateral

Management:
Minimize Ventilator
Pressures
High-Frequency
Ventilator
If Unilateral,
Intubate Unaffected
Lung

(C) Into anterior
mediastinum:
Pneumomediastinum

Clinical signs:
Hypoxemia,
cyanosis
Muffled
heart
sounds;
normal
breath
sounds
Sternal bulge
Good response
to hood O₂

X-ray:
Lateral view
diagnostic
"Sail sign" on
A-P view

Management:
Hood O₂
Minimize
Ventilator
Settings
Sedate if
Restless

(D) Into pleural space:
Pneumothorax

Clinical signs:
Hypoxemia,
acute
Chest bulge
on affected
side
Diminished
breath
sounds
ipsilateral
Mediastinal
shift contralateral
Abdominal
distention
Hypotension
Tachycardia

Rapid diagnosis:
Transillumination

X-ray:
Antecedent
PIE frequent
Pleural air,
collapsed
ipsilateral
lung
Contralateral
cardiac shift

Management:
THORACENTESIS
for Immediate
Tension Release
Chest Tube for
Continuous
Drainage

(E) Into pericardial space:
Pneumopericardium

Clinical signs:
Shock, cyanosis
Heart sounds
diminished or
absent
Pulseless

X-ray:
Radiolucent
halo completely
encircles
heart

Management:
Aspirate
Pericardial
Space
Immediately
Pericardial
Catheter
for Continuous
Drainage

(F) Into peritoneal space:
Pneumoperitoneum

Clinical signs:
Abdominal
distention
No GI abnormalities
Impaired
diaphragmatic
excursion

X-ray:
Peritoneal
air
No intestinal
abnormality
Intrathoracic
air leak

Management:
Aspirate
Peritoneal
Air if
Diaphragm
Immobile
Surgery Consult

blanched and purple skin areas. Segments of air, similar to that expected when a stopcock connection is loose, are sometimes encountered when a blood sample is drawn. There is no effective treatment for air embolus.

SBK

References

Allen RW Jr, Jung AL, Lester PD. Effectiveness of chest tube evacuation of pneumothorax in neonates. J Pediatr 1981; 99:629.

Fletcher MA, Eichelberger MR. Thoracostomy tubes. In: Fletcher MA, MacDonald MG, Avery GB, eds. Atlas of procedures in neonatology. Philadelphia: JB Lippincott Company, 1983:259.

Fletcher MA, Eichelberger MR. Pericardial tubes. In: Fletcher MA, MacDonald MG, Avery GB, eds. Atlas of procedures in neonatology. Philadelphia: JB Lippincott, 1983:281.

Korones SB. Complications. In Goldsmith JP, Karotkin EK, eds. Assisted ventilation of the neonate. 2nd ed. Philadelphia: WB Saunders, 1988:245.

BRADYCARDIA

A. Bradycardia is defined as a heart rate <100/min. The normal neonatal heart rate is in the range of 120–160/min. An ECG may suggest abnormalities in axis, chamber size, or rhythm. A low heart rate does not necessarily represent an abnormal rhythm; sinus bradycardia is often demonstrated by the ECG strip. Differential diagnosis should also take into account whether the bradycardia is intermittent or persistent. A chest film demonstrates abnormalities in heart size and contour as well as associated lung disease if present.

B. Intermittent or transient sinus bradycardia may follow apneic episodes, as in apnea of prematurity or during certain procedures that could affect vagal tone, e.g., insertion of feeding tube, oropharyngeal suctioning during intubation, or while in a bent position during lumbar puncture. Infants with CNS disorder, infection either generalized or localized (e.g., pneumonia, necrotizing entercolitis), may have apneic and bradycardic episodes. ECG shows no disturbance in rhythm, with only a slow heart rate or sinus bradycardia during these episodes.

C. Intermittent bradycardia without apneic spells may be a presenting sign of intraventricular hemorrhage (IVH) or may represent a subtle form of seizures in the newborn.

D. Persistent sinus bradycardia may be observed in respiratory failure resulting from severe respiratory disorders such as hyaline membrane disease, pneumonia, or bronchopulmonary dysplasia.

E. In perinatal asphyxia, hypoxic myocardial injury could result in impaired cardiac contractility and bradycardia.

F. Drugs such as digoxin and dilantin may cause sinus bradycardia.

G. Infections, especially those with severe myocardial ischemia or septic shock, may be associated with sinus bradycardia.

H. Metabolic acidosis, hyperkalemia, hypercalcemia, and hypomagnesemia may be associated with bradycardia. In hyperkalemia QRS and P waves are widened, and PR interval is increased, finally leading to irregular ventricular activity and then standstill. Early hypomagnesemia may show changes similar to hyperkalemia.

I. Bradycardia may be observed in conditions associated with increased intracranial pressure and in hypothyroidism.

J. Persistent bradycardia may be observed in conduction disturbances (congenital complete heart block, first-degree atrioventricular [AV] block and second-degree AV block). The ECG shows complete electrical dissociation of the atria and ventricles. Half of infants with congenital complete heart block have associated cardiac malformations, e.g., L-corrected transposition of the great arteries, ventricular septal defect, or atrial septal defect. The diagnosis of congenital complete AV block may be made during pregnancy because of sustained fetal heart rate <100 bpm; hydrops fetalis may be an associated finding. A first-degree block may be a nonspecific conduction disturbance or may be associated with a heart lesion, e.g., common atrioventricular canal. The ECG shows a prolonged PR interval beyond 0.12 sec. The second-degree AV block may occur as a nonspecific conduction disturbance, or it may occur with supraventricular tachyarrhythmias.

HSB

References

Flyer DC, Lang P. Neonatal heart disease. In: Avery GB, ed. Neonatology: Pathophysiology and management of the newborn. 3rd ed. Philadelphia: JB Lippincott, 1987:493.

Rowe RD, Freedom RM, Mehrizi A. The neonate with congenital heart disease. Philadelphia: WB Saunders, 1981:545.

BRADYCARDIA

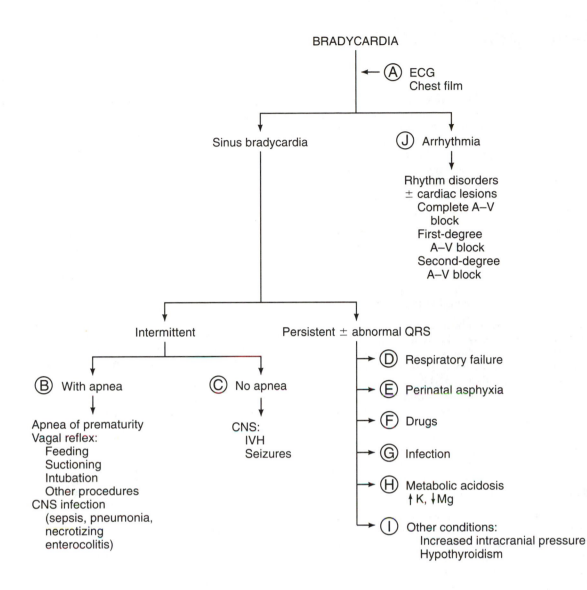

TACHYCARDIA

A. Newborn infants have heart rates of 120–160/min. *Tachycardia* is defined as a persistent heart rate ≥180/min. The assessment of an infant, particularly for color and presence or absence of respiratory distress (retractions), can give a clue to the underlying etiology of a rapid heart rate. Chest film demonstrates any abnormalities in lungs, heart size and contour, and other structures. The ECG is important in determining disturbances of rhythm as well as heart rate.

B. Sinus tachycardia in a cyanotic infant with no respiratory distress suggests an underlying nonpulmonary lesion. With an underlying cardiac defect, tachycardia may be an early sign of congestive heart failure. Sinus tachycardia may also be an early response to hypovolemia, hypoglycemia, hypothermia or infection.

C. In a cyanotic baby with chest retractions, a primary parenchymal lung disease is likely (e.g., pneumonia, respiratory distress syndrome, or extrapulmonary problems causing compromise of pulmonary air exchange, as in pneumothorax and hydrothorax). Heart abnormalities may cause severe or minimal respiratory distress with associated tachycardia, particularly with early heart failure. Abnormalities in thoracic structure may be severe enough to result in retractions, tachypnea, and tachycardia. In less severe lung, heart, or structural abnormalities, tachypnea and tachycardia may be evident but without cyanosis because Pa_{O_2} is maintained at adequate levels.

D. Tachycardia may result from drugs such as theophylline or caffeine used in apnea of prematurity or from bronchodilators such as albuterol, metaproterenol, and terbutaline, which may be utilized for treatment of bronchospasm in those with bronchopulmonary dysplasia. Pressors such as dopamine, dobutamine, and isoproterenol also cause tachycardia.

E. Tachycardia is a common manifestation of drug withdrawal (heroin, methadone, propoxyphene, pentazocine, and cocaine).

F. Pallor may be due to anemia or asphyxia. Pallor without respiratory distress with tachycardia most likely indicates chronic anemia. In asphyxia, myocardial dysfunction may be evident early as tachycardia; as hypoxia persists and significant myocardial damage occurs, bradycardia is observed. Infection (septicemia) may present with pallor and tachycardia.

G. A ruddy or plethoric infant with tachycardia suggests polycythemia/hyperviscosity syndrome. Some infants may have increased pulmonary vascular markings on chest film. In hyperthermia, both tachycardia and tachypnea may be evident.

H. Diagnosis of supraventricular tachycardia may be made in utero when fetal heart rate is >200 beats/min and when block occurs with consequent irregular tachycardia; it may be interpreted as fetal distress. Associated findings may include hydrops, congestive heart failure, or congenital heart defect. In 20%, onset is in the first week of life. Associated clinical signs include pallor, cyanosis, irritability, poor feeding, and vomiting. ECG shows a heart rate of 240–260/min and absent P waves. Wolff-Parkinson-White pattern with wide QRS may be observed in 10% of patients. Congestive heart failure results without treatment. As to treatment, digoxin is administered and is maintained for 1 year. Emergency cases require direct-current countershock (cardioversion) at 0.5-1 W sec/kg. If there is no response to digoxin, propranolol or verapamil is added; others have used amiodarone.

I. Atrial flutter is rare but may be detected in utero or at birth. Atrial rate of 400–460 beats/min and ventricular rate of 200–240/min have been observed. Because of AV block, congestive heart failure may not even develop. Treatment includes digoxin and cardioversion if necessary.

J. Atrial fibrillation is usually associated with congenital heart disease. ECG shows rapid, irregular atrial depolarization and irregular ventricular rate, 300/min. Clinical features and treatment are similar to supraventricular tachycardia.

K. Ventricular tachycardia is rare in neonates and tends to be associated with congenital heart disease, electrolyte disturbance, myocardial tumor, and infection. Idiopathic cases have been reported. Treatment includes cardioversion, infusion of lidocaine or diphenylhydantoin, or implantation of a transvenous pacemaker.

HSB

References

Flyer DC, Lang P. Neonatal heart disease. In: Avery GB, ed. Neonatology: Pathophysiology and management of the newborn. 3rd ed. Philadelphia: JB Lippincott, 1987:493.

Rowe RD, Freedom RM, Mehrizi A. The neonate with congenital heart disease. Philadelphia: WB Saunders, 1981:545.

TACHYCARDIA

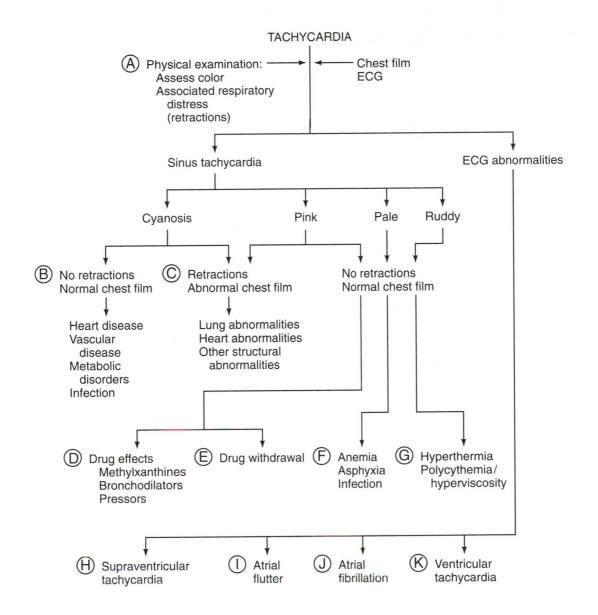

Ⓐ Physical examination: ⟶ ← Chest film
Assess color ECG
Associated respiratory
distress
(retractions)

Sinus tachycardia

ECG abnormalities

Cyanosis Pink Pale Ruddy

Ⓑ No retractions
Normal chest film

Ⓒ Retractions
Abnormal chest film

No retractions
Normal chest film

Heart disease
Vascular
disease
Metabolic
disorders
Infection

Lung abnormalities
Heart abnormalities
Other structural
abnormalities

Ⓓ Drug effects
Methylxanthines
Bronchodilators
Pressors

Ⓔ Drug withdrawal

Ⓕ Anemia
Asphyxia
Infection

Ⓖ Hyperthermia
Polycythemia/
hyperviscosity

Ⓗ Supraventricular
tachycardia

Ⓘ Atrial
flutter

Ⓙ Atrial
fibrillation

Ⓚ Ventricular
tachycardia

DIMINISHED HEART SOUNDS

A. A careful clinical assessment of an infant with diminished or muffled heart sounds is important since such findings may suggest a medical emergency. A sudden deterioration, cyanosis, severe respiratory distress, and narrow pulse pressure suggest conditions such as a pneumopericardium or tension pneumothorax. These complications should always be suspected when an infant has been requiring mechanical ventilation. Blood gases confirm a deoxygenated state as well as acidosis, which may be respiratory, metabolic, or combined respiratory and metabolic acidosis.

B. A chest film showing a radiolucent area or "halo" around a well-defined heart border indicates pneumopericardium. Needle aspiration (pericardial tap) is required in a rapidly deteriorating condition. Oxygenation is maintained by increasing FiO_2, and a continuous pericardial drainage may be necessary.

C. A normal or small heart with depressed diaphragm with lung markings observed throughout suggests overaeration from air trapping as in pulmonary interstitial emphysema.

D. Pneumomediastinum is indicated by a thymus shadow that is lifted ("sail sign") and a radiolucency is found anteriorly and around the heart.

E. In bilateral pneumothoraces, the lungs are compressed or small, but the extrapleural air depresses the diaphragm downward. Transillumination also aids in the diagnosis. Air must be aspirated immediately and a chest tube inserted.

F. Interstitial emphysema, pneumomediastinum, and pneumothoraces (air leak syndromes) are usually observed in babies requiring mechanical ventilation. Thus all these conditions benefit from additional supportive measures including oxygen therapy and adjustment of ventilator settings to lowest possible PIP, PEEP, flow rate, and rate. Patients may also require correction of associated metabolic acidosis as well as hypoperfusion that may result because of the antecedent hypoxic episode.

G. In hypoperfusion or shock, contractility of the myocardium is diminished and stroke volume is also reduced. Heart sounds may be faint and pulses thready. Volume expansion restores circulating volume; pressors improve cardiac function.

H. An enlarged globular heart suggests the presence of a pericardial effusion, primarily secondary to pericardial inflammation or pericarditis. The presence of pericardial effusion may be verified by echocardiography. This also differentiates effusion from enlarged heart. Other signs consistent with infection are usually evident. Pericardial tap would be required with clinical deterioration, and fluid is sent for Gram stain and culture (bacterial and/or viral). Continuous pericardial drainage may be needed.

HSB

References

Korones SB. High-risk newborn infants: The basis for intensive nursing care. St. Louis: Mosby–Year Book, 1986:249.

DIMINISHED HEART SOUNDS

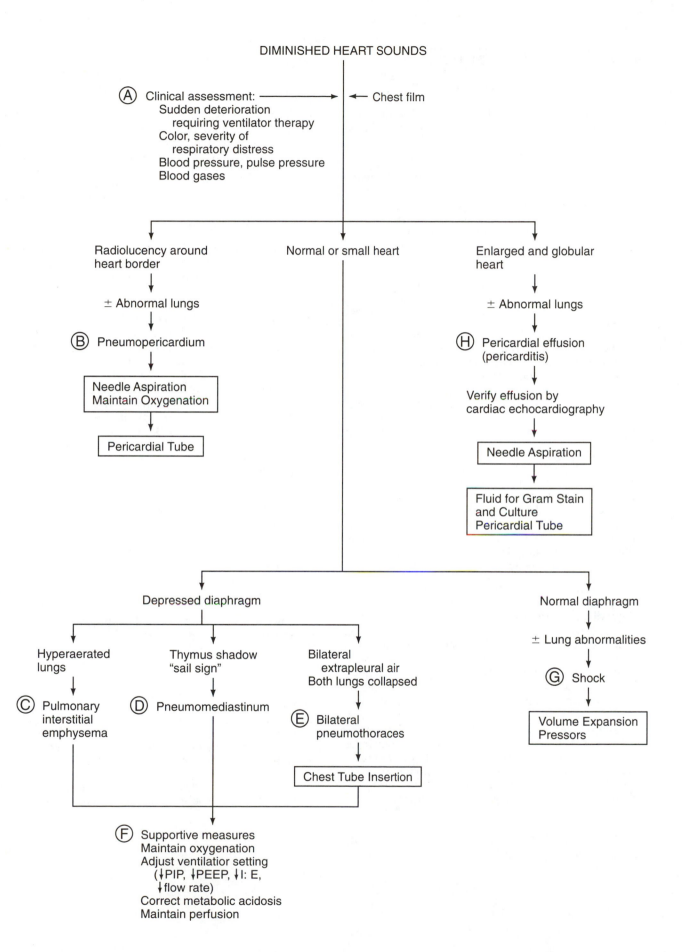

(A) Clinical assessment: ──────→ ←── Chest film
    Sudden deterioration
      requiring ventilator therapy
    Color, severity of
      respiratory distress
    Blood pressure, pulse pressure
    Blood gases

Radiolucency around   Normal or small heart   Enlarged and globular
heart border   heart

± Abnormal lungs   ± Abnormal lungs

(B) Pneumopericardium   (H) Pericardial effusion
                                                              (pericarditis)

| Needle Aspiration
Maintain Oxygenation |

                                              Verify effusion by
                                              cardiac echocardiography

| Pericardial Tube |

| Needle Aspiration |

| Fluid for Gram Stain
and Culture
Pericardial Tube |

Depressed diaphragm   Normal diaphragm

                                                  ± Lung abnormalities

Hyperaerated   Thymus shadow   Bilateral
lungs   "sail sign"   extrapleural air   (G) Shock
                                      Both lungs collapsed

(C) Pulmonary   (D) Pneumomediastinum
    interstitial   (E) Bilateral
    emphysema   pneumothoraces

| Volume Expansion
Pressors |

| Chest Tube Insertion |

(F) Supportive measures
    Maintain oxygenation
    Adjust ventilatior setting
      (↓PIP, ↓PEEP, ↓I: E,
        ↓flow rate)
    Correct metabolic acidosis
    Maintain perfusion

MEDIASTINAL SHIFT

A. Mediastinal shift is usually suspected because of a displaced PMI. The PMI palpated or heard outside its usual location may be due to dextroposition of the heart (i.e., mediastinal shift) or to dextrocardia.

B. Auscultation of breath sounds to determine whether they are diminished, absent, or normal bilaterally, unilaterally, or at specific areas (lobar or segmental) should aid in the clinical diagnosis. One needs to assess whether the abnormality in breath sounds is heard on the same side as the PMI or contralateral to the PMI.

C. Other clinical signs, e.g., the presence of cyanosis, severity of cardiorespiratory distress, and onset of cardiorespiratory distress, give clues as to the etiology of the mediastinal shift.

D. A chest film is required for a definitive diagnosis of most disorders associated with mediastinal shift. One should note the location of the cardiac apex, the presence of radiolucency without lung markings, radiodensities, air fluid level, collapsed lung lobe, lobes, or segments, hyperaeration or emphysema, and the location of the stomach bubble and liver shadow.

E. In dextrocardia, breath sounds are normal, and the PMI is on the right side. Clinically, mild to moderate respiratory distress may be evident resulting from associated cardiac defects. The liver and stomach bubble are at their appropriate sites in isolated dextrocardia. The liver is located at the left side and the stomach bubble at the right side when dextrocardia occurs with situs inversus. Asplenia may be an associated abnormality.

F. Tension pneumothorax is suspected when breath sounds are diminished contralateral to the location of the PMI and cardiorespiratory distress is severe and of abrupt onset. The patient becomes hypotensive, bradycardic, and apneic. Pulse pressure is narrowed. Transillumination and the chest film should demonstrate the pneumothorax. The chest radiograph shows an area of lucency around the collapsed lung, and the mediastinum or heart is shifted to the other side. Because of acute deterioration, air is evacuated by needle aspiration followed by chest tube insertion. Most cases of tension pneumothoraces occur as complications of mechanical ventilation. Spontaneous pneumothoraces unrelated to respirator use are of variable severity; 80%–90% are mild, requiring no therapy except for an oxygen-rich environment.

G. In a patient with significant cardiorespiratory distress in which a radiodense area causes deviation of the mediastinum to the opposite side, fluid accumulation is a probability. A fluid level is usually seen on a decubitus film. Differential diagnoses include chylothorax, hemothorax, or pleural effusion from infection, heart failure, or accompanying hydrops fetalis. Treatment is by fluid aspiration; thoracostomy may be needed for continuous drainage.

H. Atelectasis (e.g., from a mucous plug) may result in shift of the mediastinum toward the side of atelectasis. The lung segments that are not atelectatic may become emphysematous (compensatory emphysema); this overdistention further shifts the mediastinum toward the side of the atelectasis. Breath sounds are diminished or absent over the area of atelectasis and normal on the other side. Patients have mild to moderate cardiorespiratory distress. The chest film demonstrates the atelectatic lobe or segment with compensatory emphysema. Vigorous chest physiotherapy and suctioning are appropriate. In patients requiring ventilator support, interstitial air accumulation involving one lobe or one lung is not an uncommon complication; this is associated with compression of the other lobes or segments. In this condition, selective intubation of the atelectatic lung may be tried to collapse the emphysematous lung.

I. Diaphragmatic hernia needs to be considered when breath sounds are not heard, bowel sounds are audible over the chest, and the infant is in moderate to severe respiratory distress from birth. The abdomen is scaphoid, and the chest film usually demonstrates the bowel or liver in the chest cavity. Cystic adenomatous malformation of the lungs may be difficult to distinguish from bowel segments herniated into the thoracic cavity on the x-ray film and thus should be considered in the differential diagnosis.

HSB

References

Carlo WA, Martin RJ, Fanaroff AA. Pulmonary mechanics during assisted ventilation. In: Fanaroff AA, Martin RJ, eds. Neonatal-perinatal medicine: Diseases of the fetus and infant. 5th ed. St Louis: Mosby—Year Book, 1992:820.

Korones SB. High-risk newborn infants: The basis for intensive nursing care. St Louis: Mosby—Year Book, 1986:204.

Neonate with MEDIASTINAL SHIFT

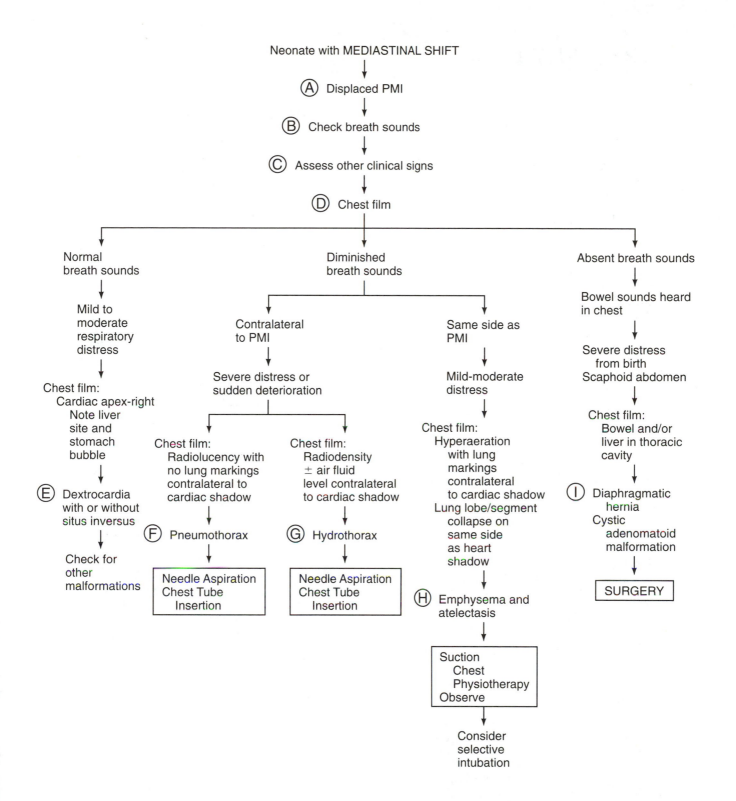

(A) Displaced PMI

(B) Check breath sounds

(C) Assess other clinical signs

(D) Chest film

Normal breath sounds

Mild to moderate respiratory distress

Chest film:
  Cardiac apex-right
  Note liver site and stomach bubble

(E) Dextrocardia with or without situs inversus

Check for other malformations

Diminished breath sounds

Contralateral to PMI

Severe distress or sudden deterioration

Chest film:
  Radiolucency with no lung markings contralateral to cardiac shadow

(F) Pneumothorax

| Needle Aspiration |
| Chest Tube |
| Insertion |

Chest film:
  Radiodensity ± air fluid level contralateral to cardiac shadow

(G) Hydrothorax

| Needle Aspiration |
| Chest Tube |
| Insertion |

Same side as PMI

Mild-moderate distress

Chest film:
  Hyperaeration with lung markings contralateral to cardiac shadow
  Lung lobe/segment collapse on same side as heart shadow

(H) Emphysema and atelectasis

| Suction |
| Chest |
| Physiotherapy |
| Observe |

Consider selective intubation

Absent breath sounds

Bowel sounds heard in chest

Severe distress from birth Scaphoid abdomen

Chest film:
  Bowel and/or liver in thoracic cavity

(I) Diaphragmatic hernia
Cystic adenomatoid malformation

| SURGERY |

HYPERTENSION

Hypertension is defined as a systolic BP >90 torr and a diastolic BP >60 torr in full-term neonates, and a systolic BP >80 torr and a diastolic BP >50 torr in preterm infants.

A. Cuff size affects BP reading when BP is determined by Doppler or by oscillometric technique; BP reading is higher with inappropriately small cuff. The BP cuff should be two thirds the length of the arm. If BP is obtained by a physiologic transducer, clot or air bubble in the line and inaccurate calibration may cause erroneous readings.

B. Renovascular etiology is likely in an infant with a history of indwelling catheter placement and hypovolemia. These conditions may predispose to thrombus formation in the aorta and its branches (e.g., renal arteries). In patent ductus arteriosus (PDA), closure promotes thrombus formation with embolization as a consequence. Other risk factors include bronchopulmonary dysplasia (BPD), CNS disorders, drugs, and hypervolemia.

C. Normally, BP readings from the lower extremities are higher than readings from the upper extremities. When lower-extremity BP is lower than upper-extremity BP, rule out coarctation of the aorta. Physical examination may reveal diminished to absent femoral pulses. Clinical manifestations depend on whether the coarctation is preductal or postductal. Preductal coarctation is usually associated with other cardiac defects (e.g., PDA, ventricular septal defect, transposition of the great arteries, and other complex lesions). In preductal coarctation, systemic blood flow may be maintained through a PDA; thus femoral pulses remain palpable, and hypertension may not be evident. In postductal coarctation, heart failure becomes evident with closure of the PDA. Echocardiography and contrast studies (aortography) demonstrate coarctation as well as other cardiac lesions. Surgery is indicated in deteriorating clinical condition.

D. When lower-extremity BP is higher than upper-extremity BP, evaluation is directed to renovascular/renal or other causes of hypertension.

E. Renovascular hypertension may be secondary to thrombosis of the aorta and renal artery resulting from an indwelling umbilical arterial catheter and/or a previous hypovolemic episode. Other vascular causes are renal vein thrombosis, intimal hyperplasia of the aorta and renal arteries, and renal artery stenosis.

F. In the absence of risk factors, intrinsic renal parenchymal disease is considered. Palpable enlarged kidneys or abdominal masses suggest cystic or metaplastic kidneys, hydronephrosis as in an obstructive uropathy, nephroblastoma, or perirenal hematoma. Other renal causes are renal dysplasia, renal hypoplasia, nephrolithiasis, pyelonephritis, and postpyeloplasty.

G. Consider endocrine disorders (e.g., pheochromocytoma, neuroblastoma, hyperthyroidism, Cushing's syndrome, hyperaldosteronism, and adrenogenital syndrome) in the absence of predisposing factors. Renal function studies and studies to rule out renal parenchymal disorders are also indicated because a renovascular or renal etiology is more common than endocrine abnormality.

H. Hypertension has been reported in babies with BPD; the mechanism is unknown. Because babies with BPD often have had umbilical catheters and episodes of hypovolemia, rule out renovascular causes.

I. Drugs such as corticosteroid, theophylline, ocular phenylephrine, and DOCA may cause hypertension, and their discontinuation normalizes BP. If hypertension persists, rule out renovascular and renal parenchymal causes.

J. CNS injury may cause hypertension. Although hypertensive episodes may predispose to the development of intracranial hemorrhage, we have not usually seen persistent hypertension after hemorrhage. Transient increase in BP occurs during seizures.

K. Hypertension may result from hypervolemia or fluid overload. Correction of fluid imbalance and diuretic therapy normalizes BP.

L. Studies such as electrolytes, fraction of sodium excretion, BUN, creatinine, calcium, base deficit, urinalysis, and urine culture screen for renal function and for pyelonephritis and hypercalciuria. Marked increase in plasma renin levels is observed in renal artery thrombosis. Abdominal ultrasound demonstrates abnormalities in kidney size and aortic and renal thrombosis, if present. Doppler flow studies detect impairment in flow in the abdominal aorta and renal vessels. In specialized situations, additional workup may include IV pyelogram, arteriography, renal scan, and voiding cystourethrography.

M. If renal and vascular studies are negative and endocrine disorders are entertained, determine plasma cortisol, aldosterone, and urinary 17-keto and 17-hydroxy steroids. Evaluate thyroid function when hyperthyroidism is suspected.

N. Essential hypertension is rare, and the diagnosis is made after excluding other causes.

HSB

References

Adelman RD. The hypertensive neonate. Clin Perinatol 1988; 15:567.

Lees MH, King DH. The cardiovascular system. In: Fanaroff AA, Martin RJ, eds. Neonatal-perinatal medicine: Diseases of the fetus and infant. St Louis: Times Mirror/Mosby College Publishing, 1987:639.

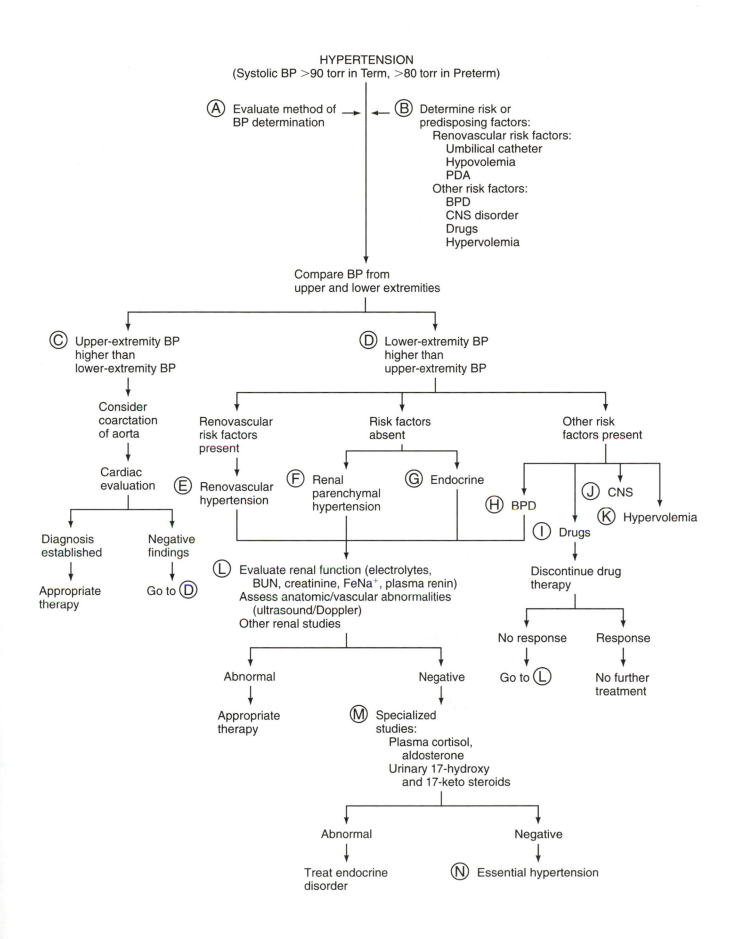

HYPERTENSION
(Systolic BP >90 torr in Term, >80 torr in Preterm)

Ⓐ Evaluate method of
BP determination

Ⓑ Determine risk or
predisposing factors:
  Renovascular risk factors:
    Umbilical catheter
    Hypovolemia
    PDA
  Other risk factors:
    BPD
    CNS disorder
    Drugs
    Hypervolemia

Compare BP from
upper and lower extremities

Ⓒ Upper-extremity BP
higher than
lower-extremity BP

Ⓓ Lower-extremity BP
higher than
upper-extremity BP

Consider
coarctation
of aorta

Renovascular
risk factors
present

Risk factors
absent

Other risk
factors present

Cardiac
evaluation

Ⓔ Renovascular
hypertension

Ⓕ Renal
parenchymal
hypertension

Ⓖ Endocrine

Ⓗ BPD

Ⓙ CNS

Ⓚ Hypervolemia

Ⓘ Drugs

Diagnosis
established

Negative
findings

Appropriate
therapy

Go to Ⓓ

Ⓛ Evaluate renal function (electrolytes,
BUN, creatinine, $FeNa^+$, plasma renin)
Assess anatomic/vascular abnormalities
(ultrasound/Doppler)
Other renal studies

Discontinue drug
therapy

No response

Response

Go to Ⓛ

No further
treatment

Abnormal

Negative

Appropriate
therapy

Ⓜ Specialized
studies:
Plasma cortisol,
aldosterone
Urinary 17-hydroxy
and 17-keto steroids

Abnormal

Negative

Treat endocrine
disorder

Ⓝ Essential hypertension

HYPERTENSION: THERAPY

A. Hypertension in the newborn may be asymptomatic or symptomatic. Although signs and symptoms may not necessarily relate to the magnitude of BP elevation, their recognition often prompts initiation of antihypertensive therapy. Generalized signs such as edema, fever, or failure to thrive may be observed; cardiorespiratory, neurological, and renal signs are also reported with hypertension. Cardiorespiratory signs (such as tachypnea, cyanosis, cardiomegaly, hepatomegaly, and poor perfusion) may indicate heart failure; ECG may show evidence of left ventricular hypertrophy. Neurological signs include alteration in tone, lethargy, coma, tremors, seizures, retinopathy, and intracranial hemorrhage. Renal-related manifestations such as polyuria, oliguria, and sodium wasting may be observed.

B. In mild hypertension, particularly when asymptomatic, observation may be adequate; a diuretic may be used on occasion.

C. Specific medical and surgical therapies may be instituted in moderate to severe hypertension, depending on the etiological factors. Thus, drug-induced hypertension may be alleviated by discontinuation of drug therapy. Hypervolemia may be corrected by decreasing amount of fluid load administered, and in some instances diuretics may be used. Renovascular hypertension resulting from aortic and/or renal artery thrombosis may require therapy with streptokinase, urokinase, or tissue plasminogen activator. Hypertension because of adrenogenital syndromes usually responds to hormone replacement therapy. Antithyroid drugs are usually administered in hyperthyroidism.

D. In general, surgical therapy needs to be reserved for cases refractory to medical therapy or when adverse side effects are observed from drug therapy. Repair of the coarctation is appropriate when evidence of clinical deterioration is present. Most patients with aortic thrombosis respond well to conservative therapy (empiric therapy at most) with resolution of hypertension. Thrombectomy/embolectomy have been tried in severe hypertension, but these surgical procedures are associated with a 33% mortality rate; rethrombosis after surgery may also occur. Nephrectomy may be considered in cases of renal parenchymal hypertension (e.g., cystic kidney). Adrenal tumors with associated hyperaldosteronism may require adrenalectomy.

E. Antihypertensive therapy is often empiric, and intravenous administration of potent vasodilators may be indicated in life-threatening situations. This is followed by weeks to months of administration of an oral antihypertensive or in combination with a diuretic. Multiple drug therapy may be necessary in resistant cases. The dose administered is tapered off four to eight weeks after normalization of BP with pharmacological therapy, and BP usually remains normal after discontinuation of therapy.

F. Diazoxide and nitroprusside are potent vasodilators and may cause hypotension in high doses. Also, diazoxide may cause hyperglycemia. Side effects of the other antihypertensive agents include hyponatremia and hypokalemia from furosemide or chlorothiazide. Hypercalciuria may occur with furosemide therapy. Hypochloremia occurs with chlorothiazide administration. Hydralazine may cause tachycardia or paroxysmal atrial tachycardia. Propranolol causes bronchospasm and bradycardia. Oliguria and hyperkalemia are reported with diazoxide.

HSB

References

Adelman RD. The hypertensive neonate. Clin Perinatol 1988; 15:567.

Kennedy LA, Drummond WH, Knight ME, et al. Successful treatment of neonatal aortic thrombosis with tissue plasminogen activator. J Pediatr 1990; 116:798.

Vailas GN, Brouillette RT, Scott JP, et al. Neonatal aortic thrombosis: Recent experience. J Pediatr 1986; 109:101.

Rasoulpour M, Marinelli KA. Systemic hypertension. Clin Perinatol 1992; 19:121.

HYPERTENSION: THERAPY

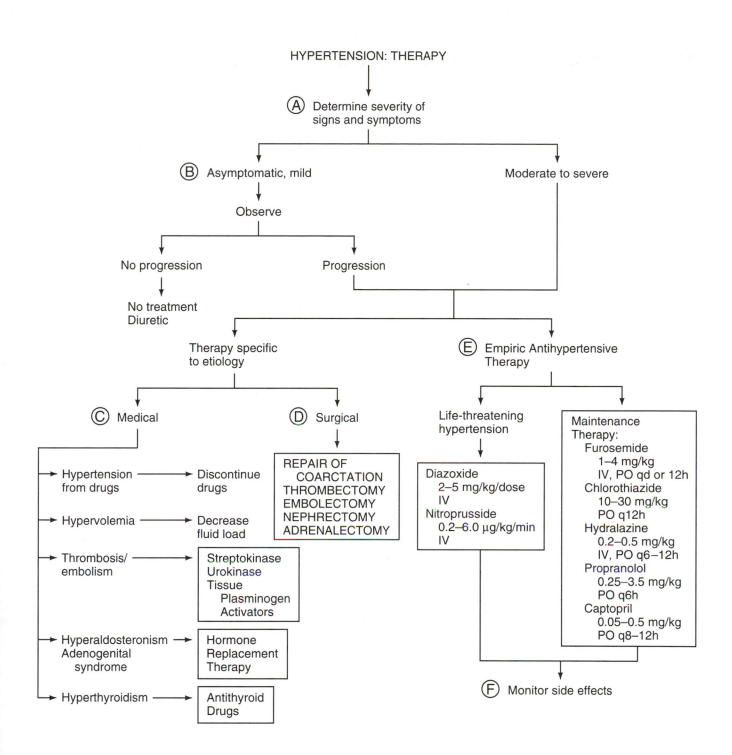

(A) Determine severity of signs and symptoms

(B) Asymptomatic, mild

Moderate to severe

Observe

No progression

Progression

No treatment
Diuretic

Therapy specific
to etiology

(E) Empiric Antihypertensive
Therapy

(C) Medical

(D) Surgical

Life-threatening
hypertension

Maintenance
Therapy:
    Furosemide
        1–4 mg/kg
        IV, PO qd or 12h
    Chlorothiazide
        10–30 mg/kg
        PO q12h
    Hydralazine
        0.2–0.5 mg/kg
        IV, PO q6–12h
    Propranolol
        0.25–3.5 mg/kg
        PO q6h
    Captopril
        0.05–0.5 mg/kg
        PO q8–12h

Hypertension
from drugs → Discontinue
drugs

Hypervolemia → Decrease
fluid load

Thrombosis/
embolism →
Streptokinase
Urokinase
Tissue
    Plasminogen
    Activators

Hyperaldosteronism
Adenogenital
syndrome →
Hormone
Replacement
Therapy

Hyperthyroidism →
Antithyroid
Drugs

REPAIR OF
    COARCTATION
THROMBECTOMY
EMBOLECTOMY
NEPHRECTOMY
ADRENALECTOMY

Diazoxide
    2–5 mg/kg/dose
    IV
Nitroprusside
    0.2–6.0 µg/kg/min
    IV

(F) Monitor side effects

ABNORMAL CENTRAL VENOUS PRESSURE

A. Central venous pressure (CVP) is determined by blood volume, vascular tone in the venous system, and the effectiveness of the heart as a pump. The normal values for CVP depend on the component at which the reading is made and the location of the tip of the catheter. The CVP waveform has three peaks or wave components, the a, v, and inspiratory waves. The a wave is produced by atrial contraction, the v wave by atrial filling, and the inspiratory wave by the negative intrathoracic pressure transmitted to the central veins and atria (thus the negative pressure wave). The ideal location for the CVP catheter tip is at the right atrium, and the a wave is observed at a mean of 5 torr ($+2$ to $+8$ torr). The accuracy of the reading may be affected by clots, air bubbles in the line, and improper calibration of the transducer. Calibration at 0 pressure is made at the level of the tricuspid valve at the midaxillary line with the patient in supine position. Patients should be assessed for signs of congestive heart failure, hypotension, dehydration, and respiratory insufficiency. Evaluation of arterial BP aids in differential diagnosis and management.

B. A low CVP should alert one to blood loss and hypotension; systemic arterial pressure is also low. Similar findings may be observed with fluid loss, i.e., dehydration, gastroenteritis, or loss to the third space (peritonitis). Treatment is volume replacement.

C. A high CVP with high arterial pressure suggests fluid overload or an early response to perinatal asphyxia. Vasoconstriction in perinatal asphyxia ultimately leads to severe acidosis with resulting hypotension. Volume expansion results in normalization of arterial pressure and CVP, and at times the CVP may decrease to subnormal values.

D. With a high CVP and low arterial BP, the primary consideration is to investigate cardiac failure. If heart failure is evident, differentiation needs to be made between intrinsic cardiac lesions and dysfunction with an anatomically normal heart. If the heart structure is normal, myocardial dysfunction resulting from hypoxia, polycythemia/hyperviscosity syndrome, or hydrops fetalis becomes a consideration. Myocardial dysfunction may require inotropic agents (pp 166, 169).

E. In the absence of heart failure, increased CVP may be observed in babies requiring mechanical ventilation with inappropriately high PIP and PEEP. On chest radiograph the lungs appear hyperaerated, the diaphragm depressed, and the heart small. The positive intrathoracic pressure may impede venous return, i.e., outflow obstruction. Adjustment of ventilator settings (e.g., $\downarrow$ PIP, $\downarrow$ PEEP, $\downarrow$ rate, $\uparrow$ expiration time) corrects the high CVP. In babies with rapidly deteriorating clinical status, pneumothorax, pneumomediastinum, or pneumopericardium is suspected and verified by chest film. Immediate air evacuation should be done.

HSB

References

Cabal LA, Siassi B, Hodgman JE. Neonatal cardiovascular and pulmonary monitoring. In: Thibeault DW, Gregory GA, eds. Neonatal pulmonary care. 2nd ed. Norwalk, CT: Appleton-Century-Crofts, 1986:321.

Crone RK. Acute circulatory failure in children. Pediatr Clin North Am 1980; 27:525.

ABNORMAL CENTRAL VENOUS PRESSURE
(Normal 4–6 torr or 5–8 cm H_2O)

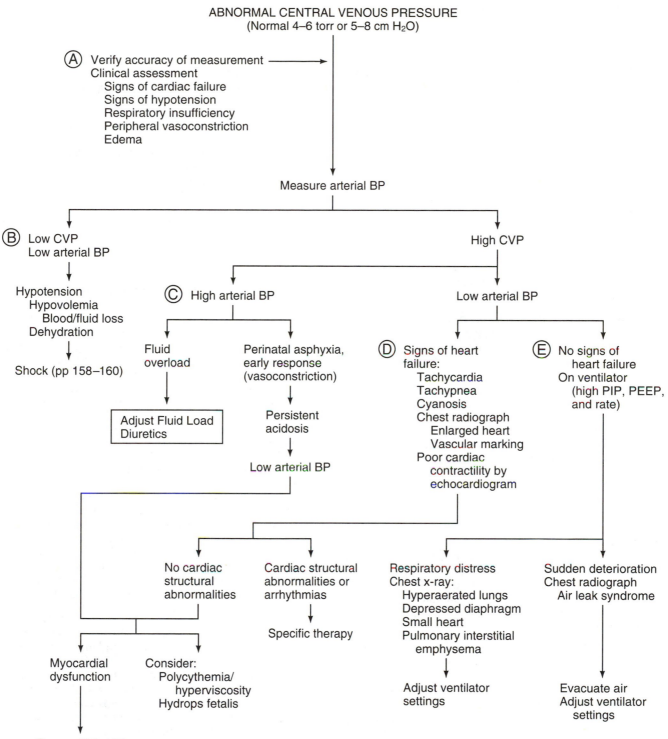

(A) Verify accuracy of measurement ⟶
Clinical assessment
  Signs of cardiac failure
  Signs of hypotension
  Respiratory insufficiency
  Peripheral vasoconstriction
  Edema

Measure arterial BP

(B) Low CVP
Low arterial BP

↓

Hypotension
Hypovolemia
  Blood/fluid loss
Dehydration

↓

Shock (pp 158–160)

High CVP

(C) High arterial BP

Low arterial BP

Fluid overload

Perinatal asphyxia, early response (vasoconstriction)

↓

Adjust Fluid Load Diuretics

Persistent acidosis

↓

Low arterial BP

(D) Signs of heart failure:
  Tachycardia
  Tachypnea
  Cyanosis
  Chest radiograph
    Enlarged heart
    Vascular marking
  Poor cardiac contractility by echocardiogram

(E) No signs of heart failure
On ventilator (high PIP, PEEP, and rate)

No cardiac structural abnormalities

Cardiac structural abnormalities or arrhythmias

↓

Specific therapy

Respiratory distress
Chest x-ray:
  Hyperaerated lungs
  Depressed diaphragm
  Small heart
  Pulmonary interstitial emphysema

↓

Adjust ventilator settings

Sudden deterioration
Chest radiograph
  Air leak syndrome

↓

Evacuate air
Adjust ventilator settings

Myocardial dysfunction

Consider:
  Polycythemia/hyperviscosity
  Hydrops fetalis

↓

See pp 166–167

SHOCK

A. Shock is a clinical condition wherein there is inadequate circulating volume to supply the metabolic demands of the body. Blood pressure ≤2 SD of normal indicates hypotension. However, accuracy of BP measurement needs to be established. Too large a cuff or an air bubble or clot in the arterial lines may cause a falsely low BP reading. One must review the history for bleeding in the perinatal or neonatal period (e.g., abruptio placentae, cord rupture, pulmonary hemorrhage, intraventricular hemorrhage), perinatal asphyxia, and the use of vasoactive drugs. The patient is assessed for signs of hypotension; more marked or severe symptoms are observed in severe cases. Signs of shock include listlessness, lethargy, tachycardia, tachypnea, weak pulses, poor perfusion, mottling, cold extremities, apnea and bradycardia, and severe metabolic acidosis.

B. Low BP is considered an emergency, and volume expansion with plasmanate at 10–15 ml/kg is administered over 1/2 hour. Response to this initial treatment (i.e., BP increase, improvement in clinical signs, and increase in urine output) is monitored while the cause of hypotension is being determined. Monitoring of central venous pressure (CVP) in addition to arterial BP is useful. In addition to the historical data and clinical assessment, acid-base and blood gas status must be evaluated, followed by correction of metabolic acidosis and hypoxemia; acidosis and hypoxia depress myocardial contractility. Correction of metabolic acidosis with sodium bicarbonate (1–3 mEq/kg) IV (diluted 1:1) in part expands intravascular volume and may improve pulmonary blood flow. Also, further workup includes hematocrit and comparison with previous values (if available), BUN, creatinine, serum electrolytes, glucose, calcium, albumin, serum and urine osmolalities to assess hydration status, and chest x-ray and echocardiography to evaluate cardiac status. An ECG should rule out cardiac arrhythmias. Septicemia workup is indicated if septic shock is considered.

C. With a history of blood loss, hypovolemia becomes the likely cause of hypotension. Decrease in circulating volume may also occur with plasma loss, as in cases of necrotizing enterocolitis or hypoproteinemia (decreased oncotic pressure). Extravascular fluid losses from excessive insensible loss, gastroenteritis, and excessive diuresis may also lead to decreased circulating blood volume.

D. Replace blood loss or fluid loss by blood transfusion, plasma, albumin, or electrolyte solutions as appropriate. Maintain CVP at 5–8 torr. Volume losses (e.g., from nasogastric drainage) must be monitored and replaced with equal volume of fluid replacement (e.g., ½ N saline). Loss to third space may require replacement volume of ≥30% of maintenance fluid volume in addition to usual daily maintenance therapy. Fluid intake and output need strict monitoring. Urine output is maintained at ≥1 ml/kg/h. Inotropic agents are sometimes administered after appropriate volume expansion (see F).

E. Myocardial dysfunction is common with perinatal asphyxia, in hypoglycemia, or in the presence of cardiac lesions such as those associated with large left-to-right shunt and outflow obstruction (e.g., aortic atresia or hypoplastic left heart syndrome). Inflow obstruction from intravascular air or increased intrathoracic pressure as in the air leak syndromes (pneumothorax, pneumopericardium) may also result in hypotension. Cardiac output may be reduced with cardiac arrhythmias, resulting in systemic hypotension.

F. Myocardial dysfunction from perinatal asphyxia may respond to inotropic agents such as epinephrine, isoproterenol, dopamine, or dobutamine initiated at low doses and titrated to desired response. Cardiac glycosides should be avoided in an acutely ill infant because of variable onset of action and toxicity. *Hypotension from air leaks needs immediate air evacuation.* Prompt recognition of arrhythmia leads to evaluation of etiology and appropriate therapy.

G. Neonatal sepsis results in increased venous capacitance or functional hypovolemia. Vasoactive substances released during sepsis are potent vasodilators, so that hypovolemia develops as capacitance increases. In babies with sepsis, additional volume expansion may be required to correct the hypotension. Sepsis may also manifest with hypoxemia and ischemia, which could be severe enough to cause myocardial dysfunction; in these instances cardiotonic agents may be beneficial. Vasoactive substances and endotoxin may be removed by exchange transfusion. Appropriate antibiotic therapy is also instituted. The use of steroids in gram-negative septic shock is controversial.

H. Functional hypovolemia may also result from administration of hypnotics, sedatives, and muscle relaxants. Tolazoline and nitroprusside, potent vasodilators, often are used in the treatment of pulmonary hypertension; hypotension is common with their administration. If the situation necessitates continuing these drugs, volume expanders may be given. Discontinuation of the drug is the specific therapy.

I. Metabolic disorders such as hypoglycemia, electrolyte imbalance, and hypocalcemia, whether they are the primary cause of hypotension or secondary to it, need to be corrected. In hypocalcemia, an empiric treatment is to give 1 ml/kg of 10% calcium gluconate IV. Low serum sodium and high serum potassium in a hypotensive neonate suggest the possibility of adrenogenital syndrome or adrenal crisis.

HSB

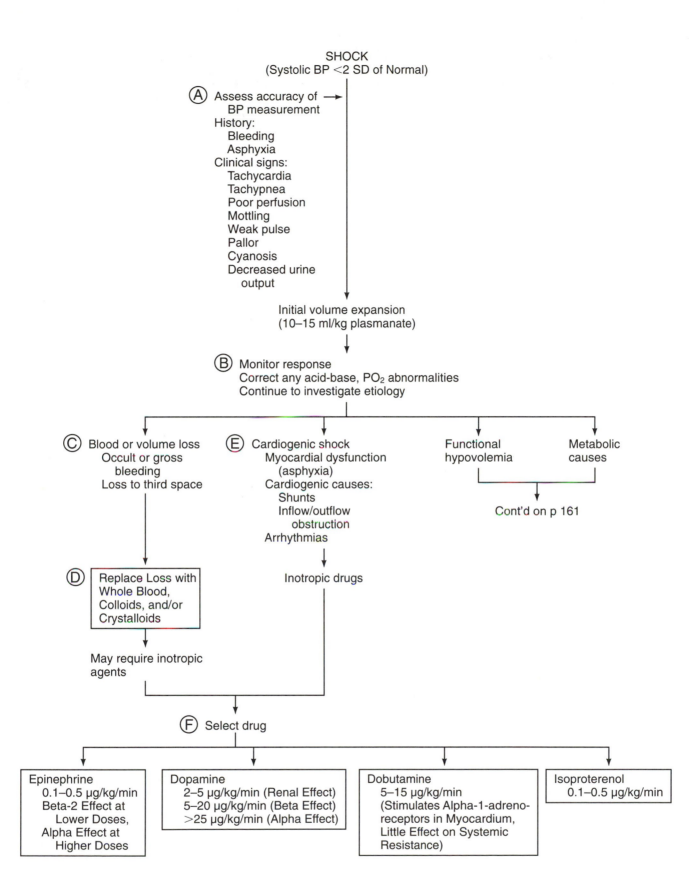

SHOCK
(Systolic BP <2 SD of Normal)

Ⓐ Assess accuracy of ⟶
    BP measurement
History:
    Bleeding
    Asphyxia
Clinical signs:
    Tachycardia
    Tachypnea
    Poor perfusion
    Mottling
    Weak pulse
    Pallor
    Cyanosis
    Decreased urine
        output

Initial volume expansion
(10–15 ml/kg plasmanate)

Ⓑ Monitor response
Correct any acid-base, PO₂ abnormalities
Continue to investigate etiology

Ⓒ Blood or volume loss
Occult or gross
    bleeding
Loss to third space

Ⓔ Cardiogenic shock
    Myocardial dysfunction
        (asphyxia)
    Cardiogenic causes:
        Shunts
        Inflow/outflow
            obstruction
    Arrhythmias

Functional
hypovolemia

Metabolic
causes

Cont'd on p 161

Ⓓ Replace Loss with
Whole Blood,
Colloids, and/or
Crystalloids

Inotropic drugs

May require inotropic
agents

Ⓕ Select drug

Epinephrine
0.1–0.5 µg/kg/min
Beta-2 Effect at
    Lower Doses,
Alpha Effect at
    Higher Doses

Dopamine
2–5 µg/kg/min (Renal Effect)
5–20 µg/kg/min (Beta Effect)
>25 µg/kg/min (Alpha Effect)

Dobutamine
5–15 µg/kg/min
(Stimulates Alpha-1-adreno-
receptors in Myocardium,
Little Effect on Systemic
Resistance)

Isoproterenol
0.1–0.5 µg/kg/min

References

Crone RK. Acute circulatory failure in children. Pediatr Clin North Am 1980; 27:525.

DiSessa TG, Leitner M, Ching CT, et al. The cardiovascular effects of dopamine in the severely asphyxiated neonate. J Pediatr 1981; 99:772.

Hohn AR, Stanton RE. Postoperative care, counseling, and medications. In: Fanaroff AA, Martin RJ, eds. Neonatal-perinatal medicine: Diseases of the fetus and infant. 5th ed. St Louis: Mosby–Year Book, 1992:931.

Roberts RJ. Drug therapy in infants. Philadelphia: WB Saunders, 1984:138.

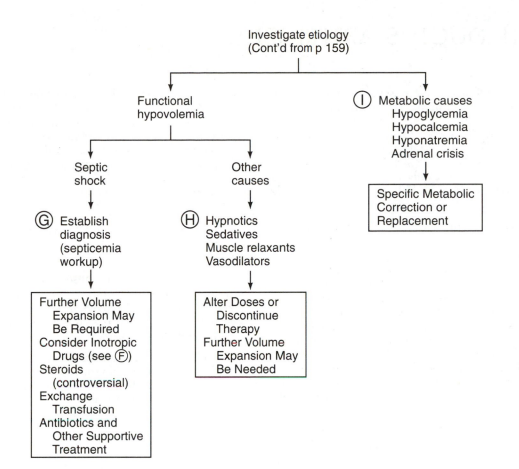

Investigate etiology
(Cont'd from p 159)

Functional
hypovolemia

Ⓘ Metabolic causes
   Hypoglycemia
   Hypocalcemia
   Hyponatremia
   Adrenal crisis

Septic
shock

Other
causes

Specific Metabolic
Correction or
Replacement

Ⓖ Establish
   diagnosis
   (septicemia
   workup)

Ⓗ Hypnotics
   Sedatives
   Muscle relaxants
   Vasodilators

Further Volume
   Expansion May
   Be Required
Consider Inotropic
   Drugs (see Ⓕ)
Steroids
   (controversial)
Exchange
   Transfusion
Antibiotics and
   Other Supportive
   Treatment

Alter Doses or
   Discontinue
   Therapy
Further Volume
   Expansion May
   Be Needed

PATENT DUCTUS ARTERIOSUS

A. The ductus arteriosus is a muscular contractile structure bridging the left pulmonary artery and the dorsal aorta at the aortic isthmus. Ductal constriction is promoted by increased oxygen tension (postnatal increase in Pao_2 as first breath is established) and affected by levels of circulating prostaglandins and available muscle mass. Other factors promoting ductal constriction include catecholamines, low pH, bradykinin, and acetylcholine.

B. In term babies the ductus arteriosus becomes functionally closed at birth; that is, right-to-left shunt ceases. Because anatomic closure may take several days as pulmonary resistance decreases postnatally, a small left-to-right shunt may exist, usually with no consequence. Persistence of the ductus arteriosus accounts for 2–5% of symptomatic cardiac diseases presenting in the first 28 days of life; the patent ductus arteriosus (PDA) may be an isolated finding or associated with other cardiac or noncardiac abnormalities (e.g., trisomy 18, congenital rubella). Echocardiography rules out other existing cardiac lesions. Ligation is the definitive treatment for the hemodynamically significant PDA.

C. In premature infants PDA is a common complication that usually becomes evident during recovery from respiratory distress syndrome. With the fall in pulmonary resistance, left-to-right shunt through the ductus develops, which is responsible for the coarse, low-pitched, rumbling, mid- and late-systolic murmur, at the left sternal border, usually first heard on the third or fourth day of life. A murmur may be absent, but other clinical signs indicate the presence of a significant ductus.

D. The presence of ductal shunt must be established by echocardiography with Doppler, which detects flow through the pulmonary artery during not only systole but diastole as well. An echocardiogram also provides information about associated lesions, if any.

E. The significance of the left-to-right shunt through the ductus must be assessed primarily by clinical criteria. Insignificant hemodynamic changes with a patent ductus require no therapy.

F. Clinical signs of decompensation include bounding pulses, wide pulse pressure, hyperactive precordium, and enlarged heart and pulmonary edema on chest x-ray; the typical murmur may be absent. Babies requiring ventilator therapy have increasing ventilator requirements; $Paco_2$ increases when distending pressure is decreased. Moist rales and apneic episodes are reported with severe pulmonary edema.

G. Distending pressure is increased to counteract pulmonary congestion and edema. Restrict fluid intake while monitoring urine output closely. Diuretics may be used.

H. In the absence of response or recurrence after a response to symptomatic treatment, pharmacologic closure is achieved by giving indomethacin (a prostaglandin inhibitor) IV at 0.2–0.3 mg/kg, repeated in 12 h for three doses.

I. The course of indomethacin may be repeated two or three times in the absence of a response with the first course. Surgical ligation is the treatment of choice when indomethacin fails.

HSB

References

Avery ME, Fletcher BD, Williams RG. The lung and its disorders in the newborn infant. Philadelphia: WB Saunders, 1981:239.

Baylen BG, Emmanouilides GC. Patent ductus arteriosus in the newborn. In: Thibeault DW, Gregory GA, eds. Neonatal pulmonary care. 2nd ed. Norwalk, Conn: Appleton-Century-Crofts, 1986:519.

Flyer DC, Lang P. Neonatal heart disease. In: Avery GB, ed. Neonatology: Pathophysiology and management of the newborn. 3rd ed. Philadelphia: JB Lippincott, 1987:506.

Korones SB. High-risk newborn infants: The basis for intensive nursing care. 4th ed. St Louis: Times Mirror/Mosby College Publishing, 1986:268.

Stahlman MT. Acute respiratory disorders in the newborn. In: Avery GB, ed. Neonatology: Pathophysiology and management of the newborn. 3rd ed. Philadelphia: JB Lippincott, 1987:421.

PATENT DUCTUS ARTERIOSUS

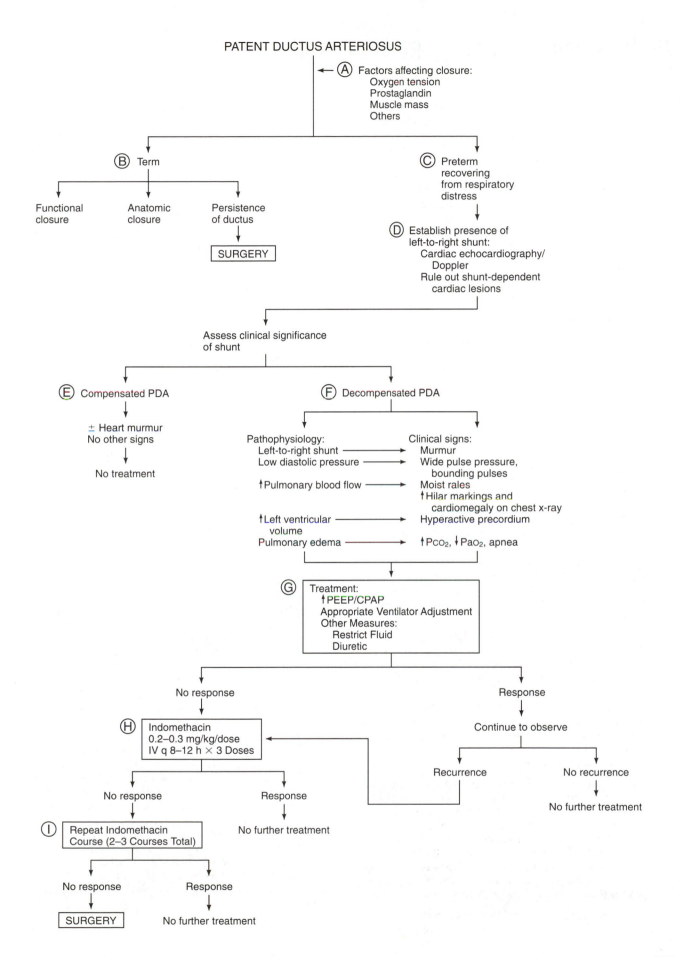

PERSISTENT FETAL CIRCULATION

Persistent fetal circulation (PFC) refers to cardiovascular hemodynamic alterations from an underlying (1) hypercontractile state of the pulmonary vessels due to substances that alter pulmonary resistance, (2) abnormal muscularization of the normally nonmuscular interacinar arteries and increased medial thickness of the muscular arteries, or (3) decreased cross-sectional area of the pulmonary bed, as in the hypoplastic lung syndromes. The typical infant with PFC is born postterm, term, or near term.

A. Clinical entities that may be associated with PFC may be grouped into those associated with pulmonary parenchymal disease such as hyaline membrane disease (HMD), pneumonia, meconium aspiration, and hypoplastic lungs (as in diaphragmatic hernia) and those conditions that are primarily vascular (e.g., asphyxia, cold stress).

B. Because of the hypercontractile state of the pulmonary vessels or decreased cross-sectional area, pulmonary resistance is increased. This results in decreased pulmonary blood flow and right-to-left (R-L) shunt through the ductus arteriosus and the foramen ovale. The admixing of venous and arterial blood becomes clinically evident as cyanosis.

C. The infant is usually cyanotic and tachypneic, with or without marked chest retractions. Chest film may be normal as in primarily vascular PFC or may demonstrate associated parenchymal lesions. By hyperoxia test, administration of Fio_2 of 1.00 results in minimal or no improvement in Pao_2. Failure of Pao_2 to increase >100 torr in Fio_2 of 1.00 suggests R-L shunt. Preductal Pao_2 (i.e., right radial, temporal artery) is 15% > postductal Pao_2 values. Echocardiography demonstrates R-L atrial shunt by saline contrast or by Doppler. Decreased cardiac contractility and/or tricuspid insufficiency suggests increased pulmonary resistance.

D. Supportive measures include administration of low-dose dopamine (2.5 μg/kg/min) in the presence of myocardial dysfunction secondary to asphyxia, administration of pressor agents (dopamine, dobutamine, or isoproterenol) to hypotensive patients, and correction of metabolic acidosis by administration of $NaHCO_3$. Pulmonary arterioles are shown to constrict with low pH; thus there is a rationale for keeping pH in alkalotic range. Muscle paralysis may facilitate ventilator management.

E. Some infants with PFC with substantial difference in preductal and postductal Pao_2 values are able to maintain preductal Pao_2 >50 torr; supportive measures may be adequate therapy. In those with normal BP, we have observed good response to a bolus of tolazoline (2 mg/kg) mixed with 10–15 ml/kg of plasmanate. A pharmacologic trial may prevent resorting to mechanical ventilation, which may further promote lung injury through barotrauma.

F. By hyperventilation, $Paco_2$ decreases and pH and Pao_2 increase. As a result, pulmonary vascular resistance decreases, leading to increased pulmonary blood flow and decreased R-L shunt. The goal of hyperventilation is to reach a "critical" $Paco_2$ range and pH so that pulmonary vasodilation occurs and oxygenation is achieved. The Pao_2 decreases once $Paco_2$ is allowed to increase above the critical value. Usually the critical $Paco_2$ is <30 torr, at times <20 torr. The pH is usually maintained >7.40. The goal of hyperventilation is achieved by (1) increasing the PIP, often to >30 cm H_2O, and (2) increasing the ventilator rate (at times >100/min). Because of the need for high PIP, flow rate must be increased. To prevent air trapping with rapid rate, inspiratory time is short and PEEP is decreased. With compliant lungs, a high PEEP may contribute to increased pulmonary resistance. Those with parenchymal disease, however, may benefit from PEEP. Pao_2 is maintained at 100–120 torr. Alternatively, or in conjunction with hyperventilation, oxygenation can be improved by continuous infusion of $NaHCO_3$ to achieve a pH ≥7.5.

G. As oxygenation improves with hyperventilation, wean from mechanical support carefully and slowly. Decrease Fio_2 by 1–2% increments to maintain Pao_2 at 100–120 torr; maintain $Paco_2$ at critical level. While $Paco_2$ is at critical level, decrease PIP by 1–2 cm H_2O and carefully monitor dependence of Pao_2 values on $Paco_2$. Defer weaning if Pao_2 is dependent on critical $Paco_2$ (danger of "flip-flop"). Once the Fio_2 is ≤0.7 and PIP ≤30 cm H_2O, rate is decreased. Continue weaning by further decreasing Fio_2 to maintain Pao_2 at 50–80 torr, $Paco_2$ at 40–50 torr, and pH at 7.25–7.4.

H. Pulmonary hypertension associated with parenchymal involvement such as pneumonia (e.g., Group B β-hemolytic streptococci) or meconium aspiration may respond to hyperventilation only transiently. A complicating air leak or the disease itself may prevent the hyperventilation regimen from decreasing $Paco_2$ levels adequately to result in pulmonary vasodilation. In these cases, therapy with tolazoline may be initiated. A bolus of 2 mg/kg is given intravenously and repeated as necessary. Our practice is to give tolazoline bolus with 10–15 ml/kg of plasmanate to minimize or prevent the hypotensive effect of tolazoline. The repeated bolus injection at a higher dose (3–5 mg/kg) may be necessary at times. The bolus dose could also be followed with a continuous drip of 1–2 mg/kg/h. Poor response to tolazoline may be related to severe acidosis, poor myocardial contractility, and hypotension. Tolazoline is less likely to be effective in severe parenchymal lung involvement (Group B β-hemolytic strep pneumonia) and in extreme cases of vascular muscularization. Nitroprusside may be used instead of tolazoline. Those unresponsive to management may be candidates for ECMO.

HSB

PERSISTENT FETAL CIRCULATION

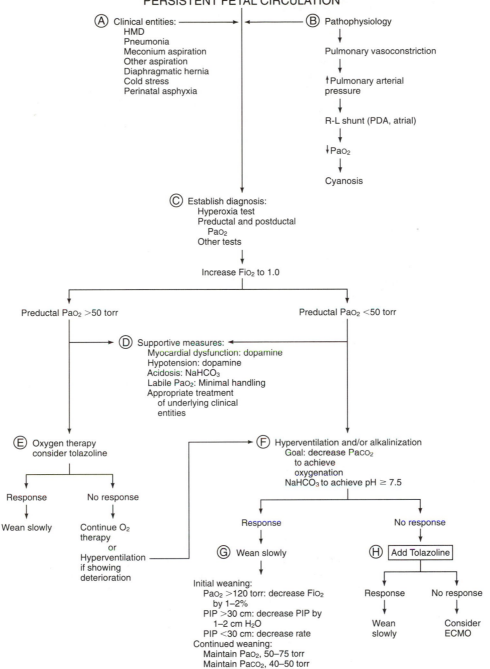

Ⓐ Clinical entities:
HMD
Pneumonia
Meconium aspiration
Other aspiration
Diaphragmatic hernia
Cold stress
Perinatal asphyxia

Ⓑ Pathophysiology
↓
Pulmonary vasoconstriction
↓
↑Pulmonary arterial pressure
↓
R-L shunt (PDA, atrial)
↓
↓Pa_{O_2}
↓
Cyanosis

Ⓒ Establish diagnosis:
Hyperoxia test
Preductal and postductal Pa_{O_2}
Other tests
↓
Increase Fi_{O_2} to 1.0

Preductal Pa_{O_2} >50 torr

Preductal Pa_{O_2} <50 torr

Ⓓ Supportive measures:
Myocardial dysfunction: dopamine
Hypotension: dopamine
Acidosis: $NaHCO_3$
Labile Pa_{O_2}: Minimal handling
Appropriate treatment of underlying clinical entities

Ⓔ Oxygen therapy consider tolazoline

Response
↓
Wean slowly

No response
↓
Continue O_2 therapy
or
Hyperventilation if showing deterioration

Ⓕ Hyperventilation and/or alkalinization
Goal: decrease Pa_{CO_2} to achieve oxygenation
$NaHCO_3$ to achieve pH ≥ 7.5

Response
↓
Ⓖ Wean slowly

Initial weaning:
Pa_{O_2} >120 torr: decrease Fi_{O_2} by 1–2%
PIP >30 cm: decrease PIP by 1–2 cm H_2O
PIP <30 cm: decrease rate
Continued weaning:
Maintain Pa_{O_2}, 50–75 torr
Maintain Pa_{CO_2}, 40–50 torr

No response
↓
Ⓗ Add Tolazoline

Response
↓
Wean slowly

No response
↓
Consider ECMO

References

Drummond WH, Gregory GA, Heymann MA, Phibbs RA. The independent effects of hyperventilation, tolazoline and dopamine on infants with persistent pulmonary hypertension. J Pediatr 1981; 98:603.

Duara S, Fox WW. Persistent pulmonary hypertension of the neonate. In: Thibeault DW, Gregory GA, eds. Neonatal pulmonary care. 2nd ed. Norwalk, Conn: Appleton-Century-Crofts, 1986;461.

Fox WW, Duara S. Persistent pulmonary hypertension of the neonate: Diagnosis and clinical management. J Pediatr 1983; 103:505.

Goetzman BW, Sunshine P, Johnson JD, et al. Neonatal hypoxia and pulmonary vasospasm: Response to tolazoline. J Pediatr 1976; 89:617.

Haworth GS, Reid LM. Persistent fetal circulation: Newly recognized structural features. J Pediatr 1976; 88:614.

MYOCARDIAL ISCHEMIA

A. Myocardial ischemia results from a decreased coronary perfusion to the myocardium with consequent decrease in cardiac output. On the other hand, a decrease in cardiac output from either intrinsically cardiac or other causes could lead to decreased coronary perfusion and myocardial ischemia. Cardiac output is the product of blood volume ejected by the left ventricle (stroke volume) and the heart rate (ejection cycles per minute). The stroke volume is determined by intrinsic myocardial contractility, preload, and afterload. Myocardial contractility, under adrenergic and neurohumoral control, is less efficient in the neonate who possesses less contractile tissue per unit of myocardium. Hypoxia, acidosis, and hypoglycemia have a negative influence on cardiac contractility. Preload is determined by the myocardial fiber end-diastolic length and the venous return to the heart. Stroke volume increases with increase in preload, but this relationship is not linear (Starling's curve). With further increase in diastolic volume, ventricular compliance and contractility diminish and stroke volume decreases. Afterload is related to the systolic ventricular wall tension and is influenced by aortic impedance, aortic wall compliance, systemic vascular resistance, and blood viscosity. Increase in vascular resistance results in decrease in stroke volume, and myocardial work increases. Because an adequate circulating blood volume, optimal oxygenation, and pH balance are crucial to maintaining cardiac output and contractility, their aberrations require appropriate correction while initiating and continuing investigation on the etiologies of myocardial dysfunction.

B. Anatomical cardiac lesions could be associated with decreased right or left ventricular output to the extent of limiting coronary perfusion. Anatomical lesions may be detected by echocardiography and Doppler evaluation. In most of the lesions, oxygenation is maintained by a patent ductus arteriosus (PDA); this patency is maintained for longer duration by prostaglandin (PGE_1) pending surgical correction, if appropriate.

C. The heart may be structurally normal, but abnormalities in heart rate could result in inadequate cardiac output and myocardial ischemia.

D. Cardiogenic shock results when the heart is unable to increase its cardiac output because of increasing demands of other organs. The neonatal cardiac function is normally at the peak of the Starling curve; myocardial contractile reserve is limited and afterload is high.

E. Myocardial ischemia and consequent dysfunction could be the result of a hypoxic-ischemic insult as in perinatal asphyxia, a poor tolerance to further demands on cardiac output as in hypovolemia, or damage from inflammation or surgical intervention.

F. In hypertensive crisis, impedance to left ventricular emptying is high (increase afterload) so that cardiac output decreases and coronary perfusion ultimately diminishes and myocardial ischemia or failure ensues.

G. Hypoglycemia, idiopathic or secondary to other metabolic disorders, is associated with decreased myocardial contractility. Thyrotoxicosis increases the body's metabolic demands that could exhaust the limited reserve of the neonatal myocardium to meet the demand of increases in cardiac output.

HSB

References

Crone RK. Acute circulatory failure in children. Pediatr Clin North Am 1980; 27:525.

Hohn AR, Stanton RE. Postoperative care, counseling, and medications. In: Fanaroff AA, Martin RJ, eds. Neonatal-perinatal medicine: Diseases of the fetus and infant. 5th ed. St Louis, Mosby–Year Book, 1992:931.

Keeley SR, Bohn DJ. The use of inotropic and afterload-reducing agents in neonates. Clin Perinatol 1988; 15:467.

MYOCARDIAL ISCHEMIA

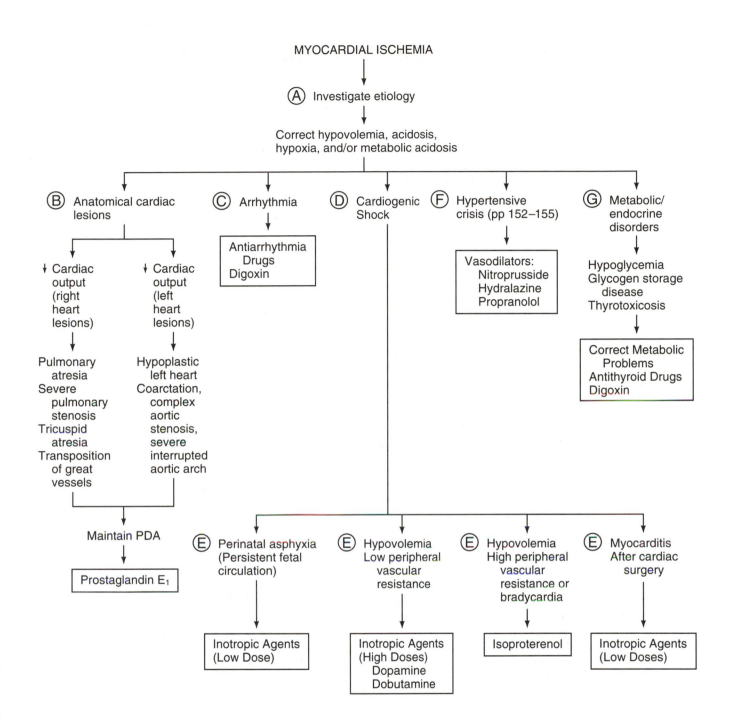

Ⓐ Investigate etiology

Correct hypovolemia, acidosis, hypoxia, and/or metabolic acidosis

Ⓑ Anatomical cardiac lesions

↓ Cardiac output (right heart lesions)

↓ Cardiac output (left heart lesions)

Pulmonary atresia
Severe pulmonary stenosis
Tricuspid atresia
Transposition of great vessels

Hypoplastic left heart
Coarctation, complex aortic stenosis, severe interrupted aortic arch

Maintain PDA

Prostaglandin E₁

Ⓒ Arrhythmia

Antiarrhythmia Drugs
Digoxin

Ⓓ Cardiogenic Shock

Ⓕ Hypertensive crisis (pp 152–155)

Vasodilators:
Nitroprusside
Hydralazine
Propranolol

Ⓖ Metabolic/ endocrine disorders

Hypoglycemia
Glycogen storage disease
Thyrotoxicosis

Correct Metabolic Problems
Antithyroid Drugs
Digoxin

Ⓔ Perinatal asphyxia (Persistent fetal circulation)

Inotropic Agents (Low Dose)

Ⓔ Hypovolemia
Low peripheral vascular resistance

Inotropic Agents (High Doses)
Dopamine
Dobutamine

Ⓔ Hypovolemia
High peripheral vascular resistance or bradycardia

Isoproterenol

Ⓔ Myocarditis
After cardiac surgery

Inotropic Agents (Low Doses)

NECROTIZING ENTEROCOLITIS: DIAGNOSIS

A. The vast majority (90%) of infants with necrotizing enterocolitis (NEC) are premature. Over 95% of infants are fed enterally at the time of onset; in most symptoms appear 5–7 days after feedings begin. Onset of disease is reported to occur as early as the first day and as late as the ninety-ninth day; but in most instances, onset occurs between 7 and 14 days.

B. NEC rarely begins gradually, rarely occurs without some degree of abdominal distention, and rarely progresses in a saltatory pattern. Severity of disease is grossly correlated with x-ray findings that delineate stages I, II, and III. Thus the clinical signs of mild disease (stage I) are often transient, usually consisting of moderate abdominal distention and increased volumes of gastric aspirate. Abdominal radiograph reveals that the bowel is distended without identifiable gas in the intestinal wall or the portal vein. This triad of abdominal distention, gastric retention, and intestinal dilatation without pneumatosis on x-ray findings is generally the result of feeding intolerance. However, NEC is a more likely diagnosis if these signs are associated with pallor, recurrent apnea and bradycardia, and frank or occult blood in stools. In babies with any of these additional signs, the distended bowel may be grossly uneven, suggesting segmental involvement and loop distention. This x-ray appearance is in distinct contrast to the homogeneous distention ("bag of bubbles") that characterizes feeding intolerance. In the list of generalized signs, the lower the position of any given sign, the more severe is the disease. Furthermore, any single sign on this list is usually associated with one or more above it. The list of gastrointestinal signs is also progressive in severity, but these abnormalities occur in varying combinations.

C. The abdominal radiograph is a diagnostic keystone. It is extremely difficult to establish the diagnosis without pneumatosis intestinalis, or portal vein air, or peritoneal air and/or fluid. Bubbles in the hepatic portal vein, not visible on radiograph, can sometimes be identified by abdominal ultrasound. Experience has shown that 90% of verified diagnoses (x-ray findings, surgery, or autopsy) are associated with an elevated C-reactive protein (CRP) in any of three samples taken at onset and at 12-hour intervals thereafter. Once elevated, the CRP persists or rises as NEC progresses, and it declines as the disease recedes. Sepsis has been reported in approximately 20%–40% of stage II and III disease, but in a recent study (unpublished) blood cultures were positive in approximately 60% of stage II and 70% of stage III disease. The clinical course of NEC is considerably more severe when complicated by septicemia.

D. A broad classification of NEC is used based on x-ray appearance because the association of specific clinical signs with radiological patterns is so often unpredictable. Stage I is thus designated by intestinal dilatation, particularly if uneven rather than homogeneous. Stage II is characterized by intestinal distention, pneumatosis intestinalis, and sometimes portal venous air. Stage III implies perforation of the gut wall, either gross or microscopic, as indicated on x-ray findings by free peritoneal air, or less often by peritoneal fluid (purulent or sanguinous).

SBK

References

Anderson DM, Kliegman RM. The relationship of neonatal alimentation practices to the occurrence of endemic necrotizing enterocolitis. Am J Perinatol 1991; 8:62–67.

Kennedy J, Holt CL, Ricketts RR. The significance of portal vein gas in necrotizing enterocolitis. Am Surg 1987; 53:231–234.

Kleigman RM, Walsh MC. Neonatal necrotizing enterocolitis: Pathogenesis, classification, and spectrum of illness. Curr Probl Pediatr 1987; 17:219–288.

Kosloske AM, Musemeche CA. Necrotizing enterocolitis of the neonate. Clin Perinatol 1989; 16:97–111.

Ostertag SG, LaGamma EF, Reisen CE, Ferrentino FL: Early enteral feeding does not affect the incidence of necrotizing enterocolitis. Pediatrics 1986; 77:275–280.

NECROTIZING ENTEROCOLITIS: DIAGNOSIS

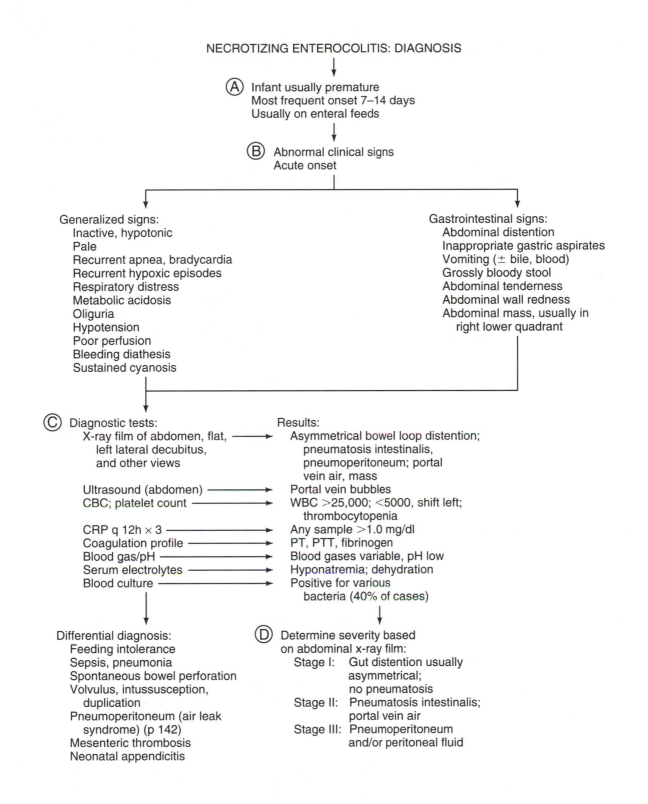

Ⓐ Infant usually premature
Most frequent onset 7–14 days
Usually on enteral feeds

Ⓑ Abnormal clinical signs
Acute onset

Generalized signs:
  Inactive, hypotonic
  Pale
  Recurrent apnea, bradycardia
  Recurrent hypoxic episodes
  Respiratory distress
  Metabolic acidosis
  Oliguria
  Hypotension
  Poor perfusion
  Bleeding diathesis
  Sustained cyanosis

Gastrointestinal signs:
  Abdominal distention
  Inappropriate gastric aspirates
  Vomiting (± bile, blood)
  Grossly bloody stool
  Abdominal tenderness
  Abdominal wall redness
  Abdominal mass, usually in
    right lower quadrant

Ⓒ Diagnostic tests: Results:
  X-ray film of abdomen, flat, ———→   Asymmetrical bowel loop distention;
    left lateral decubitus,   pneumatosis intestinalis,
    and other views   pneumoperitoneum; portal
                                             vein air, mass

  Ultrasound (abdomen) ————————→   Portal vein bubbles
  CBC; platelet count ————————————→   WBC >25,000; <5000, shift left;
                                             thrombocytopenia

  CRP q 12h × 3 ————————————————→   Any sample >1.0 mg/dl
  Coagulation profile ———————————→   PT, PTT, fibrinogen
  Blood gas/pH ————————————————→   Blood gases variable, pH low
  Serum electrolytes ————————————→   Hyponatremia; dehydration
  Blood culture ————————————————→   Positive for various
                                             bacteria (40% of cases)

Differential diagnosis: Ⓓ Determine severity based
  Feeding intolerance   on abdominal x-ray film:
  Sepsis, pneumonia   Stage I: Gut distention usually
  Spontaneous bowel perforation   asymmetrical;
  Volvulus, intussusception,   no pneumatosis
    duplication   Stage II: Pneumatosis intestinalis;
  Pneumoperitoneum (air leak   portal vein air
    syndrome) (p 142)   Stage III: Pneumoperitoneum
  Mesenteric thrombosis   and/or peritoneal fluid
  Neonatal appendicitis

NECROTIZING ENTEROCOLITIS: MANAGEMENT

A. Most episodes of stage I necrotizing enterocolitis (NEC) are "NEC scares" caused by feeding intolerance, but NEC is a hovering possibility that must be addressed. Management at the most basic level is withdrawal of enteral feedings, institution of parenteral alimentation or IV fluids, and administration of antibiotics. Duration of treatment varies from several hours to 3 days. It is not unusual for primary septicemia to present as an apparent stage I NEC.

B. Stage II may follow a short episode of stage I, but more often it is the presenting illness. Since stage II is so varied in severity, management entails detection of physiological abnormalities (none of which are unique to NEC), and attempts to minimize them, i.e., respiratory support, abdominal decompression, antibiotic therapy, correction of fluid, electrolyte, and acid-base imbalances, restoration of hemostasis, and cardiovascular support that includes volume expansion and vasoactive drugs. When needed, mechanical respiratory support for NEC is usually less vigorous than for intrinsic lung disease. Failure to breathe is presumably of central origin; difficulty with oxygenation is probably of cardiovascular origin. Antibiotics are chosen as for primary septicemia. Some consider it essential to treat the patient for the possibility of infection by anaerobes. Fluid therapy is aimed at third space losses, either anticipated or actual. Thus once the diagnosis of stage II NEC is made, the quantity of fluid administered should be greater than that used for maintenance. Metabolic acidosis can be expected in moderately and severely ill babies. Correction may be attempted by sporadic administration of sodium bicarbonate in calculated doses. For severe persistent acidosis continuous intravenous drip may be used in doses of 0.5–1.0 mEq/kg/h, sometimes more depending on the severity. Sodium and blood gas/pH determinations at least every 4 hours are indispensable while the bicarbonate drip is in progress. Bleeding diatheses are most frequently caused by thrombocytopenia; disseminated intravascular coagulopathy (DIC) develops in a substantial number of instances. Repeated platelet administration is essential for thrombocytopenia; fresh frozen plasma (FFP) is used for DIC and for volume expansion. Cardiovascular support may require dopamine and/or dobutamine. Dopamine in small doses (2.5–5.0 μg/kg/min) is intended to promote renal and mesenteric perfusion; dobutamine is used to increase cardiac output when vascular collapse occurs or when it seems imminent. As the disease recedes, the various modalities of multisystem support may be discontinued. Enteral feedings can generally be reinstituted approximately 14 days after their withdrawal. Feedings can begin earlier if the C-reactive protein (CRP) level has been normal for 3–5 days, if abnormal clinical signs have disappeared, and if the abdominal radiograph is normal.

C. Stage III requires surgical intervention. Indications for operation vary among surgeons, but there is general agreement that free peritoneal air requires operation. At some institutions failure of response to medical treatment and abrupt deterioration are also indications for surgery. Unconfirmed evidence suggests that in babies <1000 g, temporary insertion of a peritoneal drain followed later by surgical repair may be salutary. Peritoneal drainage is not recommended as a definitive alternative to laparotomy, but rather as an ameliorative procedure preceding it.

D. Among survivors of medically treated NEC, the incidence of postnecrotic intestinal stricture is 9%–44%. In most series the incidence is between 15% and 23%. Symptoms generally appear 6–10 weeks following the acute disease, but reported onset varies from 10 days–20 months. The colon is affected in 80% of cases; small bowel involvement is virtually always in the terminal ileum. There seems to be little relationship between clinical severity of the acute disease and incidence of strictures. Strictures following stage I are not rare. Mortality from complications of strictures has been estimated at 8%.

SBK

References

Cheu HW, Sukarochana K, Lloyd DA. Peritoneal drainage for necrotizing enterocolitis. J Pediatr Surg 1988; 23: 557–561.

Cikrit D, Mastandrea J, West KW, et al. Necrotizing enterocolitis: Factors affecting mortality in 101 surgical cases. Surgery 1984; 96:648–655.

Frey EE, Smith W, Franken EA, Jr, Wintermeyer KA. Analysis of bowel perforation in necrotizing enterocolitis. Pediatr Radiol 1987; 17:380–382.

Hartman GE, Drugas GT, Shochat SJ. Post-necrotizing strictures presenting with sepsis or perforation: Risk of clinical observation. J Pediatr Surg 1988; 23:562–566.

Kosloske AM, Goldthorn JF: Paracentesis as an aid to the diagnosis of intestinal gangrene. Arch Surg 1982; 117:571–575.

Walsh MC, Kliegman RM. Necrotizing enterocolitis: Treatment based on staging criteria. Pediatr Clin North Am 1986; 33:179–201.

NECROTIZING ENTEROCOLITIS: MANAGEMENT

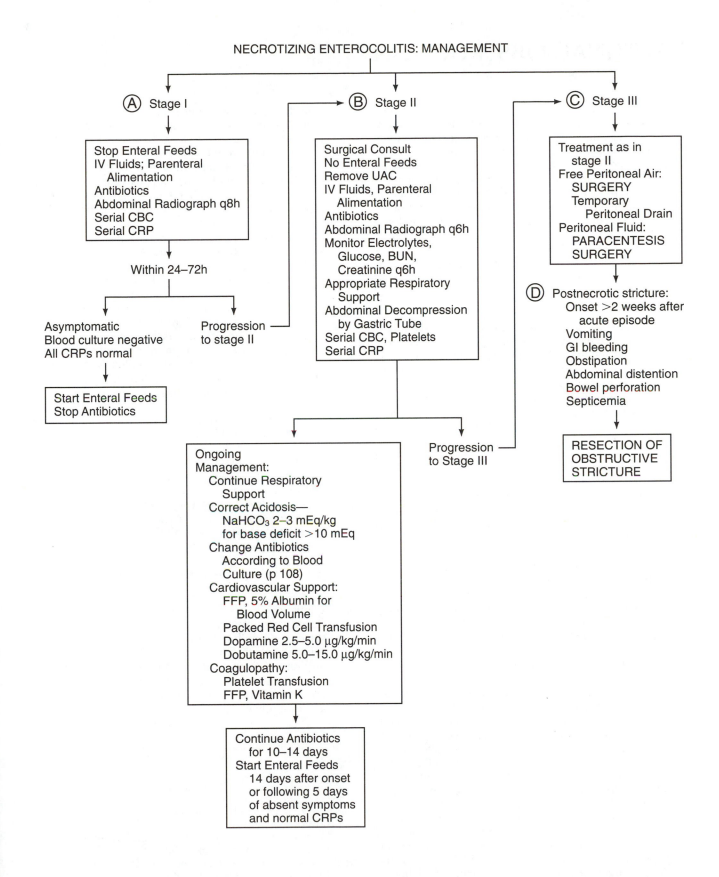

Ⓐ Stage I

Stop Enteral Feeds
IV Fluids; Parenteral
  Alimentation
Antibiotics
Abdominal Radiograph q8h
Serial CBC
Serial CRP

Within 24–72h

Asymptomatic
Blood culture negative
All CRPs normal

Start Enteral Feeds
Stop Antibiotics

Progression
to stage II

Ⓑ Stage II

Surgical Consult
No Enteral Feeds
Remove UAC
IV Fluids, Parenteral
  Alimentation
Antibiotics
Abdominal Radiograph q6h
Monitor Electrolytes,
  Glucose, BUN,
  Creatinine q6h
Appropriate Respiratory
  Support
Abdominal Decompression
  by Gastric Tube
Serial CBC, Platelets
Serial CRP

Progression
to Stage III

Ⓒ Stage III

Treatment as in
  stage II
Free Peritoneal Air:
  SURGERY
  Temporary
    Peritoneal Drain
Peritoneal Fluid:
  PARACENTESIS
  SURGERY

Ⓓ Postnecrotic stricture:
  Onset >2 weeks after
    acute episode
  Vomiting
  GI bleeding
  Obstipation
  Abdominal distention
  Bowel perforation
  Septicemia

RESECTION OF
OBSTRUCTIVE
STRICTURE

Ongoing
Management:
  Continue Respiratory
    Support
  Correct Acidosis—
    NaHCO$_3$ 2–3 mEq/kg
    for base deficit >10 mEq
  Change Antibiotics
    According to Blood
    Culture (p 108)
  Cardiovascular Support:
    FFP, 5% Albumin for
      Blood Volume
    Packed Red Cell Transfusion
    Dopamine 2.5–5.0 μg/kg/min
    Dobutamine 5.0–15.0 μg/kg/min
  Coagulopathy:
    Platelet Transfusion
    FFP, Vitamin K

Continue Antibiotics
  for 10–14 days
Start Enteral Feeds
  14 days after onset
  or following 5 days
  of absent symptoms
  and normal CRPs

INTESTINAL OBSTRUCTION

A. Abdominal distention that is localized in the upper abdomen and bilious vomiting indicate duodenal or upper jejunal obstruction. The diagnosis is often made prenatally by ultrasound, which is usually performed in response to the appearance of polyhydramnios. Vomiting without a bilious component is quite infrequent by virtue of the low incidence of preampullary obstructions. These upper intestinal obstructions are usually identifiable in plain abdominal radiographs. The double-bubble sign, caused by distention of the duodenum and stomach, is a hallmark of duodenal atresia, or more rarely of annular pancreas. In high jejunal atresia one or two distended loops are evident in the absence of distal intestinal gas.

B. The lower the obstructive lesion, the more generalized is abdominal distention, and the greater the number of distended loops on the radiograph. Bilious vomiting and impaired meconium passage are usually prominent features of the disease. Atresia of the jejunum and ileum occur with equal frequency. A history of polyhydramnios is more likely in jejunal obstruction; it is rare in ileal involvement. Plain abdominal films (supine and lateral decubitus) indicate the diagnosis clearly. Level of involvement may be surmised from the number of distended loops. Air-fluid levels are characteristic. Calcifications suggest intrauterine intestinal perforation (meconium peritonitis).

Meconium ileus is the first sign of cystic fibrosis in 10% of affected children. Intestinal involvement is infrequent in black children, corresponding to the low racial incidence of cystic fibrosis. Clinical signs are typical of ileal obstruction, making their appearance within 48 hours of age. Failure to pass meconium is associated with severe abdominal distention and bilious vomiting. Firm loops of meconium-containing bowel are easily palpated unless the abdomen is so tight as to preclude informative examination. X-ray findings reveal multiple distended loops. Tiny entrapments of air within the inspissated meconium appear as multiple bubbles in bowel. This "soap bubble" appearance also occurs in atresias, Hirschsprung's disease, and meconium plug syndrome. The usual absence of air-fluid levels distinguishes meconium ileus from jejunoileal atresia. Contrast studies demonstrate a narrow unused colon. The inspissated meconium becomes visible when contrast die refluxes into the terminal ileum. Nonsurgical treatment entails attempts to remove meconium with a hyperosmolar enema. The procedure may be complicated with hypovolemic shock (particularly in suboptimal hydration) and in perforation of the bowel. When performed in proper circumstances by experienced personnel, hyperosmolar enemas are successful in 60% of patients. Surgery is the primary therapeutic modality for meconium ileus complicated by volvulus, perforation, or peritonitis.

Midgut volvulus requires urgent surgical intervention. It generally occurs as a complication of malrotation and associated duodenal bands. Abrupt appearance of bilious vomiting and abdominal distention of varying degrees require immediate evaluation for the possibility of volvulus, as well as other obstructive intestinal disorders. Other symptoms include shock, sepsis, and grossly bloody stools. Complications of volvulus include necrosis and perforation of the bowel. The radiograph reveals a high intestinal obstruction, usually from duodenal bands. An upper gastrointestinal contrast study reveals the site of obstruction. Barium enema may reveal a highly placed cecum or alternatively the contrast medium may fail to pass beyond the transverse colon.

Failure to pass meconium by 48 hours postnatally requires consideration of Hirschsprung's disease. Obstipation is the rule but symptoms may not appear until several weeks of age. The entire colon is involved in 10% of affected infants; in the remainder involvement is rectosigmoid. X-ray diagnosis requires a contrast study that demonstrates the conical transitional zone between the narrow aganglionic segment and the distended proximal bowel. Suction rectal biopsy is the definitive diagnostic procedure in most cases.

The meconium plug syndrome is manifest in the first three days as a lower intestinal obstruction. Gentle cautious rectal examination may cause the meconium plug to pass. Contrast enema may be necessary for diagnosis; it is therapeutic as well. The radiograph demonstrates a long meconium plug. Half of affected infants are born of diabetic mothers. Additionally, cystic fibrosis is present in approximately 20%. A sweat chloride test is therefore indicated in meconium plug syndrome.

C. Continuous gastric suction is indicated for all types of severe gastrointestinal obstruction. In extreme circumstances, distention leads to bowel perforation or to splinting of the diaphragm, which causes severe respiratory distress. Fluid and electrolyte losses are inevitable and often extensive. Laboratory determinations every 6 hours are essential to monitor hydration and electrolyte status.

SBK

References

Flake AW, Ryckman FC. Selected anomalies and intestinal obstruction. In: Fanaroff AA, Martin RJ: Neonatal-perinatal medicine: diseases of the fetus and infant. 5th ed. St Louis: Mosby—Year Book, 1992:1038.

Reyes HM, Meller JL, Loeff D. Neonatal intestinal obstruction. Clin Perinatol 1989; 16:85—96.

Swischuk LE. Radiology of the newborn and young infant. 2nd ed. Baltimore: Williams & Wilkins, 1980:400.

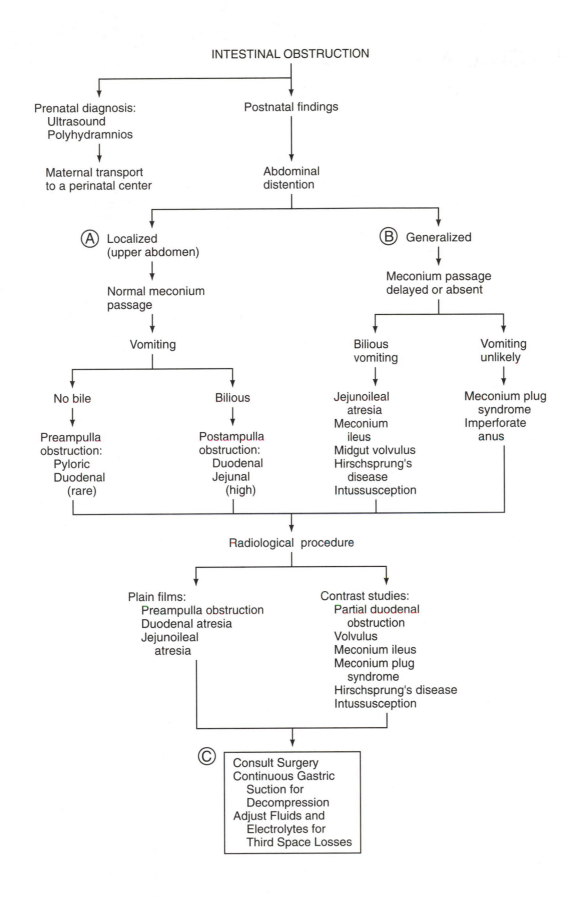

INTESTINAL OBSTRUCTION

Prenatal diagnosis:
  Ultrasound
  Polyhydramnios

Maternal transport
to a perinatal center

Postnatal findings

Abdominal
distention

Ⓐ Localized
(upper abdomen)

Normal meconium
passage

Vomiting

No bile

Preampulla
obstruction:
  Pyloric
  Duodenal
  (rare)

Bilious

Postampulla
obstruction:
  Duodenal
  Jejunal
  (high)

Ⓑ Generalized

Meconium passage
delayed or absent

Bilious
vomiting

Jejunoileal
  atresia
Meconium
  ileus
Midgut volvulus
Hirschsprung's
  disease
Intussusception

Vomiting
unlikely

Meconium plug
  syndrome
Imperforate
  anus

Radiological procedure

Plain films:
  Preampulla obstruction
  Duodenal atresia
  Jejunoileal
    atresia

Contrast studies:
  Partial duodenal
    obstruction
  Volvulus
  Meconium ileus
  Meconium plug
    syndrome
  Hirschsprung's disease
  Intussusception

Ⓒ | Consult Surgery
Continuous Gastric
  Suction for
  Decompression
Adjust Fluids and
  Electrolytes for
  Third Space Losses

ESOPHAGEAL ATRESIA AND TRACHEOESOPHAGEAL FISTULA

A. In the presence of the listed symptoms and historical factors, demonstration of the esophageal pouch must be attempted. The most direct procedure entails passage of a radiopaque catheter that curls in the atretic esophageal pouch. Occasionally it may be necessary to use air as a contrast medium to outline the pouch. With bag and mask, timing the x-ray trigger with an insufflation, the esophagus fills with air that will be clearly seen on the radiograph. Use of contrast dye is hazardous and rarely necessary. Aspiration into the airway may be severely damaging.

B. Esophageal atresia is overwhelmingly more common in association with a tracheoesophageal fistula (TEF) between the distal esophagus and the carina or close to it. Air enters the stomach and the intestinal tract and is thus visible on abdominal radiographs. Presence of an esophageal pouch associated with intestinal air is diagnostic of TEF. Abdominal distention is frequent. Reflux of gastric secretions causes chemical pneumonitis; secretions that emerge from the trachea are occasionally bilious. The absence of intestinal air on the radiograph is diagnostic of esophageal atresias without tracheal fistulae.

Fistulae between the proximal esophageal segment and the trachea are rare. More frequently but still rare, the H-type fistula connects the trachea to an intact esophagus. A large proportion of these lesions only become symptomatic several months after birth. In the neonatal period, symptoms are generally caused by a large fistula. A number of H-type fistulae have been reported during the neonatal period following recovery from pneumonia due to Group B Streptococcus.

C. Before transfer for surgery, continuous suction is essential to avoid aspiration of accumulated secretions. In the presence of the common type of TEF, the need for mechanical respiratory support imposes a hazard of severe gastric distention. The lowest effective pressures at a relatively high respiratory rate are essential. A gastrostomy tube should be in place as soon as feasible. The baby should be tilted (head up) 30–45 degrees. In this position gastric reflux through the fistula into the lungs and the accumulation of secretions in the esophageal pouch are minimized.

SBK

References

Avery ME, Fletcher BD, Williams RG. The lung and its disorders in the newborn infant. 4th ed. Philadelphia: WB Saunders, 1981:150.

Holder TM, Ashcraft KW. Developments in the care of patients with esophageal atresia and tracheoesophageal fistula. Surg Clin North Am 1981; 61:1051.

Reyes HM, Meller JL, Loeff D. Management of esophageal atresia and tracheoesophageal fistula. Clin Perinatol 1989; 16:79–84.

Sillen U. Hagberg S, Rubenson A. Management of esophageal atresia: Review of 16 years' experience. J Pediatr Surg 1988; 23:805.

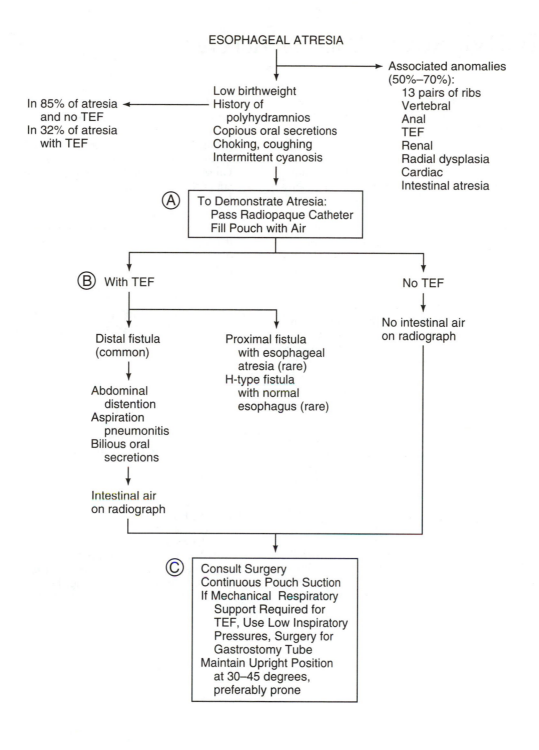

ESOPHAGEAL ATRESIA

Associated anomalies
(50%–70%):
  13 pairs of ribs
  Vertebral
  Anal
  TEF
  Renal
  Radial dysplasia
  Cardiac
  Intestinal atresia

In 85% of atresia
and no TEF
In 32% of atresia
with TEF

Low birthweight
History of
  polyhydramnios
Copious oral secretions
Choking, coughing
Intermittent cyanosis

Ⓐ To Demonstrate Atresia:
  Pass Radiopaque Catheter
  Fill Pouch with Air

Ⓑ With TEF

No TEF

Distal fistula
(common)

Proximal fistula
  with esophageal
  atresia (rare)
H-type fistula
  with normal
  esophagus (rare)

No intestinal air
on radiograph

Abdominal
  distention
Aspiration
  pneumonitis
Bilious oral
  secretions

Intestinal air
on radiograph

Ⓒ Consult Surgery
Continuous Pouch Suction
If Mechanical Respiratory
  Support Required for
  TEF, Use Low Inspiratory
  Pressures, Surgery for
  Gastrostomy Tube
Maintain Upright Position
  at 30–45 degrees,
  preferably prone

INEFFECTIVE SUCK AND SWALLOW

A. During acute and depressed phases of illness the suck and swallow is seldom challenged. The clinical conditions addressed here concern those infants who have either recovered from acute distress or were never in such a state. Suck and swallow should be effective in infants who are well or recuperative between 32 and 34 conceptual weeks. In many instances early ineffective attempts to suck and swallow can be attributed to immaturity, in others the dysfunction is pathological and permanent, although it may improve after a regimen of physical therapy. Those infants in whom suck and swallow defects persist will ultimately require gastrostomy for their enteral feeds.

B. Structural defects are either obstructive or are so defective as to preclude normal function (cleft lip and palate). Macroglossia and micrognathia are usually components of a number of congenital malformation syndromes. The cleft palate fixed tongue, microstomia, and micrognathia of Pierre-Robin syndrome prevent normal sucking but more impressively, breathing as well. Clefts of the lip and palate preclude effective sucking rather than swallowing.

C. Functional defects are the result of neurological and muscular abnormalities. Severe cerebral damage is a residuum of acute asphyxiating episodes and infections, both bacterial and nonbacterial. Myasthenia gravis (neonatal transient) occurs in 15% of neonates delivered by mothers who have the adult form of the disease. Onset is within three days of birth and frequently the most impressive initial sign is impaired function of suck and swallow. Cranial nerve impairment produces numerous troublesome manifestations such as respiratory difficulty because of pooled oral secretions and respiratory muscle weakness; the cry is weak and facial diplegia is striking. Congenital myotonic dystrophy is a heritable disease characterized by muscle weakness that is often severe. Polyhydramnios is consistent in severely affected infants, probably as a consequence of impaired swallowing in utero. Clinical problems include need for mechanical respiratory support, feeding, hypotonia, and arthrogryposis. Mortality is high among neonates. Infantile botulism is caused by ingested *Clostridium botulinum* organisms rather than the toxin that the organism has elaborated. It may begin late in the neonatal period, but more often during postneonatal infancy. Vague feeding difficulties and constipation are the usual initial signs that soon progress to impaired suck and swallow, facial diplegia, and global peripheral weakness. Premature infants who are otherwise well can first suck and swallow at approximately 33–34 conceptual weeks.

SBK

References

Gryboski J, Walker WA. Suck and swallow. In: Gastrointestinal problems in the infant. 2nd ed. Philadelphia: WB Saunders, 1983:12.

Herbst JJ. Development of suck and swallow. In: Lebenthal E, ed. Human gastrointestinal development. New York: Raven Press, 1989:229.

Ryckman FC, Flake AW, Balistreri WF. Upper gastrointestinal disorders. In: Fanaroff AA, Martin RJ, eds. Neonatal-perinatal medicine: Diseases of the fetus and infant. 5th ed. St Louis: Mosby-Year Book, 1992:1024.

Volpe JJ. The neurological exam: Normal and abnormal features. In: Neurology of the newborn. 2nd ed. Philadelphia: WB Saunders, 1987:77, 88.

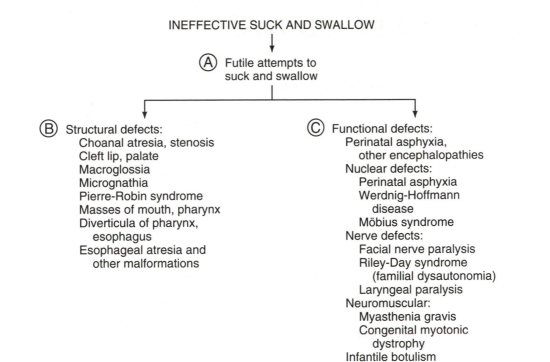

INEFFECTIVE SUCK AND SWALLOW

(A) Futile attempts to suck and swallow

(B) Structural defects:
   Choanal atresia, stenosis
   Cleft lip, palate
   Macroglossia
   Micrognathia
   Pierre-Robin syndrome
   Masses of mouth, pharynx
   Diverticula of pharynx,
      esophagus
   Esophageal atresia and
      other malformations

(C) Functional defects:
   Perinatal asphyxia,
      other encephalopathies
   Nuclear defects:
      Perinatal asphyxia
      Werdnig-Hoffmann
         disease
      Möbius syndrome
   Nerve defects:
      Facial nerve paralysis
      Riley-Day syndrome
         (familial dysautonomia)
      Laryngeal paralysis
   Neuromuscular:
      Myasthenia gravis
      Congenital myotonic
         dystrophy
   Infantile botulism
   Prematurity (<33–34 weeks)

ANEMIA DUE TO BLOOD LOSS

A. Anemia due to blood loss presents with pallor and low hematocrit. An infant with an acute blood loss has moderate to severe cardiorespiratory distress because of hypovolemia; BP is low, peripheral smear shows a macrocytic normochromic type of anemia, and reticulocyte count is normal. With chronic anemia or chronic blood loss, the pale infant is not in distress; the infant is normovolemic with a normal BP. The high reticulocyte count indicates the chronicity of the anemia. Peripheral smear is consistent with microcytic and hypochromic anemia.

B. Acute blood loss is suspected in the presence of obstetrical complications such as placenta previa, abruptio placentae, or bleeding from low-lying placental vessels. Umbilical vein rupture leads to massive hemorrhage with severe hypovolemia and hypotension. Diagnosis is easily established by careful inspection of the placenta and the umbilical cord; further histopathological studies may be necessary to confirm the diagnosis.

C. In the postnatal period, acute blood loss may result from hemorrhages or bleeding in various organ systems. Pulmonary hemorrhage is not uncommon, especially in an infant requiring ventilator therapy. In this condition, a large amount of fresh blood is suctioned from the endotracheal tube, and there is acute clinical deterioration. Chest x-ray demonstrates radiodensities, and the infant usually requires adjustment in ventilator settings: increasing oxygen requirement, peak inspiratory pressure, and distending pressure. Extracranial hemorrhage as in subgaleal hemorrhage is suspected because of a rapidly increasing head size, progressive pallor, and clinical deterioration. Subgaleal hemorrhage is often so massive that the infant requires a large volume of blood transfusion and plasma expanders. Intracranial hemorrhage such as periventricular-intraventricular hemorrhage is usually suspected in a premature infant with respiratory distress syndrome. The infant can also sustain hemorrhage in the liver, spleen, kidneys, and other viscera. Acute blood loss also occurs in disseminated intravascular coagulation (DIC), which may result from various conditions such as infection, asphyxia, and necrotizing enterocolitis. An infant may have an acute blood loss from a disconnected peripheral arterial cannula or from unsecured umbilical arterial line; blood loss is more rapid when the bleeding source is arterial versus venous. Head or abdominal ultrasound studies aid detection of intracranial or intraabdominal hemorrhages. Clotting studies (platelet count, prothrombin time, partial thromboplastin time, fibrin degradation products, and fibrinogen levels) are useful to establish the diagnosis of DIC.

D. Prenatal causes (feto-maternal, feto-fetal, and feto-placental transfusions) most often result in chronic blood loss. Maternal chills and fever have been reported in association with massive fetomaternal transfusion. Kleihauer-Betke stain on the maternal blood demonstrates fetomaternal transfusion; a large proportion of acid-resistant (fetal) cells is seen compared with the number of ghost (maternal) cells. Fetofetal transfusion, particularly of the chronic type, is always considered when twins of the same sex are discordant, the smaller twin being the donor twin with the chronic anemia while the larger twin is the recipient with polycythemia and hyperviscosity. Fetoplacental transfusion occurs with cord prolapse or a nuchal cord. In these instances, partial obstruction (i.e., umbilical vein blood flow obstruction while umbilical arterial flow continues) results in fetal hypovolemia, clinically manifesting with signs of acute blood loss.

E. Frequent intermittent blood sampling and GI disorders wherein occult bleeding occurs over a period of time need to be considered as causes of chronic blood loss.

F. In acute blood loss, the immediate goal is to normalize blood volume by volume expansion as either blood transfusion or plasma expanders. Supportive therapy (e.g., oxygen therapy or ventilator therapy) is administered to babies with severe cardiorespiratory distress.

G. In chronic blood loss, therapy is mainly supportive because infants are asymptomatic. Because the infant's iron stores are usually depleted, iron supplementation is indicated. To increase the hematocrit while maintaining normovolemia, partial exchange transfusion with packed cells may be necessary.

HSB

References

Blanchette VS, Zipursky A. Assessment of anemia in newborn infants. Clin Perinatol 1984; 11:489.

Oski FA, Naiman JL. Hematologic problems in the newborn. 3rd ed. Philadelphia: WB Saunders, 1982:56.

ANEMA DUE TO BLOOD LOSS

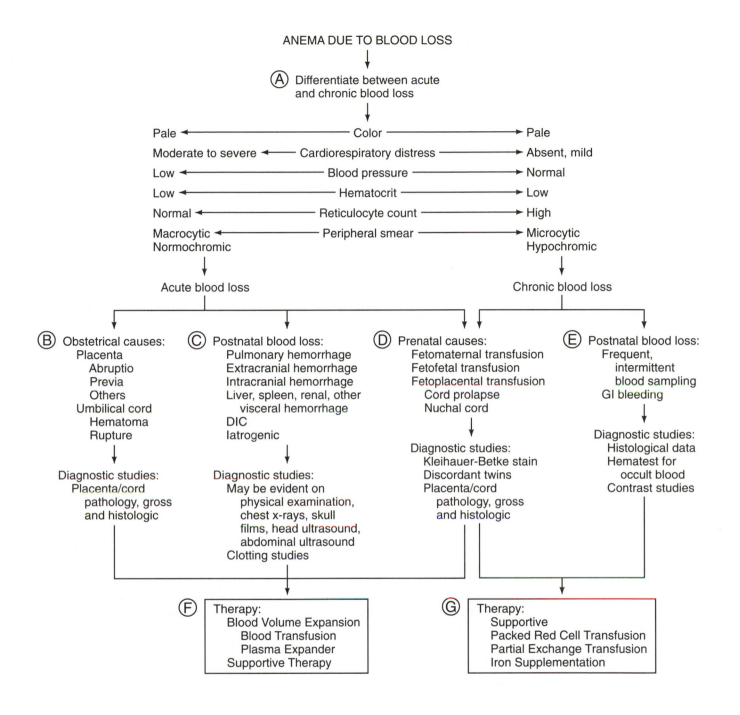

ANEMIA DUE TO HEMOLYSIS

A. Hemolysis refers to breakdown of red blood cells (RBCs), resulting in anemia that is clinically manifested as pallor. Jaundice may be observed with the breakdown of RBCs because of the synthesis of bilirubin from heme liberated from the hemolyzed RBCs. When anemia becomes severe, cardiorespiratory distress may be evident. Hepatosplenomegaly results because of extramedullary hematopoiesis triggered by rapid destruction of RBCs. Fetal anemia from hemolysis in utero is also associated not only with hepatosplenomegaly but also with myocardial dysfunction, resulting in fluid accumulation, anasarca or generalized edema, and low serum albumin.

B. In hemolytic anemia, laboratory abnormalities include a low hematocrit, a high reticulocyte count (normal 4%–5%), elevated bilirubin level, and abnormal peripheral smear. The presence of abnormally shaped RBCs, spherocytes, or nucleated RBCs in the peripheral smear suggests hemolysis. A positive Coombs' test indicates an immune process.

C. The more common immune hemolytic disorders include ABO incompatibility and Rh incompatibility. In ABO incompatibility, anti-A antibodies (7S fraction of the serum) in mothers with type O or type B blood group cross the placenta. Hemolysis develops when the infant's RBCs bear the A antigen. Hemolysis from anti-A and anti-B antibodies demonstrates spherocytes on the infant's peripheral smear, possibly a result of the removal of the portion of the RBC membrane in the spleen, releasing cells containing reduced surface area and cell volume. ABO incompatibility may be demonstrated with the first pregnancy. The clinical expression of this hemolytic disease is less severe than Rh incompatibility. In Rh incompatibility, the mother is Rh negative, i.e., homozygous d/d. The mother is usually sensitized during pregnancy when the fetal RBCs enter the maternal circulation. Approximately 1 ml of blood appears to be necessary to sensitize the mother to the fetal Rh antigen (D). Since most sensitization occurs with pregnancy, the severity of the clinical expression in the infant of Rh incompatibility increases with subsequent pregnancies. Management of Rh incompatibility or Rh hemolytic disease usually is initiated early in pregnancy; hydrops fetalis or fetal death may be prevented by intrauterine transfusion. The minor blood group antigens include Kell, Duffy, Lewis, Kidd, M, S, and the less antigenic components of the Rh system (C, c, E, and e). Sensitization to minor blood group antigens is also possible. The expression of the hemolytic disease in the newborn may vary from subclinical evidence of sensitization to hydrops fetalis. The management of severe blood group incompatibility with severe hemolysis includes supportive measures and, specifically, exchange transfusion. Phototherapy may be used as an adjunct to exchange transfusion for the treatment of the associated hyperbilirubinemia.

D. Other immune disorders that may cause hemolysis in the newborn include maternal lupus erythematosus, rheumatoid arthritis, and autoimmune hemolytic disease. The Coombs test is positive in the mother and the neonate but no antibody to the RBC antigen such as A, B, or Rh is demonstrated. Antibodies from drugs (penicillin) may also cause hemolysis.

E. Hemolysis may be acquired prenatally or postnatally as in neonatal infection. With the rising incidence of congenital syphilis, this disease must be ruled out in an infant who is anemic with a high reticulocyte count. Disseminated intravascular coagulation (DIC) is manifested by abnormal bleeding from puncture sites and/or from orifices with thrombocytopenia, prolonged partial thromboplastin time (PTT), low fibrinogen, and increased fibrin degradation products. Management of DIC includes platelet transfusion, administration of fresh frozen plasma, or exchange transfusion. Heparinization may also be an alternative therapy.

F. Hereditary RBC disorders may be divided according to whether a defect is in the RBC membrane, enzyme, or hemoglobin. Hereditary spherocytosis may be transmitted as autosomal dominant; the defect is in the binding of spectrin to actin as a result of abnormal binding of another membrane protein, band 4.1. In the autosomal recessive form, spectrin deficiency has been demonstrated. Hereditary spherocytosis may be asymptomatic, severe, or may present with chronic anemia. In spherocytosis, 25% of cases are sporadic. The other hemolytic diseases with a defect in the RBC membrane are elliptocytosis and stomatocytosis. In hereditary elliptocytosis, the defect in association with spectrin dimers results in a decreased mechanical stability of the membrane. RBCs undergo elliptical deformation, i.e., elliptocytes in the peripheral smear. In hereditary stomatocytosis, the RBCs are swollen and cup shaped. The activity of the sodium potassium pump is markedly increased in response to the increase in intracellular sodium, i.e., a defect in the cation permeability. Glucose-6-phosphate dehydrogenase (G-6-PD) deficiency is inherited as an X-linked disorder; males are most often affected. Populations with a high frequency of abnormal G-6-PD enzymes includes blacks, southern Europeans, Sephardic Jews, Chinese, southeast Asians, and Arabs. The incidence of G-6-PD deficiency among American blacks is 11%. In this disorder, the RBC survival is normal under ordinary conditions. However, exposure to certain drugs can result in acute hemolysis. A less frequent RBC enzyme defect disorder is pyruvate kinase deficiency. Hemoglobinopathies may result from abnormalities of globin chain production that are both quantitative and qualitative. The quantitative disorders include the thalassemias, alpha or beta. Qualitative disorders include sickle cell syndromes, hemoglobin E, hemoglobin C, and hemoglobin M. Severe anemia results in alpha thalassemia. Since alpha chain

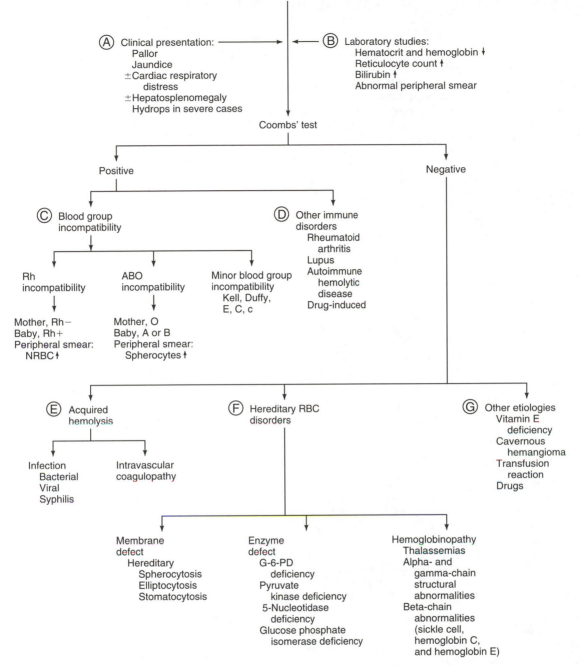

ANEMIA DUE TO HEMOLYSIS

(A) Clinical presentation:
Pallor
Jaundice
±Cardiac respiratory
distress
±Hepatosplenomegaly
Hydrops in severe cases

(B) Laboratory studies:
Hematocrit and hemoglobin ↓
Reticulocyte count ↑
Bilirubin ↑
Abnormal peripheral smear

Coombs' test

Positive

Negative

(C) Blood group
incompatibility

(D) Other immune
disorders
Rheumatoid
arthritis
Lupus
Autoimmune
hemolytic
disease
Drug-induced

Rh
incompatibility

ABO
incompatibility

Minor blood group
incompatibility
Kell, Duffy,
E, C, c

Mother, Rh−
Baby, Rh+
Peripheral smear:
NRBC ↑

Mother, O
Baby, A or B
Peripheral smear:
Spherocytes ↑

(E) Acquired
hemolysis

(F) Hereditary RBC
disorders

(G) Other etiologies
Vitamin E
deficiency
Cavernous
hemangioma
Transfusion
reaction
Drugs

Infection
Bacterial
Viral
Syphilis

Intravascular
coagulopathy

Membrane
defect
Hereditary
Spherocytosis
Elliptocytosis
Stomatocytosis

Enzyme
defect
G-6-PD
deficiency
Pyruvate
kinase deficiency
5-Nucleotidase
deficiency
Glucose phosphate
isomerase deficiency

Hemoglobinopathy
Thalassemias
Alpha- and
gamma-chain
structural
abnormalities
Beta-chain
abnormalities
(sickle cell,
hemoglobin C,
and hemoglobin E)

synthesis begins during the first trimester, early severe anemia leads to hydrops fetalis.

G. In vitamin E deficiency, thrombocytosis and acanthocytosis are also observed with hemolytic anemia and reticulocytosis. The infants may have peripheral edema. Hemolysis usually does not develop in infants with vitamin E deficiency unless their diet consists of high polyunsaturated fatty acids. However, administration of high doses of vitamin E to treat vitamin E deficiency may be detrimental. Pulmonary deterioration, liver and renal failure, and thrombocytopenia have been reported in premature infants who received intravenous vitamin E. Other etiologies of hemolysis include cavernous hemangiomas, transfusion reac-

tion, and drugs (maternal administration of synthetic vitamin K).

HSB

References

Blanchette VS, Zipursky A. Assessment of anemia in newborn infants. Clin Perinatol 1984; 11:489.

Oski FA, Naiman JL. Hematologic problems in the newborn. 3rd ed. Philadelphia: WB Saunders, 1982:56.

Shurin SB. The blood and hematopoietic system. In: Fanaroff AA, Martin RJ, eds. Neonatal-perinatal medicine: Diseases of the fetus and newborn, 5th ed. St Louis, Mosby–Year Book 1992:941.

POLYCYTHEMIA/HYPERVISCOSITY

Polycythemia is defined as a venous hematocrit (Hct) ≥65%. However, in each patient there is considerable variation in Hct according to the site and time of sampling. The highest Hct and viscosity values are obtained at 2 hours of postnatal age with subsequent decrease between 12–18 hours of age. A lower Hct is used as a criterion for polycythemia when sampling is from the umbilical vein or radial artery (≥63 %). Viscosity increases with increasing Hct, i.e., an almost linear relationship up to a Hct of 60%–65%, above which this relationship becomes exponential. Although Hct contributes largely to blood viscosity, less red blood cell (RBC) filtrability or deformability of the newborn may be an important factor. Total plasma protein concentration, individual protein fractions such as α_1-globulins, α_2-globulins, and fibrinogen correlate strongly with viscosity. Intravenous fat may also contribute to blood viscosity.

A. The initial approach to the evaluation of an infant with polycythemia/hyperviscosity is to determine the possible etiology, i.e., whether it is due to active erythropoiesis or passive transfusion. Increased RBC production may result from intrauterine hypoxia as in cases of placental insufficiency from maternal toxemia, other causes of intrauterine growth retardation, and postterm gestation. Other causes include maternal diabetes, Down syndrome and other chromosomal disorders (e.g., trisomy 13, trisomy 18), adrenal hyperplasia, thyrotoxicosis, and maternal propranolol therapy. Polycythemia, although asymptomatic, has been reported in hypothyroid infants; the precise mechanism, however, is unknown. Polycythemia/hyperviscosity may result from excessive RBC transfusion antenatally or intrapartum as in the recipient fetus of a twin-to-twin transfusion or in a maternal-to-fetal transfusion. A neonate may also receive a large volume from placental transfusion during an unassisted delivery or from delayed cord clamping. As part of intensive care management, polycythemia may result iatrogenically from excessive RBC transfusion.

B. Many babies with polycythemia/hyperviscosity are asymptomatic. However, increasing viscosity may result in alteration in organ blood flow. Thus clinical signs such as cardiorespiratory distress with or without cyanosis, lethargy, hypotonia, and irritability are observed. Often it is difficult to determine whether the clinical manifestations observed are due to polycythemia/hyperviscosity or to the underlying disease that is associated with polycythemia/hyperviscosity. Laboratory abnormalities in addition to a high Hct and hyperviscosity also may be observed. Thrombocytopenia, hypoglycemia, and hypocalcemia are not infrequent. The mechanism for hypoglycemia is not clear; it may be a consequence of increased cerebral glucose extraction or decreased hepatic glucose production because of a sluggish circulation. Reticulocytosis suggests active erythropoiesis as in intrauterine prolonged hypoxia; the reticulocyte count is usually normal in acute erythrocyte transfusion. ECG findings include chamber hypertrophy, particularly of the right heart and depressed ST segment. Chest film demonstrates pulmonary congestion and/or cardiomegaly.

C. Therapy in the form of partial plasma exchange transfusion is instituted based on the degree of polycythemia and the presence of clinical manifestations. Published data on the benefit of therapy in asymptomatic polycythemia/hyperviscosity are inconclusive. If a decision is reached to do a partial plasma exchange transfusion, treatment is best instituted within the first 24 hours of life. Thus prompt recognition of the syndrome is important.

D. The amount of blood volume to be exchanged with plasma (fresh frozen plasma, plasmanate solution, or albumin) is determined by the formula:

$$\text{Volume of exchange (ml)} = \frac{(\text{Observed Hct} - \text{Desired Hct}) \times \text{Blood volume}}{\text{Observed Hct}}$$

The blood volume is calculated as weight in kg × 100 ml. Increment for each infusion or withdrawal should not exceed 10% of the baby's blood volume.

E. Hyperbilirubinemia may become evident a few days after birth because of increased number of fetal RBCs presented and destroyed at the reticuloendothelial system. Complications that may result from decreased organ blood flow or from thrombosis include cerebral ischemia and seizures, ileus, necrotizing enterocolitis, renal failure, and/or peripheral gangrene.

HSB

References

Bada HS, Korones SB, Kolni HW, et al. Partial plasma exchange transfusion improves cerebral hemodynamics in symptomatic neonatal polycythemia. Am J Med Sci 1986; 29:157.

Black VD. Neonatal hyperviscosity syndrome, Curr Probl Pediatr 1987; 17:73.

Black VD, Lubchenco LO, Luckey DW, et al. Developmental and neurologic sequelae of neonatal hyperviscosity syndrome. Pediatrics 1982; 69:426.

Oski FA, Naiman JL. Hematologic problems in the newborn. 3rd ed. Philadelphia: WB Saunders, 1982:87.

Ramamurthy RS, Berlanga M. Postnatal alteration in hematocrit and viscosity in normal and polycythemic infants. J Pediatr 1987; 110:929.

Ramamurthy RS, Brans YW. Neonatal polycythemia. I. Criteria for diagnosis and treatment. Pediatrics 1981; 68:168.

Shohat M, Reisner SH, Mimouni F, Merlob P. Neonatal polycythemia. II. Definition related to time of sampling. Pediatrics 1984; 73:11.

Weinblatt ME, Fort P, Kochen J, DiMayio M. Polycythemia in hypothyroid infants. Am J Dis Child 1987; 141:1121.

POLYCYTHEMIA/HYPERVISCOSITY

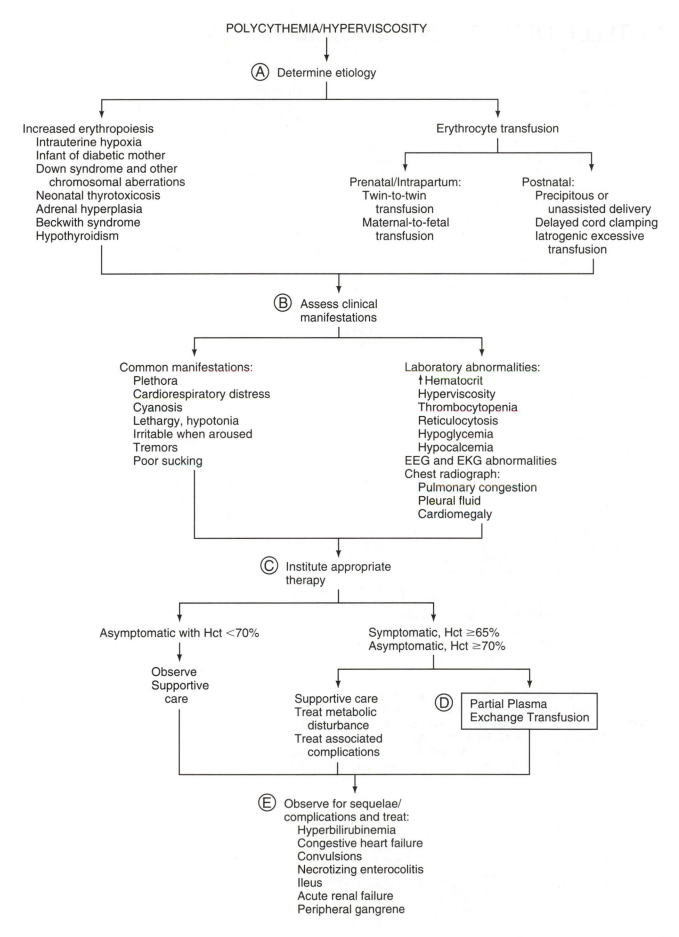

(A) Determine etiology

Increased erythropoiesis
Intrauterine hypoxia
Infant of diabetic mother
Down syndrome and other
    chromosomal aberrations
Neonatal thyrotoxicosis
Adrenal hyperplasia
Beckwith syndrome
Hypothyroidism

Erythrocyte transfusion

Prenatal/Intrapartum:
    Twin-to-twin
        transfusion
    Maternal-to-fetal
        transfusion

Postnatal:
    Precipitous or
        unassisted delivery
    Delayed cord clamping
    Iatrogenic excessive
        transfusion

(B) Assess clinical
manifestations

Common manifestations:
    Plethora
    Cardiorespiratory distress
    Cyanosis
    Lethargy, hypotonia
    Irritable when aroused
    Tremors
    Poor sucking

Laboratory abnormalities:
    ↑ Hematocrit
    Hyperviscosity
    Thrombocytopenia
    Reticulocytosis
    Hypoglycemia
    Hypocalcemia
EEG and EKG abnormalities
Chest radiograph:
    Pulmonary congestion
    Pleural fluid
    Cardiomegaly

(C) Institute appropriate
therapy

Asymptomatic with Hct <70%

Observe
Supportive
    care

Symptomatic, Hct ≥65%
Asymptomatic, Hct ≥70%

Supportive care
Treat metabolic
    disturbance
Treat associated
    complications

(D) | Partial Plasma
Exchange Transfusion |

(E) Observe for sequelae/
complications and treat:
    Hyperbilirubinemia
    Congestive heart failure
    Convulsions
    Necrotizing enterocolitis
    Ileus
    Acute renal failure
    Peripheral gangrene

183

PLATELET DISORDERS: THROMBOCYTOPENIA

A. Bleeding may occur when the platelet count falls to approximately 25,000/μl. Skin petechiae and purpura are the usual presenting signs of thrombocytopenia. Petechiae are more frequent. They are characteristically generalized in distribution; new ones appear over variable periods of time. Petechiae, acquired during delivery, are restricted to the upper body and new lesions do not appear in the normal infant. Unsuspected thrombocytopenia is often recognized by protracted oozing from puncture sites. In addition, mucosal bleeding may occur in the form of pulmonary hemorrhage, rectal bleeding, or epistaxis. Deep hemorrhage in muscle and viscera is not an expected manifestation of isolated thrombocytopenia. CNS hemorrhage occurs occasionally and is particularly associated with difficult deliveries and with isoimmune thrombocytopenia (see later). Fetal platelet deficiency has been identified by cordocentesis. Fetal thrombocytopenia requires delivery by cesarean section if platelets are <50,000/μl.

B. The phase platelet count is the most accurate available method for assessment of platelet number. Counts of 100,000–150,000/μl should be repeated to monitor the possibility of further diminution. Counts of <100,000/μl are abnormal. Examination of a peripheral blood smear reveals a paucity of platelets. If large (young) platelets abound, the disorder is likely because of destruction of circulating platelets. If platelets are inordinately small (older), underproduction of platelets is suggested.

C. Clinical signs of platelet deficiency (see Section **A**) in the presence of a normal platelet count and normal clotting screen suggest platelet dysfunction in which adhesion and/or aggregation are defective. Most commonly, dysfunction is caused by maternal aspirin and in the infant by administration of indomethacin for ductus arteriosus closure, ticarcillin, and piperacillin. Uremia also causes significant platelet dysfunction. Treatment of drug-induced thrombocytopenia includes drug withdrawal and platelet transfusion for counts below 40,000/μl.

D. Maternal autoimmune thrombocytopenia (ITP, lupus erythematosus) affects the fetus variably. Many infants are born with normal platelets; some develop thrombocytopenia several days after birth; others are born with severe platelet deficiency. Maternal administration of IVIG or corticosteroids may diminish the chances of thrombocytopenia in the fetus and neonate. IVIG levels then linger in the neonate for 3 or 4 weeks, maintaining their effectiveness for that period of time. Since autoimmune disease is destructive, platelet transfusions to the neonate are of limited value. IVIG infused over 6 to 8 hours in a dose of 700 to 1000 mg/kg is often effective treatment for autoimmune disease. The response to corticosteroids is unpredictable. Prednisone is given in a dose of 1 to 2 mg/kg/day. Other corticosteroid equivalents are also used in appropriate doses.

Isoimmune (alloimmune) thrombocytopenia is caused by a mechanism similar to Rh disease. Maternal platelets are negative for the antigen PL^{a-1}, fetal platelets are positive. Maternal antibodies to fetal platelets cross to the fetus to cause platelet destruction. Diagnosis is almost certain if the neonatal platelet count rises only after maternal platelets are administered. The first pregnancy is affected and diagnosis is unsuspected unless a familial history is identified. Subsequent pregnancies are affected and therefore, they should be anticipated. Periodic fetal platelet count, fetal transfusion of maternal platelets, and maternal IVIG administration are major elements of prenatal management. Isoimmune thrombocytopenia does not respond to steroid therapy. IVIG to the neonate is probably effective. Transfusion of the neonate will raise the platelet count only if maternal platelets are used because maternal isoimmune antibodies destroy platelets from 98% of random donors. Thrombocytopenia persists through the first 6 to 8 weeks of life, the period during which transmitted maternal antibodies persist.

SBK

References

Andrew M, Kelton J. Neonatal thrombocytopenia. Clin Perinatol 1984; 11:359–391.

Gill FM. Thrombocytopenia in the newborn. Semin Perinatol 1983; 7:201–212.

Naiman JL. Disorders of the platelets. In: Oski FA, Naiman JL. Hematologic problems in the newborn. Philadelphia: WB Saunders, 1982:175.

Stuart MJ, Kelton JG. The platelet: Quantitative and qualitative abnormalities. In: Nathan DG, Oski FA. Hematology of infancy and childhood. 3rd ed. Philadelphia: WB Saunders, 1987:1343.

THROMBOCYTOPENIA

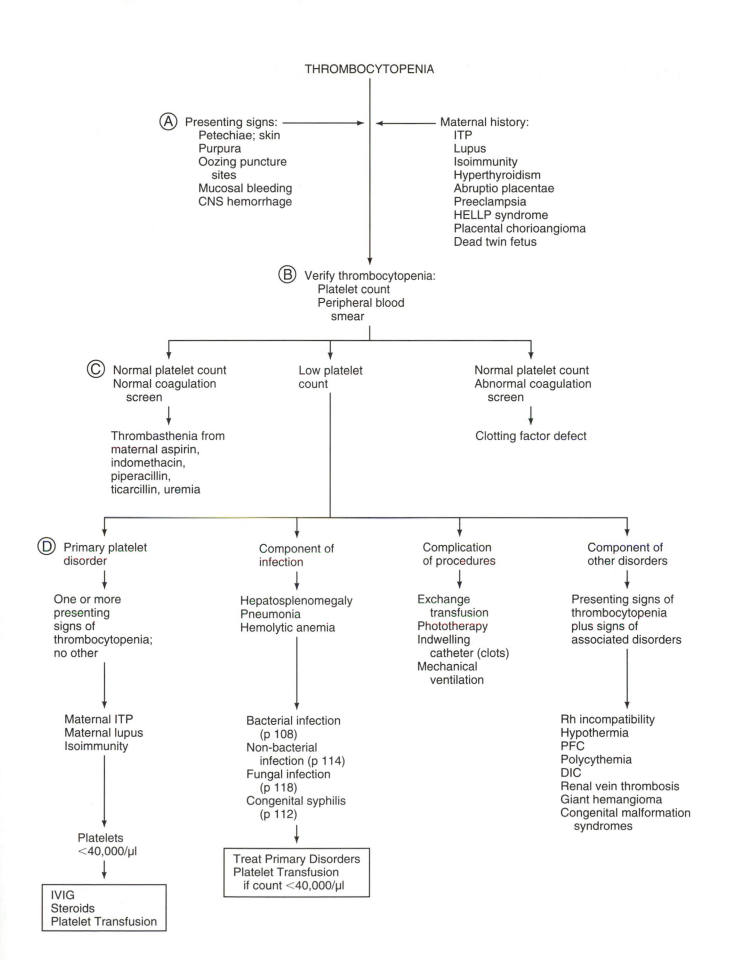

Ⓐ Presenting signs:
    Petechiae; skin
    Purpura
    Oozing puncture
      sites
    Mucosal bleeding
    CNS hemorrhage

Maternal history:
    ITP
    Lupus
    Isoimmunity
    Hyperthyroidism
    Abruptio placentae
    Preeclampsia
    HELLP syndrome
    Placental chorioangioma
    Dead twin fetus

Ⓑ Verify thrombocytopenia:
    Platelet count
    Peripheral blood
      smear

Ⓒ Normal platelet count
Normal coagulation
    screen

Low platelet
count

Normal platelet count
Abnormal coagulation
    screen

Thrombasthenia from
maternal aspirin,
indomethacin,
piperacillin,
ticarcillin, uremia

Clotting factor defect

Ⓓ Primary platelet
disorder

Component of
infection

Complication
of procedures

Component of
other disorders

One or more
presenting
signs of
thrombocytopenia;
no other

Hepatosplenomegaly
Pneumonia
Hemolytic anemia

Exchange
    transfusion
Phototherapy
Indwelling
    catheter (clots)
Mechanical
    ventilation

Presenting signs of
thrombocytopenia
plus signs of
associated disorders

Maternal ITP
Maternal lupus
Isoimmunity

Bacterial infection
    (p 108)
Non-bacterial
    infection (p 114)
Fungal infection
    (p 118)
Congenital syphilis
    (p 112)

Rh incompatibility
Hypothermia
PFC
Polycythemia
DIC
Renal vein thrombosis
Giant hemangioma
Congenital malformation
    syndromes

Platelets
<40,000/μl

Treat Primary Disorders
Platelet Transfusion
    if count <40,000/μl

IVIG
Steroids
Platelet Transfusion

PLATELET DISORDERS: THROMBOCYTOSIS

A. In older children, thrombocytosis is defined by a platelet count >750,000/μl. Platelet counts are generally lower in the normal neonate; thrombocytosis is therefore defined at a lower level. Neonatal thrombocytosis has been described in association with several primary conditions as listed in the algorithm. However, thrombocytosis itself has not been reported to cause clinical abnormalities, regardless of the underlying pathology. Maternal polydrug abuse is mentioned in literature, but only methadone maintenance is specifically described.

B. Vitamin E deficiency is seen in babies whose birthweights are <1500 g. Hemolytic anemia is the primary abnormality, but it is usually associated with thrombocytosis. Edema of the lower extremities occurs in some infants. Symptoms appear between 4 and 10 weeks of age. Prevention is accomplished by administration of oral vitamin E in a daily dose of 15 to 25 IU/kg body weight. Often the diagnosis is first suspected in a growing premature when a routine complete blood count reveals the thrombocytosis. Treatment of deficiency entails oral administration of vitamin E in a dose of 50–100 IU/kg/day.

SBK

References

Naiman JL. Disorders of the platelets. In: Oski FA, Naiman JL. Hematologic problems in the newborn. Philadelphia: WB Saunders, 1982:175.

Slagle TA, Gross SJ. Vitamin E. In: Tsang RC, Nichols BL. Nutrition during infancy. Philadelphia: Hanley and Belfus, 1988:277.

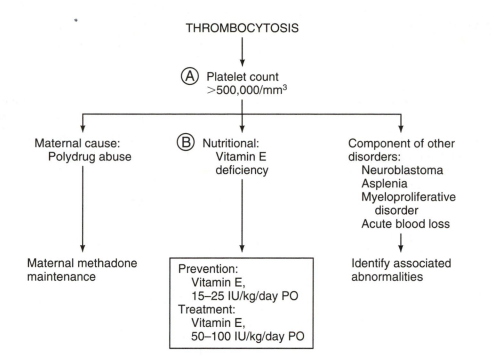

THROMBOCYTOSIS

Ⓐ Platelet count
>500,000/mm³

Maternal cause:
Polydrug abuse

Ⓑ Nutritional:
Vitamin E
deficiency

Component of other
disorders:
Neuroblastoma
Asplenia
Myeloproliferative
disorder
Acute blood loss

Maternal methadone
maintenance

Prevention:
Vitamin E,
15–25 IU/kg/day PO
Treatment:
Vitamin E,
50–100 IU/kg/day PO

Identify associated
abnormalities

NEUTROPENIA

Neutropenia is defined in terms of absolute neutrophil counts; percent of total leukocytes is a misleading parameter. Assessment of neutrophil counts must consider postnatal ages as shown in the algorithm. There is little correlation with race, sex, gestational age or birth weight, premature rupture of membranes (assuming an afebrile mother), maternal diabetes, hyaline membrane disease, transient tachypnea of the newborn, or physiologic hyperbilirubinemia.

A. Transient neutropenia is intended to designate self-limited conditions of several hours (asphyxia, maternal toxemia) to several weeks (isoimmune or autoimmune neutropenia). The principal clinical issue concerns the possible presence of treatable infection. In the circumstances listed, transient neutropenia in itself does not impose vulnerability to infection. However, it may herald impending bacterial infection or strongly support the diagnosis in an obviously ill infant whose distressing symptoms are nonspecific. Reports of low total leukocytes, high I/T (immature to total neutrophil) ratios, and their correlations with infection have been disappointingly varied. In our own experience these two parameters are in themselves unreliable as indications of infection. Severe neutropenia is more likely to be an accurate indicator. C-reactive protein (CRP) determinations have been more reliably confirmatory (not predictive) of bacterial infection if performed three times at 12-hour intervals.

B. Maternal drugs reported in association with neonatal neutropenia include sulfonamides, methimazole, and semisynthetic penicillins. The neutropenia is self-limited and asymptomatic in the neonate. Maternal lupus erythematosus entails autoantibody passage to the fetus and resultant destruction of neutrophils. The destructive IgG antibody may linger in the neonate for several weeks. Neonatal neutropenia of isoimmune origin is the result of the same maternal-fetal antibody transmission that is known to occur in Rh disease and in isoimmune thrombocytopenia (p 184). Neutropenia disappears in 2 to 4 weeks. Infants who acquire infection may fare poorly in a neutropenic state.

C. Maternal toxemia and perinatal asphyxia are the most frequent causes of neutropenia. In contrast to bacterial infection, the neutrophil count becomes normal within 24 hours.

D. In the presence of sepsis at birth (or necrotizing enterocolitis later), severe neutropenia is an ominous portent. Laboratory data and x-rays are usually procured for reasons other than neutropenia. In equivocal circumstances, persistence of neutropenia and a high I/T ratio beyond 24 hours after birth are strong suggestions of bacterial disease. In addition, a high CRP value is virtually confirmatory.

E. Persistent neutropenia during the neonatal period requires inquiries directed at disorders that will be lifelong or alternatively at conditions that cause protracted but transiently diminished absolute neutrophil counts. The lifelong conditions may be hereditary, neoplastic, or the result of inborn metabolic disorders. Involvement of other cellular elements of blood is frequent in these conditions and in those that involve a variety of congenital anomalies.

SBK

References

Curnette JT, Boxer LA. Disorders of granulopoiesis and granulocyte function. In: Nathan DG, Oski FA, eds. Hematology of infancy and childhood. 3rd ed. Philadelphia: WB Saunders, 1987:797.
Stockman JA III: Disorders of leukocytes. In: Oski FA, Naiman JL, eds: Hematologic problems in the newborn. 3rd ed. Philadelphia: WB Saunders, 1982:223.

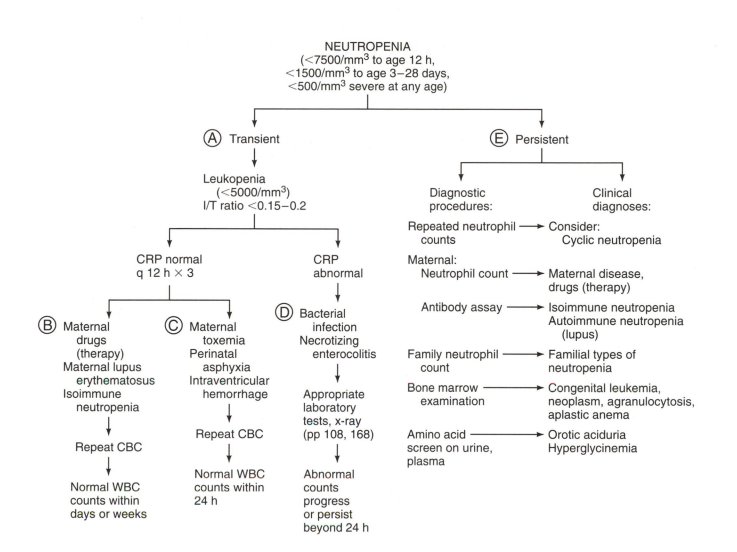

NEUTROPENIA
(<7500/mm^3 to age 12 h,
<1500/mm^3 to age 3–28 days,
<500/mm^3 severe at any age)

Ⓐ Transient

Leukopenia
(<5000/mm^3)
I/T ratio <0.15–0.2

CRP normal
q 12 h × 3

CRP
abnormal

Ⓑ Maternal
drugs
(therapy)
Maternal lupus
erythematosus
Isoimmune
neutropenia

Repeat CBC

Normal WBC
counts within
days or weeks

Ⓒ Maternal
toxemia
Perinatal
asphyxia
Intraventricular
hemorrhage

Repeat CBC

Normal WBC
counts within
24 h

Ⓓ Bacterial
infection
Necrotizing
enterocolitis

Appropriate
laboratory
tests, x-ray
(pp 108, 168)

Abnormal
counts
progress
or persist
beyond 24 h

Ⓔ Persistent

Diagnostic
procedures:

Clinical
diagnoses:

Repeated neutrophil ⟶ Consider:
counts   Cyclic neutropenia

Maternal:
    Neutrophil count ⟶ Maternal disease,
                          drugs (therapy)

    Antibody assay ⟶ Isoimmune neutropenia
                        Autoimmune neutropenia
                        (lupus)

Family neutrophil ⟶ Familial types of
count   neutropenia

Bone marrow ⟶ Congenital leukemia,
examination   neoplasm, agranulocytosis,
                 aplastic anema

Amino acid ⟶ Orotic aciduria
screen on urine,   Hyperglycinemia
plasma

DISSEMINATED INTRAVASCULAR COAGULATION

Disseminated intravascular coagulation (DIC) is secondary to an array of serious disorders. It is characterized, sequentially, by the triggering of coagulation, formation of microthrombi, and consumption of coagulation factors and platelets, culminating in diffuse hemorrhages. Sometimes hemolytic anemia is associated with the microthrombic process. Organ ischemia, bleeding into vital organs to precipitate dysfunction or failure, and on occasion major vessel thrombi are characteristic of severe disease.

A. The earliest clinical indication of DIC is bleeding from old puncture sites or protracted bleeding from punctures just inflicted. Petechiae and ecchymoses are also common. Spontaneous bleeding occurs into multiple organs (lungs, GI tract, kidneys, muscle, and/or the CNS) when DIC is particularly severe. Major vessel thrombi (aortic, renal, femoral, and other arteries) are more likely in the presence of indwelling catheters. Anemia is usual; jaundice with high total and direct bilirubin is infrequent. DIC affects only infants who are seriously ill with an underlying disease process.

B. With clinical signs of hemorrhage, laboratory data can identify the cause with little equivocation. Low platelets, abnormal coagulation times, depleted fibrinogen, and usually elevated fibrin split products (FSP) and/or d-dimer levels are together diagnostic of DIC. Low hematocrit, elevated reticulocytes, and hyperbilirubinemia may be caused by DIC, but often these abnormalities are generated by the primary antecedent disease.

C. Treatment is primarily to replace depleted elements of coagulation and to alleviate or impede major thrombus formation if it has occurred. In most instances replacement therapy suffices. Replacement with fresh frozen plasma (FFP) is most frequently employed.

Administration of 10 ml/kg of body weight increases coagulation factors by 15–20%. Administration of the same volume of platelet concentrate increases coagulation factors to the same extent and elevates the platelet count by 75,000 to 100,000/μl, depending on the ongoing rate of platelet destruction. In infants whose fibrinogen levels are particularly depressed in spite of administration of FFP, cryoprecipitate (approximately 10 ml/kg) may raise the fibrinogen level by 50 to 100 mg/dl. The goal of treatment is to rectify deficiencies to a point that hemostasis is possible, specifically platelets at 50,000/μl, fibrinogen at 100 mg/dl and PT and PTT times at 1.5 to twice normal values. To achieve this, administration of all three replacement preparations once or twice daily may be necessary. A severe, relentless process requires exchange transfusion. Anticoagulant measures must also be taken in the presence of major vessel thrombi. For this purpose heparin is used in the dose shown in the algorithm in order to maintain PTT at 1.5 to twice normal values.

SBK

References

Lusher JM. Diseases of coagulation: The fluid phase. In: Nathan DG, Oski FA, eds. Hematology of infancy and childhood. 3rd ed. Philadelphia: WB Saunders, 1987:1293.

Oski FA. Blood coagulation and its disorders in the newborn. In: Oski FA, Naiman JL, eds: Hematologic problems in the newborn. 3rd ed. Philadelphia: WB Saunders, 1982:137.

DISSEMINATED INTRAVASCULAR COAGULATION (DIC)
Sick Infant with Antecedent Primary Disorders

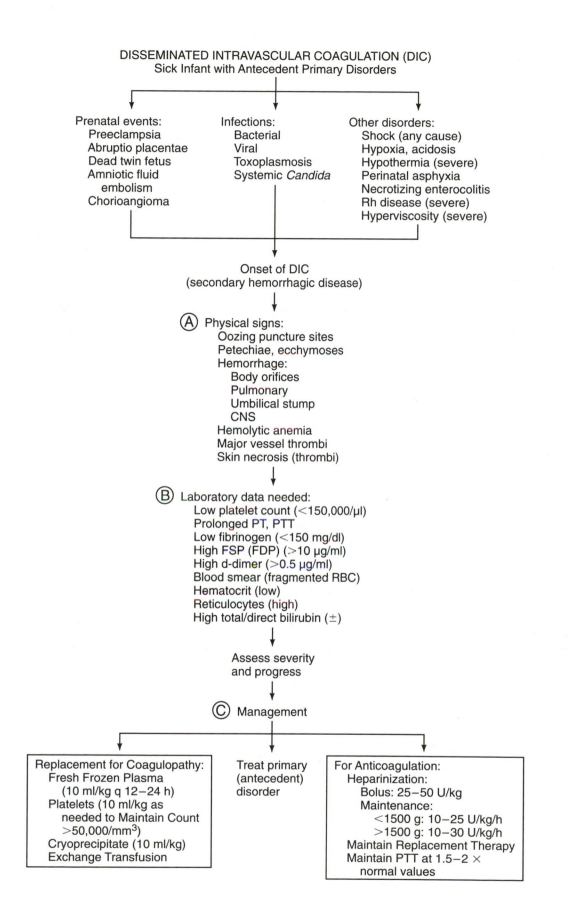

Prenatal events:
  Preeclampsia
  Abruptio placentae
  Dead twin fetus
  Amniotic fluid
    embolism
  Chorioangioma

Infections:
  Bacterial
  Viral
  Toxoplasmosis
  Systemic *Candida*

Other disorders:
  Shock (any cause)
  Hypoxia, acidosis
  Hypothermia (severe)
  Perinatal asphyxia
  Necrotizing enterocolitis
  Rh disease (severe)
  Hyperviscosity (severe)

Onset of DIC
(secondary hemorrhagic disease)

Ⓐ Physical signs:
    Oozing puncture sites
    Petechiae, ecchymoses
    Hemorrhage:
      Body orifices
      Pulmonary
      Umbilical stump
      CNS
    Hemolytic anemia
    Major vessel thrombi
    Skin necrosis (thrombi)

Ⓑ Laboratory data needed:
    Low platelet count (<150,000/µl)
    Prolonged PT, PTT
    Low fibrinogen (<150 mg/dl)
    High FSP (FDP) (>10 µg/ml)
    High d-dimer (>0.5 µg/ml)
    Blood smear (fragmented RBC)
    Hematocrit (low)
    Reticulocytes (high)
    High total/direct bilirubin (±)

Assess severity
and progress

Ⓒ Management

Replacement for Coagulopathy:
  Fresh Frozen Plasma
    (10 ml/kg q 12–24 h)
  Platelets (10 ml/kg as
    needed to Maintain Count
    >50,000/mm³)
  Cryoprecipitate (10 ml/kg)
  Exchange Transfusion

Treat primary
(antecedent)
disorder

For Anticoagulation:
  Heparinization:
    Bolus: 25–50 U/kg
    Maintenance:
      <1500 g: 10–25 U/kg/h
      >1500 g: 10–30 U/kg/h
  Maintain Replacement Therapy
  Maintain PTT at 1.5–2 ×
    normal values

BLEEDING INFANTS

A. The diagnostic approach to bleeding begins with determination of whether the baby is otherwise ill. Well infants who bleed are affected by primary clotting disorders or trauma. Platelets are probably deficient quantitatively or qualitatively (thrombasthenia or platelet dysfunction) in the presence of petechiae or small ecchymoses and occasionally with bleeding from orifices by virtue of mucosal involvement. Deeper bleeding sites, extensive ecchymoses, and subcutaneous hemorrhage imply clotting factor defects. Petechiae are not often seen in hereditary clotting defects. Abnormal PT and/or PTT suggest the diagnosis of a hereditary clotting deficiency. Specific assays for these factors are therefore in order. At least 50% to 60% of hereditary coagulopathy is manifest in the first 2 weeks of life. Bleeding may occur in the form of cephalhematomas but more dramatically in the subaponeurotic space of the scalp, where the bleeding is massive. Scalp swelling casts a bluish hue, and blood accumulates with no respect for suture lines. Intracranial hemorrhage may occur in the subdural, subarachnoid, or ventricular spaces. Umbilical hemorrhage has also been reported. Treatment of thrombocytopenia is presented on p 184. Hemangiomas may cause hemorrhage by entrapment of platelets and coagulation factor consumption (Kasabach-Merritt syndrome).

Vitamin K deficiency all but disappeared 30 years ago when administration of the vitamin soon after birth became routine. However, in the 1980s, when breast feeding became more pervasive, hemorrhagic disease reappeared at 1 to 2 months of age in babies who received no vitamin K supplement while breast-fed. Early (neonatal) disease involves cephalhematomas; bleeding from antenatal scalp probes used for monitoring fetal cardiovascular status; intracranial, gastrointestinal, and skin bleeding; and bleeding after circumcision. Bleeding infants should receive intravenous vitamin K_1, 1 to 2 mg, regardless of weight. The deficiency is corrected in a few hours. Prevention is accomplished by intramuscular administration of 1 mg soon after birth.

B. Bleeding problems arise from severe, life-threatening primary disorders. Most frequently involved are infections and other diseases that cause disseminated intravascular coagulation (DIC). Bleeding may be widespread, giving rise to hypovolemic shock. Sites of hemorrhage and diagnosis and treatment of DIC are presented on p 190. The attributes of the Kasabach-Merritt syndrome include a rapidly enlarging hemangioma with thrombocytopenia, microangiopathic hemolytic anemia, and an acute or chronic consumptive coagulopathy. Initially, the hemangiomas need not be large. As in DIC, diagnosis of hematologic status requires platelet count, PT, PTT, fibrinogen level, and fibrin split products. A blood smear reveals the abnormal number and morphology of platelets and fragmented erythrocytes. Treatment is directed at the clotting factor deficiency and at thrombocytopenia (p 184). Surgical extirpation of the hemangioma may be feasible; laser surgery has been used recently.

SBK

References

Buchanan GR. Hemorrhagic diseases. In: Nathan DG, Oski FA, eds. Hematology of infancy and childhood. 3rd ed. Philadelphia: WB Saunders, 1987:104.

Glader BE, Amylon MD. Hemostatic disorders in the newborn. In: Taeusch HW, Ballard RA, Avery ME, eds. Schaffer and Avery's diseases of the newborn. 6th ed. Philadelphia: WB Saunders, 1991:777.

Oski FA. Blood coagulation and its disorders in the newborn. In: Oski FA, Naiman JL, eds. Hematologic problems in the newborn. 3rd ed. Philadelphia: WB Saunders, 1982:137.

CLINICAL EVIDENCE OF BLEEDING

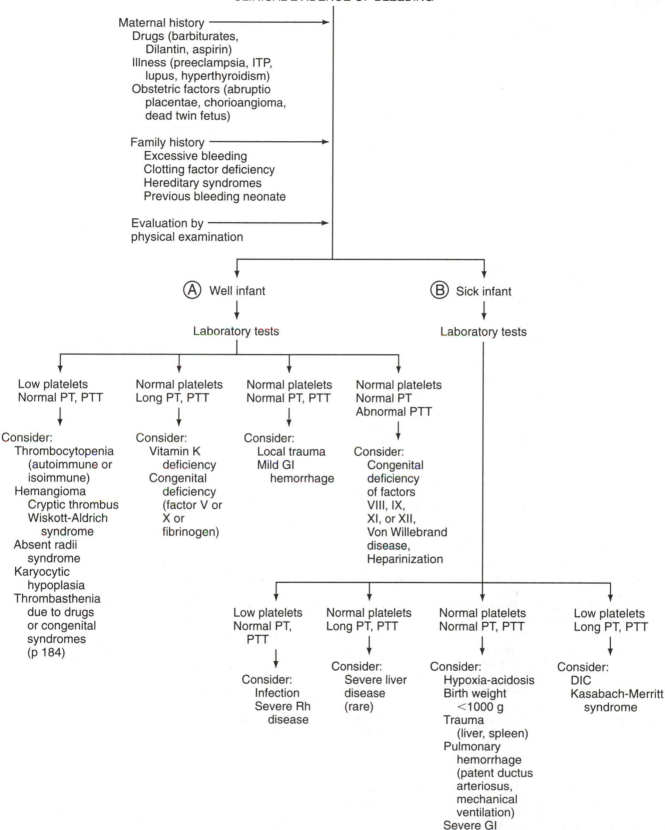

Maternal history
    Drugs (barbiturates,
        Dilantin, aspirin)
    Illness (preeclampsia, ITP,
        lupus, hyperthyroidism)
    Obstetric factors (abruptio
        placentae, chorioangioma,
        dead twin fetus)

Family history
    Excessive bleeding
    Clotting factor deficiency
    Hereditary syndromes
    Previous bleeding neonate

Evaluation by
physical examination

(A) Well infant

(B) Sick infant

Laboratory tests

Laboratory tests

Low platelets
Normal PT, PTT

Consider:
    Thrombocytopenia
        (autoimmune or
        isoimmune)
    Hemangioma
        Cryptic thrombus
        Wiskott-Aldrich
        syndrome
    Absent radii
        syndrome
    Karyocytic
        hypoplasia
    Thrombasthenia
        due to drugs
        or congenital
        syndromes
        (p 184)

Normal platelets
Long PT, PTT

Consider:
    Vitamin K
        deficiency
    Congenital
        deficiency
        (factor V or
        X or
        fibrinogen)

Normal platelets
Normal PT, PTT

Consider:
    Local trauma
    Mild GI
        hemorrhage

Normal platelets
Normal PT
Abnormal PTT

Consider:
    Congenital
        deficiency
        of factors
        VIII, IX,
        XI, or XII,
        Von Willebrand
        disease,
        Heparinization

Low platelets
Normal PT,
PTT

Consider:
    Infection
    Severe Rh
        disease

Normal platelets
Long PT, PTT

Consider:
    Severe liver
        disease
        (rare)

Normal platelets
Normal PT, PTT

Consider:
    Hypoxia-acidosis
    Birth weight
        <1000 g
    Trauma
        (liver, spleen)
    Pulmonary
        hemorrhage
        (patent ductus
        arteriosus,
        mechanical
        ventilation)
    Severe GI
        hemorrhage

Low platelets
Long PT, PTT

Consider:
    DIC
    Kasabach-Merritt
        syndrome

SEIZURES

A. Seizures occur from excessive depolarization of the CNS neurons. Because of immature neuroanatomic and physiologic development, clinical manifestations in the neonate differ from older children and adults. Seizures manifest in various patterns. *Subtle* seizures have neither clonic nor tonic components and are clinically manifested as eye deviation; sustained eye fixation; blinking or fluttering of the eyelids; sucking, smacking, or other buccolingual movements; "pedaling or swimming movements"; and/or repeated apneic spells. *Tonic* seizures involve generalized increased tone of both upper and lower extremities. *Multifocal clonic* seizures involve clonic jerking of one or more extremities with "nonordered" migration. *Focal clonic* seizures involve jerking of one extremity without loss of consciousness. *Myoclonic* seizures involve single or multiple synchronous jerks or flexion of the upper or lower extremities and are rare in the newborn. One must differentiate seizures from jitteriness (p 198), which may have no pathologic significance and requires no treatment. The age of onset and predisposing or risk factors and should guide direction and extent of workup. Other neurologic signs such as nonreactive, dilated, or unequal pupils and bulging fontanelles suggest associated ICP.

B. Investigate electrolytes and metabolic imbalance; in most such conditions, correction of metabolic abnormalities constitutes specific therapy. Most infants require evaluation for CNS infection, which includes CBC and differential, blood culture, and CSF cell count, chemistries, Gram's stain, and culture. Focal or multifocal spikes, sharp waves, or focal nonrhythmic discharges are seen on EEG. Skull films are helpful in traumatic injuries and in hydrocephalus; periventricular calcifications may be evident in congenital infection. Head ultrasound scan may reveal cerebral edema, periventricular-intraventricular hemorrhage (PV-IVH), ventriculomegaly, or periventricular leukomalacia. A CT scan may be necessary to investigate other CNS disorders, such as subdural hemorrhage and brain abscess.

C. Traumatic intracranial hemorrhage and/or cerebral contusion may occur after difficult delivery (pp 27, 35).

D. Hypoxic-ischemic encephalopathy secondary to perinatal asphyxia is a common cause of seizures in the newborn. Maternal complications (e.g., abruptio placentae, placenta previa, severe toxemia), history of fetal distress, low Apgar scores, and the need for resuscitation at delivery strongly suggest hypoxic-ischemic insult. Seizures are usually observed within the first 48 hours of life unless the encephalopathy is so severe that the infant is unconscious or comatose, and thus EEG shows electrical silence.

E. The premature infant is at risk for PV-IVH, which may develop soon after delivery or at a later age. The incidence among premature infants is about 30–50% and thus should be ruled out as a cause (p 206).

F. Posthemorrhagic hydrocephalus develops in approximately 20% of survivors of PV-IVH. Ventricles progressively enlarge, and ICP increases.

G. Seizures are also common in CNS malformations, usually resulting from prenatal insults (e.g., teratogens, infection). Deformities on physical examination may help distinguish one syndrome from another.

H. Neonatal infection manifesting within a few days of birth may have been acquired transplacentally, as an ascending infection, or during delivery from an infected vaginal canal. The etiologic organism may be a bacterium, virus, spirochete, protozoon, or fungus; manifestations depend on the organism and when the infection was acquired. Malformations are usually seen with intrauterine congenital infection. Lengthy nursery stay makes nosocomial infection more likely.

I. Intrauterine growth deviation seen in small-(SGA)-or-large-for-gestational-age (LGA) infants is often associated with metabolic problems; hypoglycemia is common. After the first few days of life, hypoglycemia may be iatrogenic or a manifestation of other systemic conditions such as sepsis or PV-IVH. Hypocalcemia is also common in SGA and LGA babies and may be related to other systemic disease such as hypoxic-ischemic encephalopathy and PV-IVH. Late hypocalcemia may result from intake of high phosphate load or from inadequate calcium intake in premature infants. Hypomagnesemia may exist in relation to hypocalcemia. In polycythemia, hyperviscosity leads to decreased or impaired blood flow; it may also predispose to cerebral vessel thrombosis.

J. Other nutritional/electrolyte problems, including electrolyte disorders or specific nutritional deficiencies related to inadequate or too much intake or as an associated finding in other systemic disorders (e.g., inappropriate ADH secretion, diabetes insipidus, overhydration, may occur in the first days of life or later.

K. Seizure is one of the neonatal withdrawal manifestations in maternal heroin, methadone, and barbiturate addiction.

L. Neonatal anesthetic intoxication is suggested by a history of prolonged bradycardia after maternal local anesthetic or nerve block injection, needle marks on the infant from accidental injection, and seizures usually occurring within hours of delivery.

M. Inborn errors of metabolism (amino acids, carbohydrate and fat metabolism) are rare; consider them when most other causes have been ruled out.

N. Hypertensive crises or drug toxicity may cause seizures. Theophylline is often used for apnea of prematurity; seizures are one of its toxic manifestations. Kernicterus is rare because of wide use of phototherapy.

O. Therapy is directed to the specific cause before or in addition to starting anticonvulsant therapy (p 196).

HSB

Reference

Brann AW Jr, Wiznitzer M. Seizures. In: Fanaroff AA, Martin RJ, eds. Neonatal-perinatal medicine: Diseases of the fetus and infant. 5th ed. St Louis: Mosby–Year Book, 1992:729.
See other references on p 196.

SEIZURES

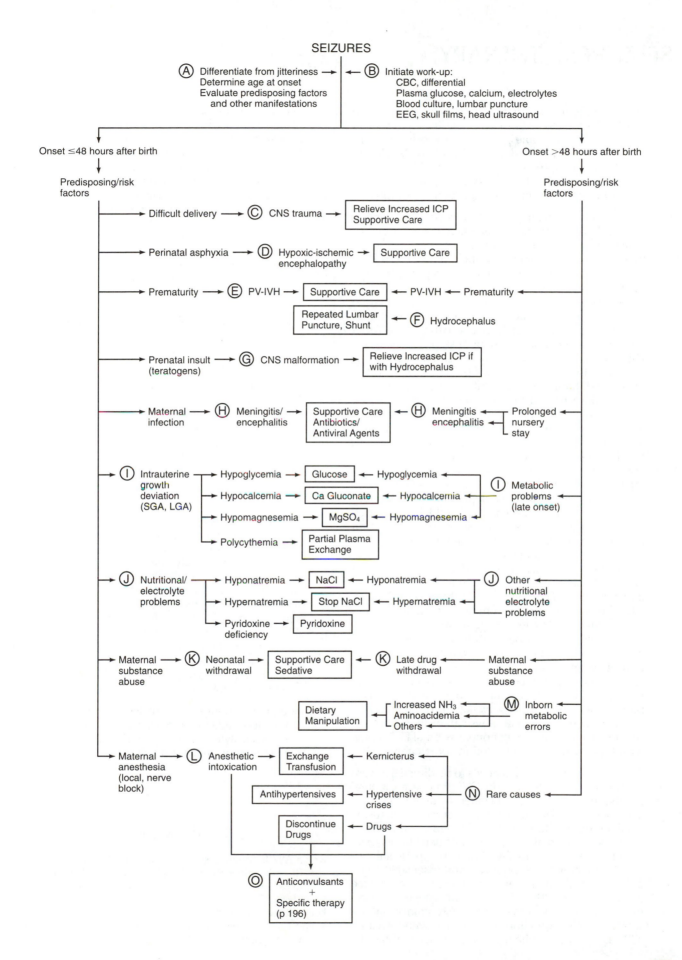

Ⓐ Differentiate from jitteriness → ← Ⓑ Initiate work-up:
Determine age at onset
Evaluate predisposing factors
and other manifestations

CBC, differential
Plasma glucose, calcium, electrolytes
Blood culture, lumbar puncture
EEG, skull films, head ultrasound

Onset ≤48 hours after birth

Onset >48 hours after birth

Predisposing/risk factors

Predisposing/risk factors

Difficult delivery → Ⓒ CNS trauma → Relieve Increased ICP / Supportive Care

Perinatal asphyxia → Ⓓ Hypoxic-ischemic encephalopathy → Supportive Care

Prematurity → Ⓔ PV-IVH → Supportive Care ← PV-IVH ← Prematurity ←

Repeated Lumbar Puncture, Shunt ← Ⓕ Hydrocephalus

Prenatal insult (teratogens) → Ⓖ CNS malformation → Relieve Increased ICP if with Hydrocephalus

Maternal infection → Ⓗ Meningitis/encephalitis → Supportive Care / Antibiotics/ Antiviral Agents ← Ⓗ Meningitis encephalitis ← Prolonged nursery stay

Ⓘ Intrauterine growth deviation (SGA, LGA) → Hypoglycemia → Glucose ← Hypoglycemia ← Ⓘ Metabolic problems (late onset)
→ Hypocalcemia → Ca Gluconate ← Hypocalcemia ←
→ Hypomagnesemia → MgSO₄ ← Hypomagnesemia ←
→ Polycythemia → Partial Plasma Exchange

Ⓙ Nutritional/electrolyte problems → Hyponatremia → NaCl ← Hyponatremia ← Ⓙ Other nutritional electrolyte problems
→ Hypernatremia → Stop NaCl ← Hypernatremia ←
→ Pyridoxine deficiency → Pyridoxine

Maternal substance abuse → Ⓚ Neonatal withdrawal → Supportive Care / Sedative ← Ⓚ Late drug withdrawal ← Maternal substance abuse

Dietary Manipulation ← Increased NH₃ ← Ⓜ Inborn metabolic errors
Aminoacidemia ←
Others ←

Maternal anesthesia (local, nerve block) → Ⓛ Anesthetic intoxication → Exchange Transfusion ← Kernicterus ←

Antihypertensives ← Hypertensive crises ← Ⓝ Rare causes ←

Discontinue Drugs ← Drugs ←

Ⓞ Anticonvulsants + Specific therapy (p 196)

SEIZURES: THERAPY

A. Seizures require immediate management. Seizures are usually associated with disturbance in respiration so that the infant becomes cyanotic, hypoxic, and apneic. Furthermore, bradycardia develops, leading to circulatory collapse. Thus airway is established, ventilation is maintained, and oxygen is given. Volume expansion becomes necessary for poor perfusion.

B. Anticonvulsant therapy is best initiated when ventilation and oxygenation are maintained because most anticonvulsants are respiratory depressants. For initial therapy, most recommend phenobarbital at a loading dose of 20 mg/kg IV, followed by 5 mg/kg IV every 5 minutes (total of 40 mg/kg loading dose) if seizures have not ceased. Phenobarbital administration may be associated with respiratory arrest and hypotension. In the absence of response to phenobarbital, phenytoin (Dilantin) is given at a loading dose of 20 mg/kg IV. Dilantin may cause bradycardia and/or cardiac arrhythmia. In our institution we prefer using a shorter-acting barbiturate, amobarbital (Amytal), at 10 mg/kg loading dose IV and the dose repeated every 2 to 4 hours when seizures recur. Respiratory depression or arrest is a common complication but less likely to be a significant clinical problem because most infants require mechanical ventilation. An alternative anticonvulsant drug is diazepam at a dose of 0.1 to 0.3 mg/kg slow IV (use 1 mg [0.2 ml] mixed with 0.8 ml saline mixture); respiratory depression and hypotension are common side effects. Paraldehyde is used when seizures persist after adequate loading doses of another anticonvulsant. It is usually given rectally at 0.1 to 0.3 ml/kg diluted 1:1 with mineral oil. For maintenance therapy, phenobarbital is the drug of choice at a dose of 3 to 4 mg/kg/day IV or PO divided into two doses (12 hours apart) and given 12 hours after the loading dose. Serum concentration is maintained at therapeutic level of 15 to 30 µg/ml. Dilantin, 4 to 8 mg/kg/day divided into two to three doses, is given for maintenance to achieve a serum concentration between 10 and 20 µg/ml. Oral formulation is poorly absorbed. Other anticonvulsants such as primidone, carbamazepine, and valproic acid are used rarely. Anticonvulsant therapy may be discontinued in the presence of normal physical examination (no seizure episodes) and with nonparoxysmal EEG. Long-term therapy may be indicated in some cases.

C. Treatment of seizures also needs to be directed toward treatment of the etiology. In CNS trauma a subdural tap should relieve increased intracranial pressure (ICP) from a subdural hemorrhage. In cerebral contusion resulting from a depressed skull fracture, elevation of the depressed cranial bone is indicated. In hypoxic-ischemic encephalopathy following perinatal asphyxia, treatment is supportive, and associated metabolic complications are monitored and treated accordingly (p 204). In cases of congenital CNS malformation, anticonvulsants are administered for seizures; if the condition is associated with increased ICP, as in hydrocephalus, a ventricular tap may be necessary, with subsequent ventriculoperitoneal shunt placement. In periventricular-intraventricular hemorrhage (PV-IVH), treatment is mainly supportive, blood loss is replaced, and anticonvulsants are given for seizures. A complicating posthemorrhagic hydrocephalus is treated by repeated lumbar puncture (LP) and/or ventriculoperitoneal shunt placement. CNS infection is treated by intravenous agents specific to the organism recovered. In complicating ventriculitis, intraventricular drug administration may be necessary. Larger brain abscesses may require surgical drainage. Neonatal withdrawal syndrome is treated with sedatives in addition to anticonvulsants for seizures. In local anesthetic intoxication the drug is removed by exchange transfusion. In polycythemia/hyperviscosity syndrome a partial plasma exchange transfusion to decrease the hematocrit to normal level improves cerebral blood flow. Partial exchange is preferable to venous phlebotomy.

D. Increased ammonia levels may result from amino acid infusion or from a disturbance in amino acid metabolism. Ammonia may be removed by peritoneal dialysis or by exchange transfusion. Most inborn errors of metabolism, whether affecting amino acid or carbohydrate or fat metabolism, require dietary manipulation.

E. Metabolic, nutritional, or electrolyte disturbances may present as isolated disorders but are often part of a systemic disease. Hypoglycemia is treated by intravenous glucose at a loading dose of 200 mg/kg (10% solution) followed by a drip at 8 mg/kg/min and increased accordingly based on plasma glucose (p 240). Hypocalcemia is treated with 200 mg/kg of calcium gluconate IV (5% solution). Hypomagnesemia is treated by IV $MgSO_4$ at 0.2 ml/kg (50% solution). If pyridoxine deficiency is suspected, 50 to 100 mg IV is given. Hyponatremia is corrected by increasing sodium supplementation in the maintenance intravenous fluid. In hypernatremia, sodium supplementation is decreased or withheld while serum sodium is monitored.

F. Supportive therapy is directed toward maintaining ventilation, adequate oxygenation, perfusion, fluid and electrolyte balance, nutritional support, and maintaining normal temperature.

HSB

References

Brann AW Jr, Wiznitzer M. Seizures. In: Fanaroff AA, Martin RJ, eds. Neonatal-perinatal medicine: Diseases of the fetus and infant. 5th ed. St Louis: Mosby—Year Book, 1992:729.

Levy SR. Neonatal seizures. Semin Perinatol 1987; 11:155.

Volpe JJ. Neurology of the newborn. 2nd ed. Philadelphia: WB Saunders, 1987:2.

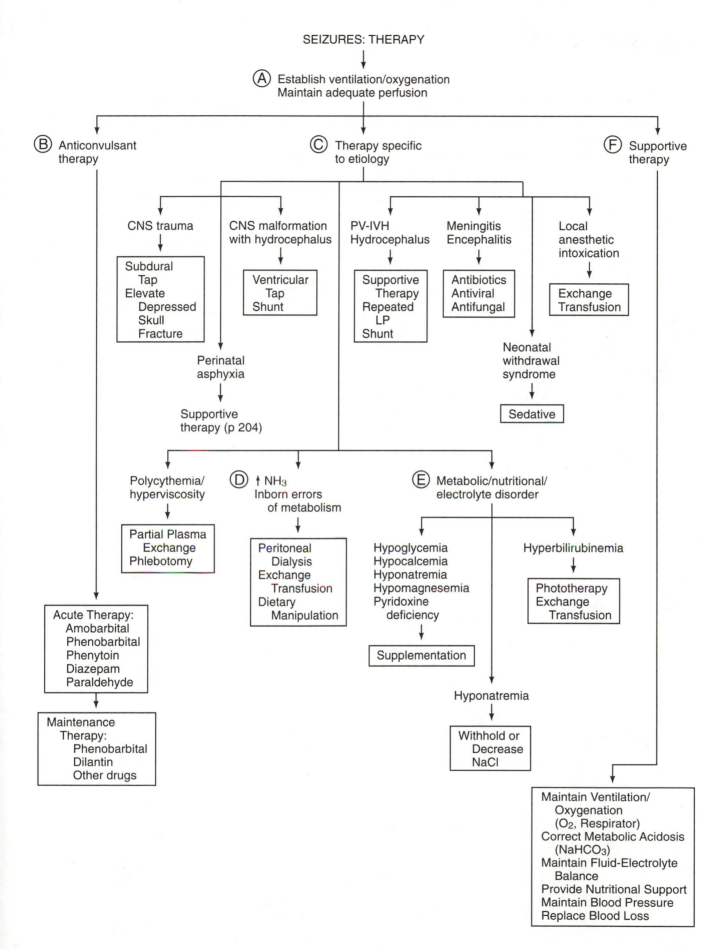

SEIZURES: THERAPY

A Establish ventilation/oxygenation
Maintain adequate perfusion

B Anticonvulsant therapy

C Therapy specific to etiology

F Supportive therapy

CNS trauma

Subdural
Tap
Elevate
Depressed
Skull
Fracture

CNS malformation with hydrocephalus

Ventricular
Tap
Shunt

PV-IVH
Hydrocephalus

Supportive
Therapy
Repeated
LP
Shunt

Meningitis
Encephalitis

Antibiotics
Antiviral
Antifungal

Local anesthetic intoxication

Exchange
Transfusion

Neonatal withdrawal syndrome

Sedative

Perinatal asphyxia

Supportive therapy (p 204)

Polycythemia/ hyperviscosity

Partial Plasma
Exchange
Phlebotomy

D ↑ NH$_3$
Inborn errors of metabolism

Peritoneal
Dialysis
Exchange
Transfusion
Dietary
Manipulation

E Metabolic/nutritional/ electrolyte disorder

Hypoglycemia
Hypocalcemia
Hyponatremia
Hypomagnesemia
Pyridoxine
deficiency

Supplementation

Hyperbilirubinemia

Phototherapy
Exchange
Transfusion

Hyponatremia

Withhold or
Decrease
NaCl

Acute Therapy:
Amobarbital
Phenobarbital
Phenytoin
Diazepam
Paraldehyde

Maintenance
Therapy:
Phenobarbital
Dilantin
Other drugs

Maintain Ventilation/
Oxygenation
(O$_2$, Respirator)
Correct Metabolic Acidosis
(NaHCO$_3$)
Maintain Fluid-Electrolyte
Balance
Provide Nutritional Support
Maintain Blood Pressure
Replace Blood Loss

JITTERINESS

A. Jitteriness (tremor, tremulousness, jerkiness, "juddery" movement, shivering, quivering) refers to a series of recurrent, involuntary movements that are oscillatory, rhythmic, and extremely stimulus sensitive. Tremor diminishes with passive flexion of the extremity and is not associated with altered gaze and consciousness and EEG abnormalities. In seizures, the movement of the extremity is jerky, nonrhythmic, and persists even with passive flexion of the extremity. Altered gaze and consciousness and EEG abnormalities are observed during seizures.

B. Tremors observed soon after birth are not necessarily pathological. In approximately two thirds of normal neonates, fine tremors are observed during the first few days of life.

C. Physiological tremors are "fine" tremors, i.e., tremor of high frequency and low amplitude. They need to be differentiated from "coarse" tremors, which are of low frequency and high amplitude. Physiological tremors are transient and usually disappear by the third day of life. Thus in the absence of risk factors and abnormal physical and neurological examination findings, physiological tremors do not require investigation. However, when fine tremors persist after 3 days or when they persist even in quiet state or in sleep, a limited work-up is suggested. Investigation needs to be directed in relation to existing risk factors. For example,

a history of difficult delivery should direct investigation to rule out intracranial hemorrhage. In the presence of other abnormal neurological findings, investigation does need to be more comprehensive (see Section **E**).

D. Coarse tremors, whether evident at birth or at a later age, have to be considered pathological and often require comprehensive work-up.

E. Risk factors should guide the clinical investigation. Electrolyte imbalance/metabolic problems may occur without necessarily an evident predisposing factor so that baseline studies need to include determination of plasma glucose, serum electrolytes, calcium, and magnesium. Infection needs to be ruled out in an infant who is critically ill. Metabolic screening may be necessary after the more common causes are ruled out.

HSB

References

Rosman NP, Donnelly JH, Braun MA. The jittery newborn and infant: A review. J Dev Behav Pediatr 1984; 5:263.

Volpe JJ. Neurology of the newborn. 2nd ed. Philadelphia: WB Saunders, 1987:2.

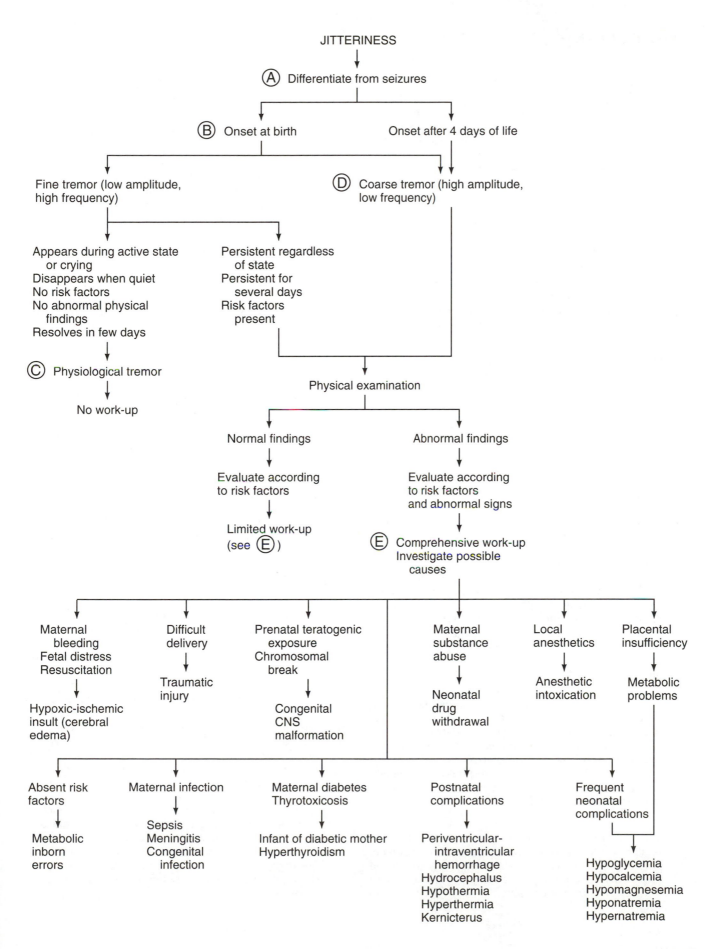

JITTERINESS

A. Differentiate from seizures

B. Onset at birth — Onset after 4 days of life

Fine tremor (low amplitude, high frequency)

D. Coarse tremor (high amplitude, low frequency)

Appears during active state or crying
Disappears when quiet
No risk factors
No abnormal physical findings
Resolves in few days

Persistent regardless of state
Persistent for several days
Risk factors present

C. Physiological tremor

No work-up

Physical examination

Normal findings

Abnormal findings

Evaluate according to risk factors

Evaluate according to risk factors and abnormal signs

Limited work-up (see E)

E. Comprehensive work-up
Investigate possible causes

Maternal bleeding
Fetal distress
Resuscitation

Difficult delivery

Prenatal teratogenic exposure
Chromosomal break

Maternal substance abuse

Local anesthetics

Placental insufficiency

Hypoxic-ischemic insult (cerebral edema)

Traumatic injury

Congenital CNS malformation

Neonatal drug withdrawal

Anesthetic intoxication

Metabolic problems

Absent risk factors

Maternal infection

Maternal diabetes
Thyrotoxicosis

Postnatal complications

Frequent neonatal complications

Metabolic inborn errors

Sepsis
Meningitis
Congenital infection

Infant of diabetic mother
Hyperthyroidism

Periventricular-intraventricular hemorrhage
Hydrocephalus
Hypothermia
Hyperthermia
Kernicterus

Hypoglycemia
Hypocalcemia
Hypomagnesemia
Hyponatremia
Hypernatremia

HYPOTONIA

A. In examinating muscle tone, evaluate postural tone based on the infant's ability to resist pull of gravity: minimal head lag when pulled to sitting position, righting of the head and trunk when held in ventral suspension, and neck extension during horizontal suspension. Muscle tone is influenced by gestational age. Risk factors and a family history of hypotonia guide the assessment. Abnormal examination findings may indicate a chromosomal or teratogenic disorder; the specific combination of findings may be unique to certain syndromes. Neonatal infection commonly presents with nonspecific signs including hypotonia; thus the basic workup usually includes a sepsis workup. Metabolic abnormalities are common in ill neonates; thus plasma glucose, serum electrolyte, and calcium determination are part of the basic investigation. Head ultrasound scan may show intracranial anatomic abnormalities, including hemorrhage.

B. When hypotonia is evident at birth, the family history is negative, and delivery was difficult, consider cerebral hypotonia due to intracranial hemorrhage or cerebral contusion and/or spinal hypotonia (primarily due to cervical cord trauma). When these conditions are ruled out, consider other causes of cerebral hypotonia.

C. Cerebral hypotonia, which may result from either acute or chronic encephalopathies, probably explains most cases of hypotonia in the newborn period.

D. In the absence of malformations, risk factors that may provide a clue to the etiology include fetal distress, maternal infection, intrauterine growth deviation, and maternal drugs (sedatives, analgesics, magnesium sulfate, general anesthesia). Hypoxic-ischemic encephalopathy is a common etiology. Signs of increased intracranial pressure, seizures, cerebral edema on head ultrasound scan, and altered consciousness may also be observed. Maternal infection may be transmitted to the neonate. In sepsis and/or meningitis, WBC count and differential are usually abnormal, blood and/or CSF cultures are positive for organisms, and CSF examination reveals pleocytosis, high protein, and low glucose. Intrauterine viral or protozoal infection may be associated with CNS malformation (see F). Maternal sedatives (barbiturates), analgesics (opiates), anesthetics (general), and magnesium sulfate are transferred transplacentally. High levels result in neonatal respiratory depression and hypotonia. Hypoglycemia and hypocalcemia are frequent metabolic problems seen in the dysmature, SGA or LGA infant.

E. When there are no risk factors, hypotonia may be related to the severity of illness in the neonate, whether term or preterm. Those having severe respiratory distress are often lethargic. Periventricular-intraventricular hemorrhage (PV-IVH) in a preterm baby may also present with hypotonia. Metabolic problems may result from systemic disorders.

F. Malformations or dysmorphism suggest chromosomal disorders, congenital intrauterine infection (TORCH), developmental disorders, or other syndromes, such as osteogenesis imperfecta and achondroplasia, that are associated with chronic encephalopathies. A positive family history may not necessarily be obtained in rare chronic and degenerative encephalopathies.

G. Dysmorphism and/or malformations may suggest a chronic or degenerative encephalopathy. *Familial dysautonomia* (Riley-Day syndrome) is an autosomal recessive disorder in Ashkenazi Jews; sporadic cases are rare. Features include IUGR, feeding difficulties, and altered consciousness and behavior. *Prader-Willi syndrome* is sporadic or familial and associated with facial dysmorphism, cryptorchidism and small penis in males or mild labial hypoplasia in females, hypotonia, and feeding difficulties. *Cerebrohepatorenal syndrome* (Zellweger syndrome) is autosomal recessive, presenting with severe hypotonia, limited arthrogryposis, peak-shaped head, full cheeks, micrognathia, biliary cirrhosis, polycystic kidneys, and cerebral malformations. *Oculocerebrorenal syndrome* (Lowe's syndrome) is an X-linked recessive disorder with features of profound hypotonia, hyporeflexia, cataracts, glaucoma, cryptorchidism and renal tubular acidosis, and aminoaciduria. Some degenerative disorders may manifest early and some at early infancy or at later age. Examples include Tay-Sachs disease, Canavan's spongy degeneration of white matter, Leigh's disease, and infantile neuroaxonal dystrophy.

H. Genetically transmitted myotonias are uncommon. A positive family history, when obtained, in addition to the associated dysmorphic features or malformations, is very helpful in making a diagnosis. Aside from the encephalopathies (see G), disorders involving the motor neuron unit may cause hypotonia in a newborn. Disorders involving the lower motor neuron include acute infantile spinal muscular atrophy (Werdnig-Hoffmann), neurogenic arthrogryposis multiplex congenita, glycogen storage disease type II (Pompe's disease), and neonatal poliomyelitis. Disorders at the level of the peripheral nerves, acute and chronic, are the least defined of the etiologies of neonatal hypotonia. Disorders of neuromuscular transmission (i.e., in the neuromuscular junction) include the different myasthenias (transitory, congenital, familial infantile myasthenia). Hypermagnesemia and antibiotics (aminoglycoside) may disturb the neuromuscular junction function. Primary degeneration of the muscle fibers or myopathies present with hypotonia in the newborn. Although muscle histology is diagnostic in some disorders, it is not diagnostic in congenital myotonic dystrophy, congenital muscular dystrophy, and polymyositis.

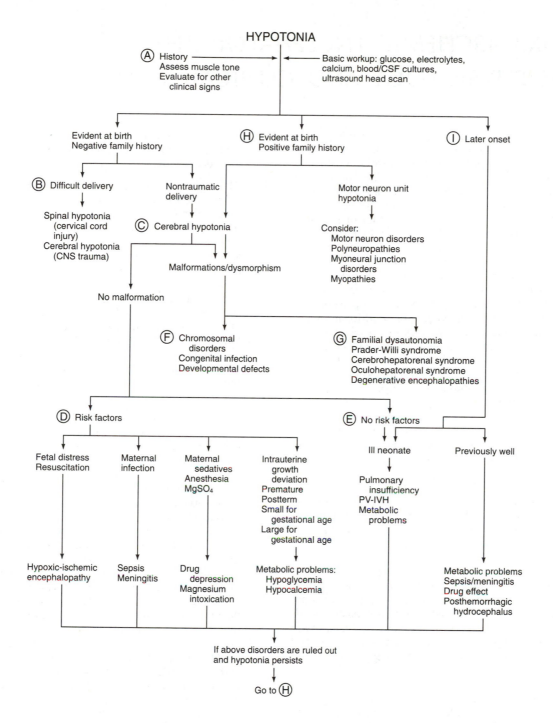

HYPOTONIA

A History ——— Basic workup: glucose, electrolytes,
Assess muscle tone | calcium, blood/CSF cultures,
Evaluate for other | ultrasound head scan
clinical signs

Evident at birth | **H** Evident at birth | **I** Later onset
Negative family history | Positive family history

B Difficult delivery | Nontraumatic delivery | Motor neuron unit hypotonia

Spinal hypotonia (cervical cord injury)
Cerebral hypotonia (CNS trauma)

C Cerebral hypotonia

Consider:
Motor neuron disorders
Polyneuropathies
Myoneural junction disorders
Myopathies

Malformations/dysmorphism

No malformation

F Chromosomal disorders
Congenital infection
Developmental defects

G Familial dysautonomia
Prader-Willi syndrome
Cerebrohepatorenal syndrome
Oculohepatorenal syndrome
Degenerative encephalopathies

D Risk factors | **E** No risk factors

Fetal distress Resuscitation | Maternal infection | Maternal sedatives Anesthesia MgSO₄ | Intrauterine growth deviation Premature Postterm Small for gestational age Large for gestational age | Ill neonate | Previously well

Pulmonary insufficiency
PV-IVH
Metabolic problems

Hypoxic-ischemic encephalopathy | Sepsis Meningitis | Drug depression Magnesium intoxication | Metabolic problems: Hypoglycemia Hypocalcemia | Metabolic problems Sepsis/meningitis Drug effect Posthemorrhagic hydrocephalus

If above disorders are ruled out
and hypotonia persists

Go to **H**

I. Some infants who may have been doing well or who were previously ill may show clinical deterioration with marked hypotonia. Investigation should be directed to ruling out metabolic problems, sepsis/meningitis, posthemorrhagic hydrocephalus, and depression from drug administration.

References

Fenichel GM. The newborn with poor muscle tone. Semin Perinatol 1982; 6:68.
Volpe JJ. Neurology of the newborn. 2nd ed. Philadelphia: WB Saunders, 1987.

HSB

HYPOXIC-ISCHEMIC ENCEPHALOPATHY: PATHOPHYSIOLOGY AND CLINICAL SIGNS

Hypoxic-ischemic encephalopathy is the neurologic syndrome resulting from perinatal asphyxia (i.e., impairment of gas exchange either at the placental level or postnatally at the pulmonary alveolar level with associated decrease in Po_2, increase in PCo_2, and decrease in pH. Predisposing factors may be of maternal, placental, obstetric, and fetal/neonatal origin. Any maternal disorder or placental disease that results in decreased O_2 transfer to the fetus may cause fetal asphyxia. A decrease in O_2 transfer may be secondary to low maternal Pao_2 as in maternal cardiac disease, impaired O_2 transport as in maternal anemia, decreased placental blood flow as in maternal diabetes, hypertension or hypotension or to decreased placental O_2 transfer as in abruptio placentae and chorioamnionitis. Obstetric complications such as prolonged labor, tetanic uterine contractions, and umbilical cord accidents (knots, prolapse, rupture) may also lead to impairment in fetal oxygenation. Fetal/neonatal diseases such as erythroblastosis fetalis, congenital pneumonia, hypoplastic lungs, and meconium aspiration syndrome predispose to asphyxia.

A. Fetal asphyxia or fetal distress is suspected when biophysical monitoring reveals lack of heart rate (beat-to-beat) variability, decelerations (variable or late), prolonged bradycardia, or sinusoidal pattern. On examination or from maternal history, fetal movements are decreased. Scalp fetal pH determination during labor usually reveals pH <7.2. A meconium-stained amniotic fluid also suggests perinatal asphyxia but is not a highly sensitive or specific indicator.

B. Soon after delivery the newborn with asphyxia is usually depressed with absent or inadequate respirations and absent or low heart rate. Apgar scores are low (pp 20, 24). The asphyxiated infant usually needs resuscitation, ranging from bag/mask ventilation with O_2 to a more aggressive intervention of intubation and manual ventilation, cardiac massage, buffer, and cardiotonic administration.

C. The clinical manifestations and prognosis of hypoxic-ischemic encephalopathy depend primarily on the severity of perinatal asphyxia (the duration of hypoxic-ischemic insult as well as the ability of the fetus or neonate to respond to the insult). Whereas cerebral blood flow (CBF) is maintained early in asphyxia at the expense of the gut and kidneys, persistence of the hypoxic-ischemic insult ultimately results in low heart rate, low BP, and ischemic injury to the brain, myocardium, and all other organs. Hypoxia results in metabolic alterations. The energy metabolism of the brain is maintained early on, but as glycolytic flux continues, glycogen reserve decreases, lactates increase, blood and cellular pH decrease further, and nerve cell death ensues. Ischemia of other organs serves as the pathophysiologic basis of various organ system injuries and manifestations after perinatal asphyxia. Brain and other tissue injury may also result from generation of free radicals during reoxygenation and reperfusion.

D. Although both premature and full-term neonates are vulnerable to hypoxic-ischemic insult, manifestations differ in these two groups. The neurologic stages of hypoxic-ischemic encephalopathy are those described in neonates near-term, term, or beyond-term gestation. Irritability, hyperactive tendon reflexes, and absent seizure activity are the major features of mild hypoxic-ischemic insult (stage 1). In stage 2, seizures, hypotonia with exaggerated tendon reflexes but weak suck and incomplete Moro reflex, and an abnormal EEG are observed. In severe encephalopathy (stage 3), the infant is unconscious, with absent reflexes and nonreactive pupils. No seizures are observed; EEG is isoelectric. This stage has the worst prognosis. Head ultrasound or CT may show encephalomalacia or periventricular leukomalacia.

E. Organ systems other than the CNS are often involved, and careful monitoring for complications is imperative. Cardiogenic shock results from myocardial dysfunction because of myocardial ischemia. CNS depression is associated with depressed respiratory effort and often requires ventilatory assistance. Hypoxia, hypercapnea, and acidosis lead to pulmonary arterial vasoconstriction; a high pulmonary vascular resistance is associated with right-to-left shunting at the level of the foramen ovale and with ductus arteriosus (pp 164–165). Decreased systemic blood flow results in acute renal tubular necrosis with consequent renal insufficiency or failure. WBC count may be abnormally high or low. Thrombocytopenia with or without disseminated intravascular coagulation (DIC) is also reported. In chronic intrauterine hypoxic insult, polycythemia/hyperviscosity is a hematologic feature. Gastric hemorrhage, necrotizing enterocolitis (NEC), and liver failure are consequences of inadequate systemic blood flow. Hypoglycemia results as glycogen reserves become depleted. Occasional hyperglycemia possibly results from an impaired glucose-regulating response through the adrenal medulla. Hyponatremia may be explained by sodium loss through the kidneys or by inappropriate ADH secretion. Various mechanisms explain hypocalcemia with hypomagnesemia and rise in serum phosphorus. $NaHCO_3$ administration increases calcium deposition in the bones. High serum phosphorus from tissue breakdown and hypoxia depresses the parathyroid gland, promoting calcium deposition. Increased calcitonin decreases bone calcium resorption. Hyperkalemia results from tissue breakdown or when kidney function fails.

HSB

See references on p 204.

HYPOXIC-ISCHEMIC ENCEPHALOPATHY: PATHOPHYSIOLOGY AND CLINICAL SIGNS

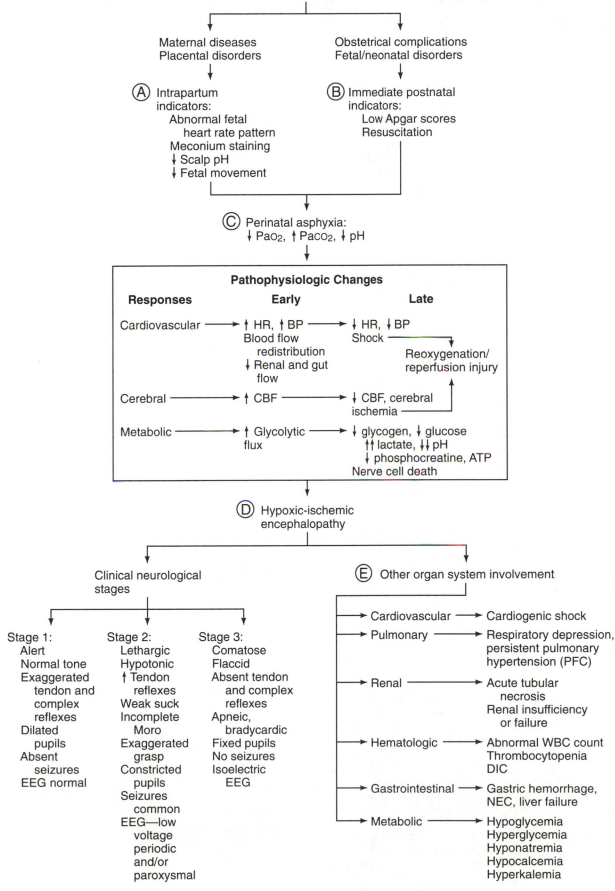

HYPOXIC-ISCHEMIC ENCEPHALOPATHY: THERAPY

A. The management of an infant with hypoxic-ischemic encephalopathy consists of two major strategies: (1) general supportive measures and (2) therapies specific to each organ system sustaining damage from the hypoxic-ischemic insult. General measures imply the routine management approach to any infant requiring intensive care. Ventilation and oxygenation have to be maintained; often mechanical ventilatory support is needed. Monitor arterial blood gases at intervals, and alter Fio_2 and ventilator settings when appropriate. In addition to respiratory acidosis, as part of the metabolic response to perinatal hypoxia, lactic acid is produced from an ongoing glycolytic flux. Blood pH further decreases so that buffer ($NaHCo_3$ administration) is indicated; the mEq of $NaHCo_3$ (diluted 1:1 with sterile H_2O) infused is calculated from the base deficit (base deficit × body weight [kg] × 0.3) and is given slowly. Oxygen delivery to the tissues must be maintained not only through O_2 therapy but also through an adequate circulating volume. In cases of poor tissue perfusion (hypotension), expand volume with plasma expanders or blood transfusion. Provide caloric and nutritional support intravenously. The infant is also maintained at neutral thermal environment so that O_2 consumption is at minimum.

B. Initiation of therapies specific to organ systems damaged by hypoxic-ischemic insult depends on prompt recognition of complications, which is best achieved by close monitoring or observation. Continuous arterial BP monitoring aids in determining a need for pressor agents. At times given at a low dose, an inotropic agent is adequate to improve cardiac function with an associated increase in BP (p 166). Simultaneous Pao_2 determination from the descending aorta through an indwelling umbilical arterial line and from the right radial artery helps in assessing right-to-left shunt at the level of the ductus arteriosus (p 164). A right-to-left shunt suggests persistent pulmonary hypertension (persistent fetal circulation), which requires maintaining preductal Pao_2 at 100 to 120 torr and $Paco_2$ below the critical level, above which Pao_2 decreases below 100 torr. A vasodilator may be necessary in some cases. Strict monitoring of fluid intake and output, as well as frequent determination of BUN, creatinine, electrolytes, glucose, calcium, and urine and serum osmolalities, screens for inappropriate ADH secretion, other metabolic problems, and renal insufficiency or failure. Normally a neonate loses weight during the first few days of life. Weight gain in the presence of oliguria or anuria, hyponatremia, and low serum osmolality suggests inappropriate ADH secretion; it requires fluid restriction and sodium supplementation. An increase in the fraction of sodium excretion (FeNa) suggests acute tubular necrosis; sodium supplementation and stabilization of BP to maintain adequate perfusion are appropriate measures. When the infant is anuric and serum BUN and creatinine values are increasing, fluid intake is restricted to insensible loss plus urine output. If anuria persists, peritoneal dialysis may be needed. Treat high potassium levels, due to either cell death or renal failure, with Kayexalate enema and/or glucose-insulin infusion. Glucose-insulin infusion is the immediate treatment in hyperkalemia-induced arrhythmias. Other complications that require treatment are disseminated intravascular coagulation (DIC), thrombocytopenia, necrotizing enterocolitis (NEC), and hepatic insufficiency or failure.

C. Seizures are frequently observed and require loading doses of anticonvulsants and maintenance therapy (pp 194, 196). Cerebral edema is manifested by alteration in consciousness, lethargy, bulging or tense fontanelles, and split sutures. An ultrasound head scan or CT may demonstrate the cerebral edema before there are overt clinical manifestations. Associated with cerebral edema is inappropriate ADH secretion. High levels of vasopressin result in excessive water retention so that serum sodium and serum osmolality are low, and the infant becomes edematous and gains weight excessively. Treatment is to restrict fluid intake to insensible loss and urine output. Sodium balance (intake and output) monitoring is helpful in determining the amount of NaCl required for supplementation. The rationale for hyperventilation is to decrease $Paco_2$ so that cerebral blood flow (CBF) decreases. Be cautious that the resultant decrease in CBF is not to the point of further ischemia; CBF velocity monitoring by Doppler technique is helpful in this regard. Osmotic diuretic (e.g., mannitol) may be administered if renal function is not impaired. Furosemide is at times given to induce diuresis. Other therapies, although experience is limited and some are experimental, include steroids, calcium channel blockers, excitatory amino acid inhibitors, and oxygen free-radical scavengers and inhibitors.

HSB

References

Brann AW, Schwartz JF. Birth injury. In: Faranoff AA, Martin RJ, eds. Neonatal-perinatal medicine: Diseases of the Fetus and infant. 5th ed. St. Louis: Mosby—Year Book, 1992:703.

Volpe JJ. Neurology of the newborn. Philadelphia: WB Saunders, 1987.

Voorhies TM, Vannucci RC. Perinatal cerebral hypoxia-ischemia: Diagnosis and management. In: Sarnat HB, ed. Topics in neonatal neurology. Orlando: Grune & Stratton, 1984:61.

HYPOXIC-ISCHEMIC ENCEPHALOPATHY: Therapy

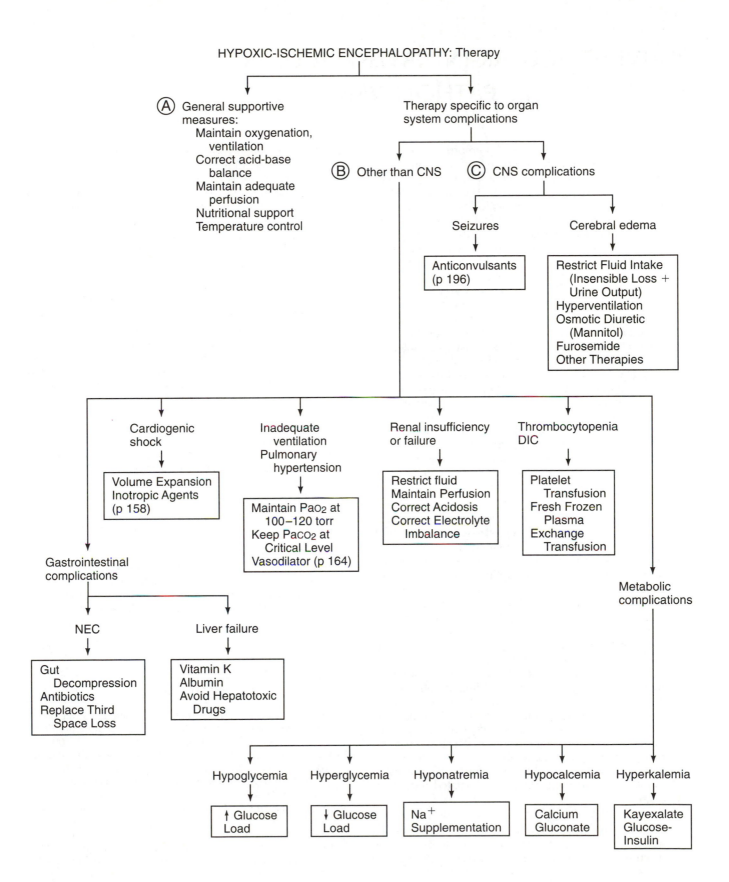

(A) General supportive measures:
- Maintain oxygenation, ventilation
- Correct acid-base balance
- Maintain adequate perfusion
- Nutritional support
- Temperature control

Therapy specific to organ system complications

(B) Other than CNS

(C) CNS complications

Seizures
→ Anticonvulsants (p 196)

Cerebral edema
→ Restrict Fluid Intake (Insensible Loss + Urine Output)
Hyperventilation
Osmotic Diuretic (Mannitol)
Furosemide
Other Therapies

Cardiogenic shock
→ Volume Expansion Inotropic Agents (p 158)

Inadequate ventilation Pulmonary hypertension
→ Maintain Pa_{O_2} at 100–120 torr
Keep Pa_{CO_2} at Critical Level
Vasodilator (p 164)

Renal insufficiency or failure
→ Restrict fluid
Maintain Perfusion
Correct Acidosis
Correct Electrolyte Imbalance

Thrombocytopenia DIC
→ Platelet Transfusion
Fresh Frozen Plasma
Exchange Transfusion

Gastrointestinal complications

NEC
→ Gut Decompression
Antibiotics
Replace Third Space Loss

Liver failure
→ Vitamin K
Albumin
Avoid Hepatotoxic Drugs

Metabolic complications

Hypoglycemia
→ ↑ Glucose Load

Hyperglycemia
→ ↓ Glucose Load

Hyponatremia
→ Na^+ Supplementation

Hypocalcemia
→ Calcium Gluconate

Hyperkalemia
→ Kayexalate Glucose-Insulin

PERIVENTRICULAR-INTRAVENTRICULAR HEMORRHAGE: PATHOPHYSIOLOGY

A. Periventricular-intraventricular hemorrhage (PV-IVH) is a common neurologic complication in premature infants; its incidence is higher at ≤32 weeks' gestation or at birth weights ≤1500 g. The preterm brain's vulnerability to this hemorrhagic lesion is explained by the prominence of the germinal matrix at this stage of development. The germinal matrix not only contains an extensive capillary bed but also may be a low-flow structure so that endothelial damage may result with minimal or abrupt changes in intravascular pressure or flow. The initial site of PV-IVH is often at the germinal matrix over the head, body, or tail of the caudate nucleus with subsequent rupture into the ventricles. Many factors have been associated with PV-IVH, including maternal factors such as antenatal bleeding, prolonged labor, and vaginal delivery and neonatal factors such as respiratory distress syndrome (RDS), particularly hyaline membrane disease (type 1 RDS), pneumothorax, low pH, hypoxia, hypotension, hypertension, impaired autoregulation of cerebral blood flow (CBF), coagulopathy, and respirator use. Each of these factors appears related to hypoxic-ischemic insult as a predisposing or etiologic factor, as an indicator of existing hypoxia or ischemia, or as a consequence of a previous hypoxic-ischemic injury.

B. Hypoxia, hypercarbia, and acidosis are biochemical changes associated with hypoxia-ischemia, an insult that may occur in utero or anytime postnatally. These biochemical derangements result in vessel endothelial injury, which leads to disruption of the vessel wall; subsequent reoxygenation and reperfusion lead to initiation of various chemical processes producing substances that may compound existing injury or modulate hemodynamic responses. Clinically, hypoxic-ischemic insult is suggested by biophysical monitoring revealing fetal distress, low scalp pH, low Apgar scores, and resuscitation. The resultant hemodynamic derangements include impairment of CBF autoregulation (i.e., CBF becomes pressure passive or CBF velocity pattern follows the arterial BP pattern). From the cardiovascular dynamics, hypoxic-ischemic injury to the myocardium results in decreased beat-to-beat variability and circulating volume. The fluctuating BP pattern may be an effect of changes in intrathoracic pressure from an associated respiratory distress.

C. With a severe hypoxic-ischemic injury to the germinal matrix capillary endothelium, the endothelium can rupture from an abrupt increase in intravascular pressure.

D. A less severe hypoxic-ischemic insult, however, requires aggravating factors to trigger PV-IVH. A tension pneumothorax is associated with marked increase in diastolic BP, decrease in $TcPo_2$, bradycardia, and hypoperfusion; thus it is no surprise that studies have shown significant association between pneumothoraces and PV-IVH. Rapid volume expansion after mild hypoxic-ischemic injury may lead to abrupt increases in BP with resultant PV-IVH.

E. The state-of-the-art diagnostic method for verifying PV-IVH is the head ultrasound scan, wherein the caudate nucleus, the periventricular area, and the ventricles can be visualized from both coronal and sagittal views. Findings may be described according to Papile's grading criteria (grade 1, hemorrhage in the germinal matrix; grade 2, IVH; grade 3, IVH with ventricular dilation; and grade 4, IVH with parenchymal extension). Others have used the categories mild, moderate, and severe or grades 1, 2, and 3, respectively. Mild or grade 1 refers to germinal matrix hemorrhage or with blood in ≤10% of the lateral ventricles. Moderate or grade 2 refers to IVH with blood filling 10% to 50% of the ventricles. In severe or grade 3, blood fills >50% of the ventricles with or without parenchymal involvement. Periventricular leukomalacia (PVL) is a common finding with PV-IVH. An area of echogenicity is seen in the periventricular area, superiorly or posteriorly. The lesion being located in the boundary zones of the brain centripetal and centrifugal arteries is generally considered an ischemic lesion. Follow-up ultrasound weeks later demonstrates small cystic or cavitary lesions or a porencephalic cyst when an extensive area is involved.

HSB

References

Bada HS, Korones SB, Perry EH, et al. Mean arterial blood pressure changes in premature infants and those at risk for intraventricular hemorrhage. J Pediatr 1990; 117:607.

Pape KE, Wigglesworth JS. Haemorrhage, ischaemia and the perinatal brain. Philadelphia: JB Lippincott, 1979.

Volpe JJ. Neurology of the newborn. 2nd ed. Philadelphia: WB Saunders, 1987.

Volpe JJ. Intraventricular hemorrhage and brain injury in the premature infant: Diagnosis, prognosis, and prevention. Clin Perinatol 1989; 16:387.

Volpe JJ. Intraventricular hemorrhage and brain injury in the premature infant: Neuropathology and pathogenesis. Clin Perinatol 1989; 16:361.

PERIVENTICULAR-INTRAVENTRICULAR HEMORRHAGE

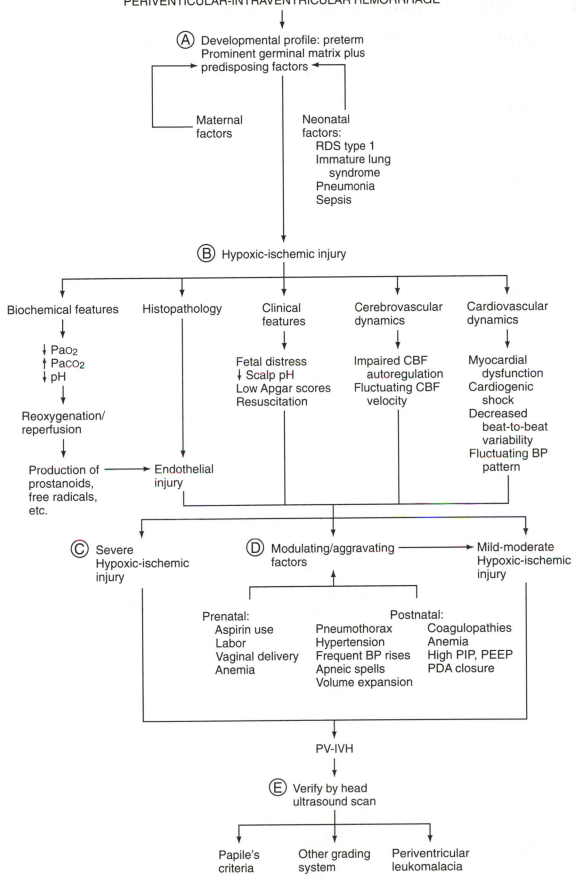

PERIVENTRICULAR-INTRAVENTRICULAR HEMORRHAGE: THERAPY

A. The clinical picture of an infant sustaining periventricular-intraventricular hemorrhage (PV-IVH) may be nonspecific with no CNS manifestations. In these "silent" cases, the presence of PV-IVH is not determined unless a head ultrasound scan is done routinely or the infant develops increasing head size because of a complicating posthemorrhagic hydrocephalus. There are cases when the infant with PV-IVH has acute deterioration (shock, severe hypoxia, acidosis, marked fall in hematocrit, apnea, bradycardia, and seizures); head ultrasound scan findings are confirmatory. With a variable clinical picture, therapy needs to be based on the infant's clinical manifestations. Once PV-IVH is determined, the infant needs to be reevaluated for evolution of the hemorrhage, the development of progressive ventriculomegaly, and an associated periventricular leukomalacia (PVL). Nonspecific CNS manifestations such as lethargy, hypotonia, hypertonia, apnea, and bradycardia need observation and O$_2$ and/or assisted ventilation if apnea and bradycardia are severe. Ventriculomegaly may occur, usually days after onset of PV-IVH. Since rapid ventricular enlargement may occur before obvious signs of increased intracranial pressure (ICP), such as increasing head size, wide sutures, and bulging fontanelles, head ultrasound scanning needs to be done weekly after the initial detection of PV-IVH. Progressive ventriculomegaly may respond to repeated lumbar puncture. Placement of a ventriculoperitoneal shunt is indicated in the absence of a response. PVL is associated with poor prognosis. No specific treatment is available at this time.

B. Similar to hypoxic-ischemic encephalopathy observed in term babies, PV-IVH is also associated with multiple organ involvement. Significant blood loss may result in circulatory hypovolemia so that volume expansion becomes necessary. Inotropic agents may be required for pressor effect and/or to treat myocardial dysfunction. Babies with PV-IVH often require respiratory support; respiratory insufficiency and/or pulmonary hemorrhage may occur. Metabolic problems are also common. Disturbances in sodium balance may result from renal involvement or from ADH excess or deficiency. Hypernatremia may also reflect a mere decrease in circulating blood volume. Renal tubular necrosis clinically manifesting as oliguria or anuria (renal insufficiency/failure) may be prevented when adequate systemic circulating volume is maintained or its decrease promptly corrected. Once renal failure ensues, fluid intake is restricted and associated electrolyte imbalance corrected. Coagulopathies may occur with PV-IVH. Hyperbilirubinemia results from the bilirubin derived from the brain hemorrhage itself so that phototherapy may be necessary. During hypoxia, blood flow is redistributed initially so that cerebral blood flow increases while gut and renal blood flow decreases. Thus the GI tract becomes highly susceptible to ischemic injury; necrotizing enterocolitis (NEC) is one manifestation of such injury.

C. Preventive measures are currently under investigation. Prenatal administration of phenobarbital or vitamin K has been shown to be associated with lower incidence of PV-IVH. Postnatally, drugs such as indomethacin, phenobarbital, vitamin E, vitamin A, ethamsylate, and pancuronium have been tried. However, prenatal or postnatal pharmacological prevention should be considered experimental at this time.

HSB

References

Pape KE, Wigglesworth JS. Haemorrhage, ischaemia and the perinatal brain. Philadelphia: JB Lippincott, 1979.
Volpe JJ. Neurology of the newborn. 2nd ed. Philadelphia: WB Saunders, 1987.

PERIVENTRICULAR-INTRAVENTRICULAR HEMORRHAGE: THERAPY

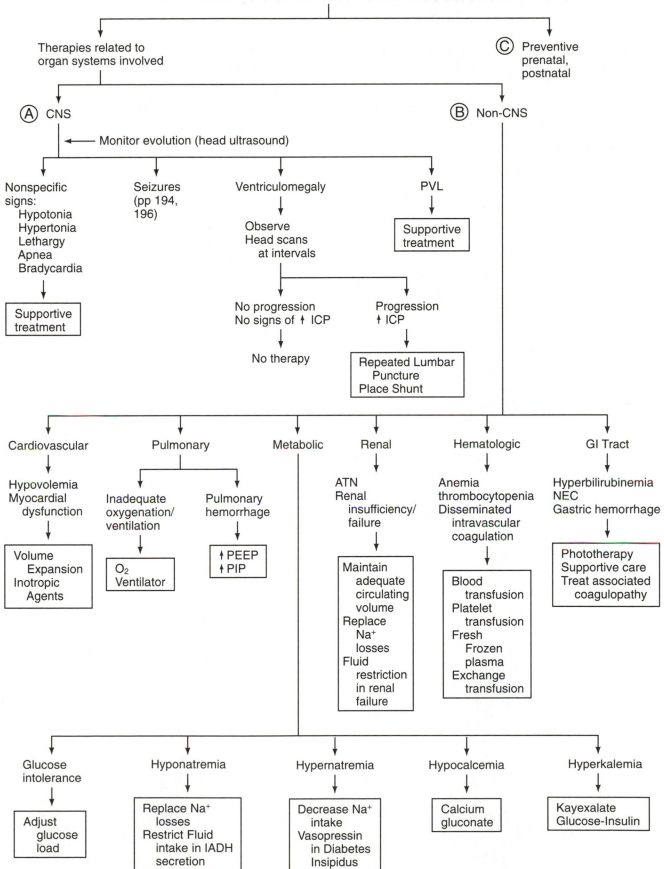

Therapies related to organ systems involved

Ⓒ Preventive prenatal, postnatal

Ⓐ CNS

Ⓑ Non-CNS

Monitor evolution (head ultrasound)

Nonspecific signs:
  Hypotonia
  Hypertonia
  Lethargy
  Apnea
  Bradycardia

Seizures (pp 194, 196)

Ventriculomegaly

PVL

Supportive treatment

Supportive treatment

Observe
Head scans at intervals

No progression
No signs of ↑ ICP

Progression
↑ ICP

No therapy

Repeated Lumbar Puncture
Place Shunt

Cardiovascular

Pulmonary

Metabolic

Renal

Hematologic

GI Tract

Hypovolemia
Myocardial dysfunction

Inadequate oxygenation/ ventilation

Pulmonary hemorrhage

ATN
Renal insufficiency/ failure

Anemia thrombocytopenia
Disseminated intravascular coagulation

Hyperbilirubinemia
NEC
Gastric hemorrhage

Volume Expansion
Inotropic Agents

O₂
Ventilator

↕PEEP
↕PIP

Maintain adequate circulating volume
Replace Na⁺ losses
Fluid restriction in renal failure

Blood transfusion
Platelet transfusion
Fresh Frozen plasma
Exchange transfusion

Phototherapy
Supportive care
Treat associated coagulopathy

Glucose intolerance

Hyponatremia

Hypernatremia

Hypocalcemia

Hyperkalemia

Adjust glucose load

Replace Na⁺ losses
Restrict Fluid intake in IADH secretion

Decrease Na⁺ intake
Vasopressin in Diabetes Insipidus

Calcium gluconate

Kayexalate
Glucose-Insulin

PUPILLARY OPACITIES (WHITE PUPILS)

A. Evaluate the red reflex (fundus reflex) first by directing an ordinary penlight to the pupil; hold it close to the eye and somewhat to the side to minimize pupillary constriction. Gross lesions such as a total cataract or end stage retinopathy of prematurity (ROP) are readily discerned. For smaller opacifying lesions, use an ophthalmoscope set at +10 diopters. Lesions that impair the red reflex may be situated in the cornea, lens, or fundus.

B. Cataractous opacities vary in their densities and therefore in their impairment of vision and ease of identification. The complete cataract is white and totally opaque. It is easily seen as a white pupil when light is directed at the eye. Other types of cataracts are less obvious and best seen with the ophthalmoscope.

C. Lesions in the vitreous obliterate the red reflex if they are sufficiently extensive. Retinoblastoma produces a white pupil when it occupies a large portion of the fundus. In the earliest stages prompt treatment results in a 95% 5-year survival rate. In the most advanced stages the 5-year survival rate is 30%. Among survivors, however, the incidence of new malignancies of other origin is high.

Persistent hyperplastic primary vitreous is a remnant of the hyaloid system of vessels, which normally resolves after the fifth gestational month to be replaced by clear mature vitreous. The vessels of the hyaloid system emanate from the disk and envelop the lens (tunica vasculosa lentis). Fragmentary, inconsequential persistence is seen in the form of a hyaloid artery remnant at the midline of the fundus that extends partially or completely from the disk to the posterior surface of the lens. Small remnants of embryonic posterior lens vessels may also be seen. When the largest portion of the embryonic vascular system fails to atrophy, a vitreous mass develops and the pupil is white as a result. The anomaly is seen in term infants, is almost always unilateral, and is associated with microphthalmia of the affected eye.

D. Extensive clouding of the cornea whitens the pupils. Corneal clouding covers the iris partially or completely; the opacity produced by lens or deeper involvement is restricted to the pupil. Herpes simplex and rubella frequently produce keratitis. Advanced glaucoma also clouds the cornea and eventually enlarges it as the eye distends from increased intraocular pressure.

SBK

References

Hamming NA, Read JE, Miller MT. The eye: Neonatal eye disease. In: Fanaroff AA, Martin RB, eds. Neonatal-perinatal medicine: Diseases of the fetus and infant. St Louis: Mosby—Year Book, 1992:1366.

Hoyt CS, Good W, Petersen R. Disorders of the eye. In: Taeusch HW, Ballard RA, Avery ME, eds. Schaffer and Avery's diseases of the newborn. 6th ed. Philadelphia: WB Saunders, 1991:1011.

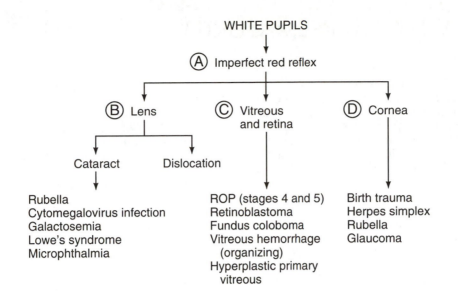

WHITE PUPILS

(A) Imperfect red reflex

(B) Lens

(C) Vitreous and retina

(D) Cornea

Cataract

Dislocation

Rubella
Cytomegalovirus infection
Galactosemia
Lowe's syndrome
Microphthalmia

ROP (stages 4 and 5)
Retinoblastoma
Fundus coloboma
Vitreous hemorrhage (organizing)
Hyperplastic primary vitreous

Birth trauma
Herpes simplex
Rubella
Glaucoma

RETINOPATHY OF PREMATURITY

A. Infants at risk for retinopathy of prematurity (ROP) should have funduscopic examination by a qualified ophthalmologist at the times shown in the algorithm. The grossly defined groups who are at risk vary slightly in definition from one institution to another. Those shown are recommendations of the American Academy of Pediatrics, except for the citation of birth weight (BW) <1500 g. Repeated examinations are required until vascularization has reached the ora serrata. Recurrence of examinations depends on the stage and location of disease and its progress since the last examination. The risk of ROP is virtually nonexistent when retinal vessels have reached the ora serrata. The risk of disease is enhanced as the distance between capillary terminals and the ora serrata increases.

B. The designated stages of disease are intended to indicate the degree of arrest in the forward progress of vascularization, the extent of fibrovascularity, and the presence of retinal detachment. In stage 1, the vessels halt in their anterior progress. A demarcating line that is flat with the retinal surface becomes visible between the vascular (posterior) retina and the more anterior avascular portion. Stage 2 describes a process of continued neovascularization that heaps up at the demarcation line rather than normally moving on in an anterior direction along the retinal plane. The flat line that was seen in stage 1 is now transformed into the typical ridge of stage 2. During stage 3, continued neovascularization produces an aggregation of capillaries that have left the ridge and entered the ocular vitreous, thus providing a basis for the fibrosis that characterizes later disease. At this stage cryotherapy is indicated. Stage 4(A) involves partial retinal detachment that spares the macula; stage 4(B) is the same process but with macular damage that virtually assures blindness. Stage 5 describes total retinal detachment.

C. Any stage of disease located in zone 1 (the most posterior zone and the area in which earliest vascu-larization occurs) is more likely to culminate in permanent ocular damage. In zone 2 the danger of poor outcome is less but still substantial, and the likelihood of spontaneous resolution is greater. Zone 3 represents the last leg of the maturational vascular journey that begins at the posterior pole (zone 1) and ends at the ora serrata. The chance of reversible disease and good outcome is considerably better in this zone than in the others.

D. The space that is occupied by the lesions in stages 1 to 3 is described by clock hours, which are intended to measure their spread. The numbers (hours) for these measurements are designated 3, 6, 9, and 12, all in standard clock positions.

E. So far, cryotherapy has been shown to diminish poor visual outcome by approximately 50%. The procedure entails freezing the anterior avascular retina when stage 3 disease is identified. Freezing the avascular area of the retina is thought to inhibit the production of an unidentified angiogenic substance that presumably promotes the abnormal neovascularization of ROP. Recently, laser surgery has been used with increased frequency.

SBK

References

Guidelines for perinatal care. 3rd ed. Elk Grove Village, Ill, and Washington, DC: American Academy of Pediatrics, American College of Obstetrics and Gynecology, and March of Dimes, 1992.

Phelps DL. The eye: Retinopathy of prematurity (part three). In: Fanaroff AA, Martin RJ, eds. Neonatal-perinatal medicine: Diseases of the fetus and infant. St Louis: Mosby—Year Book, 1992:1391.

RETINOPATHY OF PREMATURITY

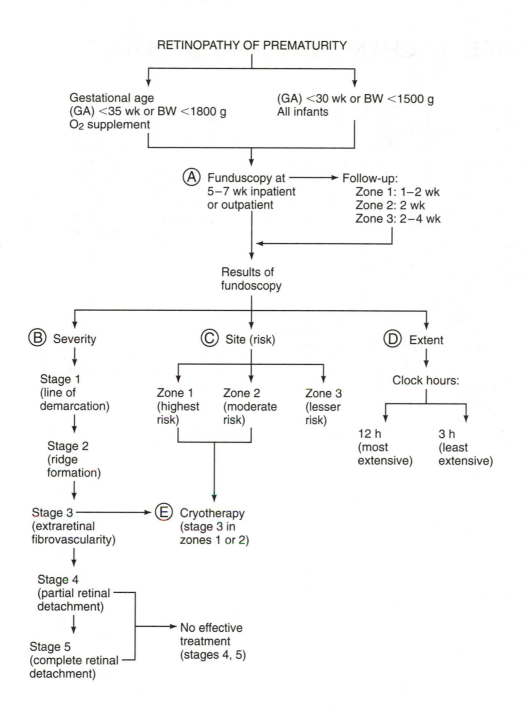

Gestational age
(GA) <35 wk or BW <1800 g
O₂ supplement

(GA) <30 wk or BW <1500 g
All infants

Ⓐ Funduscopy at ———→ Follow-up:
5–7 wk inpatient   Zone 1: 1–2 wk
or outpatient   Zone 2: 2 wk
                    Zone 3: 2–4 wk

Results of
fundoscopy

Ⓑ Severity   Ⓒ Site (risk)   Ⓓ Extent

Stage 1
(line of
demarcation)

Zone 1   Zone 2   Zone 3
(highest   (moderate   (lesser
risk)   risk)   risk)

Clock hours:

Stage 2
(ridge
formation)

12 h   3 h
(most   (least
extensive)   extensive)

Stage 3 ———→ Ⓔ Cryotherapy
(extraretinal   (stage 3 in
fibrovascularity)   zones 1 or 2)

Stage 4
(partial retinal
detachment)

No effective
treatment
(stages 4, 5)

Stage 5
(complete retinal
detachment)

PETECHIAE, ECCHYMOSES, AND BRUISES

Bleeding into the skin is the result of impaired clotting, vascular defects, or trauma. These are dramatic lesions that vary greatly in significance from sinister to benign. Diagnostic considerations should first address the presence or absence of associated physical signs, and then the occurrence of other events both antecedent and simultaneous.

A. Platelet and capillary defects listed in the algorithm are described in the indicated chapters. These disorders are not associated with other physical abnormalities.

B. Platelet deficiencies associated with other abnormal findings imply infection, Rh disease, disseminated intravascular coagulation (DIC), hereditary syndromes, congenital leukemia, or giant hemangioma. In the presence of infection, hepatosplenomegaly is virtually always in evidence, and jaundice is frequent. Hereditary syndromes include the Wiskott-Aldrich syndrome (recurrent infection resulting from immunological defect, thrombocytopenia, eczema, death in early childhood) and the syndrome of thrombocytopenia with bilaterally absent radii (platelet underproduction, leukemoid reaction, cardiac anomalies).

C. Purpuric babies with normal platelets and no other physical abnormalities have either a clotting defect (including vitamin K deficiency) or a birth injury. Benign petechiae over the upper body including the head are most common. They are the apparent result of increased venous pressure during parturition and subsequent capillary rupture. New lesions do not appear after birth. The bruising associated with breech delivery involves buttocks, perineum, and the lower extremities, often associated with edema. Bruising, usually over the head and face, is frequently encountered in the smallest premature infants who are delivered vaginally.

SBK

References

Glader BE, Amylon MD. Hemostatic disorders in the newborn. In: Taeusch HW, Ballard RA, Avery ME. Schaffer and Avery's diseases of the newborn. 6th ed. Philadelphia: WB Saunders, 1991:777.

Mangurten HH. Birth injuries. In: Fanaroff AA, Martin RJ. Neonatal-perinatal medicine: Diseases of the fetus and infant. 5th ed. St Louis: Mosby—Year Book, 1992:346.

PETECHIAE, ECCHYMOSES, BRUISES

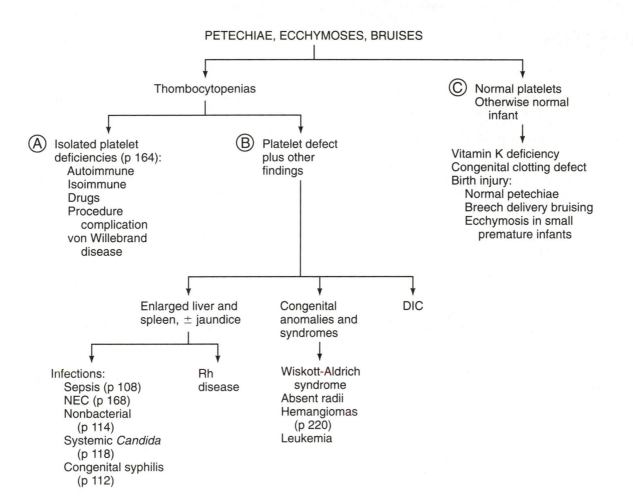

Thombocytopenias

Ⓐ Isolated platelet
deficiencies (p 164):
  Autoimmune
  Isoimmune
  Drugs
  Procedure
    complication
  von Willebrand
    disease

Ⓑ Platelet defect
plus other
findings

Ⓒ Normal platelets
Otherwise normal
infant

Vitamin K deficiency
Congenital clotting defect
Birth injury:
  Normal petechiae
  Breech delivery bruising
  Ecchymosis in small
    premature infants

Enlarged liver and
spleen, ± jaundice

Congenital
anomalies and
syndromes

DIC

Infections:
  Sepsis (p 108)
  NEC (p 168)
  Nonbacterial
    (p 114)
  Systemic *Candida*
    (p 118)
  Congenital syphilis
    (p 112)

Rh
disease

Wiskott-Aldrich
  syndrome
Absent radii
Hemangiomas
  (p 220)
Leukemia

BLISTERS

A. Bullous impetigo is a noscomial infection caused by *Staphylococcus aureus* (rarely by streptococci Groups A or B). It appears after 4 or 5 days of age. Gram's stain of blister fluid is the most rapid method for diagnosis, but culture of the fluid and an investigation for sepsis are indispensable. Treat with vancomycin pending results of culture and sensitivity. Warm saline compresses to lesions hasten their resolution. Isolation technique for staphylococcal infection is mandatory. The occurrence of two or more cases in the nursery within a 14-day interval requires full-scale epidemiologic investigation.

B. Staphylococcal scalded skin syndrome was formerly known as Ritter's disease. It, too, is a nosocomial infection. Skin manifestations are caused by an exotoxin from *S. aureus* in the group 2 phage type, but sometimes in other phage types as well. Bullae are preceded by patches or wide areas of erythema anywhere on the body, most often first on the face. As fluid accumulates in tiny flecks within the uppermost epidermal layers, ill-defined vesicles become apparent. The skin then peels, leaving behind moist red areas and a scalded appearance. The Nikolsky sign is positive. Blister fluid is sterile. The causative organism is identified in cultures from various sites, whether or not they appear normal. Although purulent conjunctivitis is common in neonates, it is more frequent in older children. Local skin treatment with compresses and systemic vancomycin therapy are indicated. Extensive involvement may cause significant loss of fluid and electrolytes. Isolation techniques are required.

C. *Pseudomonas* septicemia occasionally gives rise to purulent bullae that rupture to leave behind an ulcerated gangrenous lesion. Similar lesions have been reported in association with sepsis due to other gram-negative rods. In any case, clinical status is dominated by severe systemic signs of sepsis.

D. Diagnosis of herpes simplex or varicella begins with maternal history. Cultures should be taken from the blister fluid and other sites. For treatment of herpes and varicella, see p 114.

E. Bullous lesions are not often seen in congenital syphilis, but their appearance suggests the diagnostic possibility. Bullae caused by candidiasis may be seen in rare instances of fetal systemic infection from contamination of amniotic fluid during an invasive antepartum procedure. Ascending vaginal candidiasis may cause fetal systemic disease. For treatment of candidiasis, see p 118.

F. The lesions of erythema toxicum appear at 24–48 hours of age, sometimes later, and rarely at birth. An initial papule evolves into a small vesicle that often appears purulent. Erythematous skin surrounds each lesion. Careful aspiration and Wright's stain of a smear from the vesicle fluid reveal sheets of eosinophils, thus establishing the diagnosis. However, simple inspection of lesions usually suffices for diagnosis.

Transient neonatal pustular melanosis is present at birth. Small pustules rupture after 48 hours and pigmented macules are the aftermath. The macules persist for several weeks or months. The forehead, anterior neck, anterior legs, and lower back are most frequently involved. The entire process is benign.

Sucking blisters are uncommon. Fetal sucking presumably gives rise to relatively large bullae situated most often on the hand and wrist. Treatment is unnecessary.

SBK

References

Esterly NB, Solomon LM. Congenital and hereditary disorders of the skin. In: Taeusch HW, Ballard RA, Avery ME, eds. Schaffer and Avery's diseases of the newborn. 6th ed. Philadelphia: WB Saunders, 1991:973.

Solomon LM, Esterly NB. Vesico-bullous eruptions. In: Solomon LM, Esterly NB, eds. Neonatal dermatology. Philadelphia: WB Saunders, 1973:136.

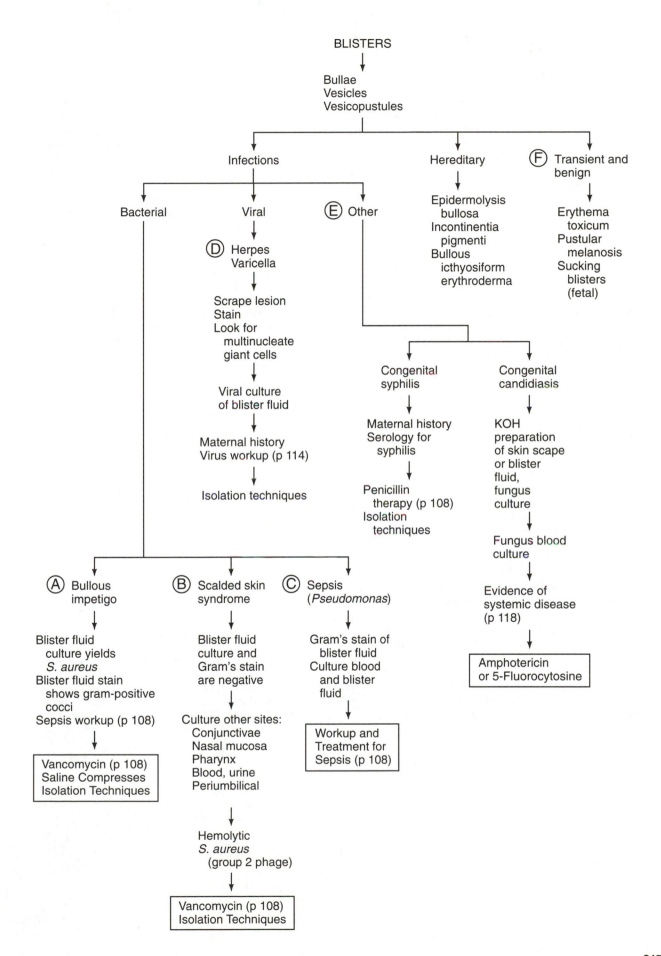

BLISTERS

Bullae
Vesicles
Vesicopustules

Infections

Bacterial

Viral

Ⓔ Other

Hereditary

Epidermolysis
 bullosa
Incontinentia
 pigmenti
Bullous
 icthyosiform
 erythroderma

Ⓕ Transient and
 benign

Erythema
 toxicum
Pustular
 melanosis
Sucking
 blisters
 (fetal)

Ⓓ Herpes
 Varicella

Scrape lesion
Stain
Look for
 multinucleate
 giant cells

Viral culture
of blister fluid

Maternal history
Virus workup (p 114)

Isolation techniques

Congenital
syphilis

Maternal history
Serology for
 syphilis

Penicillin
 therapy (p 108)
Isolation
 techniques

Congenital
candidiasis

KOH
preparation
of skin scape
or blister
fluid,
fungus
culture

Fungus blood
culture

Evidence of
systemic disease
(p 118)

Amphotericin
or 5-Fluorocytosine

Ⓐ Bullous
 impetigo

Blister fluid
 culture yields
 S. aureus
Blister fluid stain
 shows gram-positive
 cocci
Sepsis workup (p 108)

Vancomycin (p 108)
Saline Compresses
Isolation Techniques

Ⓑ Scalded skin
 syndrome

Blister fluid
 culture and
 Gram's stain
 are negative

Culture other sites:
 Conjunctivae
 Nasal mucosa
 Pharynx
 Blood, urine
 Periumbilical

Hemolytic
S. aureus
 (group 2 phage)

Vancomycin (p 108)
Isolation Techniques

Ⓒ Sepsis
 (*Pseudomonas*)

Gram's stain of
 blister fluid
Culture blood
 and blister
 fluid

Workup and
Treatment for
Sepsis (p 108)

EDEMA AND SCLEREMA

A. Sclerema is associated with sepsis and occasionally with severe hypothermia. Pervasive techniques for maintaining optimal body temperature have markedly diminished its frequency. Sclerema is a localized phenomenon that first appears on the cheeks and buttocks, later extending to the thighs and arms. It may also appear on other parts of the body in unpredictable patterns. Sclerema is the result of hardened subcutaneous fat that usually mimics in appearance the classic edema caused by fluid accumulation. In contrast to classic edema, sclerema does not pit when pressure is applied to the affected surface.

Subcutaneous fat necrosis is a clearly demarcated, localized area of subcutaneous thickening that does not pit. Occasionally, extensive areas are involved, but the usual lesion is an irregularly round plaque that is 1 to 8 cm in diameter. The overlying skin may appear normal, but it is often pale purple or red. These lesions generally resolve in days or weeks, sometimes persisting for months. Subcutaneous fat necrosis is presumably due to localized pressure on the body surface during parturition. Most affected infants are mature and large. Difficult labor is a frequent occurrence. The sites most often involved are the most vulnerable to trauma (forceps application, shoulders, buttocks).

B. Pitting edema may be localized or general. In the latter instance a number of underlying diseases may cause hydrops, which subcutaneous edema is a prominent component (p 16). Localized edema is most often a consequence of labor and delivery. Except for bone fractures, the lesions of edema listed in the algorithm resolve spontaneously.

Other forms of localized pitting edema may strongly suggest an underlying generalized disorder. Edema of the feet in female infants should trigger an awareness of Turner's syndrome. Affected babies are females with normal external genitalia. They are usually small for gestational age and have low-set ears, a low nuchal hairline, and micrognathia. Lymphedema of the hands may also be evident. Skin over the neck is loose (webbed neck); nails are sometimes hypoplastic. The more extensive manifestations of edema include ascites, pericardial or pleural effusions, and universal subcutaneous edema. Pleural effusion and ascites have been reported to clear spontaneously. Renal anomalies (hypoplasia, duplications, and horseshoe contour) are common in this syndrome. Coarctation of the aorta, hypoplastic left heart, and anomalous pulmonary venous return are often associated with webbed neck. Diagnosis is by karyotype analysis in consultation with a geneticist.

Congenital lymphedema may be diffuse, but it most often appears in the lower extremities. The edema is the result of lymphatic stasis. Chylothorax and ascites are sometimes associated abnormalities. The eponym Milroy's disease is applicable to infants in whom autosomal dominance is identified and in whom the legs are solely involved.

Vitamin E deficiency may be suspected in the presence of peripheral edema, usually of the lower extremities but sometimes including the upper extremities as well. Vitamin E deficiency occurs primarily in infants whose birth weight is <1500 g and at postnatal ages of 6 to 10 weeks. The hematologic findings include anemia, reticulocytosis, acanthocytosis, and thrombocytosis.

C. The array of underlying disorders in which edematous involvement is generalized requires a carefully considered diagnostic approach. Intrauterine cardiac disorders, infections, hematologic and pulmonary disorders often produce hydrops fetalis (p 16). Generalized edema indicates a serious underlying disorder.

SBK

References

Anand SK. Clinical evaluation of renal disease. In: Taeusch HW, Ballard RA, Avery ME, eds. Schaffer and Avery's diseases of the newborn. 6th ed. Philadelphia: WB Saunders, 1991:848.

Mangurten HH. Birth injuries. In: Fanaroff AA, Martin RJ, eds. Neonatal-perinatal medicine: Diseases of the fetus and infant. 5th ed. St Louis: Mosby—Year Book, 1992:346.

EDEMA OR SCLEREMA

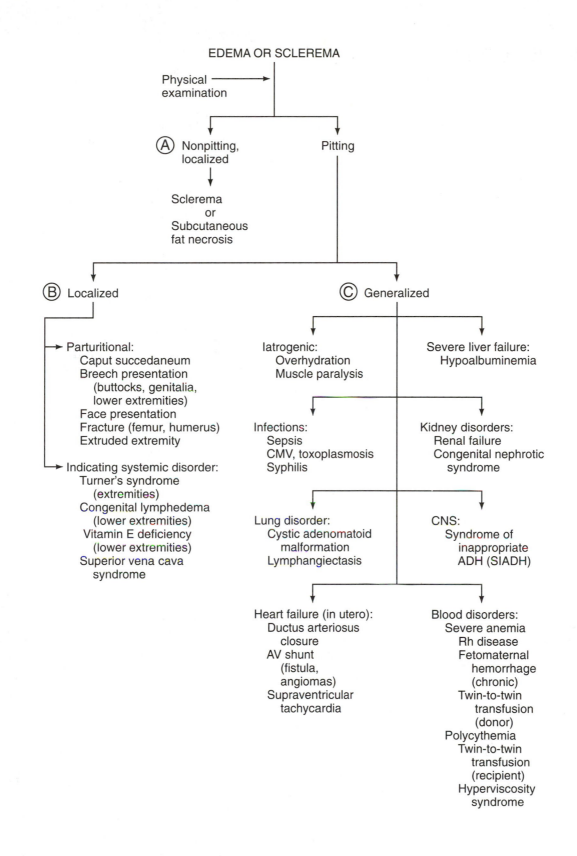

Physical examination

(A) Nonpitting, localized → Sclerema or Subcutaneous fat necrosis

Pitting

(B) Localized

Parturitional:
  Caput succedaneum
  Breech presentation
    (buttocks, genitalia,
    lower extremities)
  Face presentation
  Fracture (femur, humerus)
  Extruded extremity

Indicating systemic disorder:
  Turner's syndrome
    (extremities)
  Congenital lymphedema
    (lower extremities)
  Vitamin E deficiency
    (lower extremities)
  Superior vena cava
    syndrome

(C) Generalized

Iatrogenic:
  Overhydration
  Muscle paralysis

Infections:
  Sepsis
  CMV, toxoplasmosis
  Syphilis

Lung disorder:
  Cystic adenomatoid
    malformation
  Lymphangiectasis

Heart failure (in utero):
  Ductus arteriosus
    closure
  AV shunt
    (fistula,
    angiomas)
  Supraventricular
    tachycardia

Severe liver failure:
  Hypoalbuminemia

Kidney disorders:
  Renal failure
  Congenital nephrotic
    syndrome

CNS:
  Syndrome of
    inappropriate
    ADH (SIADH)

Blood disorders:
  Severe anemia
  Rh disease
  Fetomaternal
    hemorrhage
    (chronic)
  Twin-to-twin
    transfusion
    (donor)
  Polycythemia
  Twin-to-twin
    transfusion
    (recipient)
  Hyperviscosity
    syndrome

HEMANGIOMAS

Angiomatous skin lesions raise four immediate questions: Will they disappear? Will they grow? Are they associated with deeper hemangiomas? Do they indicate a serious generalized disorder?

A. The classic strawberry hemangioma first appears several days after birth as a pink or red macule. It proliferates for several weeks or months and evolves into a bright red raised lesion with a leathery surface. The lesion is a conglomeration of proliferated capillaries that are restricted to the epidermis. They vary in number from one to several hemangiomas. They are often associated with an underlying cavernous hemangioma (mixed). Cavernous hemangiomas are dilated venules that also occur as isolated lesions. The overlying skin is bluish, puffy, and spongy when palpated. Strawberry and cavernous hemangiomas involute spontaneously in several months or sometimes later. The cosmetic outcome is optimal when treatment is avoided.

B. Kasabach-Merritt syndrome (giant hemangioma with thrombocytopenia) is characterized by spontaneous bleeding in the presence of a cavernous hemangioma that usually enlarges with onset of hemorrhage. The signs of bleeding include ecchymoses, petechiae, oozing from orifices, circumcision, and puncture wounds. Hematologic abnormalities consist of thrombocytopenia and consumption coagulopathy, which have been attributed to hemangiomatous trapping of platelets and a subsequent accelerated consumption of coagulation factors. Treatment is urgent. Depending upon the hematologic abnormality, blood transfusion, fresh frozen plasma, platelets, and systemic prednisone may each be indicated. Surgical removal, if feasible, is curative.

C. Diffuse hemangiomatosis involves multiple skin lesions that may or may not be associated with visceral involvement. With deeper involvement the disease is usually fatal. The organs most frequently affected are the GI tract, lungs, and central nervous system. Death occurs in the first few months from intractable bleeding or congestive heart failure. Treatment with systemic steroids may be helpful.

D. Nevi at the nape, eyelid, and forehead are telangiectatic, consisting of mature capillaries beneath the epidermis. They form macular patches that vary from pale pink to deep red. They disappear eventually; the nuchal lesions are less likely to involute, however.

E. Port-wine stains may occur anywhere over the body. They are telangiectatic lesions composed of dilated subepidermal capillaries. They do not disappear, often presenting a cosmetic problem on the face. Occasionally the port-wine stain is a clinical marker of serious generalized disease. In particular, the Sturge-Weber syndrome must be considered when unilateral facial port-wine lesions are distributed over the area supplied by the trigeminal nerve (forehead and upper eyelid). Ipsilateral eye abnormalities, including glaucoma, buphthalmos, choroidal angiomas, and optic atrophy, are often associated with port-wine stains. Angiomatous CNS lesions are also ipsilateral to the port-wine stain, usually involving the occipital and parietal lobes. Neurologic signs include seizures and contralateral hemiplegia.

SBK

References

Margileth AM. Dermatologic conditions. In: Avery GB, ed. Neonatology: Pathophysiology and management of the newborn. 3rd ed. Philadelphia: JB Lippincott, 1987:1230.

Solomon LM, Esterly NB. Nevi and cutaneous tumors. In: Taeusch HW, Ballard RA, Avery ME, eds. Schaffer and Avery's diseases of the newborn. 6th ed. Philadelphia: WB Saunders, 1991:997.

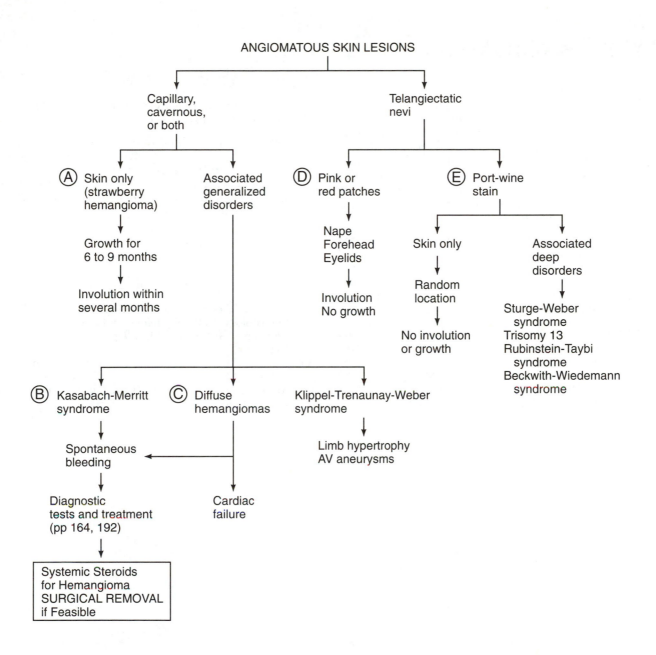

ANGIOMATOUS SKIN LESIONS

Capillary, cavernous, or both

Telangiectatic nevi

(A) Skin only (strawberry hemangioma)

↓

Growth for 6 to 9 months

↓

Involution within several months

Associated generalized disorders

(D) Pink or red patches

↓

Nape
Forehead
Eyelids

↓

Involution
No growth

(E) Port-wine stain

Skin only

↓

Random location

↓

No involution or growth

Associated deep disorders

↓

Sturge-Weber syndrome
Trisomy 13
Rubinstein-Taybi syndrome
Beckwith-Wiedemann syndrome

(B) Kasabach-Merritt syndrome

↓

(C) Diffuse hemangiomas

Klippel-Trenaunay-Weber syndrome

↓

Limb hypertrophy
AV aneurysms

Spontaneous bleeding

↓

Diagnostic tests and treatment (pp 164, 192)

↓

Cardiac failure

Systemic Steroids for Hemangioma
SURGICAL REMOVAL if Feasible

LYMPHANGIOMAS

A. Four basic types of lymphangioma are clinically identifiable. Their histologic characteristics are identical: dilated or cystic lymph channels lined by normal simple lymphatic endothelium. Except for cystic hygroma, these tumors grow little if at all. Occasionally some bleeding occurs into the cystic structures. The only known treatment is surgical extirpation; the outcome varies from optimal effectiveness to impossibility of complete removal.

B. Lymphangioma circumscriptum is the most common lymphatic tumor. It is composed of thick-walled vesicles that are usually localized but may extend to underlying tissue. The most frequent sites are the neck, shoulders, axillae, tongue, buccal mucosa, and perineum. Surgical excision is generally effective.

C. Cystic hygromas are large, unilocular (sometimes multilocular) cysts that occur most often in the neck and axilla. They are also found in the popliteal fossa and the inguinal area. In the retroperitoneal region these lesions are mesenteric cysts. Rapid growth or spontaneous involution may occasionally occur. Excise surgically as early as feasible because of the possibility of rapid growth.

D. Diffuse lymphangiomas are microscopically cavernous. They permeate subcutaneous and subjacent muscle tissue. They are particularly troublesome in the lips, tongue, and face. Generally these lesions are extensively infiltrative and diffuse; complete extirpation is usually impossible.

SBK

References

Margileth AM. Dermatologic conditions. In: Avery GB, ed. Neonatology: Pathophysiology and management of the newborn. 3rd ed. Philadelphia: JB Lippincott, 1987:1230.

Solomon LM, Esterly NB. Nevi and cutaneous tumors. In: Taeusch HW, Ballard RA, Avery ME, eds. Schaffer and Avery's diseases of the newborn. 6th ed. Philadelphia: WB Saunders, 1991:997.

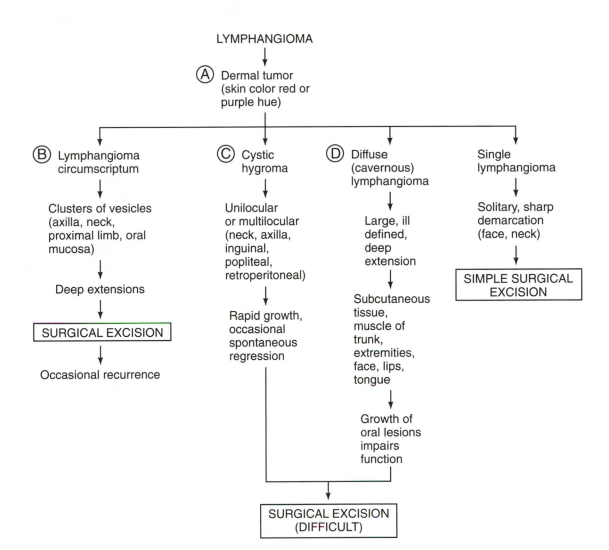

LYMPHANGIOMA
↓
(A) Dermal tumor
(skin color red or
purple hue)

(B) Lymphangioma circumscriptum
↓
Clusters of vesicles (axilla, neck, proximal limb, oral mucosa)
↓
Deep extensions
↓
SURGICAL EXCISION
↓
Occasional recurrence

(C) Cystic hygroma
↓
Unilocular or multilocular (neck, axilla, inguinal, popliteal, retroperitoneal)
↓
Rapid growth, occasional spontaneous regression

(D) Diffuse (cavernous) lymphangioma
↓
Large, ill defined, deep extension
↓
Subcutaneous tissue, muscle of trunk, extremities, face, lips, tongue
↓
Growth of oral lesions impairs function

SURGICAL EXCISION (DIFFICULT)

Single lymphangioma
↓
Solitary, sharp demarcation (face, neck)
↓
SIMPLE SURGICAL EXCISION

PIGMENTED LESIONS

Faced with one or more pigmented skin blemishes in a neonate, the clinician must know (1) if the lesions indicate a serious disease and (2) if they are permanent. Thus the algorithm is organized according to absence or presence of a more widespread disorder, rather than by histologic appearance or shape and contour of the lesion.

A. Mongolian spots are most common in black infants and more frequent in those of Asian and southern European ancestry than in other infants. They are usually distributed over the sacrum and buttocks but are also seen over the back and extensor surfaces of the extremities. They disappear spontaneously by 4 years of age.

B. A pigmented melanocytic nevus may be flat or raised. It is often a single lesion and is permanently removed surgically.

C. Transient neonatal pustular melanosis begins with small pustules that rupture, leaving pigmented macules in their place. If the process is initiated in utero, the baby presents with macules that may be sparse or dense in their distribution. Stained smears (Wright's stain) reveal debris and polymorphonuclear leukocytes. The pustules disappear in 48–72 hours, the macules within 3 months.

D. Café au lait spots are light brown. Single patches less than 2 cm in diameter occur in ≤20% of otherwise normal children. Larger lesions may be extensive. A clinical rule of thumb has long held that fewer than six lesions, each <1.5–2 cm in diameter, have only local significance.

E. Suspect neurofibromatosis with six or more café au lait spots. In some instances <6 lesions during the neonatal period may become more numerous in the ensuing 5 years. A family history of neurofibromatosis is pivotal among diagnostic considerations. Large, elongated café au lait spots (≥1) suggest McCune-Albright syndrome (polyostotic fibrous dysplasia and sexual precocity in females later on).

F. Peutz-Jeghers syndrome is characterized by small bowel polyposis that becomes apparent as a bout of intussusception during adolescence. However, pigmented oval macules in the oral mucosa and about the nose and mouth may be seen during the neonatal period or soon thereafter.

G. Giant (hairy) nevi indicate potential malignancy and severe CNS disease. Malignant melanoma within the nevus evolves in approximately 10% of affected infants. The lesion is composed of melanocytes that sometimes invade subjacent muscle and fascia. Melanocytes may also be present in the leptomeninges, causing seizures and other neurologic abnormalities. The lesion is grotesquely large. At its worst it may involve 35% of the body surface, distributed in a classic "bathing suit" pattern. Pigmentation is characteristically black, often with interspersed smaller areas of brownish discoloration. Hair within the lesion may be present at birth or appear soon thereafter. The involved skin is thick and literally leathery. The unsightliness of the lesion and the severe pruritus it occasionally causes require early planning for surgical removal. Surgery for this lesion is extensive, with multiple procedures and grafting. Thus the infant must be sufficiently grown to withstand multiple operations.

H. Pigmented whorls represent the end stage of incontinentia pigmenti, which at its onset is a process of blistering. The pigmented phase rarely appears before 3 months of age.

SBK

References

Esterly NB, Solomon LM. The skin. In: Fanaroff AA, Martin RJ, eds. Neonatal-perinatal medicine: Diseases of the fetus and infant. 5th ed. St Louis: Mosby–Year Book, 1992:1328.

Solomon LM, Esterly NB. Pigmentary abnormalities. In: Solomon LM, Esterly NB, eds. Neonatal dermatology. Philadelphia: WB Saunders, 1973:97.

Solomon LM, Esterly NB. Nevi and cutaneous tumors. In: Taeusch HW, Ballard RA, Avery ME, eds. Schaffer and Avery's diseases of the newborn. 6th ed. Philadelphia: WB Saunders, 1991:997.

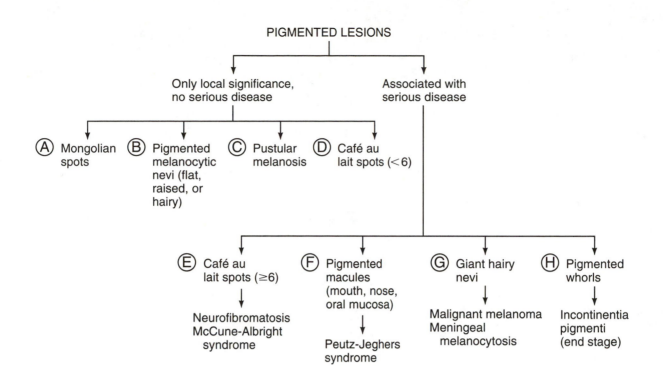

PIGMENTED LESIONS

Only local significance,
no serious disease

Associated with
serious disease

Ⓐ Mongolian
spots

Ⓑ Pigmented
melanocytic
nevi (flat,
raised, or
hairy)

Ⓒ Pustular
melanosis

Ⓓ Café au
lait spots (<6)

Ⓔ Café au
lait spots (≥6)

Neurofibromatosis
McCune-Albright
syndrome

Ⓕ Pigmented
macules
(mouth, nose,
oral mucosa)

Peutz-Jeghers
syndrome

Ⓖ Giant hairy
nevi

Malignant melanoma
Meningeal
melanocytosis

Ⓗ Pigmented
whorls

Incontinentia
pigmenti
(end stage)

NEONATAL SEQUELAE OF MATERNAL DRUG ABUSE

Maternal Cocaine Abuse
Maternal Heroin/Methadone Abuse

Maternal Alcohol Consumption
Maternal Amphetamine Use

MATERNAL COCAINE ABUSE

A. Cocaine is an amino alcohol base similar to synthetic local anesthetic lidocaine. It is derived from *Erythroxylon coca*, a plant indigenous to the mountains of South America. Cocaine is a CNS stimulant that prevents reuptake of neurotransmitters (norepinephrine, dopamine, serotonin, and acetylcholine) and delays inactivation of norepinephrine and epinephrine at the nerve terminals. The drug is administered by snorting, smoking, or by intravenous route and is well absorbed regardless of site of administration. In adults, sympathetic stimulation from cocaine causes tachycardia, vasoconstriction, and hypertension. Vasoconstriction may be associated with decreased uterine and placental blood flow in the pregnant woman.

B. The effects of cocaine during pregnancy and on the fetus are difficult to assess because of coexisting factors known to also affect fetal neonatal outcome, e.g., low socioeconomic status, lack of prenatal care, malnutrition, and abuse of alcohol and/or other drugs. These factors render it difficult to sort out effects solely attributable to cocaine.

C. The vasoconstrictive properties of cocaine and its hypertensive effects are said to result in abnormal uterine contractions, abruptio placentae, retroplacental hemorrhages, premature labor, and spontaneous abortions. Premature rupture of membranes is almost twice as common in pregnancies complicated by cocaine abuse compared with those not complicated by cocaine use. Aside from prematurity, other neonatal complications of maternal cocaine use include low birthweight or intrauterine growth retardation (IUGR), decreased head circumference and length, and low Apgar scores. These complications occur because of impaired placental blood flow resulting from the vasoconstrictive effect of cocaine.

D. Cocaine is also a teratogenic substance. Eye defects and skeletal defects from cocaine are reported in mice. Neonatal CNS, craniofacial, cardiovascular, genitourinary tract, GI tract, and musculoskeletal defects have been associated with maternal cocaine abuse. Aside from malformations, physiological and behavioral aberrations have been reported. Infants exposed to cocaine have depressed interactive behavior and poor organizational response to environmental stimuli. The risk of sudden infant death syndrome (SIDS) is also increased almost seven times in infants born to cocaine-abusing mothers compared with infants of nonsubstance-abusing mothers.

E. Confirmation of neonatal cocaine exposure is essential, particularly in cases when the mother denies cocaine use during pregnancy. If administered within 48 hours of delivery, cocaine and its metabolites may be present in the neonatal urine for 96 hours. Meconium and hair may also be analyzed for presence of cocaine.

F. Sexually transmitted diseases, such as syphilis, *Chlamydia*, gonorrhea, and acquired immunodeficiency syndrome, are prevalent among drug addicts. Hepatitis B is also a consideration among intravenous drug abusers. Mothers admitting drug abuse during prenatal care need to be tested for the above diseases so that neonatal diagnostic work-up, prophylaxis, or treatment may be instituted promptly. Treatment for neonatal cocaine effects is mainly supportive. Some of the malformations or congenital defects may require surgical treatment.

HSB

References

Chasnoff IJ, Burns WJ, Schnoll S, Burns KA. Cocaine use in pregnancy. N Engl J Med 1985; 313:666.

Davidson SL, Bautista D, Chan L, et al. Sudden infant death syndrome in infants of substance-abusing mothers. J Pediatr 1990; 117:876.

Doering PL, Davidson CL, LaFauce L, Williams CA. Effects of cocaine on the human fetus: A review of clinical studies. Ann Pharmacother 1989; 23:639.

Farar HC and Kearns GL. Cocaine: clinical pharmacology and toxicology. J Pediatr 1989; 115:665.

Frank DA, Zuckerman BS, Amaro H, et al. Cocaine use during pregnancy: Prevalence and correlates. Pediatrics 1988; 82:888.

Hoyme HE, Jones KL, Dixon SD, et al. Prenatal cocaine exposure and fetal vascular disruption. Pediatrics 1990; 85:743.

MATERNAL COCAINE ABUSE

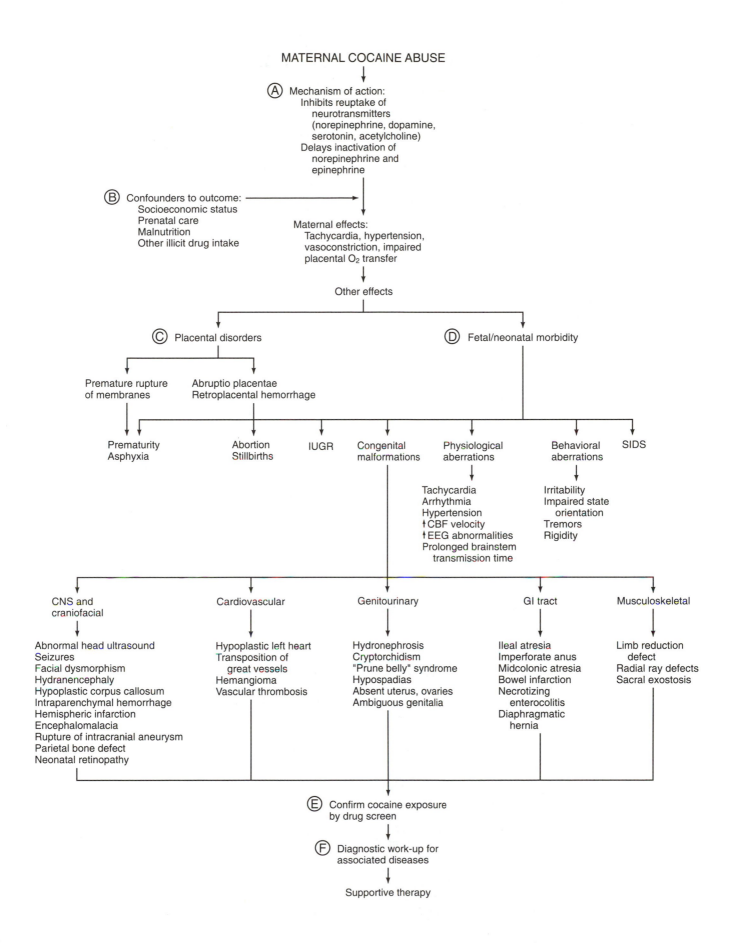

(A) Mechanism of action:
Inhibits reuptake of
neurotransmitters
(norepinephrine, dopamine,
serotonin, acetylcholine)
Delays inactivation of
norepinephrine and
epinephrine

(B) Confounders to outcome:
Socioeconomic status
Prenatal care
Malnutrition
Other illicit drug intake

Maternal effects:
Tachycardia, hypertension,
vasoconstriction, impaired
placental O_2 transfer

Other effects

(C) Placental disorders

(D) Fetal/neonatal morbidity

Premature rupture
of membranes

Abruptio placentae
Retroplacental hemorrhage

Prematurity
Asphyxia

Abortion
Stillbirths

IUGR

Congenital
malformations

Physiological
aberrations

Behavioral
aberrations

SIDS

Tachycardia
Arrhythmia
Hypertension
↑CBF velocity
↑EEG abnormalities
Prolonged brainstem
transmission time

Irritability
Impaired state
orientation
Tremors
Rigidity

CNS and
craniofacial

Cardiovascular

Genitourinary

GI tract

Musculoskeletal

Abnormal head ultrasound
Seizures
Facial dysmorphism
Hydranencephaly
Hypoplastic corpus callosum
Intraparenchymal hemorrhage
Hemispheric infarction
Encephalomalacia
Rupture of intracranial aneurysm
Parietal bone defect
Neonatal retinopathy

Hypoplastic left heart
Transposition of
great vessels
Hemangioma
Vascular thrombosis

Hydronephrosis
Cryptorchidism
"Prune belly" syndrome
Hypospadias
Absent uterus, ovaries
Ambiguous genitalia

Ileal atresia
Imperforate anus
Midcolonic atresia
Bowel infarction
Necrotizing
enterocolitis
Diaphragmatic
hernia

Limb reduction
defect
Radial ray defects
Sacral exostosis

(E) Confirm cocaine exposure
by drug screen

(F) Diagnostic work-up for
associated diseases

Supportive therapy

MATERNAL HEROIN/METHADONE ABUSE

A. Heroin is diacetyl morphine and is deacetylated in the liver to monoacetyl morphine and then to morphine. Methadone, a synthetic opiate, is a treatment for heroin addiction; it blocks the euphoric effects of heroin. Methadone is also metabolized in the liver; its metabolites are found in bile, urine, and feces. Both heroin and methadone cross the placenta. Heroin is widely distributed in fetal tissues and compartments with concentrations likely to be higher than in the maternal tissues. Methadone is found at a lower concentration in the fetus (maternal:cord concentration of 2.7:1). The incidence of neonatal withdrawal signs and symptoms varies according to the drug dosage, duration of maternal addiction, and time of last maternal drug intake. Heroin intake of <6 mg/kg/day is associated with mild withdrawal manifestations or none at all. Maternal addiction of <1 year is associated with 55% incidence of neonatal drug withdrawal; this incidence increases to >70% if addiction is of longer duration. A higher incidence of withdrawal is observed when heroin intake occurred within 24 hours of delivery. Incidence of withdrawal in neonates of mothers on methadone is 70%–90%. The higher the maternal methadone plasma levels, the greater the incidence of moderate-to-severe neonatal withdrawal manifestations. The final maternal methadone dose taken within 20 hours of delivery results in onset of withdrawal, usually after 24 hours or later, whereas earlier onset of withdrawal symptoms is observed when mother's final dose was taken >20 hours before delivery.

B. Neonatal signs and symptoms of methadone withdrawal are more severe and prolonged compared with heroin withdrawal. Intrauterine growth retardation (IUGR) is common in babies born to heroin-addicted mothers because of maternal malnutrition and possibly growth-inhibiting effect of heroin. Organs at autopsy show decreased cell number but normal cell size. The high prematurity rate may be related to associated placental disorders, e.g., chorioamnionitis, abruptio placentae. In methadone-dependent pregnancies, the incidence of IUGR is lower; the infants however tend to have decreased head circumference. Postnatal growth and behavioral disturbances are reported with narcotic withdrawal. A high incidence of sudden infant death syndrome (SIDS) is reported in babies born to mothers dependent on methadone during pregnancy. Common neonatal manifestations of drug withdrawal include irritability, tremors, diarrhea, excessive diaphoresis, and skin abrasions. Their extreme irritability results in feeding and sleep disturbances. These infants have hyperactive behavior, and constant movement results in skin abrasions. Other manifestations include fever, salivation, and tachypnea. Seizures are more common in methadone withdrawal than in heroin withdrawal. Some reported effects of methadone are thrombocytosis and abnormal thyroid function studies and thus should necessi-

tate monitoring the neonatal platelet count and evaluating thyroid function.

C. A confirmation of drug dependence in the maternal history is helpful in the diagnosis. Screening for drugs may be performed using maternal or infant's blood or urine. Meconium may also be tested for drugs taken even early in gestation.

D. The prevalence of sexually transmitted disease among drug abusers and of hepatitis B among intravenous drug users warrants screening for disorders in both the drug-addicted mothers and their neonates. Neonatal signs of drug withdrawal such as jitteriness, tremors, irritability, or seizures are manifestations common to other disorders such as hypocalcemia, hypoglycemia, and hypomagnesemia. Diarrhea and vomiting may also be manifestations of sepsis. One must also consider these diagnoses even with positive drug screen results or history.

E. Treatment in mild cases is primarily supportive. Swaddling, for example, can diminish irritability, allowing these babies to take feedings. Frequent feedings may also be given in small amounts so that adequate calories are provided. In moderate-to-severe withdrawal symptoms, pharmacological agents may be initiated and when desired effect is achieved, the medication is tapered off over 2–3 weeks or longer. The goal of therapy is to stop the symptoms and make the infant comfortable but not to the point of sedation. The mother will require counseling, and appropriate referral to various agencies may be necessary. Infants born to addicted mothers are at high risk for child abuse and SIDS.

HSB

References

Burstein Y, Giardina PJV, Rausen AR, et al. Thrombocytosis and increased circulating platelet aggregates in newborn infants of polydrug users. J Pediatr 1979; 94:895.

Chasnoff IJ, Hatcher R, Burns WJ. Polydrug- and methadone-addicted newborns: A continuum of impairment? Pediatrics 1982; 70:210.

Herzlinger RA, Kandall SR, Vaughan HG Jr. Neonatal seizures associated with narcotic withdrawal. J Pediatr 1977; 91:638.

Oro AS, Dixon SD. Perinatal cocaine and methamphetamine exposure: Maternal and neonatal correlates. J Pediatr 1987; 111:571.

Roberts RJ. Drug therapy in infants: Pharmacologic principles and clinical experience. Philadelphia: WB Saunders, 1984:337.

Rosen TS, Pippenger CE. Pharmacologic observations on the neonatal withdrawal syndrome. J Pediatr 1976; 88:1044.

Zelson C, Lee SJ, Casalino M. Neonatal narcotic addiction: Comparative effects of maternal intake of heroin and methadone. N Engl J Med 1973; 289:1216.

MATERNAL ABUSE OF HEROIN OR METHADONE

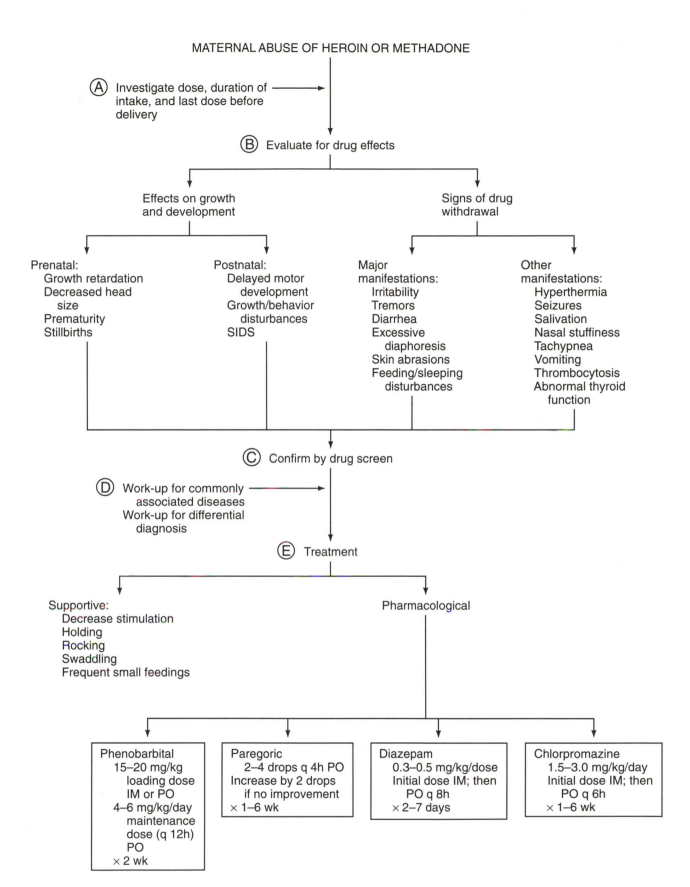

Ⓐ Investigate dose, duration of intake, and last dose before delivery

Ⓑ Evaluate for drug effects

Effects on growth and development

Signs of drug withdrawal

Prenatal:
　Growth retardation
　Decreased head
　　size
　Prematurity
　Stillbirths

Postnatal:
　Delayed motor
　　development
　Growth/behavior
　　disturbances
　SIDS

Major
manifestations:
　Irritability
　Tremors
　Diarrhea
　Excessive
　　diaphoresis
　Skin abrasions
　Feeding/sleeping
　　disturbances

Other
manifestations:
　Hyperthermia
　Seizures
　Salivation
　Nasal stuffiness
　Tachypnea
　Vomiting
　Thrombocytosis
　Abnormal thyroid
　　function

Ⓒ Confirm by drug screen

Ⓓ Work-up for commonly associated diseases
Work-up for differential diagnosis

Ⓔ Treatment

Supportive:
　Decrease stimulation
　Holding
　Rocking
　Swaddling
　Frequent small feedings

Pharmacological

| Phenobarbital
15–20 mg/kg
loading dose
IM or PO
4–6 mg/kg/day
maintenance
dose (q 12h)
PO
× 2 wk | Paregoric
2–4 drops q 4h PO
Increase by 2 drops
if no improvement
× 1–6 wk | Diazepam
0.3–0.5 mg/kg/dose
Initial dose IM; then
PO q 8h
× 2–7 days | Chlorpromazine
1.5–3.0 mg/kg/day
Initial dose IM; then
PO q 6h
× 1–6 wk |

MATERNAL ALCOHOL CONSUMPTION

A. Alcohol crosses the placenta rapidly reaching the fetus. Up to 98% of alcohol is metabolized by alcohol dehydrogenase to acetaldehyde, which is converted to coenzyme A; lactate production and hyperuricemia are accompanying metabolic changes. Both high levels of acetaldehyde and lactate in the fetal compartment may explain some of the chronic fetal effects. The fetal and neonatal effects of alcohol may result from acute intoxication and/or from chronic exposure. Neonates of mothers intoxicated from drinking alcohol or from intravenous alcohol for suppression of labor eliminate alcohol more slowly than their mothers. The neonate with acute intoxication or withdrawal from alcohol has breath odor of alcohol several hours from birth, a hyperactivity phase with tremors and/or seizures for 72 hours followed by lethargy for 48 hours, and then a return to normal activity and responsiveness. The chronic effects of alcohol from in utero exposure depend on the amount of maternal intake per day, the pattern of alcohol consumption, the time of gestation at which alcohol was consumed, and individual susceptibility. The risk of congenital anomalies is 10% if mothers had 1–2 ounces of absolute alcohol per day and 40% if consumption was >5 ounces per day. The features of chronic alcohol effects are often subtle, and their combination comprises the fetal alcohol syndrome. The effects of alcohol may be compounded by effects of other drugs such as caffeine and marijuana as well as nutritional deficiencies sustained during pregnancy.

B. Chronic intrauterine exposure to alcohol results in intrauterine growth retardation that continues postnatally. Infants with fetal alcohol syndrome often fail to thrive.

C. Craniofacial anomalies are common. Babies have small head, short palpebral fissures, small nose, and hypoplastic philtrum. Occasionally hydrocephalus is a feature as well as cleft lip with or without a cleft palate.

D. Babies with fetal alcohol syndrome are irritable and have fine motor disturbances. Apnea, seizures, and opisthotonus are observed. Irritability may persist for several months. Low IQ and hyperactivity are reported in children.

E. Skeletal abnormalities vary from the common small distal phalanges to a more severe and less frequent rib and neck malformation.

F. Cardiac defects (coarctation of the aorta, tetralogy of Fallot, or ventricular septal defect), hypoplasia of the external genitalia, skin hemangiomas, and CNS malformations such as meningomyelocele, heterotopias, or faulty migration of neurons have been reported with fetal alcohol syndrome.

HSB

References

Jones KL. Smith's recognizable patterns of human malformation. 4th ed. Philadelphia: WB Saunders, 1988:491.
Rosen TS. Infants of addicted mothers. In: Fanaroff AA, Martin RJ, eds. Neonatal-perinatal medicine: Diseases of the fetus and infant. 5th ed. St Louis: Mosby–Year Book, 1992:574.

MATERNAL ALCOHOL CONSUMPTION

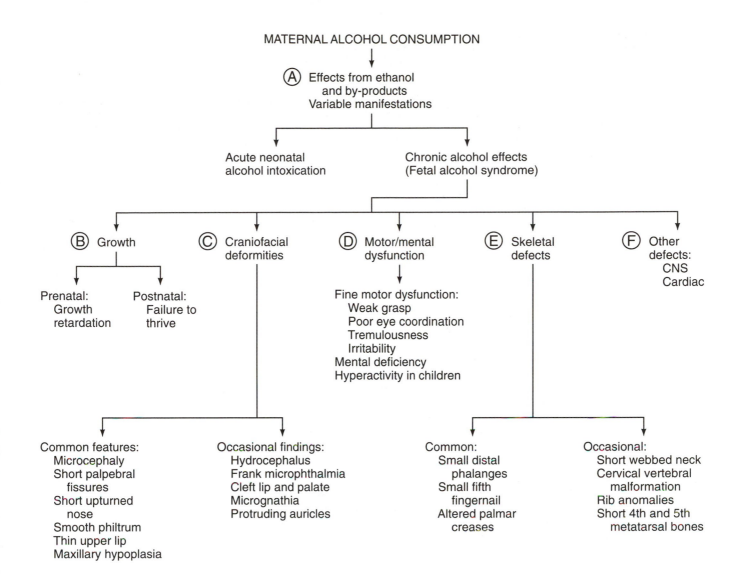

(A) Effects from ethanol
and by-products
Variable manifestations

Acute neonatal
alcohol intoxication

Chronic alcohol effects
(Fetal alcohol syndrome)

(B) Growth

(C) Craniofacial
deformities

(D) Motor/mental
dysfunction

(E) Skeletal
defects

(F) Other
defects:
CNS
Cardiac

Prenatal:
Growth
retardation

Postnatal:
Failure to
thrive

Fine motor dysfunction:
Weak grasp
Poor eye coordination
Tremulousness
Irritability
Mental deficiency
Hyperactivity in children

Common features:
Microcephaly
Short palpebral
fissures
Short upturned
nose
Smooth philtrum
Thin upper lip
Maxillary hypoplasia

Occasional findings:
Hydrocephalus
Frank microphthalmia
Cleft lip and palate
Micrognathia
Protruding auricles

Common:
Small distal
phalanges
Small fifth
fingernail
Altered palmar
creases

Occasional:
Short webbed neck
Cervical vertebral
malformation
Rib anomalies
Short 4th and 5th
metatarsal bones

MATERNAL AMPHETAMINE USE

A. Amphetamine is frequently used by young adults as diet inducer or stimulant. It is a sympathomimetic and a potent central nervous system stimulant. It may be smoked in the form of methamphetamine or "ice." Stimulation occurs or lasts for a period of 10 to 24 hours. There are few reports in the literature regarding the effect of amphetamine in the fetus and the newborn. Often amphetamine or methamphetamine is used with other drugs such as heroin or methadone and/or with alcohol. Thus the effects reported on the fetus and the newborn from amphetamine use may be compounded or influenced by use of other drugs and alcohol.

B. Amphetamine, like cocaine, can cause vasoconstriction; this effect may be selective, i.e., to the uterine vessels. Vasoconstriction leads to placental insufficiency and decreased perfusion to the fetus. Hypoxia-ischemia could result in spontaneous abortion, congenital malformation, intrauterine growth retardation (IUGR), and decrease in head growth. If amphetamine is discontinued after early gestation, its effects on the fetus may still be manifested as prematurity, increase in perinatal mortality (increase in stillbirths and neonatal deaths), and in low birthweight without necessarily associated decrease in head size.

C. Amphetamine may still be recovered for a few days postnatally in the urine of neonates born to mothers abusing the drug. Thus the reported symptoms of tremors, irritability, abnormal sleep patterns, and poor feeding in these infants may actually be related to direct effect of the drug on the newborn.

D. The neonate may also manifest signs of classic drug withdrawal. Signs and manifestations such as diaphoresis, miotic pupils, hypoglycemia, vomiting, restlessness, tremulousness, eye deviation, staring, drowsiness, prolonged sleep, and seizures have been reported.

E. The effect of amphetamine on the fetus and the neonate may also extend to long-term sequelae. Poor weight gain, delayed motor development, and abnormal behavior have been reported in babies born to mothers abusing amphetamine. However, environmental effects must be considered. Long-term sequelae are reportedly more common in babies who lived with their drug-abusing mothers compared with those discharged to foster homes or families other than the mother.

HSB

References

Larsson G. The amphetamine addicted mother and child. Acta Paediatr Scand Suppl 1980; 278:7.

Naeye RL. Maternal use of dextroamphetamine and growth of the fetus. Pharmacology 1983; 26:117.

Oro AS, Dixon SD. Perinatal cocaine and methamphetamine exposure: Maternal and neonatal correlates. J Pediatr 1987; 111:571.

Ramer CM. The case history of an infant born to an amphetamine-addicted mother. Clin Pediatr 1974; 13:596.

MATERNAL AMPHETAMINE USE

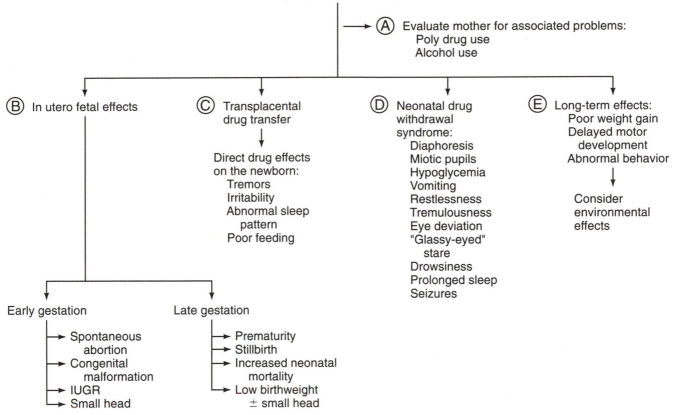

→ Ⓐ Evaluate mother for associated problems:
      Poly drug use
      Alcohol use

Ⓑ In utero fetal effects

Ⓒ Transplacental drug transfer

Direct drug effects on the newborn:
  Tremors
  Irritability
  Abnormal sleep
    pattern
  Poor feeding

Ⓓ Neonatal drug withdrawal syndrome:
  Diaphoresis
  Miotic pupils
  Hypoglycemia
  Vomiting
  Restlessness
  Tremulousness
  Eye deviation
  "Glassy-eyed"
    stare
  Drowsiness
  Prolonged sleep
  Seizures

Ⓔ Long-term effects:
  Poor weight gain
  Delayed motor
    development
  Abnormal behavior

Consider environmental effects

Early gestation
→ Spontaneous abortion
→ Congenital malformation
→ IUGR
→ Small head

Late gestation
→ Prematurity
→ Stillbirth
→ Increased neonatal mortality
→ Low birthweight ± small head

BLOOD CHEMISTRY ABNORMALITIES

Transient Neonatal Hypoglycemia:
    Clinical and Biochemical Screening
Transient Neonatal Hypoglycemia: Therapy
Acidosis
Alkalosis
Hyponatremia
Hypernatremia
Potassium Abnormalities

Hyperkalemia: Therapy
Hypocalcemia
Hypercalcemia
Hypomagnesemia
Hypermagnesemia
Hyperammonemia
Hyperammonemia: Therapy

TRANSIENT NEONATAL HYPOGLYCEMIA: CLINICAL AND BIOCHEMICAL SCREENING

A. Neonatal risk factors (clinical disorders) may produce transient hypoglycemia by one or more of the following mechanisms: (1) hepatic glycogen stores are suboptimal (premature, small for gestational age, and postdates infants; low birthweight twins); (2) hepatic glycogen is rapidly depleted (asphyxia, hypothermia); (3) gluconeogenesis is impaired (severe asymmetrical intrauterine undergrowth); and (4) excessive insulin is produced (infant of diabetic mother, maternal therapy, Rh disease). Hypoglycemia is thus secondary to a host of underlying disorders that cause low levels of glucose with sufficient frequency to warrant assiduous biochemical screening when these clinical disorders are identified.

B. Color (glucose oxidase reagent) strips are used pervasively for screening infants at risk. The inadequacies of these strips have been cited in literature repeatedly. Their use should at least be minimized, and at best eliminated. The strips are significantly influenced by hematocrit (Hct); errors of $\pm5-15$ mg/dl are common especially at glucose levels <50 mg/dl; and they are exquisitely sensitive to imprecise performance. Apparently meter readings of color changes does little to improve strip accuracy.

C. Traditional practice relies on specific glucose values for the delineation of "hypoglycemia," which vary with gestational age (or birthweight) and postnatal age. This numerical approach is based on data published in the 1960s and it may very well be currently inapplicable. There is little agreement on an absolute glucose level at which the risk of abnormal neurological outcome increases. Nor is there evidence to support the contention that asymptomatic "hypo-glycemia" is benign. With such a paucity of information, it has been suggested that specific glucose levels, purporting to define hypoglycemia, may no longer serve as the absolute therapeutic guide. Thus it may be preferable to maintain plasma glucose concentration at generous normal levels that are known to be unassociated with later CNS dysfunction and are themselves not risky. Glucose levels in the algorithm that indicate a need for therapy are somewhat higher than the traditional values used for infants at risk, because these values are not known to be associated with abnormal sequelae.

SBK

References

Conrad PD, Sparks JW, Osberg I, et al. Clinical application of a new glucose analyzer in the neonatal intensive care unit: Comparison with other methods. J Pediatr 1989; 114:281–7.

Cornblath M, Schwartz R, Aynsley-Green A, Lloyd JK: Hypoglycemia in infancy: The need for a rational definition (a Ciba Foundation discussion meeting). Pediatrics 1990; 85:834–837.

Holtrop PC, Madison KA, Kiechle FL, et al. A comparison chromogen test strip (Chemstrip bG) and serum glucose values in newborns. Am J Dis Child 1990; 144:183–185.

Ogata ES. Carbohydrate metabolism in the fetus and neonate and altered neonatal glucoregulation. Pediatr Clin North Am 1986; 33:25–45.

Pildes RS, Pyati SP. Hypoglycemia and hyperglycemia in tiny infants. Clin Perinatol 1986; 13:351–375.

Neonate at Risk for TRANSIENT NEONATAL HYPOGLYCEMIA

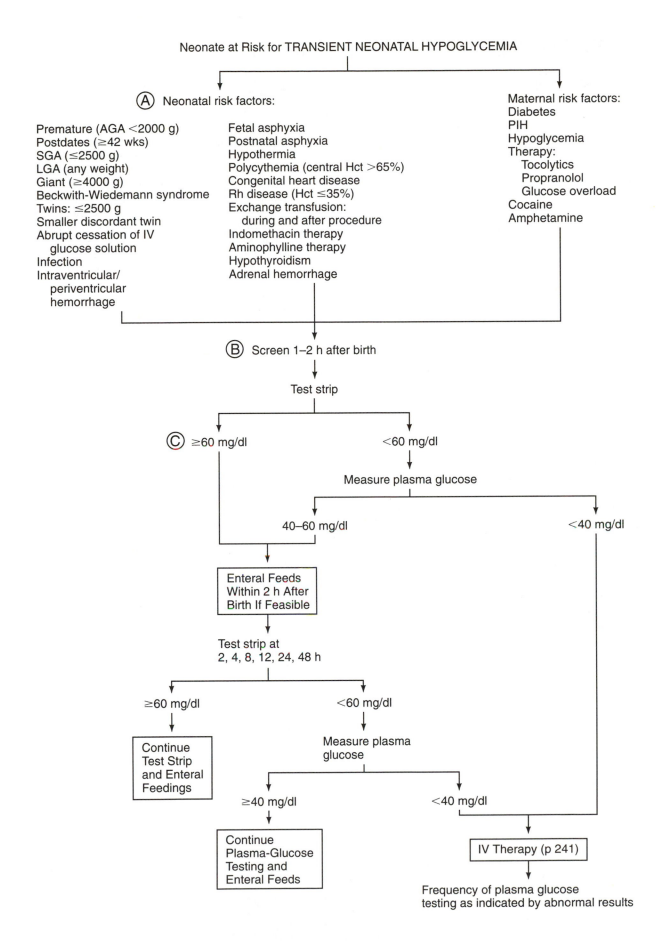

Ⓐ Neonatal risk factors:

Premature (AGA <2000 g)
Postdates (≥42 wks)
SGA (≤2500 g)
LGA (any weight)
Giant (≥4000 g)
Beckwith-Wiedemann syndrome
Twins: ≤2500 g
Smaller discordant twin
Abrupt cessation of IV
   glucose solution
Infection
Intraventricular/
   periventricular
   hemorrhage

Fetal asphyxia
Postnatal asphyxia
Hypothermia
Polycythemia (central Hct >65%)
Congenital heart disease
Rh disease (Hct ≤35%)
Exchange transfusion:
   during and after procedure
Indomethacin therapy
Aminophylline therapy
Hypothyroidism
Adrenal hemorrhage

Maternal risk factors:
Diabetes
PIH
Hypoglycemia
Therapy:
   Tocolytics
   Propranolol
   Glucose overload
Cocaine
Amphetamine

Ⓑ Screen 1–2 h after birth

Test strip

Ⓒ ≥60 mg/dl

<60 mg/dl

Measure plasma glucose

40–60 mg/dl

<40 mg/dl

Enteral Feeds
Within 2 h After
Birth If Feasible

Test strip at
2, 4, 8, 12, 24, 48 h

≥60 mg/dl

<60 mg/dl

Continue
Test Strip
and Enteral
Feedings

Measure plasma
glucose

≥40 mg/dl

<40 mg/dl

Continue
Plasma-Glucose
Testing and
Enteral Feeds

IV Therapy (p 241)

Frequency of plasma glucose
testing as indicated by abnormal results

TRANSIENT NEONATAL HYPOGLYCEMIA: TREATMENT

A. Laboratory determination of plasma glucose is the only acceptable method for identification and management of hypoglycemia. The circumstances and approach to therapy outlined in this decision tree are based solely on laboratory determinations. For these purposes, there is no place for reagent color strips.

B. There is little agreement on the lowest "safe" level of plasma glucose, and there is mounting evidence that traditionally accepted values may be too low. A prudent maintenance range of 60 to 150 mg/dl is suggested. Neural dysfunction occurs at plasma glucose levels of 45 mg/dl as shown by abnormal auditory and somatosensory evoked potentials, whereas abnormal CNS function is not known to occur at levels $\geq$ 60 mg/dl. Hyperglycemia (usually >200 mg/dl) causes osmotic diuresis at a serum osmolality >300 mOsm.

C. Asymptomatic hypoglycemia may not necessarily be benign insofar as CNS function is concerned. Current evidence for dysfunctional outcomes in asymptomatic infants warrants therapy for low glucose levels, even in the absence of abnormal signs. These abnormalities, when they do occur, include apnea and cyanosis; jitteriness, tremors, eye-rolling, seizures, inordinate hypotonicity, lethargy, and reduced responsiveness, as well as pallor and perspiration (the latter beyond 34 conceptional weeks). Because these signs also occur with similar frequency among normoglycemic infants, they can be attributed to hypoglycemia only when restoration of normal glucose levels is followed within minutes by their alleviation.

D. Persistent hypoglycemia is due to insulin overproduction or glucose underproduction. Nesidioblastosis is the most frequent cause of hyperinsulinism during the first year of life. Islet adenoma (insulinoma) is rare. Neither of these lesions is distinguishable clinically nor biochemically, and their only definitive treatment is surgery. Underproduction of glucose is due to endocrinopathies and certain inborn errors of metabolism. The hormone deficiencies include congenital hypopituitarism, glucagon deficiency, isolated congenital glucocorticoid deficiency, adrenal hemorrhage, and adrenogenital syndrome. Hypoglycemia is also a prominent feature of certain inborn metabolic disorders such as type I glycogen storage disease (glucose 6-phosphatase deficiency); galactosemia, fructose intolerance, and errors of amino acid metabolism. Hepatomegaly is a common feature in these disorders.

SBK

References

Commentary: Brain damage by neonatal hypoglycaemia. Lancet 1989; 1:882.

Cornblath M, Schwartz R, Aynsley-Green A, Lloyd JK. Hypoglycemia in infancy: The need for a rational definition (a Ciba Foundation discussion meeting). Pediatrics 1990; 85:834.

Koh THHG, Aynsley-Green A, Tarbit M, Eyre JA. Neural dysfunction during hypoglycaemia. Arch Dis Child 1988; 63:1353.

Koh THHG, Eyre JA, Aynsley-Green A. Neonatal hypoglycaemia: The controversy regarding definition. Arch Dis Child 1988; 63:1386.

Pildes RS. Neonatal hyperglycemia. J Pediatr 1986; 109:905.

Srinivasan G, Pildes RD, Cattamanchi G, et al. Plasma glucose values in normal neonates: A new look. J Pediatr 1986; 109:114.

TRANSIENT HYPOGLYCEMIA: THERAPY

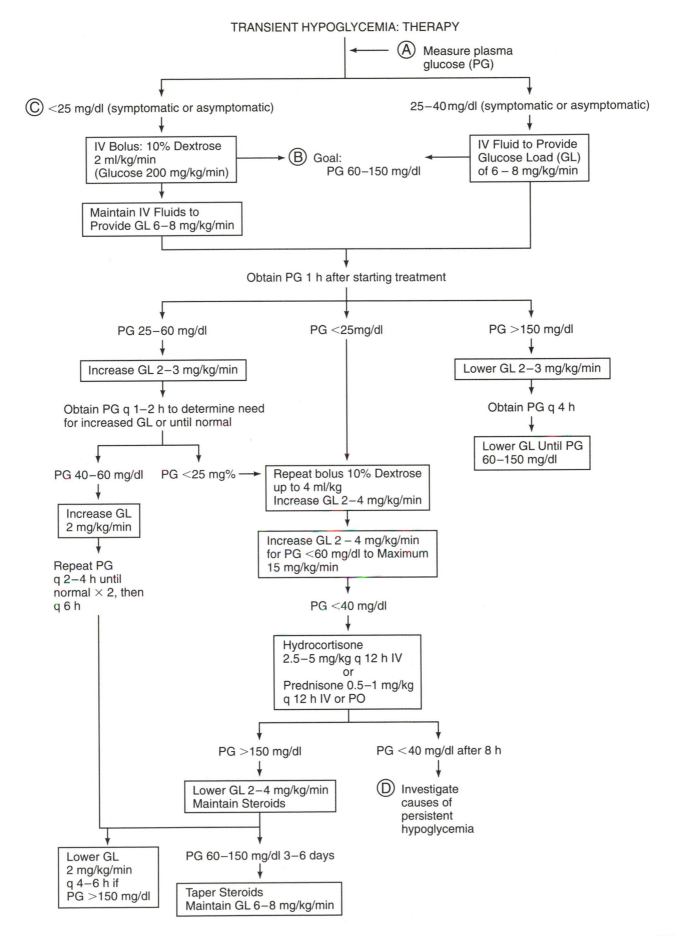

Ⓐ Measure plasma glucose (PG)

Ⓒ <25 mg/dl (symptomatic or asymptomatic)

25–40 mg/dl (symptomatic or asymptomatic)

IV Bolus: 10% Dextrose
2 ml/kg/min
(Glucose 200 mg/kg/min)

Ⓑ Goal:
PG 60–150 mg/dl

IV Fluid to Provide
Glucose Load (GL)
of 6 – 8 mg/kg/min

Maintain IV Fluids to
Provide GL 6–8 mg/kg/min

Obtain PG 1 h after starting treatment

PG 25–60 mg/dl

PG <25mg/dl

PG >150 mg/dl

Increase GL 2–3 mg/kg/min

Lower GL 2–3 mg/kg/min

Obtain PG q 1–2 h to determine need
for increased GL or until normal

Obtain PG q 4 h

Lower GL Until PG
60–150 mg/dl

PG 40–60 mg/dl

PG <25 mg%

Repeat bolus 10% Dextrose
up to 4 ml/kg
Increase GL 2–4 mg/kg/min

Increase GL
2 mg/kg/min

Increase GL 2 – 4 mg/kg/min
for PG <60 mg/dl to Maximum
15 mg/kg/min

Repeat PG
q 2–4 h until
normal × 2, then
q 6 h

PG <40 mg/dl

Hydrocortisone
2.5–5 mg/kg q 12 h IV
or
Prednisone 0.5–1 mg/kg
q 12 h IV or PO

PG >150 mg/dl

PG <40 mg/dl after 8 h

Lower GL 2–4 mg/kg/min
Maintain Steroids

Ⓓ Investigate
causes of
persistent
hypoglycemia

Lower GL
2 mg/kg/min
q 4–6 h if
PG >150 mg/dl

PG 60–150 mg/dl 3–6 days

Taper Steroids
Maintain GL 6–8 mg/kg/min

241

ACIDOSIS

A. Normal blood pH is between 7.35–7.45. At a given moment pH is determined by the concentration of hydrogen ions (H^+ in the body fluids, the net effect of various processes (production, neutralization, and elimination of acids). A disturbance in acid-base equilibrium is often detected because of a blood pH outside the normal range. A decrease in pH is termed acidosis. In metabolic acidosis, the decrease in pH is secondary to nonrespiratory mechanisms, i.e., loss of acid or gain of base or buffer. However, the decrease in pH is in part influenced by compensatory responses, the secondary physiological process occurring in response to the disturbance in acid-base equilibrium. In case of metabolic acidosis, the compensatory mechanism is the respiratory response of increasing alveolar ventilation so that normal P_{CO_2} indicates no compensation (uncompensated metabolic acidosis) whereas a low P_{CO_2} denotes a compensated metabolic acidosis either partially (pH still low, not normal) or fully (pH becomes normal). In the presence of metabolic acidosis wherein compensatory response is defective, i.e., alveolar hypoventilation exists, then a mixed metabolic and respiratory acidosis occurs and pH remains low.

In respiratory acidosis, pH decreases as a result of alveolar hypoventilation, which triggers compensatory response through the kidneys, i.e., elimination of acids as titrable acids and ammonium and reabsorption of bicarbonate. Thus normal plasma bicarbonate denotes uncompensated respiratory acidosis whereas high plasma levels are found in compensated respiratory acidosis so that pH returns to normal in the fully compensated condition.

B. The etiology of metabolic acidosis can be categorized into those resulting from gain of acid and those resulting from loss of base or buffer. In renal failure or insufficiency excretion of acid is impaired so that acids accumulate in the body fluid. Hypoperfusion or shock also leads to renal insufficiency, which then results in metabolic acidosis. This is often a finding in sepsis, necrotizing enterocolitis (NEC), asphyxia, periventricular-intraventricular hemorrhage (PV-IVH), and patent ductus arteriosus (PDA) associated with significant left-to-right shunt. Inborn errors of metabolism (e.g., organic acidurias), ketosis, lactic acidosis, amino acid infusion, toxins, and late metabolic acidosis are other conditions associated with accumulation of acids in the body fluid with resultant decrease in blood pH.

C. Bicarbonate loss occurs through the kidneys or through the GI tract. Inappropriate renal bicarbonate loss occurs in renal tubular acidosis (RTA) or dysplasia. GI losses of alkaline intestinal fluid can be excessive in diarrheal conditions or in "dumping" as in the short bowel syndrome.

D. Treatment of metabolic acidosis should be directed to treating the cause. Buffer administration may be necessary; $NaHCO_3$ is the drug of choice provided serum or plasma sodium is within normal range. The amount of $NaHCO_3$ to be given is calculated by:

$$NaHCO_3 \text{ (mEq)} = \text{base deficit} \times \text{wt(kg)} \times 0.3$$

The 10% $NaHCO_3$ solution should be diluted 1:1 with sterile water and given slowly IV, over one to several hours. THAM or Tromethamine may be used instead of $NaHCO_3$ in infants with high serum or plasma sodium or high P_{CO_2}.

E. Respiratory acidosis results from hypoventilation that may be due to depression of the respiratory center in the CNS by either diseases or drugs. Severe perinatal asphyxia, CNS infection, CNS hemorrhage, or administration of barbiturates, sedatives, or $MgSO_4$ may result in either inadequate breathing or apnea with resultant respiratory acidosis.

F. Diseases intrinsic to the airway or the lungs are associated with impaired ventilation and CO_2 diffusion, and thus respiratory acidosis. Infants who are already on mechanical ventilation may have abnormally high P_{CO_2} because of inappropriate ventilator settings, e.g., PEEP—too high, PIP—too low, inspiratory time—too short.

G. Chest wall deformities or muscular disorders result in ineffective chest wall excursions so that alveolar ventilation becomes inadequate and respiratory acidosis occurs.

H. The increase in P_{CO_2} because of hypoventilation is corrected by mechanical ventilation with the appropriate ventilator settings to provide adequate tidal volumes. Treatment of the underlying condition or etiology should be part of the management of respiratory acidosis.

HSB

References

Dell RB. Normal acid-base regulation. In: Winters RW, ed. The body fluids in pediatrics. Boston: Little, Brown, 1973:23.

Korones SB. High-risk newborn infants: The basis for intensive nursing care. 4th ed. St Louis: Mosby–Year Book, 1986:177.

Stork JE, Stork EK: Acid-base physiology and disorders in the neonate. In: Fanaroff AA, Martin RJ, eds. Neonatal-perinatal medicine: Diseases of the fetus and infant. 5th ed. St Louis: Mosby–Year Book, 1992:536.

Winters RW, ed. The body fluids in pediatrics. Boston: Little, Brown, 1973:46.

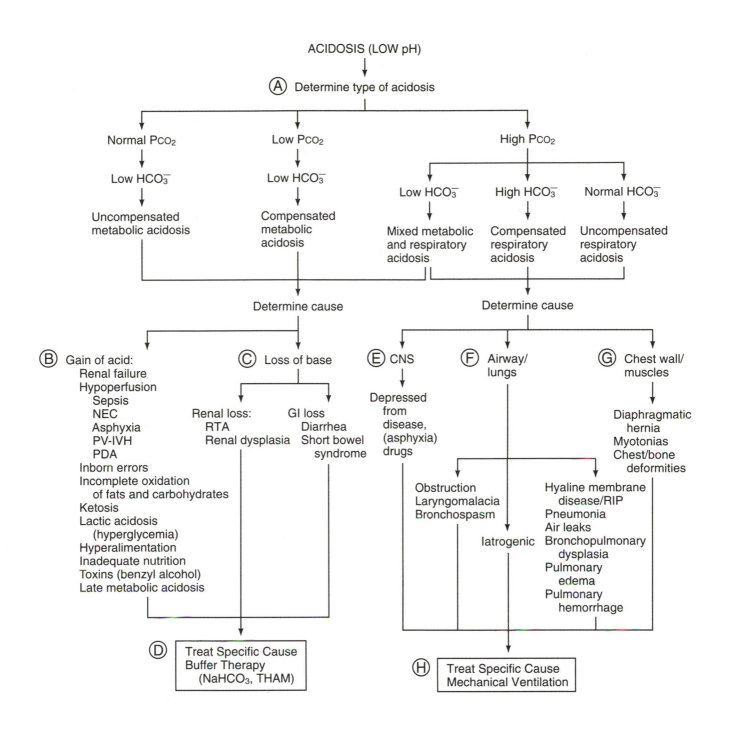

ACIDOSIS (LOW pH)

(A) Determine type of acidosis

Normal P_{CO_2} → Low HCO_3^- → Uncompensated metabolic acidosis

Low P_{CO_2} → Low HCO_3^- → Compensated metabolic acidosis

High P_{CO_2}
- Low HCO_3^- → Mixed metabolic and respiratory acidosis
- High HCO_3^- → Compensated respiratory acidosis
- Normal HCO_3^- → Uncompensated respiratory acidosis

Determine cause

(B) Gain of acid:
Renal failure
Hypoperfusion
  Sepsis
  NEC
  Asphyxia
  PV-IVH
  PDA
Inborn errors
Incomplete oxidation
  of fats and carbohydrates
Ketosis
Lactic acidosis
  (hyperglycemia)
Hyperalimentation
Inadequate nutrition
Toxins (benzyl alcohol)
Late metabolic acidosis

(C) Loss of base
Renal loss:
  RTA
  Renal dysplasia
GI loss
  Diarrhea
  Short bowel
  syndrome

(D) Treat Specific Cause
Buffer Therapy
(NaHCO$_3$, THAM)

Determine cause

(E) CNS → Depressed from disease, (asphyxia) drugs

(F) Airway/lungs
Obstruction
Laryngomalacia
Bronchospasm

Iatrogenic

Hyaline membrane disease/RIP
Pneumonia
Air leaks
Bronchopulmonary dysplasia
Pulmonary edema
Pulmonary hemorrhage

(G) Chest wall/muscles → Diaphragmatic hernia
Myotonias
Chest/bone deformities

(H) Treat Specific Cause
Mechanical Ventilation

ALKALOSIS

A. In alkalosis, blood pH increases because of one of two mechanisms: (1) a gain in HCO_3 or loss of acid (metabolic component) and (2) an increase in alveolar ventilation or decrease in Pa_{CO_2} (respiratory component). As in acidosis, both metabolic and respiratory components come into play in maintenance of acid-base equilibrium so that compensatory changes occur. Theoretically in metabolic alkalosis, an increase in blood HCO_3 should trigger a compensatory respiratory response, i.e., an increase in Pa_{CO_2} and CO_2 would be available for hydration reaction to form H_2CO_3. However, clinical experiences indicate that respiratory compensation in metabolic alkalosis is so irregular and unpredictable that this physiological phenomenon remains unexplained.

   When respiratory alkalosis occurs, immediate response to blowing off CO_2 is an abrupt rise in blood base excess followed by a slower fall towards normal when Pa_{CO_2} continues to remain low. The early rise in base excess is the effect of acute bicarbonate redistribution (from the interstitial fluid into blood). This early increase in bicarbonate is fortuitously offset by a slower increase in lactic acid that may be due to a regional circulatory adjustment, an intracellular pH change, or a combination of both. Compensatory response to respiratory alkalosis is through renal excretion of bicarbonate with sodium and potassium; the plasma concentrations of these ions determine the efficacy of the renal mechanism to excrete bicarbonate. With an effective compensatory metabolic response, pH therefore can normalize in sustained respiratory alkalosis. Both metabolic and respiratory alkalosis may exist at the same time (mixed disturbance). The net effect is a very high pH. Both compensated metabolic alkalosis and compensated respiratory alkalosis have to be differentiated from mixed disturbances. In the mixed disturbances, the directional change in pH may be normal, low, or high depending on the intensities of the disturbances.

B. Metabolic alkalosis may result from exogenous administration of $NaHCO_3$ or oxidation of salts of organic acids such as citrate, lactate, and acetate. These causes of metabolic alkalosis are often iatrogenic.

C. Acid is lost in gastrointestinal conditions such as pyloric stenosis because of vomiting of gastric contents with high hydrochloric acid concentration. Diuretic therapy results in potassium depletion that augments renal excretion of H^+ as well as causes extrarenal shifts of H^+ into the intracellular space.

D. Treatment is primarily directed to correction or treatment of the cause of metabolic alkalosis. The correction therefore should provide for adequate ions (so-dium, potassium, chloride), the deficiency of which limits the ability of the kidney to excrete HCO_3. The deficiency of sodium and potassium should be suspected in paradoxical aciduria; the kidneys excrete H^+ in exchange of sodium in existing metabolic alkalosis.

E. Alveolar hyperventilation results when drugs such as salicylates stimulate the CNS. Diseases such as meningitis and hypoxic-ischemic encephalopathy may be associated with stimulation of the respiratory center so that respiratory alkalosis becomes a feature, especially if these conditions occur in the absence of pulmonary lung disease.

F. The respiratory center may be stimulated through reflex mechanisms either through the peripheral chemoreceptors (hypoxia) or through the intrathoracic stretch receptors (localized pulmonary disease).

G. In neonatal intensive care management, hyperventilation is sometimes used as in persistent pulmonary hypertension or persistent fetal circulation (PFC). Low P_{CO_2} is expected to result in pulmonary vasodilation and decreased pulmonary resistance. Thus pulmonary blood flow increases with resultant improvement in oxygenation (increased Pa_{O_2}). At times, infants require mechanical ventilation for causes other than pulmonary; inappropriately delivered high tidal volume may result in hyperventilation.

H. Therapy of respiratory alkalosis should also be directed to the treatment of its cause. When infants are using mechanical ventilation, appropriate blood gas monitoring and ventilator setting adjustments need to be done to maintain Pa_{CO_2} in the normal range unless hyperventilation is a therapeutic objective.

HSB

References

Dell RB. Normal acid-base regulation. In: Winters RW, ed. The body fluids in pediatrics. Boston: Little, Brown, 1973:23.

Korones SB. High-risk newborn infants: The basis for intensive nursing care. 4th ed. St Louis: Mosby—Year Book, 1986:177.

Stork JE, Stork EK. Acid-base physiology and disorders in the neonate. In: Fanaroff AA, Martin RJ, eds. Neonatal-perinatal medicine: Diseases of the fetus and infant. 5th ed. St Louis: Mosby—Year Book, 1992:536.

Winters RW, ed. The body fluids in pediatrics. Boston: Little, Brown, 1973:46.

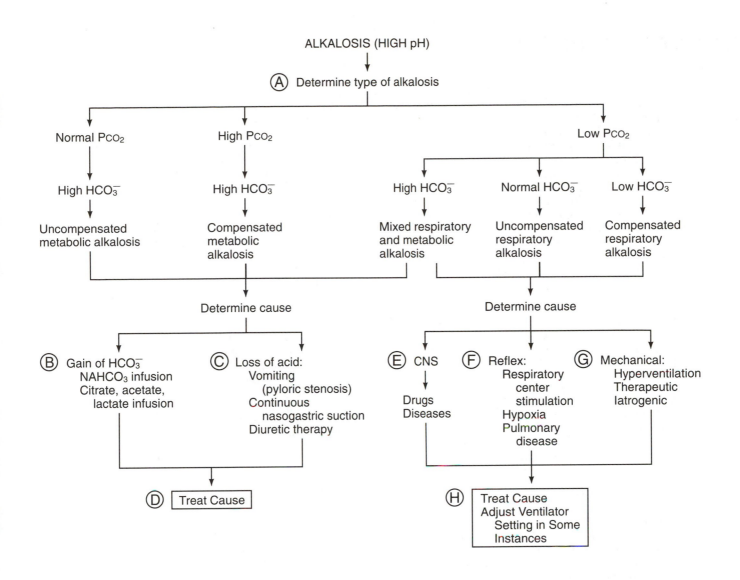

ALKALOSIS (HIGH pH)

(A) Determine type of alkalosis

Normal P_{CO_2}

High HCO_3^-

Uncompensated metabolic alkalosis

High P_{CO_2}

High HCO_3^-

Compensated metabolic alkalosis

Low P_{CO_2}

High HCO_3^-

Mixed respiratory and metabolic alkalosis

Normal HCO_3^-

Uncompensated respiratory alkalosis

Low HCO_3^-

Compensated respiratory alkalosis

Determine cause

(B) Gain of HCO_3^-
NAHCO₃ infusion
Citrate, acetate, lactate infusion

(C) Loss of acid:
Vomiting
(pyloric stenosis)
Continuous
nasogastric suction
Diuretic therapy

(D) Treat Cause

Determine cause

(E) CNS

Drugs
Diseases

(F) Reflex:
Respiratory
center
stimulation
Hypoxia
Pulmonary
disease

(G) Mechanical:
Hyperventilation
Therapeutic
Iatrogenic

(H) Treat Cause
Adjust Ventilator
Setting in Some
Instances

HYPONATREMIA

A. *Hyponatremia* is defined arbitrarily as a serum sodium (Na^+) of <130 mEq/L. Symptoms (e.g., seizures) may not be evident until serum Na^+ is <120 mEq/L, which requires urgent correction of the electrolyte imbalance. Assessment of hydration status is important. Diminished skin turgor, dry and scaly skin, dry mucous membranes, and weight loss indicate dehydration or depletion of intravascular volume. Edema and abnormal weight gain indicate overhydration or increase in intravascular or extracellular fluid volume (EFV). Careful calculation of fluid and electrolyte intake as well as urine output and losses from other sites helps to determine whether low serum Na^+ is secondary to inadequate intake, dilutional, or due to excessive losses.

B. Laboratory studies and electrolyte determinations assess renal function as well as the possible effect of other substances (e.g., high glucose, low albumin) on fluid-electrolyte balance.

C. Rapid infusion of isotonic salt-free solution may result in hyponatremia with a normal serum osmolality and hydration and without increased urinary Na^+ losses; treatment is Na^+ supplementation. Hyperlipidemia and hyperproteinemia are rare causes of hyponatremia with normal serum osmolality; treatment consists of correcting the underlying etiology.

D. With high serum osmolality, the infant may show signs of dehydration, especially when output is inappropriately large for intake. The high serum osmolality, even with low serum sodium, is contributed by high concentrations of hyperosmolar solutions during mannitol administration or in hypertonic glucose infusion. Hyperglycemia from endogenous causes may also raise serum osmolality, usually resulting in diuresis and salt wasting. Treat hyponatremia by Na^+ supplementation to replace losses and by correction of the underlying disorder responsible for the hyperosmolality.

E. When serum osmolality is low, hydration status helps distinguish certain groups of etiologic factors. Signs of dehydration with increased urine Na^+ losses and increased urine volume suggest losses through the kidneys, as in salt-losing nephropathies, and, more commonly, in the low-birth-weight premature infant with immature renal function. Excessive use of diuretics may lead to hyponatremia and dehydration. Adrenal insufficiency can be associated with severe salt wasting, dehydration, and shock. Treatment consists of managing the underlying disorder. Sodium supplementation should replace urine losses and provide the daily maintenance requirement of 2 to 3 mEq/kg/day. Sodium replacement for correction of hyponatremia is calculated as follows:

$$Na^+ \text{ deficit (mEq/L)} = [\text{normal } Na^+ \text{ (mEq/L)} - \text{actual } Na^+ \text{ (mEq/L)}] \times \text{wt (kg)} \times 0.3$$

Correction is made slowly over at least 24 hours while serum Na^+ levels are monitored every 6 to 8 hours.

F. In dehydrated babies with hyponatremia but with no renal salt and water losses, consider increased Na^+ and water losses through the GI tract, the skin, or repeated paracenteses (e.g., peritoneal) or lumbar punctures. GI losses occur in necrotizing enterocolitis ("third space"), severe diarrhea, and vomiting. Skin losses from increased insensible water loss occur when using radiant warmer or phototherapy. Increased insensible loss is estimated at 20 ml/kg/day, and this volume is added to the daily maintenance volume of electrolyte solution being infused.

G. Edema indicates increased EFV because of fluid retention, as in cardiac, liver, or renal failure (i.e., dilutional hyponatremia). Myocardial failure secondary to overwhelming infection or to intrinsic heart disease leads to impaired perfusion. As a result, renal perfusion becomes impaired, urine output diminishes, and fluid accumulates intravascularly. In liver failure and in nephrotic syndrome, hypoalbuminemia leads to increase in EFV but with ineffective perfusion because of a decrease in oncotic pressure. Hypoperfusion leads to a decrease in urine output. Water is also preferentially retained after administration of indomethacin so that hyponatremia is not uncommon. Prolonged muscle paralysis as an adjunct to ventilator therapy results in immobilization with consequent fluid retention. Treatment consists of treating the underlying cause and restricting fluid or both fluid and Na^+ intake. Albumin may be infused in hypoalbuminemia. Inotropic agents may be beneficial in myocardial dysfunction.

H. The syndrome of inappropriate antidiuretic hormone secretion (SIADH) is common in ill premature or term neonates. Physical examination in the early stages may reveal normal hydration and no weight loss. In more pronounced cases, excessive weight gain and edema become evident. Causes of SIADH include postoperative states, pulmonary disorders (e.g., positive pressure ventilation, pneumothorax), CNS disorders (perinatal asphyxia, meningitis, subdural hemorrhage, intraventricular hemorrhage), and drugs (opiates, diuretics, barbiturates, carbamazepine). Treatment is primarily fluid restriction and treatment of the underlying disorder. Sodium replacement, in addition to maintenance requirement, may be needed if serum Na^+ levels are dangerously low. Fluid restriction usually constitutes providing intake to merely cover insensible losses (45–65 ml/kg/day). Premature infants require a higher fluid volume (90–120 ml/kg/day) because of their increased insensible loss secondary to a wider surface area. Furosemide may be an added therapy in SIADH.

HSB

246

HYPONATREMIA
(Serum Na$^+$ <130 mEq/L)

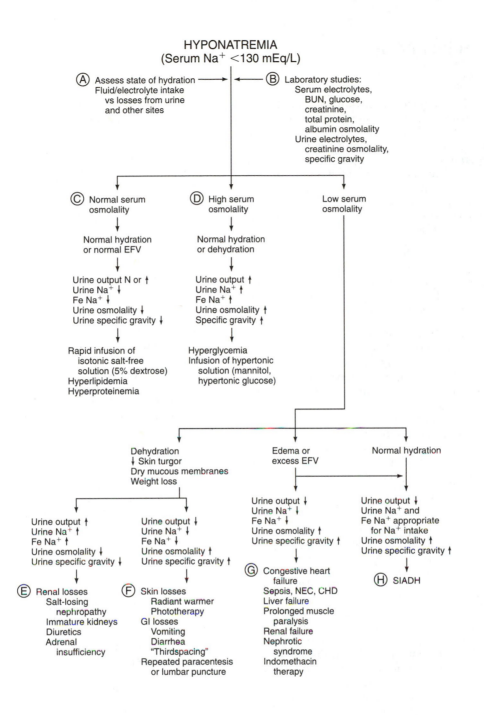

(A) Assess state of hydration
Fluid/electrolyte intake
vs losses from urine
and other sites

(B) Laboratory studies:
Serum electrolytes,
BUN, glucose,
creatinine,
total protein,
albumin osmolality
Urine electrolytes,
creatinine osmolality,
specific gravity

(C) Normal serum
osmolality

Normal hydration
or normal EFV

Urine output N or ↑
Urine Na$^+$ ↓
Fe Na$^+$ ↓
Urine osmolality ↓
Urine specific gravity ↓

Rapid infusion of
isotonic salt-free
solution (5% dextrose)
Hyperlipidemia
Hyperproteinemia

(D) High serum
osmolality

Normal hydration
or dehydration

Urine output ↑
Urine Na$^+$ ↑
Fe Na$^+$ ↑
Urine osmolality ↑
Specific gravity ↑

Hyperglycemia
Infusion of hypertonic
solution (mannitol,
hypertonic glucose)

Low serum
osmolality

Dehydration
↓ Skin turgor
Dry mucous membranes
Weight loss

Urine output ↑
Urine Na$^+$ ↑
Fe Na$^+$ ↑
Urine osmolality ↓
Urine specific gravity ↓

Urine output ↓
Urine Na$^+$ ↓
Fe Na$^+$ ↓
Urine osmolality ↑
Urine specific gravity ↑

(E) Renal losses
Salt-losing
nephropathy
Immature kidneys
Diuretics
Adrenal
insufficiency

(F) Skin losses
Radiant warmer
Phototherapy
GI losses
Vomiting
Diarrhea
"Thirdspacing"
Repeated paracentesis
or lumbar puncture

Edema or
excess EFV

Urine output ↓
Urine Na$^+$ ↓
Fe Na$^+$ ↓
Urine osmolality ↑
Urine specific gravity ↑

(G) Congestive heart
failure
Sepsis, NEC, CHD
Liver failure
Prolonged muscle
paralysis
Renal failure
Nephrotic
syndrome
Indomethacin
therapy

Normal hydration

Urine output ↓
Urine Na$^+$ and
Fe Na$^+$ appropriate
for Na$^+$ intake
Urine osmolality ↑
Urine specific gravity ↑

(H) SIADH

References

Baliga R, Lewy JE. Pathogenesis and treatment of edema. Pediatr Clin North Am 1987; 34:639.

Engle WD. Evaluation of renal function and acute renal failure in the neonate. Pediatr Clin North Am 1986; 33:129.

Feld LG, Kaskel FJ, Schoeneman MJ. The approach to fluid and electrolyte therapy in pediatrics. In: Barness LA, ed. Advances in pediatrics. vol. 35. Chicago: Year Book Medical Publishers, 1988:497.

Oh W. Fluid, electrolytes, and acid-base homeostasis. In: Fanaroff AA, Martin RJ, eds. Neonatal-perinatal medicine: Diseases of the fetus and infant. 5th ed. St Louis: Mosby−Year Book, 1992:527.

Robillard JE, Segar FG, and Jose PA. Regulation of sodium metabolism and extracellular fluid volume during development. Clin Perinatal 1992; 19:15.

HYPERNATREMIA

A. Hypernatremia is defined as a serum concentration of sodium >150 mEq/L. As in other electrolyte imbalances, assessment of hydration based on physical examination is important in determining the etiology of the hypernatremia. Furthermore, calculation of fluid and electrolyte intake and output, both from the kidneys and other sites, is essential in patient evaluation. The finding of edema suggests increased extracellular fluid volume; calculated fluid intake significantly exceeds that of output.

B. Furthermore, physical findings need to be assessed with laboratory determinations that reflect adequacy of renal function. These studies include but are not limited to serum BUN, creatinine, electrolytes, and urine Na^+, and fraction of sodium excretion.

C. In an edematous infant with normal renal function, excessive extracellular fluid volume is likely because of volume overload with fluid containing high sodium concentration. Without impaired renal function, Na^+ excretion is increased with an increase in urine volume. Mineralocorticoid excess is also associated with both sodium and water retention. Elimination of excess exogenous Na^+ should result in a decrease in serum Na^+ concentration. Diuretic may also be used in some instances. Sodium retention from steroid therapy usually resolves with dosage modification.

D. Babies who are dehydrated and hypernatremic have contracted extracellular volume resulting from either excessive renal losses of fluid with minimal Na^+ loss or of both fluid and Na^+. In diabetes insipidus, the deficiency of vasopressin or antidiuretic hormone leads to excessive water loss through the kidneys without the corresponding loss of Na^+. Thus serum concentration of Na^+ is increased with a contracted intravascular volume while urine volume is excessive and urine osmolality and specific gravity are low. Central diabetes insipidus has been reported with periventricular-intraventricular hemorrhage. Before therapy, central diabetes insipidus needs to be differentiated from the nephrogenic diabetes insipidus. Central diabetes insipidus is treated with pitressin administration. In nephrogenic diabetes insipidus, which is usually a hereditary disorder, the kidneys do not respond to vasopressin therapy. Treatment is primarily carried out by having copious volume of fluid available while providing a low solute load. By some unknown mechanism, thiazide diuretic has been shown effective in diabetes insipidus.

E. In a dehydrated infant with hypernatremia with a large urine volume and a high fraction of sodium excretion ($FeNa^+$), renal disorders, the use of diuretics, or adrenal insufficiency need to be considered. Although sodium is lost, the water loss is in excess of sodium so that serum concentration of sodium is increased. Premature infants have immature renal function with high $FeNa^+$ and increased urine output. This may result in dehydration and hypernatremia.

F. Dehydration and hypernatremia in an infant with a low urine volume suggest sodium and fluid losses occurring from sites other than renal. Hypernatremia develops when fluid loss is in excess of sodium losses so that intravascular space becomes contracted or decreased. Extrarenal fluid and electrolyte losses occur in diarrhea, vomiting, or when an infant is under radiant warmer or under phototherapy and additional fluid volume is not provided equivalent to the increase in insensible water loss. Treatment is by replacement of fluid deficit in addition to maintenance therapy. A decrease in the amount of sodium administered may not be indicated since the hypernatremia is not necessarily indicative of sodium excess. Regardless of the etiology of the hypernatremia, monitoring serum and urine electrolyte concentrations as well as the fluid intake and output is part of the total management and should be the basis for modifying amount of fluid and concentration of electrolytes being infused.

HSB

References

Costarino A, Baumgart S. Modern fluid and electrolyte management of the critically ill premature infant. Pediatr Clin North Am 1986; 33:153.

Feld LG, Kaskel FJ, Schoeneman MJ. The approach to fluid and electrolyte therapy in pediatrics. In: Barness LA, ed. Advances in pediatrics. vol 35. Chicago: Mosby—Year Book, 1988:497.

Oh W. Fluid, electrolytes, and acid-base homeostasis. In: Fanaroff AA, Martin RJ, eds. Neonatal-perinatal medicine: Diseases of the fetus and infant. 5th ed. St Louis, Mosby—Year Book, 1992:527.

HYPERNATREMIA

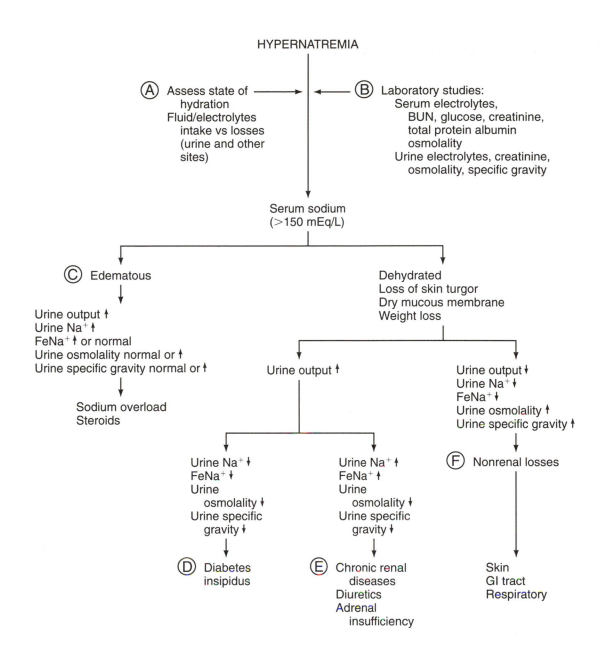

(A) Assess state of
    hydration
    Fluid/electrolytes
    intake vs losses
    (urine and other
    sites)

(B) Laboratory studies:
    Serum electrolytes,
      BUN, glucose, creatinine,
      total protein albumin
      osmolality
    Urine electrolytes, creatinine,
      osmolality, specific gravity

Serum sodium
($>$150 mEq/L)

(C) Edematous

Urine output ↑
Urine Na$^+$ ↑
FeNa$^+$ ↑ or normal
Urine osmolality normal or ↑
Urine specific gravity normal or ↑

Sodium overload
Steroids

Dehydrated
Loss of skin turgor
Dry mucous membrane
Weight loss

Urine output ↑

Urine output ↓
Urine Na$^+$ ↓
FeNa$^+$ ↓
Urine osmolality ↑
Urine specific gravity ↑

Urine Na$^+$ ↓
FeNa$^+$ ↓
Urine
  osmolality ↓
Urine specific
  gravity ↓

(D) Diabetes
    insipidus

Urine Na$^+$ ↑
FeNa$^+$ ↑
Urine
  osmolality ↓
Urine specific
  gravity ↓

(E) Chronic renal
    diseases
    Diuretics
    Adrenal
    insufficiency

(F) Nonrenal losses

Skin
GI tract
Respiratory

POTASSIUM ABNORMALITIES

A. Assessment of the neonate for hydration status, other physical signs, and fluid and electrolyte intake and output balance are important in determining the etiology of potassium disorders. Signs of dehydration (i.e., decreased skin turgor, sunken fontanelles), abdominal distention with decreased urine output, previous episodes of diuresis, and continuous nasogastric suction are consistent with the possibility of hypokalemia. However, minimal-to-absent urine output in an edematous infant suggests renal insufficiency or failure with associated hyperkalemia. Disorders of potassium balance may be associated with ECG abnormalities.

B. Serum electrolytes indicate severity of hyperkalemia or hypokalemia. BUN, serum creatinine, and urine electrolytes and creatinine indicate adequacy of renal function. Serum and urine osmolalities and urine specific gravity reflect hydration status.

C. *Hypokalemia* is defined as serum K^+ <3.5 mEq/L. A rhythm strip or ECG may show depressed ST segment, prolonged QT interval, and U waves.

D. Hypokalemia may result from inadequate intake. Maintenance potassium ranges from $1-2$ mEq/kg/day. If inadequate intake is established, therapy consists primarily of providing maintenance potassium plus additional supplementation to correct the deficit.

E. When intake is normal, hypokalemia may result from excessive potassium losses through renal or nonrenal mechanisms. Diuretics such as furosemide and thiazides may be associated with hypokalemia as well as hyponatremia. Renal toxic drugs such as carbenicillin, gentamicin, and amphoterocin B may induce renal potassium loss. Hypomagnesemia or hypercalcemia promotes potassium wasting. Potassium losses through nonrenal mechanisms may occur from continuous nasogastric drainage, diarrhea, and vomiting or from deficiency of certain adrenal enzymes. In hypertensive adrenogenital syndromes (i.e., 11 β-hydroxylase deficiency and 17 α-hydroxylase deficiency), serum sodium tends to be high or high-normal with associated hypokalemia. Females with 11 β-hydroxylase deficiency demonstrate virilization, whereas males may not have recognizable penile enlargement. In 17 α-hydroxylase deficiency, females have normal external genitalia, whereas males may show feminization. In both conditions, ACTH and deoxycorticosterone levels are elevated, and the production rate of aldosterone is low.

F. In the presence of normal intake, redistribution of potassium (i.e., increase in intracellular uptake) may occur when pH increases from either hyperventilation or bicarbonate therapy. Insulin also promotes intracellular uptake of potassium. β-2 Agonists (catecholamines, isoproterenol, albuterol, or terbutaline) also enhance intracellular uptake of potassium. These effects should be taken into account during vasopressor therapy or as an effect of prolonged prenatal therapy for premature labor.

G. The treatment of hypokalemia is directed primarily to replacing potassium loss or deficit in addition to providing maintenance requirement. Drugs causing potassium losses may need to be discontinued. Hypokalemia resulting from renal defects, metabolic disorders, or adrenal disorders require therapy specific to the disorder in addition to potassium supplementation.

H. *Hyperkalemia* is defined as serum K^+ >6 mEq/L. ECG changes include peaked T waves, wide QRS, depressed P waves, prolonged PR interval, and ventricular tachycardia that may progress to ventricular fibrillation.

I. Hyperkalemia may occur even in the presence of normal intake and is thus called *pseudohyperkalemia*. It results from redistribution of potassium as in either respiratory or metabolic acidosis, decreased insulin levels, and during digoxin therapy. Serum K^+ level continues to increase even after evidence of recovery from acidosis. In digitalis overdose, acute impairment of sodium potassium ATPase pump leads to hyperkalemia. With hypertonicity of the extracellular fluid (e.g., high glucose load or mannitol infusion), plasma K^+ increases by 0.5 mEq/L when plasma osmolality increases 20 mOsm/kg.

J. Hyperkalemia may also result from decreased renal losses, either from acute renal failure or from renal immaturity in very-low-birth-weight babies. In these tiny babies, the high ratio of sodium to potassium excretion decreases with postnatal age; potassium excretion overall is quite low. Associated findings in salt-losing adrenal insufficiency include impaired aldosterone synthesis and hyperkalemia. Low aldosterone and calcium levels may also result in potassium retention. Diuretics that are K^+ sparing are associated with decreased K^+ losses. β-receptor blockers (propranolol) and α-adrenergic agonists (phenylephrine) abolish the renal and extrarenal effect of epinephrine on potassium so that serum K^+ increases.

K. High serum K^+ levels may occur as a result of K^+ administration. It may be due to administration of drugs containing potassium or may be iatrogenic. Cell destruction as in perinatal asphyxia or severe hemolysis may also result in hyperkalemia.

HSB

References

Danish RK. Abnormalities of sexual differentiation. In: Fanaroff AA, Martin RJ, eds. Neonatal-perinatal medicine: Diseases of the fetus and infant. 5th ed. St Louis: Mosby—Year Book, 1992:1222.

Guignard J-P, John EG. Renal function in the tiny, premature infant. Clin Perinatol 1986; 13:377.

POTASSIUM ABNORMALITIES

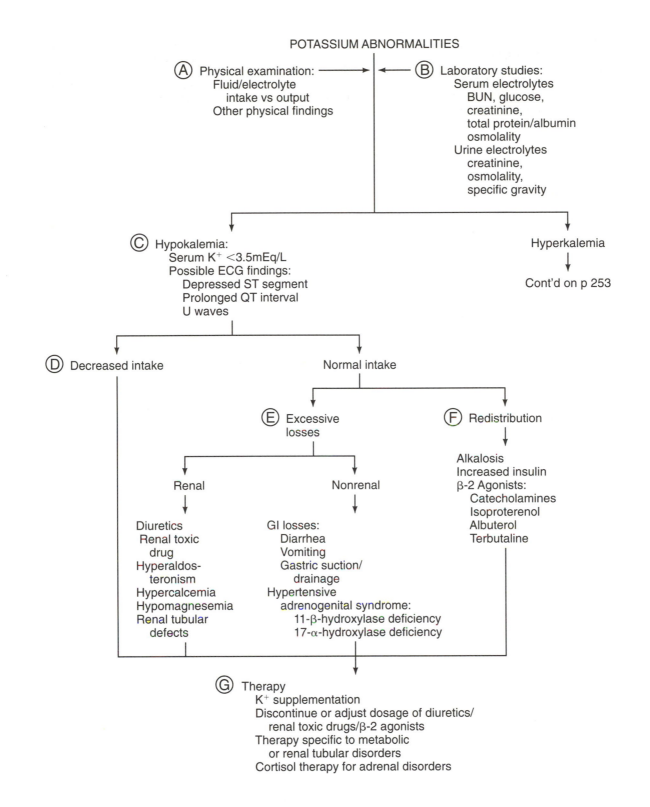

(A) Physical examination:
  Fluid/electrolyte
    intake vs output
  Other physical findings

(B) Laboratory studies:
  Serum electrolytes
    BUN, glucose,
    creatinine,
    total protein/albumin
    osmolality
  Urine electrolytes
    creatinine,
    osmolality,
    specific gravity

(C) Hypokalemia:
  Serum K$^+$ <3.5mEq/L
  Possible ECG findings:
    Depressed ST segment
    Prolonged QT interval
    U waves

Hyperkalemia

Cont'd on p 253

(D) Decreased intake

Normal intake

(E) Excessive
  losses

(F) Redistribution

Alkalosis
Increased insulin
β-2 Agonists:
  Catecholamines
  Isoproterenol
  Albuterol
  Terbutaline

Renal

Nonrenal

Diuretics
  Renal toxic
    drug
  Hyperaldos-
    teronism
  Hypercalcemia
  Hypomagnesemia
  Renal tubular
    defects

GI losses:
  Diarrhea
  Vomiting
  Gastric suction/
    drainage
  Hypertensive
    adrenogenital syndrome:
      11-β-hydroxylase deficiency
      17-α-hydroxylase deficiency

(G) Therapy
  K$^+$ supplementation
  Discontinue or adjust dosage of diuretics/
    renal toxic drugs/β-2 agonists
  Therapy specific to metabolic
    or renal tubular disorders
  Cortisol therapy for adrenal disorders

Jones DP, Chesney RW. Development of tubular function. Clin Perinatol 1992; 19:33.

Linshaw MA. Potassium homeostasis and hypokalemia. Pediatr Clin North Am 1987; 34:649.

Spitzer A, Bernstein J, Boichis H, Edelmann CM Jr. Kidney and urinary tract. In: Fanaroff AA, Martin RJ, eds. Neonatal-perinatal medicine: Diseases of the fetus and infant. 5th ed. St Louis: Mosby–Year Book, 1992:1293.

Stapleton FB, Jones DP, Green RS. Acute renal failure in neonates: Incidence, etiology, and outcome. Pediatr Nephrol 1987; 1:314.

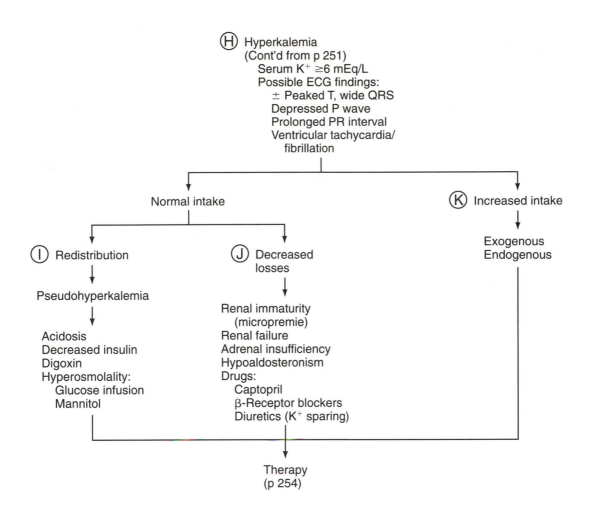

H Hyperkalemia
(Cont'd from p 251)
    Serum K$^+$ ≥6 mEq/L
    Possible ECG findings:
        ± Peaked T, wide QRS
        Depressed P wave
        Prolonged PR interval
        Ventricular tachycardia/
            fibrillation

Normal intake

K Increased intake

I Redistribution

J Decreased
    losses

Exogenous
Endogenous

Pseudohyperkalemia

Acidosis
Decreased insulin
Digoxin
Hyperosmolality:
    Glucose infusion
    Mannitol

Renal immaturity
    (micropremie)
Renal failure
Adrenal insufficiency
Hypoaldosteronism
Drugs:
    Captopril
    β-Receptor blockers
    Diuretics (K$^+$ sparing)

Therapy
(p 254)

HYPERKALEMIA: THERAPY

A. Hyperkalemia requires emergency measures, particularly when there are associated EKG changes. In addition to discontinuation of potassium supplementation, sodium bicarbonate is administered intravenously to correct existing metabolic acidosis. The ventilator settings are adjusted to provide adequate tidal volume and improved ventilation. Calcium gluconate infusion is given slowly intravenously. Glucose insulin infusion is prepared by mixing 48 ml of 50% dextrose in water and 8 units of regular insulin (1 unit insulin for 3 g glucose). A dose of 3 ml/kg of this glucose-insulin mixture (1.5 g glucose and 0.5 unit insulin) given IV push usually results in normalization of the ECG complexes. Insulin promotes intracellular uptake of K^+. Kayexalate is a cation exchange resin; Na^+ is exchanged for K^+. At a dose of 1 to 1.5 g/kg, it is mixed with 10% dextrose in water and administered rectally as a retention enema (15−30 min; 1 g of resin removes 1 mEq of K^+). ECG changes should be monitored during therapy.

B. The goal of maintenance therapy is to keep serum potassium levels in the normal range. A normal acid-base balance as well as a normal serum calcium level must be maintained. Kayexalate enema may be repeated q 6−8 hours until the serum potassium level is in the normal range.

C. Determination of the etiology of hyperkalemia is important, especially when specific therapy is to be instituted. Hyperkalemia from drug therapy may be corrected by either discontinuation or by adjusting the dose of the drug that promotes potassium retention. In the presence of renal insufficiency or failure, fluid restriction while maintaining renal perfusion is necessary. Hormonal replacement is effective in cases of adrenal insufficiency. In the very premature infant ($\leqq$800 g birthweight) with immature kidney function, providing adequate fluid volume maintenance and close monitoring of serum electrolytes (q 6 hours) are important if severe renal insufficiency and hyperkalemia are to be prevented. Should hyperkalemia develop, emergency measures are indicated to normalize ECG changes as well as treatment of renal insufficiency or failure.

HSB

References

Danish RK. Abnormalities of sexual differentiation. In: Fanaroff AA, Martin RJ, eds. Neonatal-perinatal medicine: Diseases of the fetus and infant. 5th ed. St Louis: Mosby−Year Book, 1992:1222.

Guignard J-P, John EG. Renal function in the tiny, premature infant. Clin Perinatol 1986; 13:377.

Linshaw MA. Potassium homeostasis and hypokalemia. Pediatr Clin North Am 1987; 34:649.

Spitzer A, Bernstein J, Boichis H, Edelmann CM Jr. Kidney and urinary tract. In: Fanaroff AA, Martin RJ, eds. Neonatal-perinatal medicine: Diseases of the fetus and infant. 5th ed. St Louis: Mosby−Year Book, 1992:1293.

Stapleton FB, Jones DP, Green RS. Acute renal failure in neonates: Incidence, etiology, and outcome. Pediatr Nephrol 1987; 1:314.

HYPERKALEMIA: THERAPY

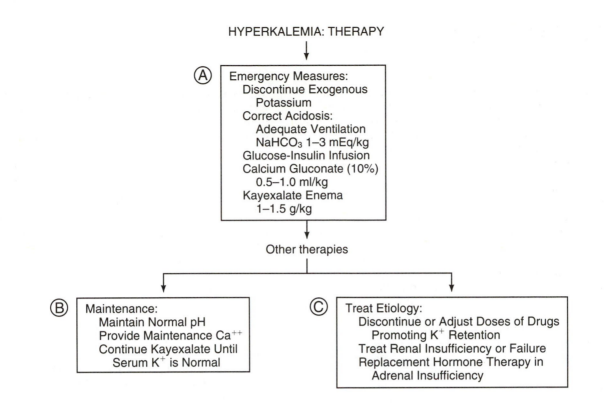

(A) Emergency Measures:
  Discontinue Exogenous
    Potassium
  Correct Acidosis:
    Adequate Ventilation
    NaHCO$_3$ 1–3 mEq/kg
  Glucose-Insulin Infusion
  Calcium Gluconate (10%)
    0.5–1.0 ml/kg
  Kayexalate Enema
    1–1.5 g/kg

Other therapies

(B) Maintenance:
  Maintain Normal pH
  Provide Maintenance Ca^{++}
  Continue Kayexalate Until
    Serum K$^+$ is Normal

(C) Treat Etiology:
  Discontinue or Adjust Doses of Drugs
    Promoting K$^+$ Retention
  Treat Renal Insufficiency or Failure
  Replacement Hormone Therapy in
    Adrenal Insufficiency

HYPOCALCEMIA

A. Most hypocalcemic disorders are asymptomatic. Manifestations of hypocalcemia include apnea, tremors, rarely seizures, and, when associated with severe osteopenia, pathologic fractures. An amount of 100–150 mg/kg of Ca^{++} is transferred transplacentally during the last trimester of pregnancy so that ionized fetal serum calcium level is higher than that of the mother. At delivery, abrupt termination of calcium supply results in regulation of fetal calcium homeostasis through increased calcium flux from fetal bones unless calcium is provided from an exogenous source. Contributing to low neonatal serum Ca^{++} level is the increase in serum phosphorus concentrations from active placental transfer, increase in tissue glycogen breakdown and release of phosphorus into the extracellular space, and decrease in renal phosphorus excretion because of a decrease in renal glomerular filtration rate and increased tubular reabsorption secondary to hypoparathyroidism. In the neonate, the action of calcitonin on the bone site is also augmented; that is, it antagonizes the effect of parathyroid hormone, thereby decreasing the amount of Ca^{++} released from bone. Moreover, calcitonin has calciuric and phosphaturic effects. The neonates also have a low serum concentration of $1\alpha,25$-dihydroxycholecalciferol (the most active vitamin D metabolite). These metabolites are responsible for increasing intestinal absorption of Ca and P, mobilizing Ca and P from bone, and conserving renal Ca and P. Preterm infants also are said to have end organ resistance to $1\alpha,25$-dihydroxycholecalciferol, which may also contribute to low serum Ca^{++} levels.

B. Determination of total serum calcium levels may not be adequate because the active physiologic fraction is the ionized calcium. In the presence of low plasma protein, total blood concentration of calcium is low, but physiologic changes may be absent if the concentration of ionized calcium is normal. The high correlation between serum ionized calcium levels and total serum calcium does not equate to excellent predictability of ionized calcium levels from the total calcium values. Determination of serum magnesium is useful because hypomagnesemia and hypocalcemia may coexist. ECG changes in hypocalcemia include prolongation of QT or QoT intervals. Osteopenia and fractures may be seen on bone x-rays.

C. Certain maternal conditions may predispose to early neonatal hypocalcemia. Severe maternal vitamin D deficiency could result in deficient levels of vitamin D in the neonate and consequently hypocalcemia; this early hypocalcemia may be aggravated by neonatal intake of milk with a high phosphate load. Similarly, maternal deficiency of vitamin D and its active metabolites may occur with chronic intake of anticonvulsants (e.g., phenobarbital and phenylhydantoin), with resultant early neonatal hypocalcemia. The severity of neonatal hypocalcemia increases with the severity of maternal diabetes. With maternal diabetes, the increased urinary magnesium losses lead to deficient maternal serum magnesium levels and decreased transfer to the fetus. Fetal hypomagnesemia and associated secondary hypoparathyroidism may account for the neonatal hypocalcemia. At birth, regardless of whether pregnancy is complicated by diabetes, serum calcitonin levels are also increased, preventing mobilization of calcium from the bones. Maternal hyperparathyroidism or increase in maternal calcium levels leads to increased transfer of calcium to the fetus, fetal hypercalcemia, and suppression of the fetal parathyroids. With fetal and neonatal hypoparathyroidism, neonatal serum calcium levels are decreased. Hypocalcemia has also been reported among babies with withdrawal symptoms from maternal narcotic drug use.

D. The incidence of hypocalcemia is higher among premature and low-birth-weight infants than in term neonates. Approximately 30–90% of premature infants may develop early hypocalcemia. The mechanisms are related to various physiologic changes related to calcium balance at the time of birth. Stress may be significant as in perinatal asphyxia, respiratory distress syndrome (RDS), sepsis, shock, and intraventricular hemorrhage (IVH), so that associated marked decrease of serum calcium may require higher doses of calcium gluconate not only for maintenance therapy but also for correction.

E. Hypocalcemia from iatrogenic causes may occur at any age. Alkali therapy (sodium bicarbonate) and transfusion of blood containing citrate are associated with increased blood pH, promoting binding of calcium and thus a decrease in ionized calcium. Thus symptoms may be evident, even with a normal total serum calcium level. Lipid administration promotes calcium-albumin binding. Phototherapy is believed to stimulate a complex system of extraretinal photoreception associated with neuroendocrine sequelae and hypocalcemia. Diuretics may be calciuric, and their chronic use may be associated with metabolic alkalosis and thus hypocalcemia results from either increased urinary loss and/or alkalosis.

F. Either late or early hypocalcemia could occur with congenital hypoparathyroidism as in parathyroid hypoplasia or agenesis (e.g., DiGeorge syndrome); in these disorders, hypocalcemia is permanent and requires continuous therapy. In vitamin D deficiency, active metabolites of vitamin D may also be deficient and cause hypocalcemia. In hepatic diseases, as in neonatal hepatitis, impaired hepatic 25-hydroxylation of vitamin D could lead not only to hypocalcemia but also to hypophosphatemia and rickets. Infants with renal disease may have a congenital block in the conversion of 25-hydroxycholecalciferol to $1\alpha,25$-dihydroxycholecalciferol. Reduction in this final active vitamin D metabolite results in hypocalcemia and rickets. In certain renal disorders, end organ unresponsiveness to $1\alpha,25$-dihydroxycholecalciferol from

(Continued on page 258)

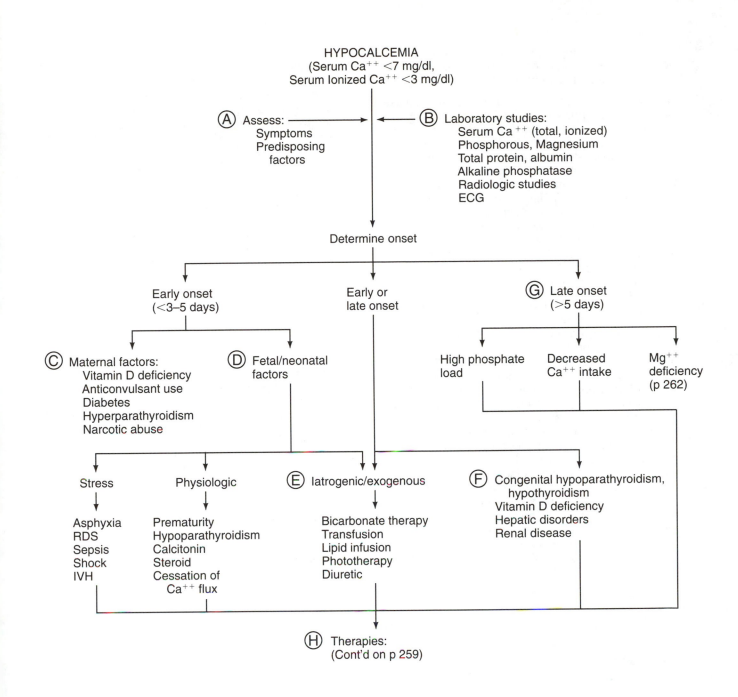

HYPOCALCEMIA
(Serum Ca⁺⁺ <7 mg/dl,
Serum Ionized Ca⁺⁺ <3 mg/dl)

Ⓐ Assess:
Symptoms
Predisposing
factors

Ⓑ Laboratory studies:
Serum Ca⁺⁺ (total, ionized)
Phosphorous, Magnesium
Total protein, albumin
Alkaline phosphatase
Radiologic studies
ECG

Determine onset

Early onset
(<3–5 days)

Early or
late onset

Ⓖ Late onset
(>5 days)

Ⓒ Maternal factors:
Vitamin D deficiency
Anticonvulsant use
Diabetes
Hyperparathyroidism
Narcotic abuse

Ⓓ Fetal/neonatal
factors

High phosphate
load

Decreased
Ca⁺⁺ intake

Mg⁺⁺
deficiency
(p 262)

Stress

Physiologic

Ⓔ Iatrogenic/exogenous

Ⓕ Congenital hypoparathyroidism,
hypothyroidism
Vitamin D deficiency
Hepatic disorders
Renal disease

Asphyxia
RDS
Sepsis
Shock
IVH

Prematurity
Hypoparathyroidism
Calcitonin
Steroid
Cessation of
Ca⁺⁺ flux

Bicarbonate therapy
Transfusion
Lipid infusion
Phototherapy
Diuretic

Ⓗ Therapies:
(Cont'd on p 259)

a receptor or postreceptor defect is associated with rickets, although high concentrations of the final active vitamin D metabolite exist.

G. Late hypocalcemia in general may be a result of intake of a high phosphate load, decreased or deficient calcium intake, or magnesium deficiency. A high phosphate intake probably leads to increased tricalcium phosphate deposition in bone and soft tissues, which enhances the effect of calcitonin and inhibits the calcemic response to parathyroid hormone. Calcium deficiency is a finding in short bowel syndrome and in other small bowel disorders; hypocalcemia is a result of calcium malabsorption. Magnesium depletion also occurs with intestinal disorders associated with malabsorption, and, unless magnesium deficiency is corrected, hypocalcemia persists even with adequate calcium supplementation.

H. Prior to therapy, in addition to symptomatology, possible etiologies and results from workup must be considered. Hypocalcemia of early onset is usually symptom free or mild, whereas seizures may be observed with late hypocalcemia. Interval determination of serum calcium is recommended in the first few days of life in premature babies because early hypocalcemia is common and/or when maternal predisposing factors exist. Persistence of hypocalcemia after the first 3 – 5 days of life necessitates investigation of other causes, including determination of concentrations of vitamin D and its metabolites. Although specific therapy is directed to specific etiology, immediate therapy is indicated in the presence of seizures, ECG changes, and other manifestations. Give calcium gluconate (10%) at 1 – 2 ml/kg intravenously over 5 minutes while strictly monitoring the heart rate. Rapid calcium infusion may result in bradycardia and/or dysrhythmia. Calcium solution is sclerosing; tissue necrosis and calcium deposits result from extravasation. Hepatic necrosis may complicate intraumbilical vein infusion, and intestinal necrosis has been reported from rapid umbilical arterial administration. Incompatibility of calcium solution with $NaHCO_3$ results in precipitation of calcium carbonate. If calcium chloride is used, hyperchloremic acidosis is an associated complication. The goal of maintenance therapy is to maintain or increase calcium levels towards normal values over time. Expectant therapy may help prevent decreases in calcium levels resulting from physiologic mechanism or exaggeration of these physiologic responses in the very stressed neonate. Intravenous calcium is also administered daily to supplement daily requirements in infants who do not receive adequate oral calcium intake with feedings.

HSB

References

Campbell DE, Fleischman AR. Rickets of prematurity: Controversies in causation and prevention. Clin Perinatol 1988; 15:879.

Greer FR, Tsang RC. Calcium, phosphorus, magnesium, and vitamin D requirements for the preterm infant. In: Tsang RC, ed. Vitamin and mineral requirements in preterm infants. New York: Marcel Dekker, 1985:99.

Koo WWK, Tsang RC. Neonatal calcium and phosphorus disorders. In: Lifshitz F, ed. Pediatric endocrinology: A clinical guide. 2nd ed. New York: Marcel Dekker, 1990: 569.

Demarini S,, Tsang RC. Disorders of calcium and magnesium metabolism. In: Fanaroff AA, Martin RJ, eds. Neonatal-perinatal medicine: diseases of the fetus and infant. St Louis: Mosby–Year Book, 1992:1181.

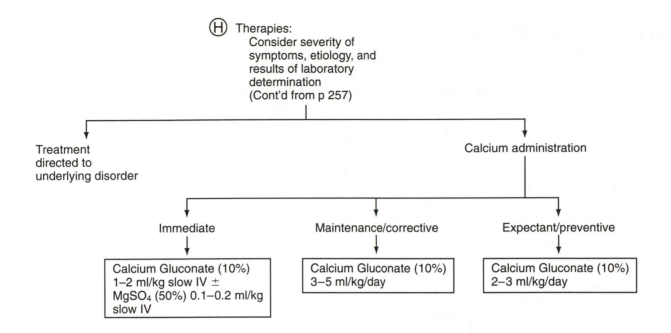

HYPERCALCEMIA

A. In the evaluation of an infant with hypercalcemia, assess predisposing factors as well as physical examination findings. Hypercalcemia is often asymptomatic, but severe clinical manifestations have been reported. Polyuria, which may be associated with poor feeding and polydipsia, results from interference by hypercalcemia with ADH action. Calcium also has a direct vasoconstrictive effect so that hypertension may result when the serum calcium level is high. Encephalopathy from hypertension may be evident from signs such as vomiting, hypotonia, lethargy, and seizures. Chronic hypercalcemia may result in tissue calcifications and nephrocalcinosis. Investigate maternal history for calcium disorders, parathyroid disorders, nephrocalcinosis, unexplained fetal losses, dietary intake, and drug history. Also determine whether there is a family history of hypercalcemia or familial hypocalciuric hypercalcemia. Excessive doses of vitamin A or vitamin D may result in hypercalcemia. It is also important to determine whether intake of phosphate and calcium is adequate, particularly in the preterm infant. Physical findings may help in determining the etiology of hypercalcemia. Abnormalities may include: SGA, craniotabes, fractures, elfin faces, heart murmur, indurated localized skin lesions (subcutaneos fat necroses) or blue discoloration of diaper.

B. Of primary importance in the laboratory studies are neonatal serum calcium, phosphorus, and alkaline phosphatase levels, as well as urinary calcium to urinary creatinine ratio. In premature infants, an elevated serum calcium level may indicate primary hyperparathyroidism or phosphate depletion. A very low ratio of urine calcium to urine creatinine suggests familial hypocalciuric hypercalcemia. Serum alkaline phosphatase level is increased in the presence of bone resorption. Determination of levels of vitamin D, its metabolites, and parathyroid hormone (PTH) may be necessary. Low maternal serum calcium levels and PTH levels may indicate a secondary neonatal hyperparathyroidism. Radiographs of bones, particularly hands and wrists, may demonstrate demineralization, subperiosteal resorption, or submetaphyseal rarefaction.

C. Parathyroid causes of hypercalcemia need to be distinguished from nonparathyroid disorders. The underlying physiologic mechanism in hypercalcemia is the increase in PTH and 1,25-dihydroxycholecalciferol ($1,25(OH)_2D$) synthesis with resultant increase in calcium mobilization from the bone, absorption from the intestines, and decrease in renal excretion. The common causes of hypercalcemia of nonhyperparathyroid origin are iatrogenic or excessive calcium supplementation in an infant who initially was being treated for hypocalcemia and subcutaneous fat necrosis. Subcutaneous fat necrosis may result from trauma or asphyxia. These granulomatous, necrotic lesions may be a factor in unregulated $1,25(OH)_2D$ synthesis. Phosphate depletion in a preterm infant stimulates $1,25(OH)_2D$ production, thereby mobilizing phosphate and calcium from the bone into the extracellular fluid compartment. Idiopathic neonatal or infantile hypercalcemia is part of Williams syndrome, which, in addition to hypercalcemia, includes supravalvular aortic stenosis or other cardiac defects, "elfin" faces, and psychomotor retardation; proposed mechanisms include increased calcium absorption, vitamin D sensitivity, and impaired calcitonin secretion. Defect in intestinal transport of tryptophan (blue diaper syndrome) is associated with hypercalcemia, but the pathogenesis is not known.

D. Secondary hyperparathyroidism due to maternal hypoparathyroidism is usually transient and resolves over several weeks. Primary hyperparathyroidism may be autosomal recessive, as in parathyroid adenomas, or autosomal dominant, as in familial hypocalciuric hypercalcemia. In recessive familial hyperparathyroidism, serum calcium level is elevated up to 25 mg/dl with associated hypophosphatemia, hyperphosphatasia, hypercalciuria, phosphaturia, and occasional aminoaciduria and albuminuria. Long bones on radiographs show diffuse demineralization, subperiosteal resorption, osteitis fibrosa, and spontaneous fractures. Prognosis is poor if untreated, with progressive deterioration and death. Familial hypocalciuric hypercalcemia is a benign autosomal-dominant disorder. It is usually symptom free, and complications are infrequent (chondrocalcinosis, pancreatitis). In this condition, there appears to be an altered PTH response to calcium.

E. Treatment can be divided into emergency therapy and other therapies. In emergencies, hydration and sodium administration promote urinary calcium excretion. Furosemide is given to promote calcium excretion. Side effects of furosemide therapy, however, are potassium and magnesium depletion; monitor their levels and supplement as necessary. The use of inorganic phosphate also lowers calcium levels in hypercalcemia with hypophosphatemia. Phosphate inhibits bone resorption and promotes bone mineral accretion. Oral administration of phosphate is preferred to parenteral. Parenteral phosphate is not advisable when total serum calcium is >12 mg/dl because of the danger of extraskeletal calcification; it is reserved for severe hypophosphatemia. Glucocorticoids inhibit both bone resorption and intestinal calcium absorption. Their use is primarily in hypervitaminosis A and D and subcutaneous fat necrosis. Other therapies include providing low calcium and low vitamin D intake, an adjunctive therapy in hypervitaminosis A or D, subcutaneous fat necrosis, and Williams syndrome. There is limited experience in the use of calcitonin in the neonate. In severe neonatal hyperparathyroidism, parathyroidectomy with autologous reimplantation may be indicated.

HSB

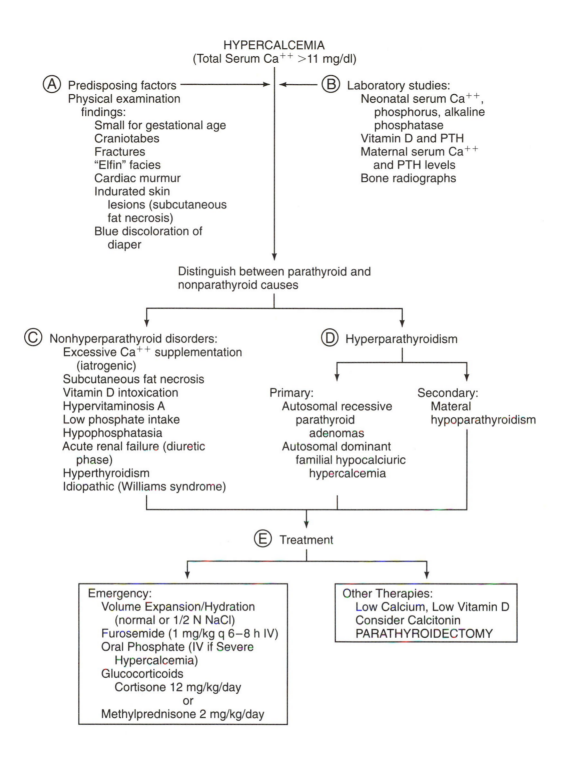

HYPERCALCEMIA
(Total Serum Ca^{++} >11 mg/dl)

Ⓐ Predisposing factors ──────→ ←────── Ⓑ Laboratory studies:
Physical examination   Neonatal serum Ca^{++},
   findings: phosphorus, alkaline
     Small for gestational age   phosphatase
     Craniotabes   Vitamin D and PTH
     Fractures   Maternal serum Ca^{++}
     "Elfin" facies   and PTH levels
     Cardiac murmur   Bone radiographs
     Indurated skin
       lesions (subcutaneous
       fat necrosis)
     Blue discoloration of
       diaper

Distinguish between parathyroid and
nonparathyroid causes

Ⓒ Nonhyperparathyroid disorders: Ⓓ Hyperparathyroidism
   Excessive Ca^{++} supplementation
    (iatrogenic)
   Subcutaneous fat necrosis   Primary: Secondary:
   Vitamin D intoxication   Autosomal recessive   Materal
   Hypervitaminosis A   parathyroid   hypoparathyroidism
   Low phosphate intake   adenomas
   Hypophosphatasia   Autosomal dominant
   Acute renal failure (diuretic   familial hypocalciuric
    phase)   hypercalcemia
   Hyperthyroidism
   Idiopathic (Williams syndrome)

Ⓔ Treatment

Emergency:
   Volume Expansion/Hydration
    (normal or 1/2 N NaCl)
   Furosemide (1 mg/kg q 6–8 h IV)
   Oral Phosphate (IV if Severe
    Hypercalcemia)
   Glucocorticoids
    Cortisone 12 mg/kg/day
      or
    Methylprednisone 2 mg/kg/day

Other Therapies:
   Low Calcium, Low Vitamin D
   Consider Calcitonin
   PARATHYROIDECTOMY

References

Campbell DE, Fleischman AR. Rickets of prematurity: Controversies in causation and prevention. Clin Perinatol 1988; 15:879.

Greer FR, Tsang RC. Calcium, phosphorus, magnesium, and vitamin D requirements for the preterm infant. In: Tsang RC, ed. Vitamin and mineral requirements in preterm infants. New York: Marcel Dekker, 1985:99.

Koo WWK, Tsang RC. Neonatal calcium and phosphorus disorders. In: Lifshitz F, ed. Pediatric endocrinology: A clinical guide. 2nd ed. New York: Marcel Dekker, 1990:569.

Demarini, Tsang RC. Disorders of calcium and magnesium metabolism. In: Fanaroff AA, Martin RJ, eds. Neonatal-perinatal medicine: Diseases of the fetus and infant. St Louis: Mosby–Year Book, 1992:1181.

HYPOMAGNESEMIA

Normal magnesium serum level is in the range of 1.6–2.8 mg/dl. Magnesium is primarily an intracellular rather than an extracellular cation, with 65% of body magnesium in the mineral space of the skeleton, 34% in the intracellular space, and 1% in the extracellular fluid. Thus it is difficult to assess magnesium stores based on serum magnesium concentration. In the circulation, 35% of magnesium is bound to proteins. Magnesium is important in many enzyme systems, in energy production, cell membrane function, and in the regulation of mitochondrial function. The kidneys are primarily responsible for regulation of serum magnesium concentration; 70%–95% of magnesium is reabsorbed by the kidneys. Thus in magnesium-deficient state, urinary magnesium excretion is minimal. On the other hand, hypercalcemia and phosphorus depletion increase urinary magnesium excretion. Parathyroid hormone increases magnesium mobilization from the bones and intestinal magnesium absorption as well as decreases renal magnesium excretion; an end result is increased serum magnesium concentration. The effect of serum magnesium on the parathyroid hormone secretion is similar to that of calcium, i.e., an increase in serum magnesium decreases parathyroid hormone secretion, and a decrease in serum magnesium increases parathyroid hormone secretion. However, when magnesium deficiency is chronic, parathyroid hormone secretion is also decreased. Vitamin D excess results in increased intestinal absorption of calcium, a process competing with magnesium absorption. Increase in calcitonin levels may decrease serum magnesium concentrations.

A. When serum magnesium level falls below 1.6 mg/dl, an investigation as to etiology is indicated. In infants of diabetic mothers and growth-retarded infants, diminished transplacental transfer of magnesium from mother to fetus results in hypomagnesemia. Birth asphyxia has been associated with low magnesium concentrations. Repeated exchange transfusion using citrated blood with low magnesium content may also lead to hypomagnesemia. Increased magnesium loss occurs in intestinal fistulas or short bowel syndrome; these disorders may also be associated with magnesium malabsorption. Hypoparathyroidism may also be associated with hypomagnesemia. Hyperphosphatemia causes both hypocalcemia and hypomagnesemia. Thus high phosphate intake from cow's milk may result in both hypocalcemia and hypomagnesemia.

B. In hypomagnesemia, the signs and symptoms represent hyperexcitability. Infants may manifest muscle twitching, irritability, and seizures that are tonic, clonic, generalized, or focal.

C. Hypomagnesemia should be suspected when an infant has persistent hypocalcemia unresponsive to administration of calcium or vitamin D therapy. Because of this interrelationship between calcium and magnesium metabolism, the laboratory work-up for hypomagnesemia needs to include serum calcium, phosphorus, and alkaline phosphatase determinations. Since both hypomagnesemia and hypocalcemia can occur with hypoparathyroidism, it may be necessary to assess parathyroid hormone function as well as the infant's vitamin D status. It may be difficult to determine whether hypoparathyroidism led to hypocalcemia and hypomagnesemia, or the magnesium deficiency led to secondary hypoparathyroidism with subsequent hypocalcemia. Thus an intravenous magnesium load of 6 mg elemental magnesium per kg over one hour distinguishes between primary and secondary hypoparathyroidism. After magnesium loading, an increase in parathyroid hormone indicates secondary hypoparathyroidism from magnesium deficiency whereas the absence of increase of parathyroid hormone indicates primary hypoparathyroidism unrelated to the magnesium deficiency. Hypomagnesemia may also be associated with electrocardiographic changes; these include t wave inversion and ST segment depression.

D. The treatment of choice for hypomagnesemia is to administer magnesium sulfate at a dose of 0.25 ml/kg body weight of a 50% solution of magnesium sulfate given intramuscularly. This is followed by maintenance dose of 0.25 ml/kg daily of the same magnesium sulfate solution given PO.

HSB

References

Campbell DE, Fleischman AR: Rickets of prematurity: Controversies in causation and prevention. Clin Perinatol 1988; 15:879.

Greer FR, Tsang RC: Calcium, phosphorus, magnesium, and vitamin D requirements for the preterm infant. In: Tsang RC, ed. Vitamin and mineral requirements in preterm infants. New York: Marcel Dekker, 1985:99.

Koo WWK, Tsang RC. Neonatal calcium and phosphorus disorders. In: Lifshitz F, ed. Pediatric endocrinology: A clinical guide. 2nd ed. New York: Marcel Dekker, 1990:569.

Mimouni F, Tsang RC. Disorders of calcium and magnesium metabolism. In: Fanaroff AA, Martin RJ, eds. Neonatal-perinatal medicine: Diseases of the fetus and infant. 4th ed. St Louis: Mosby–Year Book, 1987:1077.

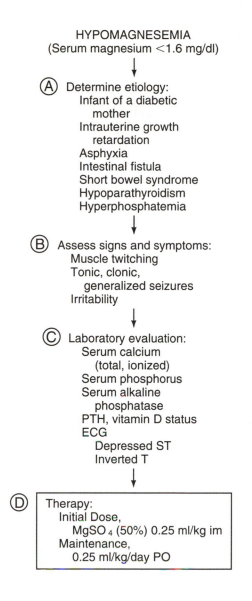

HYPOMAGNESEMIA
(Serum magnesium <1.6 mg/dl)

Ⓐ Determine etiology:
   Infant of a diabetic
      mother
   Intrauterine growth
      retardation
   Asphyxia
   Intestinal fistula
   Short bowel syndrome
   Hypoparathyroidism
   Hyperphosphatemia

Ⓑ Assess signs and symptoms:
   Muscle twitching
   Tonic, clonic,
      generalized seizures
   Irritability

Ⓒ Laboratory evaluation:
   Serum calcium
      (total, ionized)
   Serum phosphorus
   Serum alkaline
      phosphatase
   PTH, vitamin D status
   ECG
      Depressed ST
      Inverted T

Ⓓ | Therapy:
      Initial Dose,
         MgSO₄ (50%) 0.25 ml/kg im
      Maintenance,
         0.25 ml/kg/day PO

HYPERMAGNESEMIA

A. Hypermagnesemia refers to serum magnesium levels over 2.8 mg/dl. In the neonatal period, the most important cause of neonatal hypermagnesemia is maternal magnesium sulfate therapy for either toxemia of pregnancy or for tocolysis or prevention of progression of premature labor. Hypermagnesemia may also result from intake of excessive amount of magnesium that is added to the parenteral nutrition fluid or when given antacid therapy.

B. A neonate with hypermagnesemia is usually depressed and hypotonic and may have signs of hypotension, urinary retention, respiratory depression or apnea, and coma; the manifestations are more severe with higher serum magnesium levels.

C. In addition to monitoring serum magnesium levels in hypermagnesemia, determination of serum calcium (both total and ionized), serum phosphorus, and alkaline phosphatase may be helpful, especially when excessive intake and maternal magnesium therapy have been ruled out. Neonatal parathyroid function is suppressed by hypermagnesemia. Among hypermagnesemic infants, magnesium has a direct effect on facilitating the release of calcium from the bone and thus with resulting high serum calcium concentration. ECG changes include tachycardia or bradycardia, increased atrial ventricular contraction time, and increased ventricular contraction time.

D. Calcium gluconate may be administered to antagonize the effect of magnesium as in cases of neonatal hypermagnesemia resulting from maternal magnesium sulfate therapy. Since magnesium is excreted through the kidneys, magnesium level would decrease over a few days. Thus maintenance of adequate hydration ensures adequate renal flow and magnesium excretion. Diuretics may be administered to increase magnesium urinary excretion. Exchange transfusion may be performed in severe magnesium intoxication.

HSB

References

Campbell DE, Fleischman AR: Rickets of prematurity: Controversies in causation and prevention. Clin Perinatol 1988; 15:879.

Greer FR, Tsang RC: Calcium, phosphorus, magnesium, and vitamin D requirements for the preterm infant. In: Tsang RC, ed. Vitamin and mineral requirements in preterm infants. New York: Marcel Dekker, 1985:99.

Koo WWK, Tsang RC: Neonatal calcium and phosphorus disorders. In: Lifshitz F, ed. Pediatric endocrinology: A clinical guide. 2nd ed. New York: Marcel Dekker, 1990:569.

Mimouni F, Tsang RC: Disorders of calcium and magnesium metabolism. In: Fanaroff AA, Martin RJ, eds. Neonatal-perinatal medicine: Diseases of the fetus and infant. 4th ed. St Louis, Mosby—Year Book, 1987:1077.

HYPERMAGNESEMIA
(Serum Magnesium Level >2.8 mg/dl)

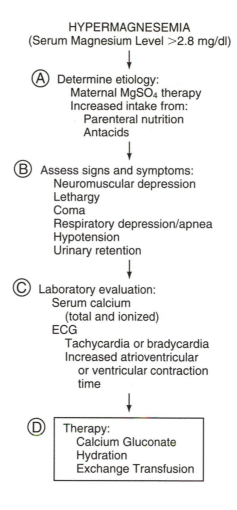

A Determine etiology:
    Maternal MgSO₄ therapy
    Increased intake from:
        Parenteral nutrition
        Antacids

B Assess signs and symptoms:
    Neuromuscular depression
    Lethargy
    Coma
    Respiratory depression/apnea
    Hypotension
    Urinary retention

C Laboratory evaluation:
    Serum calcium
      (total and ionized)
    ECG
      Tachycardia or bradycardia
      Increased atrioventricular
        or ventricular contraction
        time

D Therapy:
    Calcium Gluconate
    Hydration
    Exchange Transfusion

HYPERAMMONEMIA

A. Hyperammonemia is often the result of inborn errors of metabolism. However, the signs and symptoms associated with inborn errors of metabolism are similar to more common neonatal disorders, which should be ruled out. Particular attention must be paid to family history and history of consanguinity; some of these inborn errors of metabolism are autosomal recessive. Metabolic disorders are suspected in babies presenting with an acute onset of respiratory distress or lethargy, vomiting, or seizures after they have had normal feeding intake. Some infants may have dysmorphic physical features. One should also pay attention to unusual odor (sweet odor from acetone, maple syrup odor from branch chain ketoacids, sweaty feet odor from isovaleric acid, rancid butter odor from tyrosinemia, cat urine odor from β-hydroxy-isovalerate, and rotten fish odor from trimethyl-amine).

B. Laboratory evaluations, in addition to either a venous or capillary ammonia determination, include arterial blood gases, electrolytes, glucose, BUN, lactate and pyruvate, CBC, platelet count, and liver function tests. Test urine for glucose-reducing substances, ferric chloride, pH, and ketones. The presence of metabolic acidosis, hypoglycemia, and ketonuria directs attention to certain groups of disorders.

C. High ammonia levels may be detected in cases of prolonged specimen handling, when air in the tube is mixed with the specimen, when ammonia-containing reagent water is used during the tests, and when using ammonium heparin tubes. Thus false-positive results need to be ruled out before initiating an extensive workup for metabolic disorders.

D. Conditions other than inborn errors of metabolism associated with hyperammonemia include transient hyperammonemia of prematurity, perinatal asphyxia, liver failure and the administration of total parenteral nutrition. Suspect transient hyperammonemia of prematurity in a premature infant who has an acute onset of respiratory distress. This is followed by coma in the second day of life, with an elevated ammonia level and a normal anion gap; citrulline may be mildly elevated. Administration of intravenous amino acid solutions may also cause hyperammonemia.

E. Evaluation proceeds next to consideration of rare causes of hyperammonemia. In the presence of metabolic acidosis and hypoglycemia, determine whether ketosis is absent or ketonuria is present. In the absence of ketosis, defect in fatty acid oxidation and some organic acidurias are possible. In the presence of ketonuria, determine whether lactate levels are normal or high. Congenital lactic acidosis and branch chain aminoacidurias are possible when lactate levels are high.

F. In the presence of normal pH and normal glucose, additional workup includes quantitation of plasma and urine amino acids; urine orotic acid also needs to be determined. The citrulline level distinguishes between the rare aminoacidurias and the urea cycle disorders. In the presence of a normal citrulline level, the rare aminoacidurias are to be considered. If the citrulline level is abnormal, low orotic acid in the urine distinguishes carbamyl-phosphate synthetase deficiency from the ornithine transcarbamylase deficiency. Mildly elevated and markedly elevated citrulline levels are seen in argininosuccinic acidemia and citrullinemia, respectively.

HSB

References

Arn PH, Valle DL, Brusilow SW. Inborn errors of metabolism: Not rare, not hopeless. Contemp Pediatr 1988; 5:47.

Burton BK. Inborn errors of metabolism: The clinical diagnosis in early infancy. Pediatrics 1987; 79:359.

Goodman SI. Inherited metabolism disease in the newborn: Approach to diagnosis and treatment. Adv Pediatr 1986; 33:197.

Greene CL, Blitzer MG, Shapira E. Inborn errors of metabolism and Reye syndrome: Differential diagnosis. J Pediatr 1988; 113:156.

Ward JC. Inborn errors of metabolism of acute onset in infancy. Pediatr Rev 1990; 11:205.

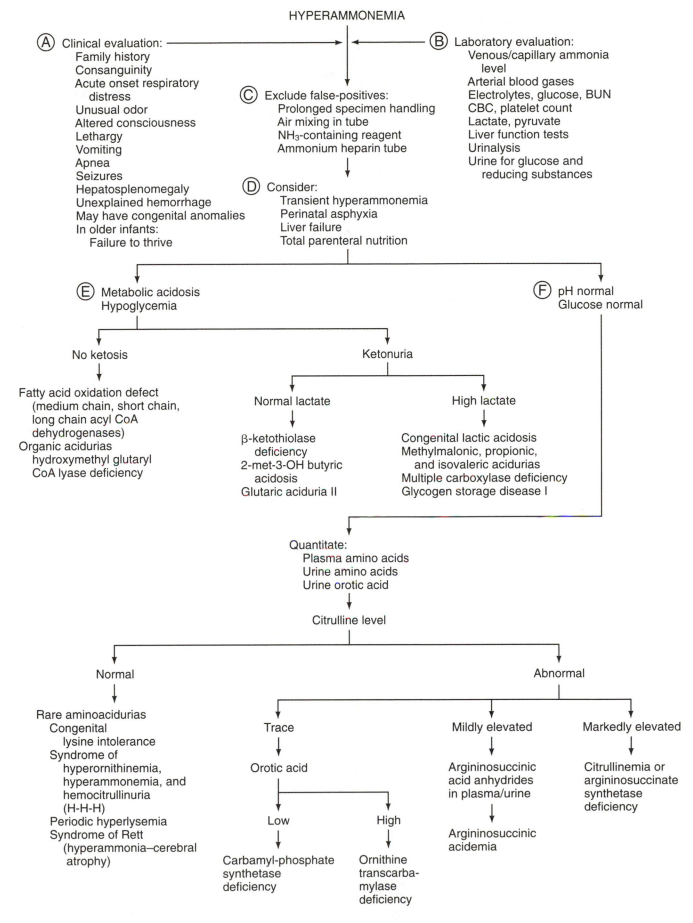

HYPERAMMONEMIA

(A) Clinical evaluation:
- Family history
- Consanguinity
- Acute onset respiratory distress
- Unusual odor
- Altered consciousness
- Lethargy
- Vomiting
- Apnea
- Seizures
- Hepatosplenomegaly
- Unexplained hemorrhage
- May have congenital anomalies
- In older infants:
  - Failure to thrive

(B) Laboratory evaluation:
- Venous/capillary ammonia level
- Arterial blood gases
- Electrolytes, glucose, BUN
- CBC, platelet count
- Lactate, pyruvate
- Liver function tests
- Urinalysis
- Urine for glucose and reducing substances

(C) Exclude false-positives:
- Prolonged specimen handling
- Air mixing in tube
- NH_3-containing reagent
- Ammonium heparin tube

(D) Consider:
- Transient hyperammonemia
- Perinatal asphyxia
- Liver failure
- Total parenteral nutrition

(E) Metabolic acidosis
Hypoglycemia

(F) pH normal
Glucose normal

No ketosis

Fatty acid oxidation defect
(medium chain, short chain, long chain acyl CoA dehydrogenases)
Organic acidurias
hydroxymethyl glutaryl
CoA lyase deficiency

Ketonuria

Normal lactate

β-ketothiolase deficiency
2-met-3-OH butyric acidosis
Glutaric aciduria II

High lactate

Congenital lactic acidosis
Methylmalonic, propionic, and isovaleric acidurias
Multiple carboxylase deficiency
Glycogen storage disease I

Quantitate:
- Plasma amino acids
- Urine amino acids
- Urine orotic acid

Citrulline level

Normal

Rare aminoacidurias
Congenital lysine intolerance
Syndrome of hyperornithinemia, hyperammonemia, and hemocitrullinuria (H-H-H)
Periodic hyperlysemia
Syndrome of Rett (hyperammonia–cerebral atrophy)

Abnormal

Trace

Orotic acid

Low

Carbamyl-phosphate synthetase deficiency

High

Ornithine transcarbamylase deficiency

Mildly elevated

Argininosuccinic acid anhydrides in plasma/urine

Argininosuccinic acidemia

Markedly elevated

Citrullinemia or argininosuccinate synthetase deficiency

HYPERAMMONEMIA: THERAPY

A. Immediate measures for treatment of hyperammonemia include discontinuation of protein intake, intravenous glucose administration, and sodium bicarbonate administration. Intravenous glucose administration corrects hypoglycemia, and sodium bicarbonate administration corrects existing metabolic acidosis.

B. Other supportive measures should be administered. The etiology of catabolism needs to be treated. If increased catabolism is secondary to infection, then appropriate antibiotic therapy should be initiated. If the increased catabolism is secondary to hypoxia, then oxygen therapy and adequate ventilation have to be provided. The infant also needs to be maintained on adequate caloric intake. This can be done by administration of glucose, complex carbohydrates, and intravenous lipid.

C. Excess ammonia can be removed in the neonate primarily by exchange transfusion. However, this is not as effective in older infants. In older infants, the immediate removal of excess ammonia may be done by peritoneal dialysis and followed later by hemodialysis.

D. Alternative pathways for nitrogen excretion may be provided by administration of sodium benzoate, sodium phenylacetate, or arginine. However, experience in this area is limited.

HSB

References

Arn PH, Valle DL, Brusilow SW. Inborn errors of metabolism: Not rare, not hopeless. Contemp Pediatr 1988; 5:47.

Burton BK. Inborn errors of metabolism: The clinical diagnosis in early infancy. Pediatrics 1987; 79:359.

Goodman SI. Inherited metabolism disease in the newborn: Approach to diagnosis and treatment. Adv Pediatr 1986; 33:197.

Greene CL, Blitzer MG, Shapira E: Inborn errors of metabolism and Reye syndrome: Differential diagnosis. J Pediatr 1988; 113:156.

Ward JC. Inborn errors of metabolism of acute onset in infancy. Pediatr Rev 1990; 11:205.

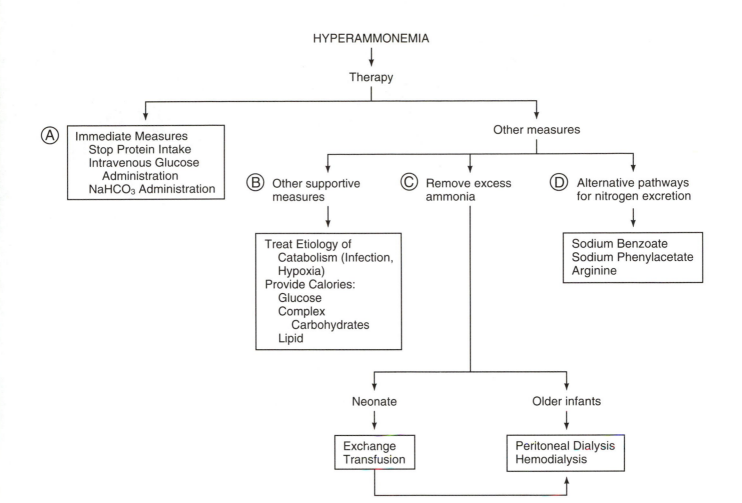

HYPERAMMONEMIA

Therapy

A Immediate Measures
　Stop Protein Intake
　Intravenous Glucose
　　Administration
　NaHCO₃ Administration

Other measures

B Other supportive
　　measures

Treat Etiology of
　Catabolism (Infection,
　Hypoxia)
Provide Calories:
　Glucose
　Complex
　　Carbohydrates
　Lipid

C Remove excess
　　ammonia

Neonate

Exchange
Transfusion

Older infants

Peritoneal Dialysis
Hemodialysis

D Alternative pathways
　　for nitrogen excretion

Sodium Benzoate
Sodium Phenylacetate
Arginine

INDEX

A

Abdomen
  ascites and, 92–95
  distention of, 84
    intestinal obstruction and, 172
    necrotizing enterocolitis and, 168
  enlargement of, 88–89
  injury to, 34
  mass in, 90–91
    enlarged kidney or bladder as, 100–101
    hepatomegaly and, 96–97
    splenomegaly and, 98–99
  small thorax and, 80
ABO incompatibility
  anemia and, 180
  jaundice and, 54
Abruptio placentae, 28–29
Acardiac twin, 8
Acceleration of intrauterine growth, 4–5
Acidosis
  jaundice and, 54
  necrotizing enterocolitis and, 170
  prolapse of cord and, 30
  shock and, 158
Adenomatous malformation of lung, 150
Adrenal function, potassium and, 250
Adrenal hemorrhage, 90
  as birth trauma, 34
Agenesis
  parathyroid, 256
  renal, 46
Air, necrotizing enterocolitis and, 168, 170
Air embolus, 142–143
Air hunger, 64
  retractions and, 82
Air leak
  cyanosis and, 58
  pulmonary, 142–143
Airway
  apnea and, 64
  asphyxia of newborn and, 22–23
  retractions and, 82
Albumin, hydrops fetalis and, 16, 18
Alcohol abuse, effects of, 2, 232–233
Alkali therapy, hypocalcemia and, 256
Alkalosis, 244–245
Altitude, fetal effects of, 2
Alveolar hemorrhage, 136
Alveolar hyperventilation, 244
Alveolar rupture
  air leak and, 142
  cyanosis and, 58
Amikacin, dosages of, 110
Ammonia
  hyperammonemia and, 266–269
  seizures and, 196
Amnion nodosum, 12

Amniotic fluid
  meconium-stained, 128–129
  oligohydramnios and, 12–13
  polyhydramnios and, 10
Amniotic membrane rupture
  cocaine abuse and, 228
  respiratory distress and, 122
Amobarbital, 196
Amphetamine abuse, 234–235
Amphotericin, candidiasis and, 118
Ampicillin, 110
Amytal, 196
Anal fissure, 86
Anastomosis, vascular, twins and, 8
Anemia
  blood loss and, 178–179
  hemolytic, 180–181
    thrombocytosis and, 186
  hydrops fetalis and, 16, 18
  pallor and, 60
  tachycardia and, 146
Anencephaly, polyhydramnios and, 10
Anesthetic intoxication, seizures and, 194
Angiomatous lesion, 220–221
Antenatal diagnosis
  of diaphragmatic hernia, 138
  of pleural effusion, 134
Antibiotic
  choice of, 108
  dosages of, 110
  necrotizing enterocolitis and, 170
Anticonvulsant therapy, 196–197
Antidiuretic hormone
  hypoxic-ischemic encephalopathy and, 204
  oliguria and, 46
  syndrome of inappropriate secretion of, 246
Antihypertensive therapy, 154
Apgar score
  of 0–3, 22–23
  of 4–10, 24–25
  placenta previa and, 28
Aplasia, pure red cell, 60
Apnea, 62–64
  bradycardia and, 144
Apt test, 84
  bloody stools and, 86
Arginine vasopressin, polyuria and, 50
Arm, paralysis of, 32
Arteriovenous malformation, 78
Artery-to-artery anastomosis in twins, 8
Ascites
  hydrops fetalis and, 18
  isolated, 92–95
Asphyxia
  apnea and, 62
  bradycardia and, 144
  difficult labor and, 4

Asphyxia—cont'd.
  hydrops fetalis and, 18
  hypoxic-ischemic encephalopathy and, 202
  management of, 22–23
  meconium aspiration and, 128
  placenta previa and, 28
  prolapse of cord and, 30
  seizures and, 194
  shock and, 158
  tachycardia and, 146
Aspirate, gastric, excessive, 84–85
Aspiration
  apnea and, 62
  meconium, 128–129
  needle, of pneumopericardium, 142, 148
Asymmetrical undergrowth of infant, 2
Asymmetry
  of chest, 80
  retractions and, 82
Atelectasis, 122
  mediastinal shift and, 150
  postextubation, 139
Atresia
  duodenal, vomiting and, 84
  esophageal, 174–175
Atrial flutter, 146
Atrioventricular block, bradycardia and, 144

B

Bacterial infection; *see also* Infection
  diagnosis and management of, 108–111
  etiology and signs of, 106–107
  maternal-fetal transmission of, 104–105
Bag of bubbles as sign of necrotizing enterocolitis, 168
Barbiturate, seizures and, 196
Barotrauma, bronchopulmonary dysplasia and, 132
Barrel chest, 80
BDP; *see* Bronchopulmonary dysplasia
Beckwith-Wiedemann syndrome, difficult labor and, 4
Betamethasone, respiratory distress and, 126
Bicarbonate
  acidosis and, 242
  alkalosis and, 244
  hydrops fetalis and, 18
  hypocalcemia and, 256
  hypoxic-ischemic encephalopathy and, 204
Biliary duct, ruptured, 92
Bilious ascitic fluid, 92
Bilious vomiting, 84
  intestinal obstruction and, 172
Bilirubin
  infant of diabetic mother and, 6
  jaundice and, 54, 56
  periventricular-intraventricular hemorrhage and, 208
Birthweight
  high, 4–5
  hydrops fetalis and, 16
  large head and, 70
  low, 2–3
    fluid balance and, 44
    hypocalcemia in, 256

placenta previa and, 28
  small head and, 72
Bladder
  as abdominal mass, 90
  enlargement of, 100–101
  oliguria and, 46
Bleb
  bronchopulmonary dysplasia and, 132
  subpleural, 142
Bleeding; *see* Hemorrhage
Blister, 216–217
Block, atrioventricular, 144
Blood
  anemia and; *see* Anemia
  coagulation of; *see* Disseminated intravascular coagulation
  hemangioma and, 220
  hematemesis and, 84
  hyperviscosity of, 182–183
    infant of diabetic mother and, 6
  hypoxic-ischemic encephalopathy and, 202
  jaundice and, 54
  misshaped head and, 74
  neutropenia and, 188–189
  petechia or ecchymosis and, 214
  platelet disorders of, 184–187
  in stool, 86–87
Blood cells
  hemolysis of, 180
  infection and, 108
  syphilis and, 112
Blood chemistry abnormality, 237–269
  acidosis and, 242–243; *see also* Acidosis
  hypoglycemia and, transient, 238–241
Blood flow, cerebral, 204
Blood gas analysis
  cyanosis and, 58
  hypoxic-ischemic encephalopathy and, 204
Blood loss; *see* Hemorrhage
Blood pressure
  hypertension and, 152–155
  hypoxic-ischemic encephalopathy and, 204
  shock and, 158
Blood type incompatibility, 180
Body temperature
  hyperthermia and, 42–43
  hypothermia and, 40–41
Bone
  birth trauma to, 36–37
  breech birth and, 26
Botulism, infantile, 176
Brachial nerve palsy, 32
Brachycephaly, 74
Bradycardia, 144–145
  hydrops fetalis and, 16
Brain
  misshaped head and, 74
  small head and, 72
Breast milk jaundice, 54
Breath sounds, mediastinal shift and, 150
Breathing
  apnea and, 62–63

cyanosis and, 58
stridor and, 68–69
tachypnea and, 66–67
Breech birth, 26–27
head shape and, 74
trauma from, 34
Bronchodilator, bronchopulmonary dysplasia and, 132
Bronchopulmonary dysplasia, 132–133
hypertension and, 152
Bruise, 214–215
Bruising, periorbital, 34
Bubble, intestinal obstruction and, 172
Bulging fontanelle, 78–79
Bullous impetigo, 216

C

Café-au-lait spots, 224
Caffeine, apnea and, 62
Calcitonin, 256
Calcium
cephalhematoma and, 34
disorders of, 256–261
infant of diabetic mother and, 6
seizures and, 194, 196
Calcium gluconate
hypermagnesemia and, 264
severe asphyxia and, 22
Candida albicans, 118–119
Capsule, liver, rupture of, 90
Caput succedaneum, 74
Carbenicillin, dosages of, 110
Carbon dioxide
bronchopulmonary dysplasia and, 132
partial pressure of, acidosis and, 242
persistent fetal circulation and, 164
Cardiogenic shock, myocardial ischemia and, 166
Cardiomegaly, infant of diabetic mother and, 6
Cardiorespiratory distress, mediastinal shift and, 150
Cardiovascular system; *see also* Heart
apnea and, 62
blood and; *see* Blood
central venous pressure and, 156–157
hypertension and, 152–155
necrotizing enterocolitis and, 170
pallor and, 60
patent ductus arteriosus and, 162–163
persistent fetal circulation and, 164–165
shock and, 158–160
Cataractous opacities, 210
Catheter
oliguria and, 46
umbilical vein, 22
Cavernous hemangioma, 220
Cefotaxim, dosages of, 110
Cell, hepatomegaly and, 96
Central cyanosis, 58
Central diabetes insipidus, hypernatremia and, 248
Central nerve paralysis, 32
Central nervous system
angiomatous lesions of, 220

hypotonia and, 200
hypoxic-ischemic encephalopathy and, 202–205; *see also* Hypoxic-ischemic encephalopathy
infection of, 114
lesion of
acidosis and, 242
hypertension and, 152
tachypnea and, 66
seizure and, 194–197
Central venous pressure, abnormal, 156–157
Cephalhematoma, 34, 74
Cephalic index, 74
Cerebral blood flow, 204
Cerebral edema
bulging fontanelles and, 78
hypoxic-ischemic encephalopathy and, 204
large head and, 70
Cerebral hypotonia, 200
Cerebrohepatorenal syndrome, 200
Cerebrospinal fluid
hypotonia and, 200
infection and, 108
syphilis and, 112
Cervical spine injury, 34
Cesarean delivery, head shape and, 74
Chest, abnormal contour of, 80–81
Chest radiograph, tachypnea and, 66
Chest wall deformity, acidosis and, 242
Chylothorax, pleural effusion and, 134–135
Chylous ascites, 92–95
Circulation, persistent fetal, 164–165
cyanosis and, 58
meconium aspiration and, 128
Circumference of head
large, 70
small, 72
Clavicular fracture, as birth injury, 36
Clonic seizures, 194
Clouding of cornea, 210
Coagulation, disseminated intravascular, 190–191
anemia and, 178
bleeding and, 192
bloody stools and, 86
hydrops fetalis and, 18
necrotizing enterocolitis and, 170
Coarse tremors, 198
Cold stress, 40–41
apnea and, 62, 64
Colon, Hirschsprung's disease and, 172
Compressed umbilical cord, 30–31
Compression, oligohydramnios and, 12
Conduction heat loss, 40
Congenital disorder
bulging fontanelles and, 78
chest contour and, 80
cyanosis and, 58
diaphragmatic hernia and, 138
edema and, 218
hypocalcemia and, 256
hypotonia and, 200
infant of diabetic mother and, 6

Congenital disorder—cont'd
  infection as
    ascites and, 92
    fungal, 118–119
    syphilis and, 112–113
    viral, 114–117
  jaundice and, 54
  large head and, 70
  laryngeal stridor as, 68
  myocardial ischemia and, 166
  oliguria and, 46, 48
  placenta previa and, 28
  seizures and, 194
  suck and swallow abnormalities and, 176
  twins and, 8
Congestive heart failure
  bulging fontanelles and, 78
  hepatomegaly and, 96
Continuous positive airway pressure, 124
Contour of chest, 80–81
Contraction, diaphragmatic, cyanosis and, 58
Convection heat loss, 40
Coombs' test, jaundice and, 54
Cord
  spinal
    birth trauma to, 32
    shoulder dystocia and, 34
  vocal, paralysis of, 32
    stridor and, 68
Cornea, clouding of, 210
Coronal suture, intracranial pressure and, 76
Coxsackievirus, 116
Cranial bone abnormality, 74
Craniofacial anomaly, alcohol abuse and, 232
Cranium, unusual shape of, 74
C-reactive protein, infection and, 108
Creatinine, ascites and, 92
Cryotherapy, for retinopathy of prematurity, 210
Cyanosis, 58–59
  persistent fetal circulation and, 164
Cyst
  mesenteric, 90
  splenic, 98
  vitelline, 90
Cystic adenomatous malformation of lung, 150
Cystic fibrosis, meconium ileus and, 172
Cystic hydroma, 222-223
Cystourethrography, voiding, 100
Cytomegalovirus, 114

D

Degenerative disease, hypotonia and, 200
Dehydration, 44
  hypernatremia and, 248
  hyponatremia and, 246
  oliguria and, 46
Dexamethasone, respiratory distress and, 126
Dextrocardia, mediastinal shift and, 150–151
Dextrose, infant of diabetic mother and, 6
Dextrotransposition of great vessels, 4
Diabetes, maternal, 6–7
  calcium and, 256
  fetus of, 6–7
  head circumference of infant and, 72
  intrauterine growth acceleration and, 4
  intrauterine growth retardation and, 2
  polyhydramnios and, 10
Diabetes insipidus, hypernatremia and, 248
Diacetyl morphine, 230
Diamond-Blackfan syndrome, 60
Diaphragmatic contraction, cyanosis and, 58
Diaphragmatic hernia, 138–139
  mediastinal shift and, 150
Diaphragmatic paralysis, 32
Diazepam, seizures and, 196
Diazoxide, for hypertension, 154
Diffuse hemangioma, 220
Diffuse lymphangioma, 222
DiGeorge syndrome, hypocalcemia and, 256
Digitalization, bulging fontanelles and, 78
Dilantin, seizures and, 196
Discoloration, jaundice and, 54–55
Dislocation, vertebral, 36
Disseminated infection
  candidal, 118
  herpes simplex virus, 114
Disseminated intravascular coagulation, 190–191
  anemia and, 178
  bleeding and, 192
  bloody stools and, 86
  hydrops fetalis and, 18
  necrotizing enterocolitis and, 170
Distention
  abdominal, 88–89
    intestinal obstruction and, 172
    necrotizing enterocolitis and, 168
    vomiting and, 84
  bladder, 100
Diuretic
  bronchopulmonary dysplasia and, 132
  hydrops fetalis and, 18
  hypoxic-ischemic encephalopathy and, 204
  potassium and, 250
Diverticulum, Meckel's, vitelline cyst with, 90
Dizygous twins, 8
Dobutamine, necrotizing enterocolitis and, 170
Dolicocephaly, 74
Dopamine
  necrotizing enterocolitis and, 170
  persistent fetal circulation and, 164
Double-bubble sign, intestinal obstruction and, 172
Drainage
  necrotizing enterocolitis and, 170
  of pleural effusion, 134
Drug abuse, maternal, 227–235
  alcohol, 232–233
  amphetamine, 234–235
  cocaine, 228–229
  fetal effects of, 2
  heroin or methadone, 230–231
Drug therapy
  bronchopulmonary dysplasia and, 132

for hypertension, 154
periventricular-intraventricular hemorrhage and, 208
tachycardia as, 146
Drug-induced disorder
gastric hemorrhage as, 84
gastrointestinal bleeding as, 86
hyperkalemia as, 254
hypertension as, 152
hypovolemia as, 158
jaundice as, 54
neutropenia as, 188
polyuria and, 50
Duchenne-Erb palsy, 32
Duct, biliary, ruptured, 92
Ductal shunt, right-to-left, 58
Duodenal atresia, 84
Duodenal obstruction, 84
Duplication cyst, intestinal, 90
Dwarfism
chest contour and, 80
large head and, 70
Dysmorphism, hypotonia and, 200
Dysplasia, bronchopulmonary, 132–133
hypertension and, 152
Dystocia, shoulder, 34
Dystrophy, myotonic, 176

E

Ear, birth injury to, 34
Ecchymosis, 214–215
ECHO virus, 116
Edema, 218–219
cerebral
bulging fontanelles and, 78
hypoxic-ischemic encephalopathy and, 204
large head and, 70
hydrops fetalis and, 14, 16
hypernatremia and, 248
hyponatremia and, 246
laryngeal, endotracheal intubation and, 139
pulmonary, patent ductus arteriosus and, 162
subcutaneous, 80
Effusion
pericardial, heart sounds and, 148
pleural, 134–135
Electrocardiography
bradycardia and, 144
tachycardia and, 146
Electroencephalogram, seizures and, 194
Electrolyte imbalance, seizures and, 196
Elliptosis, 180
Embolus, air, 142–143
Emphysema
interstitial, heart sounds and, 148
pulmonary interstitial, 142
Encephalitis, herpes simplex virus and, 114
Encephalocele, 74
Encephalopathy
hypotonia and, 200
pathophysiology of, 202–203

periventricular-intraventricular hemorrhage and, 206
seizures and, 194
End-expiratory pressure, positive; see Positive end-expiratory pressure
Endocrine disorder
hypertension and, 152
jaundice and, 54
Endophthalmitis, candidiasis and, 118
Endotracheal intubation
complications of, 139
massive hemorrhage and, 136
meconium aspiration and, 128
severe asphyxia and, 22
Enema, for meconium ileus, 172
Enlargement
abdominal, 88–89
of bladder, 100–101
of head, 70–71
of liver, 96–97
renal, 100–101
of spleen, 98–99
Enteric infection, 108
Enterocolitis, necrotizing
ascites and, 92
bloody stools and, 86
diagnosis of, 168–169
management of, 170–171
neutropenia and, 188
vomiting and, 84
Enterovirus infection, 116, 117
Entire arm paralysis, 32
Epidermis, heat loss and, 40
Epidural hemorrhage, 34
Epinephrine, severe asphyxia and, 22
Epiphysis, humeral fracture and, 36
Erythema toxicum, 216
Erythrocyte precursor, hepatomegaly and, 96
Erythrogenesis imperfecta, 60
Erythropoiesis, hepatomegaly and, 96
Esophageal atresia, 174–175
polyhydramnios and, 10
Evaporative heat loss, 40
Exchange transfusion
hydrops fetalis and, 18
hyperammonemia and, 268
jaundice and, 56
magnesium and, 262
polycythemia and, 182
Exsanguination
placenta previa and, 28
twin gestation and, 8
Extracellular fluid
hypernatremia and, 248
hyponatremia and, 246
Extracranial birth injury, 34
Extremity, blood pressure readings and, 152
Eye
birth injury to, 34
candidiasis and, 118
optic nerve injury and, 32
port-wine stain and, 220

Eye—cont'd
pupillary opacity of, 210–211
retinopathy of prematurity and, 212–213

F

Face
birth injury to, 34, 36
oligohydramnios and, 12
Facial nerve palsy, 32
Facies, stridor and, 68
Familial dysautonomia, 200
Fat necrosis, subcutaneous, 218
Feeding
apnea and, 62
maternal heroin abuse and, 230
necrotizing enterocolitis and, 168, 170
pleural effusion and, 134
suck and swallow abnormalities and, 176
Femoral fracture, 36
Femoral pulse, 152
Fetal alcohol syndrome, 2, 232–233
Fetal circulation, persistent, 164–165
cyanosis and, 58
meconium aspiration and, 128
Fetomaternal transfusion, 178
Fetoplacental transfusion, 178
Fetus, 1–20
of diabetic mother, 6–7
hydrops fetalis of, 14–19
hypoxic-ischemic encephalopathy and, 202
intrauterine growth acceleration and, 4–5
intrauterine growth retardation and, 2–3
oligohydramnios and, 12–13
polyhydramnios and, 10–11
respiratory distress and, 122
thermal gradient and, 42
transmission of infection to, 104–105
twin gestation and, 8–9
Fetus papyraceus, 8
Fibrillation, atrial, 146
Fissure, anal, 86
Fistula, tracheoesophageal, 174–175
Fluid
airway management and, 22
amniotic
meconium-stained, 128–129
oligohydramnios and, 12–13
polyhydramnios and, 10
ascites and, 92–95
blister, 216
cerebrospinal
hypotonia and, 200
infection and, 108
syphilis and, 112
extracellular
hypernatremia and, 248
hyponatremia and, 246
hydrops fetalis and, 16, 18
hypoxic-ischemic encephalopathy and, 204
oliguria and, 48

pleural, hepatomegaly and, 96
pleural effusion and, 134–135
tachypnea and, 66
Fluid balance, 44–45
Flutter, atrial, 146
Focal clonic seizures, 194
Fontanelle, large head and, 70
Forceps injury, 34
Formula, pleural effusion and, 134
Fractional inspired oxygen concentration
bronchopulmonary dysplasia and, 132
transient tachypnea and, 130
Fracture
as birth injury, 36
breech birth and, 26
Fresh frozen plasma, 190
FTA-ABS test for syphilis, 112
Fundus reflex, 210
Fungal infection, 118–119
Furosemide, hypercalcemia and, 260

G

Gangrene, ascites and, 92
Gas, abdominal distention from, 88–89
Gastric aspirate, excessive, 84–85
Gastric suction, obstruction and, 172
Gastric tube, diaphragmatic hernia and, 138
Gastrointestinal system
abdominal distention and, 88–89
abdominal mass and, 90–91
ascites and, 92–93
bloody stools and, 86–87
esophageal atresia and, 174–175
necrotizing enterocolitis and; see Necrotizing enterocolitis
obstruction of, 172–173
tracheoesophageal fistula and, 174–175
vomiting and, 84–85
Gentamicin, dosages of, 110
Gestational age, heat loss and, 40
Giant hemangioma, 220
Giant nevus, 224
Gluconate, infant of diabetic mother and, 6
Glucose
Beckwith-Wiedemann syndrome and, 4
cerebrospinal, infection and, 108
hypoglycemia and, 238–239
infant of diabetic mother and, 6
seizures and, 194, 196
Glucose-6-phosphate dehydrogenase deficiency
hemolysis and, 180
jaundice and, 54
Glycogen, hepatic, 238
Gram-negative infection, 108
Great vessels, transposition of, intrauterine growth
acceleration and, 4
Growth acceleration, intrauterine, 4–5
Growth retardation, intrauterine, 2–3
placenta previa and, 28
seizures and, 194
small head and, 72

H

Hairy nevus, 224
Head
  birth injury to, 34
  bulging fontanelles and, 78–79
  large, 70–71
  misshaped, 74–75
  small, 72–73
  wide sutures of, 76–77
Head injury, seizures and, 196
Heart
  acardiac twin and, 8
  alcohol abuse and, 232
  apnea and, 62
  bradycardia and, 144–145
  central venous pressure and, 156
  cyanosis and, 58
  diminished sounds of, 148–149
  hydrops fetalis and, 16, 18
  infant of diabetic mother and, 6
  mediastinal shift and, 150–151
  myocardial ischemia of, 166–167
  patent ductus arteriosus and, 162–163
  persistent fetal circulation and, 164
  shock and, 158
  tachycardia and, 146–147
  tachypnea and, 66
Heart block, 144
Heart failure
  bulging fontanelles and, 78
  hepatomegaly and, 96
Heart rate
  asphyxia and
    moderate, 24
    severe, 22
  bradycardia and, 144–145
  tachycardia and, 146–147
Heat
  hyperthermia and, 42–43
  hypothermia and, 40–41
Heat shield, fluid balance and, 44
Hemangioma, 220–221
  bloody stools and, 86
Hematemesis, 84
Hematocrit
  anemia and, 178
  jaundice and, 54
  massive hemorrhage and, 136
  pallor and, 60
  polycythemia and, 182
Hematoma
  intestinal intramural, 34
  liver, 34
Hemodynamic disorder, hydrops fetalis and, 16
Hemoglobinopathy, hemolysis and, 180–181
Hemolysis
  anemia due to, 180–181
  jaundice and, 54
  pallor and, 60
Hemolytic anemia, thrombocytosis and, 186

Hemorrhage, 192–193
  adrenal, 90
  anemia and, 178–179
  as birth trauma, 34
  birth trauma and, 34
  breech birth and, 26
  cephalhematoma and, 34
  disseminated intravascular coagulation and, 190–191
  intracranial, hypertension and, 152
  intraventricular, bradycardia and, 144
  misshaped head and, 74
  pallor and, 60
  periventricular-intraventricular
    apnea and, 62
    bulging fontanelles and, 78
    pathophysiology of, 206–207
    pneumothorax and, 142
    seizures and, 194, 196
    therapy of, 208–209
  placenta previa and, 28
  pulmonary, 136–137
  severe asphyxia and, 22
  shock and, 158
  subdural, bulging fontanelles and, 78
  subgaleal, large head and, 70
  thrombocytopenia and, 184
Hepatic glycogen, 238
Hepatocyte, hepatomegaly and, 96
Hepatomegaly, 90, 96–97
  splenomegaly and, 98
Hereditary disorder
  hemolysis and, 180
  hypotonia and, 200
  petechia or ecchymosis and, 214
  suck and swallow abnormalities and, 176
Hernia, diaphragmatic, 138–139
  mediastinal shift and, 150
Heroin abuse, 230–231
Herpes simplex virus infection, 114
Hirschsprung's disease, 172
Hormone
  antidiuretic, 204
  parathyroid, 262
Horseshoe kidney, 90
Humeral fracture, as birth injury, 36
Hunger, air, 64
  retractions and, 82
Hyaline membrane disease, 122
  apnea and, 62
  infant of diabetic mother and, 6–7
Hyaloid vessels, 210
Hydration
  hyponatremia and, 246
  potassium and, 250
Hydrocephalus
  bulging fontanelles and, 78
  large head and, 70
  seizures and, 196
Hydrocortisone, respiratory distress and, 126
Hydrogen ions, alkalosis and, 244

Hydroma, cystic, 222–223
Hydrometrocolpos, 90
Hydrops fetalis, 14–19
  antenatal diagnosis of, 14–15
  management of, 18–19
  postnatal diagnosis of, 16–17
Hydrothorax, pleural effusion and, 134–135
Hyperaeration of lung, tachypnea and, 66
Hyperammonemia, 266–269
Hyperbilirubinemia
  jaundice and, 54
  periventricular-intraventricular hemorrhage and, 208
  polycythemia and, 182
Hypercalcemia, 260–261
Hyperglycemia
  infant of diabetic mother and, 6–7
  polyuria and, 50
Hyperkalemia, 250, 252–255
  hypoxic-ischemic encephalopathy and, 204
  renal disease and, 48
Hypermagnesemia, 264–265
Hypernatremia, 248–249
  polyuria and, 50
  seizures and, 196
Hyperosmolar enema for meconium ileus, 172
Hyperosmolar syndrome, 44
Hyperparathyroidism, hypercalcemia and, 260
Hyperplastic primary vitreous, 210
Hypertension, 152–155
  myocardial ischemia and, 166
  pulmonary, 164
Hyperthermia, 42–43
Hypertonia, breech birth and, 26
Hypertrophy, myocardial, 6
Hyperventilation
  alkalosis and, 244
  persistent fetal circulation and, 164
Hyperviscosity of blood, 182–183
  cyanosis and, 58
  infant of diabetic mother and, 6
  seizures and, 196
Hypervolemia, hypertension and, 154
Hypoalbuminemia, 16
Hypocalcemia, 256–259
  hypomagnesemia and, 262
  infant of diabetic mother and, 6
  seizures and, 194, 196
Hypoglycemia
  Beckwith-Wiedemann syndrome and, 4
  myocardial ischemia and, 166
  seizures and, 194, 196
  transient, 238–241
Hypokalemia, 250–251
Hypomagnesemia, 262–263
  hypocalcemia and, 256
  infant of diabetic mother and, 6
  seizures and, 196
Hyponatremia, 246–247
Hypoparathyroidism, hypocalcemia and, 256
Hypoperfusion, heart sounds and, 148

Hypoplasia
  parathyroid, hypocalcemia and, 256
  pulmonary, oligohydramnios and, 12
  renal, oliguria and, 46
Hypoplastic anemia, 60
Hypoplastic undergrowth of infant, 2
Hypotension, 158
Hypothermia, 40–41
  apnea and, 62, 64
Hypothyroidism, large head and, 70
Hypotonia, 200–201
  breech birth and, 26
Hypotrophic undergrowth of infant, 2
Hypoventilation, acidosis and, 242
Hypovolemia
  pallor and, 60
  renal disease and, 48
  severe asphyxia and, 22
  shock and, 158
Hypoxemia
  cyanosis and, 58
  respiratory distress and, 130
Hypoxia
  hydrops fetalis and, 18
  myocardial ischemia and, 166
  prolapse of cord and, 30
Hypoxic-ischemic encephalopathy
  hypotonia and, 200
  pathophysiology of, 202–203
  periventricular-intraventricular hemorrhage and, 206
  seizures and, 194
  therapy for, 204–205

I

Ileus, meconium
  abdominal mass and, 90
  intestinal obstruction and, 172
Immature lung, respiratory distress and, 122
Immature lung syndrome, apnea and, 62
Immune hydrops fetalis, 12
Implantation of placenta, placenta previa and, 28
Inborn errors of metabolism
  hyperammonemia and, 266
  seizures and, 194
  splenomegaly and, 98
Incontinentia pigmenti, 224
Incubator, hyperthermia and, 42
Indomethacin
  gastrointestinal rupture caused by, 88
  patent ductus arteriosus and, 162
Infantile botulism, suck and swallow abnormalities and, 176
Infection
  apnea and, 62
  ascites and, 92
  bacterial
    diagnosis and management of, 108–111
    etiology and signs of, 106–107
    maternal-fetal transmission of, 104–105
  bloody stools and, 86

bradycardia and, 144
bulging fontanelles and, 78
cocaine abuse and, 228
fungal, 118–119
hemolysis and, 180
hepatosplenomegaly caused by, 90
neutropenia and, 188
seizures and, 194, 196
shock and, 158
syphilitic, 112–113
viral, 114–117
Infiltrate, hepatomegaly and, 96
Injury; see Trauma, birth
Insulin
Beckwith-Wiedemann syndrome and, 4
lung maturity and, 6
Intercostal retraction, 80
respiratory distress and, 82
Interstitial emphysema
heart sounds and, 148
pulmonary, 142
Intestinal bleeding, 86–87
Intestinal disorder; see Gastrointestinal system
Intestinal intramural hematoma, 34
Intoxication
alcohol, 232
seizures and, 194, 196
Intracellular fluid, magnesium and, 262
Intracranial hemorrhage, 192
anemia and, 178
breech birth and, 26
bulging fontanelles and, 78
hypertension and, 152
Intracranial pressure
bulging fontanelles and, 78–79
large head and, 70
seizures and, 196
sutures and, 76
Intramural hematoma of intestine, 34
Intraperitoneal air, 88
Intrauterine growth acceleration, 4–5
Intrauterine growth retardation
alcohol abuse and, 232
placenta previa and, 28
seizures and, 194
small head and, 72
Intrauterine infection, candidal, 118
Intravascular coagulation, disseminated, 190–191
anemia and, 178
bleeding and, 192
bloody stools and, 86
hydrops fetalis and, 18
necrotizing enterocolitis and, 170
Intravenous pyelography, renal disorder and, 100
Intraventricular hemorrhage, bradycardia and, 144
Intubation
complications of, 139
diaphragmatic hernia and, 138
endotracheal, severe asphyxia and, 22
massive hemorrhage and, 136

meconium aspiration and, 128
pulmonary air leak and, 142
Ischemia, myocardial, 166–167
Isoimmune disorder
hydrops fetalis and, 18
jaundice and, 54
thrombocytopenia as, 184
Isolated ascites, 92–95
Isotonic solution, hyponatremia and, 246

J
Jaundice, 54–57
Jitteriness, 198–199

K
Kasabach-Merritt syndrome, 220
Kidney
abdominal mass and, 90
enlargement of, 100–101
renovascular hypertension and, 152
Klumpke's palsy, 26, 32
Kupffer cells, hepatomegaly and, 96

L
Labor and delivery, 21–38
abruptio placentae/placenta previa and, 28–29
Apgar score of 0–3, 22–23
Apgar score of 4–10, 24–25
breech birth and, 26–27
prolapse or compression of cord, 30–31
transmission of infection during, 104
trauma during
to bones, 36–37
to peripheral nerves, 32–33
to viscera and soft tissue, 34–35
Laceration of lung, 136
Large for gestational age infant, 4–5
Large head, 70–71
bulging fontanelles and, 78
Larynx
clearing of, 22
endotracheal intubation and, 139
stridor and, 68
Leak, air
cyanosis and, 58
pulmonary, 142–143
Lecithin/sphingomyelin ratio, 122
Left-to-right shunt, 162
Leukopenia, 108
Liver
enlargement of, 96–97
hematoma of, 34
hydrops fetalis and, 16
Liver disease, bloody stools and, 86
Low birthweight, 2–3
fluid balance and, 44
hypocalcemia in, 256
Lower extremity, blood pressure readings and, 152
Lowe's syndrome, 200
Lumbar puncture, infection and, 108

Lung; *see also* Respiratory *entries*
  air leak and, 142–143
  chest contour and, 80
  immature, respiratory distress and, 122
  massive hemorrhage of, 136–137
  mediastinal shift and, 150
  overexpanded, hepatomegaly and, 96
  pulmonary hypoplasia and, 12
  tachypnea and, 66
Lung disease, cyanosis and, 58
Lung maturity, infant of diabetic mother and, 6
Lupus erythematosus, neutropenia and, 188
Lymphangioma, 222–223
Lymphedema, 218

M

Macrosomia, infant of diabetic mother and, 6
Macular damage, 210
Magnesium
  disorders of, 262–265
  hypocalcemia and, 256, 258
  infant of diabetic mother and, 6
  seizures and, 196
Malformation, hypotonia and, 200
Malignancy
  abdominal mass and, 90
  giant nevus and, 224
Malnutrition, 2
Mandibular injury, 36
Mass, abdominal, 90–91
  enlarged kidney or bladder as, 100–101
  hepatomegaly and, 96–97
  splenomegaly and, 98–99
Massive pulmonary hemorrhage, 136–137
Maternal blood, swallowing of, 84
Maternal drug abuse, 227–235
Maternal-fetal transmission of infection, 104–105
Maxilla, birth injury to, 36
Mechanical ventilation; *see* Ventilation
  complications of, 139–140
  massive hemorrhage and, 136
Meckel's diverticulum, vitelline cyst with, 90
Meconium, ascites and, 92
Meconium aspiration, 128–129
Meconium ileus
  abdominal mass and, 90
  intestinal obstruction and, 172
Meconium plug syndrome, 172
Mediastinal shift, 150–151
Megacephaly, breech birth and, 26
Melanocytic nevus, 224
Melanosis, pustular, 216, 224
Meningitis, apnea and, 62, 64
Mesenteric cyst, 90
Metabolic acidosis
  causes of, 242
  necrotizing enterocolitis and, 170
Metabolic alkalosis, 244
Metabolic disorder
  bradycardia and, 144
  hyperammonemia and, 266–269

  infant of diabetic mother and, 6
  jaundice and, 54
  seizures and, 194, 196
  shock and, 158
  splenomegaly and, 98
  tachypnea and, 66
Metalloporphyrins, jaundice and, 56
Metastasis, abdominal mass and, 90
Methamphetamine, 234
Methemoglobinemia, cyanosis and, 58
Methylxanthine, apnea and, 62
Micturition, frequency of, 46
Midgut volvulus, 172
Milk sensitivity, bloody stools and, 86
Milky ascitic fluid, 92, 94
Misshaped head, 74–75
  bulging fontanelles and, 78
Mongolian spot, 224
Monoamniotic twins, 8
Monochorionic twins, 8
Monozygous twins, 8
Moro reflex, humeral fracture and, 36
Mortality
  candidiasis and, 118
  cytomegalovirus infection and, 112
  diaphragmatic hernia and, 138
  necrotizing enterocolitis and, 170
  pneumopericardium and, 142
  spinal cord trauma during birth and, 32
  of twin gestation, 8
Motor neuron disorder, 200
Multicystic kidney, 90, 100
Multifocal seizures, 194
Multiple fetuses, 2
Muscle disorder
  hypotonia and, 200
  suck and swallow abnormalities and, 176
Muscle function, breech birth and, 26
Myocardial hypertrophy, infant of diabetic mother and, 6
Myocardial ischemia, 166–167
Myocardium
  hydrops fetalis and, 18
  shock and, 158; *see also* Heart
Myoclonic seizures, 194
Myotonia, 200
Myotonic dystrophy, 176

N

Nafcillin, 110
Nasotracheal intubation, 139
Necrosis, subcutaneous fat, 218
Necrotizing enterocolitis
  ascites and, 92
  bloody stools and, 86
  diagnosis of, 168–169
  management of, 170–171
  neutropenia and, 188
  vomiting and, 84
Needle aspiration of pneumopericardium, 142, 148
Neovascularization in eye, 210
Neuroblastoma, 90

Neurofibromatosis, pigmented lesions of, 224
Neurogenic bladder, 90
Neurologic disease, viral, 114
Neurologic function
    seizures and, 194–195
    suck and swallow abnormalities and, 176
Neuromuscular disorder
    apnea and, 62
    cyanosis and, 58
Neuromuscular transmission disorder, 200
Neurulation, head and, 74
Neutropenia, 188–189
Nevus, 220
    pigmented, 224
Nitroprusside, for hypertension, 154
Nodule, amnion nodosum and, 12
Nosocomial infection, 108

O

Obstruction
    ascites and, 92
    of endotracheal tube, 139
    hepatomegaly and, 96
    intestinal, 172–173
    renal, 100
    retractions and, 82
    stridor and, 68
    urinary, 90
    vomiting and, 84
Occlusion, of endotracheal tube, 139
Occult prolapse of cord, 30
Oculocerebrorenal syndrome, 200
Oligohydramnios, 12–13
Oliguria, 46–49
Omental cyst, 90
Omphalomesenteric cyst, 90
Opacity, pupillary, 210–211
Optic nerve injury, 32
Orbit, birth injury to, 36
Osmolality, hyponatremia and, 246
Otitis media, fetal transmission of, 104
Overaeration of heart, 148
Overexpanded lung, hepatomegaly and, 96
Overhydration, 44
Oversedation, apnea and, 62
Oxygen
    cyanosis and, 58
    diaphragmatic hernia and, 138
    hypoxic-ischemic encephalopathy and, 202, 204
    moderate asphyxia and, 24
    persistent fetal circulation and, 164
    respiratory distress and, 130

P

Pallor, 60–61
    anemia and, 178
    tachycardia and, 146
Palsy
    Duchenne-Erb, 32
    facial nerve, 32
    Klumpke's, 26, 32

Parabiotic syndrome
    hydrops fetalis and, 14
    oligohydramnios and, 12
Paracentesis, ascites and, 92
Paraldehyde, seizures and, 196
Paralysis
    diaphragmatic, 32
    peripheral, 32
    vocal cord, 32
        stridor and, 68
Parathyroid hormone
    hypercalcemia and, 260
    hypomagnesemia and, 262
Parathyroid hypoplasia, 256
Parenchymal lung disease, 58
Partial pressure of arterial carbon dioxide
    bronchopulmonary dysplasia and, 132
    persistent fetal circulation and, 164
Partial pressure of arterial oxygen
    cyanosis and, 58
    diaphragmatic hernia and, 138
    persistent fetal circulation and, 164
Partial pressure of carbon dioxide, acidosis and,
    242
Patent ductus arteriosus, 162–163
    apnea and, 62
    hypertension and, 152
Pectus excavation, 80–81
Penicillin, dosages of, 110
    for syphilis, 112
Pepile's grading of periventricular-intraventricular
    hemorrhage, 206
Pericardial effusion, 148
Pericardial tap of pneumopericardium, 142, 148
Perinatal infection, 104–105
Periorbital bruising, 34
Peripheral cyanosis, 58
Peripheral nerve trauma during birth, 32–33
Peritoneal air, necrotizing enterocolitis and, 170
Peritonitis, meconium, 92
Periventricular calcification, 78
Periventricular-intraventricular hemorrhage, 206–209
    apnea and, 62
    bulging fontanelles and, 78
    pathophysiology of, 206–207
    pneumothorax and, 142
    seizures and, 194, 196
    therapy of, 208–209
Persistent fetal circulation, 164–165
    cyanosis and, 58
    meconium aspiration and, 128
Persistent hyperplastic primary vitreous, 210
Petechia, 214–215
Peutz-Jeghers syndrome, pigmented lesions of, 224
pH
    acidosis and, 242–243
    alkalosis and, 244–245
Phenobarbital
    jaundice and, 56
    seizures and, 196
Phenytoin, seizures and, 196

Phosphate
  hypercalcemia and, 260
  hypocalcemia and, 258
Phosphatidylglycerol, respiratory distress and, 122
Phototherapy, jaundice and, 56
Phrenic nerve injury, 32
Physiologic jaundice, 54
Physiological tremors, 198
Pigmented lesion, 224–225
Pitting edema, 218
Placenta
  abruptio placentae and, 28–29
  cytomegalovirus and, 114
  fetoplacental transfusion and, 178
  hydrops fetalis and, 16
  intrauterine growth retardation and, 2
  transmission of infection across, 104
Placenta previa, 28–29
Plasma, 190
Platelets
  bleeding and, 192
  petechiae and ecchymosis and, 214–215
  thrombocytopenia and, 184–185
  thrombocytosis and, 186–187
Pleural effusion, 134–135
Pleural fluid, hepatomegaly and, 96
Pleuroamniotic shunt, 134
Plexiglas heat shield, 42
Plug, meconium, 172
PMI, 150
Pneumomediastinum
  heart sounds and, 148
  spontaneous, 142
  tachypnea and, 66
Pneumonia
  apnea and, 64
  fetal transmission of, 104
  respiratory distress and, 130
Pneumonitis, meconium aspiration and, 128
Pneumopericardium, 142
  heart sounds and, 148
Pneumoperitoneum, air leak and, 142
Pneumothorax
  abdominal distention and, 88
  diagnosis of, 142
  heart sounds and, 148
  hepatomegaly and, 96
  mediastinal shift and, 150
  splenomegaly and, 98
  tachypnea and, 66
Poland syndrome, 80
Polycystic kidney, 100
Polycythemia, 182–183
  cyanosis and, 58
  infant of diabetic mother and, 6
  seizures and, 196
Polyhydramnios, 10–11
Polyuria, 50–51
Port-wine stain, 220
Positive end-expiratory pressure
  central venous pressure and, 156

  massive hemorrhage and, 136
  persistent fetal circulation and, 164
  severe asphyxia and, 22
Positive pressure ventilation, 132
Postextubation atelectasis, 139
Posthemorrhagic hydrocephalus, 78
Postmaturity, size of infant, 4
Potassium
  disorders of, 250–255
  hypoxic-ischemic encephalopathy and, 204
  polyuria and, 50
Potter syndrome, 12
Prader-Willi syndrome, 200
Premature rupture of membranes, cocaine abuse and, 228
Prenatal diagnosis
  of diaphragmatic hernia, 138
  of pleural effusion, 134
Prerenal failure, 48
Pressor agent for persistent fetal circulation, 164
Pressure
  blood
    hypertension and, 152–155
    hypoxic-ischemic encephalopathy and, 204
  central venous, 156–157
  intracranial
    bulging fontanelles and, 78–79
    large head and, 70
    seizures and, 196
    sutures and, 76
  positive end-expiratory; see Positive end-expiratory pressure
Preterm infant
  anemia of, 60
  apnea and, 62
  bulging fontanelles and, 78
  hypercalcemia and, 260
  hypocalcemia in, 256
  patent ductus arteriosus and, 162
  placenta previa and, 28
  retinopathy in, 212–213
  seizures and, 194
Probe, skin, hyperthermia and, 42
Prolapsed cord, 30–31
Protein, C-reactive, 108
Protrusions from chest, 80
Pseudohyperkalemia, 250
Pseudomonas infection of skin, 216
Pulmonary air leak, 142–143
Pulmonary edema, 162
Pulmonary hemorrhage, 136–137
  anemia and, 178
Pulmonary hypertension, persistent fetal circulation and, 164
Pulmonary hypoplasia, 12
Pulmonary interstitial emphysema, 142
Pulmonary vessel, tachypnea and, 66
Pulse, hypertension and, 152
Puncture, lumbar, infection and, 108
Pupillary opacity, 210–211
Pure red cell aplasia, 60

Purpura, 214
Purulent ascitic fluid, 92
Pustular melanosis, 216, 224
Pyelography, intravenous, 100
Pyrimethamine, toxoplasmosis and, 114

Q
Quivering, 198–199

R
Radiant heat loss, 40
Radiographic evaluation
    bronchopulmonary dysplasia and, 132
    bulging fontanelles and, 78
    diaphragmatic hernia and, 138
    hydrops fetalis and, 16
    intestinal obstruction and, 172
    massive hemorrhage and, 136
    mediastinal shift and, 150
    necrotizing enterocolitis and, 168
    pneumopericardium and, 142
    respiratory distress and, 130
    seizures and, 194
Radioisotope studies, oliguria and, 46
Reagent strips for glucose, 238
Recurrent laryngeal nerve, 32
Red blood cells
    hemolysis of, 180
    jaundice and, 54
    pallor and, 60
    polycythemia and, 182
Red reflex, 210
Reflex
    Moro, humeral fracture and, 36
    red, 210
Renal function
    abdominal mass and, 90
    edema and, 218
    enlargement of kidney and, 100–101
    fluid balance and, 44
    oligohydramnios and, 12
    oliguria and, 46–47, 46–49, 48
    polyuria and, 50–51
    potassium and, 250
Renal hemorrhage, as birth injury, 34
Renovascular hypertension, 152
    therapy for, 154
Respiratory acidosis, 242
Respiratory alkalosis, 244
Respiratory distress
    apnea and, 62
    breech birth and, 26
    hydrops fetalis and, 16
    management of, 124–125
    meconium aspiration and, 128–129
    mediastinal shift and, 150
    pathogenesis and diagnosis of, 122–123
    retractions and, 82–83
    stridor and, 68
    therapy for, 126–127
    transient tachypnea and, 130–131

Respiratory system
    acidosis and, 242
    air leak and, 142–143
    apnea and, 62–63
    bronchopulmonary dysplasia and, 132–133
    cyanosis and, 58
    hepatomegaly and, 96
    hydrops fetalis and, 18
    massive hemorrhage of, 136–137
    mediastinal shift and, 150
    pleural effusion and, 134–135
    pulmonary hypoplasia and, 12
    tachypnea and, 66
    ventilation and; see Ventilation
Retardation, intrauterine growth, 2–3
    placenta previa and, 28
    seizures and, 194
    small head and, 72
Retinopathy of prematurity, 212–213
Retraction
    chest contour and, 80
    respiratory distress and, 82–83
Retractions, cyanosis and, 58
Retroperitoneal hemorrhage, 34
Rh disease, hydrops fetalis and, 18
Rib, absence of, 80
Right-to-left ductal shunt, cyanosis and, 58
Riley-Day syndrome, 200
Rubella, 114, 116, 117
Rupture
    alveolar
        air leak and, 142
        cyanosis and, 58
    of amniotic membranes, cocaine abuse and, 228
    of extrahepatic biliary duct, 92
    gastrointestinal, indomethacin as cause of, 88
    of liver capsule, 90

S
Sail sign, 148
Scalp
    birth injury to, 34
    misshaped head and, 74
Scaphocephaly, 74
Sclerema, 218–219
Seizures, 194–197
    hypoxic-ischemic encephalopathy and, 204
Sepsis
    apnea and, 62, 64
    necrotizing enterocolitis and, 168
    neutropenia and, 188
    sclerema and, 218
    shock and, 158
Serosanguineous fluid, ascitic, 92
Serum osmolality, hyponatremia and, 246
Setting-sun irises
    bulging fontanelles and, 78
    large head and, 70
    wide sutures and, 76

Sexually transmitted disease
  cocaine abuse and, 228
  methadone or heroin abuse and, 230
Shield, heat, 42
Shift, mediastinal, 150–151
Shivering, 198–199
Shock, 158–161
  cardiogenic, 166
  heart sounds and, 148
Shoulder dystocia, 34
Shunt
  patent ductus arteriosus and, 162
  pleuroamniotic, 134
  vascular, twins and, 8
Sideroblastic anemia, 60
Sign
  double-bubble, 172
  sail, 148
Sinus bradycardia, 144
Sinus tachycardia, 146
Skeletal abnormality, alcohol abuse and, 232
Skin
  blisters and, 216–217
  hemangioma and, 220–221
  jaundice and, 54–55
  lymphangioma of, 222–223
  petechia of, 214–215
  pigmented lesions of, 224–225
Skin probe, hyperthermia and, 42
Skull, calcifications of, 78
Skull fracture
  as birth injury, 36
  breech birth and, 26
Small for gestational age infant, 2–3
  seizures and, 194
  small head and, 72
Small head, 72–73
Smoking, fetal effects of, 2
Soap bubble appearance, 172
Sodium
  hypernatremia and, 248–249
  hyponatremia and, 246–247
  oliguria and, 46
  periventricular-intraventricular hemorrhage and, 208
  polyuria and, 50
  seizures and, 196
Sodium bicarbonate
  acidosis and, 242
  alkalosis and, 244
  hydrops fetalis and, 18
  hypocalcemia and, 256
  hypoxic-ischemic encephalopathy and, 204
  severe asphyxia and, 22
Soft tissue, misshaped head and, 74
Sounds
  breath, 150
  heart, 148–149
Spherocytosis, 180
Spinal cord injury
  birth trauma to, 32
  breech birth and, 26

shoulder dystocia and, 34
vertebral dislocation and, 36
Spiramycin, toxoplasmosis and, 114
Spleen
  birth injury to, 34
  hydrops fetalis and, 16
Splenomegaly, 98–99
Spot, Mongolian, 224
Stain, port-wine, 220
Staphylococcal infection
  management of, 108
  risk of, 106
  of skin, 216–217
Staphylococcal scalded skin syndrome, 216–217
Sternal defect, 80–81
Sternal/xiphoid retractions, 82
Stomatocytosis, 180
Stool, bloody, 86–87
Strawberry hemangioma, 220–221
Stress ulcer, 86
Stricture, necrotizing enterocolitis and, 170
Stridor, 68–69
Sturge-Weber syndrome, port-wine stain and, 220
Subarachnoid hemorrhage, 34
Subcostal retraction, 82
Subcutaneous edema, 80
Subcutaneous fat necrosis, 218
Subdural hemorrhage
  as birth trauma, 34
  bulging fontanelles and, 78
Subgaleal hemorrhage, 34
  anemia and, 178
  large head and, 70
  misshaped head and, 74
Subpleural bleb, 142
Subtle seizures, 194
Sucking, ineffective, 176–177
Sucking blister, 216
Suction
  airway management and, 22
  intestinal obstruction and, 172
  massive hemorrhage and, 136
  meconium aspiration and, 128
Sudden infant death syndrome, cocaine abuse by mother
  and, 228
Sulfadiazine, toxoplasmosis and, 114
Sun-setting irises
  bulging fontanelles and, 78
  large head and, 70
  wide sutures and, 76
Supraventricular tachycardia, 146
Surfactant, respiratory distress and, 126
Suture
  large head and, 70
  misshaped head and, 74
  wide, 76–77
    bulging fontanelles and, 78
Swallowing
  fetal, polyhydramnios and, 10
  ineffective, 176–177
Symmetrical undergrowth of infant, 2

Symmetry of chest, 80
Syndrome of inappropriate secretion of antidiuretic hormone
    hyponatremia and, 246
    oliguria and, 46
Syphilis, 112–113

T
Tachycardia, 146–147
    hydrops fetalis and, 16
Tachypnea, 66–67
    cyanosis and, 58
    persistent fetal circulation and, 164
    retractions and, 82
    transient, 130–131
Tap, pericardial, 142
Tay-Sachs disease, 200
Teleangiectasia, port-wine stain as, 220
Temperature
    hyperthermia and, 42–43
    hypothermia and, 40–41
Temporal bone, birth injury to, 36
Tension pneumothorax
    abdominal distention and, 88
    hepatomegaly and, 96
    mediastinal shift and, 150
    splenomegaly and, 98
Teratogenicity, of cocaine, 228
Thalassemia, 180–181
Theophylline
    apnea and, 62
    bronchopulmonary dysplasia and, 132
    gastrointestinal bleeding caused by, 86
    seizures and, 194
Thorax, abnormal contour of, 80
Thrombocytopenia, 184–185
    giant hemangioma with, 220
Thrombocytosis and, platelets, 186–187
Thrombosis, 154
Thyrotoxicosis, myocardial ischemia and, 166
Ticarcillin, dosages of, 110
Tobramycin, dosages of, 110
Tolazoline
    gastric hemorrhage and, 84
    persistent fetal circulation and, 164
Tonic seizures, 194
TORCH infections, 78
Toxemia, neutropenia and, 188
Toxicity, cyanosis and, 58
Toxoplasmosis, 114–117, 117
Trachea, intubation injury to, 139
Tracheoesophageal fistula, 174–175
Transcutaneous water loss, 44
Transfusion
    exchange
        hyperammonemia and, 268
        jaundice and, 56
        magnesium and, 262
        polycythemia and, 182
    fetoplacental or fetomaternal, 178
    hydrops fetalis and, 18
    necrotizing enterocolitis and, 170

    severe asphyxia and, 22
    shock and, 158
    twin-to-twin, 8
Transient tachypnea, 130–131
Transillumination
    bulging fontanelles and, 78
    pneumothorax and, 142
Transposition of great vessels, 4
Trauma, birth
    to bones, 36–37
    breech birth and, 26
    bulging fontanelles and, 78
    misshaped head and, 74
    to peripheral nerves, 32–33
    seizures and, 196
    to viscera and soft tissue, 34–35
Traumatic birth injury, infant of diabetic mother and, 6–7
Tremor, 198–199
Treponema pallidum, 112–113
Triphyllocephaly, 74
Tumor
    abdominal, 90–91
    renal, 100
    thoracic, 80
Twin gestation, 8–9
    intrauterine growth retardation and, 2

U
Ulcer, stress, 86
Ultrasound
    hydrops fetalis and, 14, 16
    periventricular-intraventricular hemorrhage and, 206
    renal disorder and, 100
    seizures and, 194
Umbilical cord
    prolapsed or compressed, 30–31
    twin gestation and, 8
Umbilical vein catheter, 22
Urea, ascites and, 92
Uremia, thrombocytopenia and, 184
Urinary ascites, 92
Urinary disorder, abdominal mass and, 90
Urine
    fetal, oligohydramnios and, 12
    hypernatremia and, 248
    polyuria and, 50–51
Urine output, oliguria and, 46–47
Uterus
    abdominal mass and, 90
    breech birth and, 26

V
Vaginal delivery of breech birth, 26
Vaginal organism, transmission of, 104
Vancomycin, dosages of, 110
Vasa previa, twin gestation and, 8
Vascular disorder, maternal diabetes and, 6
Vascular shunt, twins and, 8
Vascular system
    bronchopulmonary dysplasia and, 132
    central venous pressure and, 156–157

Vascular system—cont'd
  diaphragmatic hernia and, 138
  hypertension and, 152
  necrotizing enterocolitis and, 170
  ocular
      pupillary opacities and, 210
      retinopathy and, 212–213
  patent ductus arteriosus and, 162–163
  persistent fetal circulation and, 164–165
  pulmonary, tachypnea and, 66
  transposition of great vessels and, 4
Vasoconstriction, cocaine and, 228
Vasodilator, for hypertension, 154
Vasopressin, polyuria and, 50
VDRL test for syphilis, 112
Vein-to-vein anastomosis in twins, 8
Velamentous insertion of cord, twin gestation and, 8
Venous catheter, umbilical, severe asphyxia and, 22
Venous pressure, central, 156–157
Ventilation
  alkalosis and, 244
  central venous pressure and, 156
  complications of, 139–140
  diaphragmatic hernia and, 138
  diminished heart sounds and, 148
  hydrops fetalis and, 18
  massive hemorrhage and, 136
  persistent fetal circulation and, 164
  positive pressure, bronchopulmonary dysplasia and, 132
  pulmonary air leak and, 142
Ventricular tachycardia, 146
Vertebra
  anomaly of, chest contour and, 80
  dislocation or fracture of, 36
Vertical transmission of infection, 104–105
Vessels; see Vascular system
Viral infection, 114–117
Visceral trauma during birth, 34–35
Vitamin A, hypercalcemia and, 260

Vitamin B$_{12}$ transport protein transcobalamin II deficiency, 60
Vitamin D
  calcium and, 256
  hypercalcemia and, 260
  hypomagnesemia and, 262
Vitamin E, thrombocytosis and, 186
Vitamin E deficiency, 181
  edema and, 218
Vitamin K
  bleeding and, 192
  bloody stools and, 86
Vitelline cyst, 90
Vitreous lesion, 210
Vocal cord paralysis, 32
  stridor and, 68
Voiding cystourethrography, 100
Volvulus, midgut, 172
Vomiting, 84–85
  intestinal obstruction and, 172

W

Weight; see Birthweight
White's classification of diabetic pregnancies, 6–7
Wide suture, 76–77
  bulging fontanelles and, 78
Williams syndrome, 260
Withdrawal
  amphetamine, 234
  methadone or heroin, 230
  seizures and, 194, 196

Y

Yellow skin color, 54–55

Z

Zellweger syndrome, 200
Zixoryn, jaundice and, 56